E-learning Strategies

E-learning Strategies

How to get implementation and delivery right first time

Don Morrison

WILEY

Other Wiley Editorial Offices

John Wiley & Sons Inc., 111 River Street, Hoboken, NJ 07030, USA

Jossey-Bass, 989 Market Street, San Francisco, CA 94103-1741, USA

Wiley-VCH Verlag GmbH, Boschstr. 12, D-69469 Weinheim, Germany

John Wiley & Sons Australia Ltd, 33 Park Road, Milton, Queensland 4064, Australia

John Wiley & Sons (Asia) Pte Ltd, 2 Clementi Loop #02-01, Jin Xing Distripark, Singapore
129809

John Wiley & Sons Canada Ltd, 22 Worcester Road, Etobicoke, Ontario, Canada M9W 1L1

Wiley also publishes its books in a variety of electronic formats. Some content that appears
in print may not be available in electronic books.

Library of Congress Cataloging-in-Publication Data

Morrison, Don.
    E-learning strategies : how to get implementation and delivery right first time / Don Morrison.
        p. cm.
    Includes bibliographical references and index.
    ISBN 0-470-84922-3 (alk. paper)
    1. Internet in education. 2. Employees — Training of — Computer-assisted instruction. I.
Title.

    LB1044.87.M65 2003
    658.3'124'02854678 — dc21

                                                                        2002192444

British Library Cataloguing in Publication Data

A catalogue record for this book is available from the British Library

ISBN 0-470-84922-3

Typeset in 10/12pt Garamond by Laserwords Private Limited, Chennai, India
Printed and bound in Great Britain by Antony Rowe Ltd, Chippenham, Wiltshire
This book is printed on acid-free paper responsibly manufactured from sustainable forestry
in which at least two trees are planted for each one used for paper production.

For ABB and NTD

Contents

Acknowledgements

I first want to thank Julia Collins who was a partner at PwC Consulting with global responsibility for Knowledge Management until the summer of 2002 when she decided it was time for a dramatic change in lifestyle. Without her very practical and effective support, there might not have been a book.

I would also like to express my thanks to everyone who helped me develop the case studies. I had been sceptical about including e-learning case studies because those I'd come across previously had proved disappointing. In the end, the four case studies turned out to be some of the most interesting material to research and write. That was due to the generosity of Amy Wright, David Dockray and David Stirling at PWC Consulting, David Appleton at BP, David Buglass and Brian McLaren at The Royal Bank of Scotland Group, and Sonya Davis at The Dow Chemical Company.

Other people at PwC Consulting were very supportive too — providing advice, feedback and miscellaneous contributions. My thanks to Frank Barczak, Ian Bird, Martin Black, Holger Heuss and Patrice Pope. I am also grateful to the following souls for their kind help. Andrew Abboud, PricewaterhouseCoopers; Clark Aldrich, SimuLearn; Virginia Barder; Chuck Barritt, Cisco Systems; Laurie Bassi, Human Capital Dynamics; Amy Corrigan, Technology Solutions Company; Rob Edmonds, SRI Consulting Business Intelligence; Bryan Eldridge, Sunset Learning; Alan Gabrel; Bill Lee, American Airlines; Victoria Macdonald, BMW of North America; Lindsay Mann, Click2Learn; Shiree Moreland, University of Notre Dame; Gabriel Morrison, Lee Newbold, PricewaterhouseCoopers; Harold Stolovitch, Harold Stolovitch Associates; Eilif Tronsden, SRI Consulting Business Intelligence; Alison Walker, BizMedia; Richard Winter, Winter Corporation. Many thanks — and grovelling apologies to anyone I've left out.

Introduction

... people learn in order to achieve desired forms of participation in communities and activity, in order to affect positively their sense of their meaning in the world. People learn not just in order to do, but in order to become ... we stress the learners' sense that they are contributing to the life and success of an enterprise that matters to them and to others, and that they in turn matter to that enterprise. A worker engaged in mindless or meaningless activity learns a good deal — about meaninglessness. Learning in and for Participation in Work and Society[1]

Show me the army with better trained soldiers and I will show you the victor of the battle. Sun Tzu

In just a few days, Massachusetts Institute of Technology (MIT) will publish the first tranche of material in its OpenCourseWare programme. The aim over the next 10 years is to make the university's materials for nearly all its courses freely available on the Internet. OpenCourseWare is a such a remarkable undertaking that the university has admitted to being surprised at its own audacity. MIT's programme is just one of many signs that the long term success of e-learning is inevitable. The ability to deliver cost-effective, personalized, relevant, interactive learning whenever and wherever it is needed is simply too beneficial to teachers and learners alike not to succeed.

The challenges for e-learning lie in the short and medium term: in the short term because enterprise learning departments are being tasked with making e-learning work effectively using what are still embryonic tools; in the medium term because all e-learning practitioners are struggling to develop a clear and imaginative vision that will give direction to their current efforts and mollify those making substantial investments in e-learning's promises. This book is about meeting those challenges in a post dot-com reality and in the context of learning in the enterprise.

Everyone has learning needs; no one has e-learning needs. That tells us e-learning is a solution not an end in itself. Implemented right, it can be a powerful way of meeting learning needs. It's turned out that implementing e-learning successfully is harder than we at first thought. There are technology hurdles to get over, and e-learning creates significant change across the enterprise — if it doesn't, there's no point. As everyone knows, change is almost always uncomfortable. For

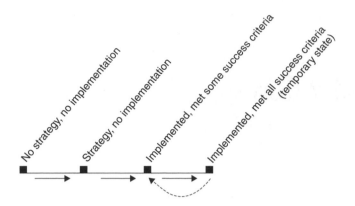

Figure 1 — The e-learning continuum

some time to come, anyone working on an e-learning project will be a pioneer but not an early pioneer. There have been enough implementation successes and failures for lessons to have been learned and best practices forged. You'll find many of them in the pages of this book. They will help you get implementation and delivery right first time.

It seems to me that there is an e-learning continuum and every enterprise finds itself at one of four key points on it (see Figure 1). The aim of this book is to provide strategic guidance for decision-makers, implementation teams and delivery teams at all four points.

Since the dot-com crash, I don't hear people talking about e-business. That doesn't mean it's gone away, just the opposite. The e-business lessons we learned about nimbleness and connectedness are applied routinely in every business that aims to stay in business. The same thing happened with e-learning. Even though many enterprises have moved into a comfort zone where the traditional learning delivery channel — face-to-face training in a classroom — is used alongside e-learning channels as a matter of policy, the lessons e-learning taught us have changed everything. The headline lessons are:

- Learning should be driven by business requirements not training requirements.
- The learner not the training department is at the centre of learning in the enterprise.

When training met learning

Expressions can be Trojan horses delivering radical messages hidden inside conspicuous ones. In the early 1960s, Avis Rent A Car launched an advertising campaign with a tag line that is reckoned to be one of the 10 best ever: "We're No. 2. We try harder." By turning self-deprecation into a selling point,

Avis's advertising agency, Doyle Dane Bernbach, resurrected an ailing car rental company. But the campaign secreted a message into the consumer's consciousness — that Avis was the number two company in car rental. It wasn't. The sleight of hand enabled Avis to leapfrog over a slew of competitors and wrest second place from the incumbent.

"E-learning" was a Trojan horse too. While everyone focused on the "e", the hidden message — that training was being replaced by learning — slipped into our collective unconscious. So what is the difference between training and learning? In David Mamet's film *State and Main*, a Hollywood film crew descends on a small town in Vermont. Joe White, the film within a film's screenwriter, makes the acquaintance of Ann Black who runs the town's bookstore and amateur theatrical group. Making conversation, Joe observes: "... small town. I suppose you have to make your own fun." With homespun wisdom, Ann teaches the writer something about his own business: "Everybody makes their own fun. F'you don't make it yourself, it ain't fun, it's entertainment."[2]

For me that exchange goes some way to explaining the difference between training and learning. Everybody makes their own learning. It's a commitment we make to ourselves and our employers — to remain capable of consistent peak performance through a process of lifelong learning. If you don't make it yourself, if you don't have a role to play in the process, if you just sit back and consume what's pushed at you, it ain't learning, it's training. The raw content of learning and training might be the same; everything else, as you'll see, is different.

What you need to know, what you need to do

The head of the technology team on an internal e-learning project at PricewaterhouseCoopers would routinely interrupt meetings with the caution: "We've started talking about how. We should be talking about why." He was right. But making strategic decisions about e-learning is tough. Skipping over the thinking and jumping straight into the doing is very attractive; it's also dumb. In the course of implementation and delivery, there are hundreds, maybe thousands of questions you need to answer. Without sound strategies to guide the process, you might end with e-learning but chances are you won't end up with an e-learning solution. To help you move towards the solution that's right for your enterprise, I've designed most chapters in two parts:

- *What you need to know* to answer the question Why?
- *What you need to do* to answer the question How?

Controversial topics

Two of the most controversial topics in e-learning are return on investment (ROI) and instructional design (ISD). There is a wide range of opinion about the most appropriate models for both and even a debate about whether either has a place in e-learning. Although ROI and ISD have nothing in common, they share a common cause for the controversy that surrounds them. Both practices are rooted in pre-Web, industrial models that struggle to stay relevant in the knowledge economy. At the same time, newer more appropriate models are struggling to establish themselves. The gap between old and new is characterized by a—possibly apocryphal—retort fired at a disgruntled investor by Intel's chairman Andy Grove: "What's my return on investment in e-commerce? Are you crazy? This is Columbus in the New World. What was his return on investment?" Chapter 3 tells you what you need to know and do about ROI; Chapter 16, about ISD.

Clarifying terms

When you're new to a subject, it can be confusing if a number of expressions are used to mean the same thing. Let me clarify some common e-learning synonyms used here.

Online learning and *e-learning* mean the same thing. *Generic content, off-the-shelf content* and *third-party content* all refer to the same thing: courses or learning objects that have been developed by content publishers for use in more than one enterprise. *Custom content* and *bespoke content* have equivalent meanings: courses or learning objects that have been developed to meet a specific business need in a specific enterprise. Custom content is always used in the USA; bespoke content is common in the UK. *Self-paced learning* and *asynchronous learning* both describe e-learning courses taken by learners on their own at a time of their choosing. *Face-to-face learning, classroom learning* and *instructor-led learning* are synonymous. Finally, *live e-learning, synchronous learning* and *virtual classroom* all mean the same thing.

Depending on context, I refer to dollars ($) or pounds (£) when talking about money. Dollars always refers to US dollars; pounds, to British pounds.

References and the Internet

Much of the research I did was on the Internet. Wherever possible, I have provided a URL as part of references to online material. Unfortunately, the widespread adoption of Content Management Systems by content publishers—a good thing, by the way—means that URLs are getting both longer and more abstract which is fine for computer systems but unhelpful to us humans. I apologise for the unwieldiness of some URLs. I operated on the principle that you'd rather know than not know.

There is a second shortcoming to online research. The ephemeral quality of the Internet means that some of the pages and documents I refer to will have been removed by the time you try to access them. All is not lost. Google, my idea of a great search engine, has responded to the Net's constantly changing landscape by keeping a snapshot of every page it indexes. Even when the original page vanishes, there's a copy in Google. To access the copy, just click on Cached near the end of a search hit. You'll find Google at <http://www.google.com>.

There is another place to search for pages that have been removed from Web sites: the Wayback Machine <http://www.archive.org>. Remarkably, 10 billion pages are stored in this Web archive. Maybe the page you're looking for will be there.

The Mission Statement for the Learning Organization

As I've already indicated, implementing and delivering e-learning isn't easy. Team morale is important, so I've tried to keep the substantial benefits of e-learning in focus throughout the book. If you keep sight of what you're struggling towards, it helps — and on that note, I recommend The Mission Statement for the Learning Organization as an antidote to sagging spirits:

> "The world changes and we cannot stop it. Our products will change, our markets will change, our customers will change, and some of our employees will move on — we hope to greater things.
>
> But these things will not change.
> We will learn faster than our competitors,
> We will learn across our organization from each other, and from teams,
> We will learn externally from our suppliers and our customers,
> We will learn vertically from top to bottom of our organization,
> We will ask the right questions; and use action learning.
> We will anticipate the future and create scenarios to learn from it,
> We will practice what we learn, and learn from practice,
> We will learn faster than our environment changes,
> We will learn where no man or woman has learned before,
> Therefore we will survive and prosper."[3]

If you would like to share any insights about e-learning or to comment on anything you read here, e-mail me at: don.morrison@knowledgedonut.com

References

1   Greeno JG Eckert P Stucky SU Sachs P and Wenger E (1999) *Learning in and for Participation in Work and Society* [Presentation] How Adults Learn Washington DC, 6–8 April 1998 [Internet] Available from <http://www.ed.gov/pubs/HowAdultsLearn/Greeno.html> Accessed 12 Oct 2001.
2   Mamet D (2001) *State and Main: The Shooting Script* New York, Newmarket Press.
3   Fulmer R Gibbs P and Bernard Keys J (1998) *The Second Generation Learning Organizations: New Tools For Sustaining Competitive Advantage* Organizational Dynamics Vol 27 No 2 pp 6–21.

Part I
E-learning primer

1

Defining terms: get comfortable with e-learning

... the promise of the Internet:
- *To center learning around the student instead of the classroom*
- *To focus on the strengths and needs of individual learners*
- *To make lifelong learning a practical reality* Report of the Web-based Education Commission to the US President and Congress[1]

A digitally literate citizen will be able to:
- *communicate digitally;*
- *choose, apply and keep up to date with digital tools;*
- *search, process and use information in a discriminating and responsible manner;*
- *learn and take responsibility for continuous, personal learning development and employability.* European cLearning Summit [2]

What you need to know

E-learning is to training what e-business is to business. Using technology as an enabler and process as a framework, e-learning has the power to transform how employees and enterprises learn in the new economy where knowledge is prized and change is constant. With power comes the responsibility — placed on the enterprise and the employee — of creating a learning partnership. The enterprise needs to invest in its human capital by delivering high-quality learning experiences to employees through multiple channels. Employees need to engage with the learning that is provided with the aim of achieving a state of readiness to compete. If either partner ducks their responsibility, some learning might take place but no transformation.

If e-learning is a response to the information age, we need to know something about what we are responding to. Dr Charles Reigeluth, Professor of Education at Indiana University and an authority on learning theory, provides what he describes as "key markers" to help us understand the environment in which e-learning needs to function (see Figure 1.1). What is interesting is how closely the characteristics of e-learning are aligned with Reigeluth's key markers for the information age.

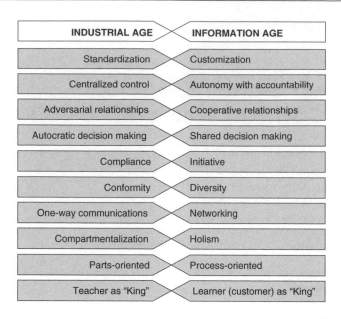

Figure 1.1—Key markers of the information age paradigm[3]

Towards a definition

E-learning means different things to different people. It's understandable. The telephone, television, even the book all mean different things to different people. There are dictionary definitions but we prefer to define these everyday media according to how we use them—and how we use them defines how we buy them. That's important. How you use e-learning should define how you buy e-learning.

Most definitions of e-learning you'll encounter reflect agendas you might not share. A custom content developer talks about *e-learning* differently than a generic content publisher. A Learning Management System vendor influences prospective buyers to think about *e-learning* differently than the vendor of a content authoring tool. In the end, you need to develop your own understanding that reflects the needs of your business. For now it is important that you understand how the term *e-learning* is used in this book.

Here is my definition:

> E-learning is the continuous assimilation of knowledge and skills by adults stimulated by synchronous and asynchronous learning events—and sometimes Knowledge Management outputs—which are authored, delivered, engaged with, supported, and administered using Internet technologies.

Let's focus on some of the key words and phrases in the definition.

Adults

E-learning in the enterprise, the main focus of this book, is almost always for the benefit of learners who have finished their formal education. They are adults who have become lifelong learners, some motivated by certification or compliance requirements but most by the desire to reach high performance levels—they want to be good at their jobs. "We are living in a world where what you earn is a function of what you can learn," observed Bill Clinton and that resonates with adult learners.[4] While much of what is covered in this book can be applied to e-learning in primary, secondary and higher education, it's important to recognize that the characteristics of adult learners—their attitudes, expectations, life experiences, and goals—are not interchangeable with those of full-time students. The design of adult learning needs to reflect the differences.

In his book *The Modern Practice of Adult Education* Malcolm S. Knowles, an influential professor of adult learning, appropriated the term *andragogy* to differentiate the principles of adult learning from those of pedagogy. For all their demographic diversity, Knowles held that all adult learners share these characteristics:

- Adults need to know why they have to learn something. They want control and responsibility over their learning—and must believe it will deliver a personal benefit.
- Adults need to learn experientially. They have had rich life experiences and want to bring them to their learning.
- Adults approach learning as problem-solving. A practical solution-centric approach to learning works better for adults than a theoretical approach.
- Adults learn best when content is of immediate value. Assimilation is facilitated when adults can put learning into practice soon.

In 1970 Knowles anticipated e-learning with surprising accuracy: "We are nearing the end of the era of our edifice complex and its basic belief that respectable learning takes place only in buildings and on campuses. Adults are beginning to demand that their learning take place at a time, place, and pace convenient to them. In fact, I feel confident that most educational services by the end of this century (if not decade) will be delivered electronically ... Our great challenge now is to find ways to maintain the human touch as we learn to use the media in new ways."[5]

Stimulated

I have used the word *stimulated* to keep the definition honest. Real learning, the assimilation of knowledge or skill, usually happens only when what has been "learned" is applied. That might be during an interactive exercise, simulation or discussion that forms part of an e-learning event but it is just as likely to be in a real-world context after the learning event has ended. E-learning has a responsibility to stimulate the learner by providing explicit knowledge but the responsibility of transforming explicit knowledge into tacit knowledge — taking personal ownership of it — can only ever be the learner's.

Synchronous events

A telephone conversation is a good example of a synchronous event. Both parties are present — remotely — and spontaneous interaction happens with no time delay. A video conference is another form of synchronous event. Synchronous learning is a learning event that takes place in real time, for example, a virtual class or peer-to-peer communication based on Instant Messaging technologies. In the virtual class there is real-time interaction between instructor and learners. The learner can interrupt the instructor to ask for clarification. The instructor can ask the virtual class if everyone understands a concept that has just been explained. Usually, synchronous learning happens at a fixed time. Like their physical counterparts, virtual classes are scheduled — so everyone knows when to "turn up".

When synchronous learning is instructor-led, it is sometimes called *distance learning* which is defined as online learning that takes place without the instructor being physically present. Confusingly, for many years before the arrival of e-learning, the term distance learning was used to describe any training that was delivered using any media, for example, videotape, broadcast television, satellite, CBT and CD-ROM. Today, a number of terms have emerged to describe synchronous learning: live e-learning (LEL), virtual classrooms, real-time learning and real-time collaboration.

Asynchronous

A book is a good example of asynchronous communication. The reading process is time-independent of the writing process; a book can be read any time after it has been written. E-mail is asynchronous communication. The nature of e-mail technology means interactions between sender and receiver can never happen in real time — unlike Instant Messaging technology. Asynchronous learning takes place when the learner, not the author, wants it to. Usually, authors have no idea when their learning content is being used; learners engage with a self-paced e-learning course without any interaction with the author. The creative use of interactivity in a self-paced course can give the impression of a synchronous learning event but it is just an impression. Like the book, all content has been authored and locked down in advance of the learning event.

Asynchronous learning is sometimes called *distributed learning* which is defined as online learning that takes place anywhere and any time it is needed.

The flexibility of Internet technology creates grey areas around the notions of synchronous and asynchronous. While a virtual class starts life as synchronous learning, it can be "recorded" and "played back" at any time even by learners who were not "present" at the original event. The instructor and the learners who participated in the original class become the authors of an asynchronous learning event that can be viewed by other learners at a time and place of their choosing.

Simulations are another interesting discussion point. In the past, what passed for e-learning simulations were no more than simulations of simulations — elaborately constructed exercises in branching that gave the learner the impression anything could happen when in reality all outcomes had been scripted in advance of the learning event. E-learning developers are starting to build authentic simulations based on rules engines and vast databases. These simulations contain an almost infinite number of variables. No one — not even the author — can predict all outcomes. Aircraft flight simulators are a classic example of genuine simulations. They happen in real time and the only constraints on the outcome of the crew's actions are the engineering constraints of the aircraft itself. The question arises, are authentic e-learning simulations synchronous or asynchronous events? The answer comes in two parts.

- They are synchronous in the sense that there are real-time spontaneous interactions that produce unscripted outcomes.
- They are asynchronous is the sense that the "world" of the simulation — whether a potentially explosive boardroom meeting or a factory floor process — has been defined before the learner interacts with it. The learner cannot move outside the boundaries of that world.

Knowledge Management (KM)

In *Smart Business* Dr Jim Botkin offers a crisp high-level definition of Knowledge Management: "... the process of capturing, sharing, and leveraging a company's collective expertise".[6] That could pass for a high-level description of the e-learning cycle. (See Chapter 4 for more about e-learning cycles.) In fact, the overlap between e-learning and Knowledge Management is now widely recognized and smart enterprises are already in the process of integrating the two to better leverage learning resources and eliminate duplicate activities. (Chapter 18 provides a case study of just such an initiative.) (See Figure 1.2.)

E-learning and Knowledge Management do the same thing in different ways. E-learning delivers *processed* knowledge — it takes subject matter expertise, puts it through an instructional design process and presents the result in an obvious framework. KM delivers *raw* or, at the very least, less processed knowledge. Nancy Dixon, organizational knowledge consultant and author of *Common Knowledge: How Companies Thrive by Sharing What They Know*, makes the same

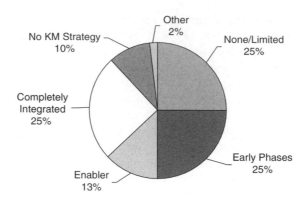

Figure 1.2—What is e-learning's role in your KM strategy?[7]
Reproduced by permission of Linkage, Inc

point slightly differently when she talks about *sanctioned* and *local* knowledge: "Most knowledge sharing is done between peers, and the organizational "sanction" for this kind of exchange, is an implicit recognition that local knowledge is important ... Local knowledge always competes with "sanctioned knowledge", i.e. knowledge that the organization has declared as valid. Sanctioned knowledge may come from outside the organization, or it may come from internal experts or task forces."[8] A holistic view of learning would provide learners with access to both processed/sanctioned and raw/local knowledge.

You can have a successful implementation of e-learning without KM which is why my definition isn't absolute about its inclusion.

Internet technologies

Internet technologies—and protocols—are the enablers of e-learning. Self-paced e-learning courses are hosted on Web servers and always delivered in a Web browser though some browsers are so customized, they look like something else. Peer-to-peer collaboration through Instant Messaging is an example of e-learning delivered outside a Web browser but still using Internet technologies. To leverage the power of the network, e-learning support and administration should also be browser-based. Telephone support is usually delivered using conventional telephone systems but using Voice over IP technology, it could be browser-based. By contrast, most mainstream content authoring tools are desktop applications.

Others define e-learning more loosely. I have seen definitions that include any learning delivered through any electronic media including CD-ROM, videotape, audio cassette, SMS text message, broadcast telephone message, and so on. These might all be effective channels for the delivery of learning but they are not e-learning any more than a fax—no matter how effective—is e-mail.

The e-learning industry

Content, technology and services are the three key segments in the e-learning industry (see Figure 1.3). No single e-learning vendor provides a true end-to-end solution though many have formed alliances and partnerships with the aim of providing everything an enterprise needs through a single umbrella contract. For example, Docent, a Learning Management System vendor, has alliances with the big five business consultancies and more than 50 content publishers. Increasingly, e-learning vendors border-hop to provide offerings in more than one of the three segments. Large generic content publishers like SkillSoft and NetG offer Learning Management Systems and hosting services. (To learn more about e-learning vendors, see Chapter 9.)

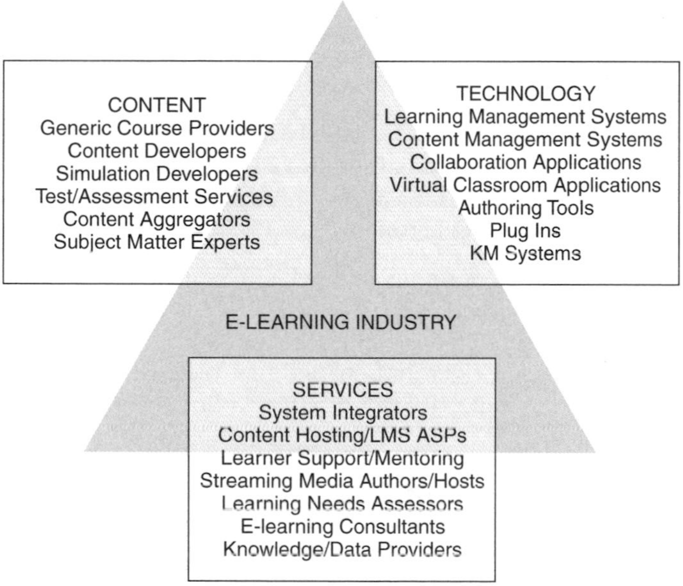

CONTENT
Generic Course Providers
Content Developers
Simulation Developers
Test/Assessment Services
Content Aggregators
Subject Matter Experts

TECHNOLOGY
Learning Management Systems
Content Management Systems
Collaboration Applications
Virtual Classroom Applications
Authoring Tools
Plug Ins
KM Systems

E-LEARNING INDUSTRY

SERVICES
System Integrators
Content Hosting/LMS ASPs
Learner Support/Mentoring
Streaming Media Authors/Hosts
Learning Needs Assessors
E-learning Consultants
Knowledge/Data Providers

Figure 1.3 — E-learning industry sectors

Time-critical: the key differentiator

Human attention is our most valuable and scarce commodity. When our time is what we have to offer the world, we look at technology differently. We aren't distracted by the sheer novelty of what it can do. We want to know how quickly it can help us get where we want to go, do what we need to do.
Wayne Hodgins, Director of Worldwide Learning Strategies Autodesk Inc [9]

When it comes down to it, learning is about one thing: the time-critical value of information. Tom Kelly, Vice-President of Worldwide Training Cisco Systems [10]

For your business and your competitors, time is either a competitive asset or a competitive disadvantage. There's no middle road. If your business makes decisions and implements them faster than your competitors, time is an asset; if you don't, it isn't. E-learning can help your business operate, as Bill Gates says, at the speed of thought. It's that quality that sets e-learning apart from every other channel in your learning value chain. E-learning leverages time in four ways.

Speed of delivery: E-learning can deliver content anywhere in the world *as soon as possible*—no other learning channel delivers faster. If your business needs just-in-time learning, your business needs e-learning.

Efficiency of delivery: E-learning means that once delivery has been made, learning happens *as fast as possible*. E-learning reduces time to performance by about one-third. Today no employee has a surplus of time or attention; every task is in competition with every other task for a share of both. Because e-learning enables a learner to learn about three times faster or three times as much in the same time, downtime and opportunity costs are minimized.[11]

Continuous delivery: Because it is available whenever and wherever the learner needs it, e-learning overcomes the barriers associated with time zones. Availability is critical for enterprises that work across continents and time zones and need to keep their employees' learning harmonized.

Dynamic delivery: No other learning channel is as responsive to the dynamics of e-business as e-learning. Whether your learner base is local, regional or global, e-learning delivers the shortest lead times for updating and publishing. Design your e-learning application right and change that originates in the board room can be communicated to a global learner based in hours—day after day.

By leveraging asynchronous and synchronous learning as well as collaborative tools, e-learning is able to support both an established curriculum and ad hoc responses to those events no amount of business planning can forecast. No other learning channel provides this degree of flexibility. Cisco Systems delivers both "structured learning" and what it calls "emergency learning". The emergency doesn't need to be at enterprise level—if one employee feels under-prepared for an important meeting, that's an emergency and one that can be quelled with an ad hoc e-learning session. All the employee needs is a computer and access to the intranet.

The elements of e-learning

Looking at the e-learning experience from the learner's point of view, e-learning appears as combinations of the following elements:

- Logon process
- Registration process

- Personal profile
- Competency and skills assessments
- Course catalogues
- Course enrolment processes
- Pre-defined learning paths
- Personal learning path
- Customizable home page
- Online courses — custom built or bought off-the-shelf, usually containing some combination of these elements:

  - Pre-assessment
  - Text
  - Graphics, photographs
  - Streaming animations, audio, video
  - Simulations
  - Interactive exercises
  - Online and downloadable tools
  - Quizzes
  - Bookmarks
  - Online notepads
  - Post-assessment
  - Feedback forms

- Downloadable courses or course elements
- Electronic Performance Support Systems (EPSS)
- Moderated message boards (formal peer-to-peer communication)
- Peer-to-peer message boards (informal peer-to-peer communication)
- Peer-to-peer Instant Messaging (informal peer-to-peer communication)
- Virtual classrooms — live and archived
- Online mentoring
- Other collaborative applications, e.g. Lotus Anytime, Webex, Groove
- Web casts — live and archived
- Links to public or subscription Web sites
- Access to proprietary or third-party Knowledge Management databases
- Online help files
- Online help desks
- Telephone help desks

From the enterprise's point of view, you need to decide which of these elements your learners need and whether to buy or build them. In addition, there are elements which the learner does not see but which are essential from the enterprise perspective. They include:

- Activity tracking mechanisms
- Reporting tools
- Certification processes

- Course catalogue management tools
- Competencies and skills profiles database
- Links to HR and other enterprise-wide applications
- Classroom resource management tools
- Localization tools
- Content authoring tools

E-learning content

All e-learning content has three dimensions:

- subject matter—the content of content
- focus—an indicator of the breadth of the learner base
- intention—how the learning is intended to affect learners

Subject matter

At first, e-learning subject matter was dominated by technology. In 2000, according to IDC (International Data Corporation), IT subject matter accounted for 72% of content demand worldwide.[12] That shouldn't come as a surprise. First, there is harmony between form and content—you're using technology to learn technology. Secondly, you can assume that learners who need to learn about technology will know how to use it well enough to take advantage of e-learning. Thirdly, it's easier to develop learning content about hard skills than soft—and technology learning is based on hard skills. The dominance of technology-based subject matter won't last; enterprises have too many other important learning needs. The amount of technology learning will grow but its proportion of all e-learning will fall. IDC predicts that by 2004 non-IT content will account for over 54% of worldwide revenues.[13]

Typical non-IT e-learning subject matter includes:

- business skills
- communication and interpersonal skills
- customer service
- executive development
- financial skills
- management skills
- sales and marketing skills
- team work

There is a bias against using e-learning for soft skills, based on the perceived difficulty of (1) handling soft content and (2) influencing learners' behaviours. It is more difficult to handle soft content than hard content but providing you can bring creativity, humanity and technological innovation to the design process, it is very possible. As the technology becomes more powerful and interfaces richer, I believe that we will see increasingly more soft skills content in e-learning, for example, in the form of simulations.

Focus

The focus of e-learning content extends from low to high. The lower the focus, the larger the potential learner base; the higher the focus, the smaller the learner bases. Focus can be expressed under four content headings:

- generic — low focus
- sector-specific — medium focus
- legislation-specific — medium focus
- business-specific — high focus

There is a hierarchy of content sources that reflects both the cost of acquisition and the value to an enterprise in terms of performance improvement. The most valuable content is business-specific; next comes industry- or sector-specific content, and then generic content.

Generic

Generic content can be used across a number of industries. Typical generic content includes courses about how to use Microsoft Office applications or courses about soft skills like team leadership and how to conduct a job interview. Generic content is relatively inexpensive and can be made available very quickly. However, because it does not touch on core knowledge and skills, its impact on an enterprise's performance is limited. Thousands of generic e-learning courses are available from content publishers like SkillSoft and NetG.

Sector-specific

Industry- or sector-specific content is sourced from knowledge that is common to an industry or sector. It can be sourced from within the enterprise and from industry-wide databases where these exist. It can be bought from third-party information vendors, for example, Gartner focuses on a number of specific markets including telecommunications, healthcare and government.

Where a sector is large enough or in sectors that are learning-intensive, third-party publishers will recognize a market and develop e-learning courses designed to meet sector-specific needs. Financial services and telecommunications are examples of sectors well served by sector-specific content. For example, DigitalThink offers a series of courses developed with the American Bankers Association and aimed at the financial services sector.

Legislation-specific

There are areas of learning that are driven by legislation, whether at regional, national or, in the case of Europe, EU level. Learning content about health and safety issues, for example, tends to be driven by legislation. Most countries have data protection laws that impact on daily business. Employment law is another important area that will require legislation-specific learning content. Here again, content publishers will recognize a market and develop e-learning content that reflects local legislation.

Business-specific

Most enterprises have learning needs that cannot be met with content published by third parties. Areas where there are specific learning needs include corporate culture, proprietary processes or technologies, and intellectual property owned or developed by the enterprise. Usually, learning in these critical areas will be the most important learning the enterprise does. It is also in these areas where enterprises will be prepared to invest in the development of custom e-learning content, drawing on their own subject matter experts as a source of knowledge. The process of content development makes tacit knowledge explicit and accessible across the enterprise. This does not mean that the whole process of developing business-specific content needs to take place in-house. The experience and skills of external content designers and developers should be leveraged. It does mean that the enterprise has to initiate development and provide the raw content, simply because it is not available anywhere else.

Intention

The intention of e-learning content should be determined by an up-front performance gap analysis designed to answer the question, why aren't employees performing at required levels? The answer will point to one or more intentions.

Information: If the performance gap is the result of a lack of information, the intention is to tell learners what they don't know. That might be details of a new business strategy emanating from the board room, the features and prices of a new product range, or updates about how a newly acquired business will be integrated with the parent company. Learning information uses the learner's cognitive skills.

Process: Process builds on information by turning it into action. The reason employees aren't performing the way they're expected to is because they don't know how to do something. It could be something as simple as raising a purchase order, or something as complex as managing a global project. Some processes are strictly cognitive—filling in an expenses claim; others have a psychomotor aspect — giving a patient an injection. E-learning excels at delivering and assessing the cognitive aspect of a process — understanding the correct sequence of events, the functions of different controls, the settings to use under different circumstances, but most people assume that it has little to offer for psychomotor aspects. That's not true — providing designers are prepared to move beyond the keyboard and mouse as input devices. One of the most interesting applications of technology-based learning I have ever seen was developed in the 1980s for the College of Aeronautics at La Guardia Airport. As part of its aircraft maintenance courses, the college taught oxyacetylene welding. It's a complex, hard to master skill; it's also dangerous and dirty. Traditional training proved expensive and took too long. The solution, developed by David Hon's Ixion Inc, was based on synthetic reality and tactile interfaces. Briefly, a touch-screen PC monitor was set facing up — the screen acting like the top of a work bench. Two photo-realistic metal plates were displayed on the monitor screen; the learner's task was to weld them together. The learner worked with a real welding rod and an authentic mechanically-simulated torch. The skills and knowledge of experienced welders were built into the system's responses, so the appearance and quality of the weld developing on the screen accurately reflected the skill with which the learner manipulated the torch. Because a typical learner was unlikely to be either computer- or text-literate, no computing or reading skills were required to use the system. The approach also had the advantage of integrating feedback and evaluation with content; you don't need a text or spoken message to tell you that you've moved the torch too slowly, you can see a puddle form on the screen. Video was used to display the weld; today we might use real-time graphics. The point is, it is possible to realize this type of psychomotor simulation using e-learning technology. All it takes is imagination and inventive implementation.

Behavioural/Attitudinal: Here employees are performing below requirements, not because they don't know something or how to do something but because they are not behaving the way they should. This situation often arises during periods of change. A new process or tool has been introduced; employees have learned how to use it but *choose* not to. It can arise with corporate culture; employees know from their induction learning that they should back up their data regularly yet they *choose* not to. In other cases, employees in a call centre might not know the best behaviours to use with customers who complain, or the best behaviours for maximizing cross-selling. Used creatively, e-learning has the power to persuade; it can change behaviours. It can also provide learners with a safe area where they can try out new behaviours.

Build e-learning around the learner

Adoption is a land mine on the road to e-learning. Other higher profile challenges you can see a mile off: management support, project management, infrastructure, security, vendor selection, system integration. When you've dealt successfully with all those — and are beginning to feel invincible — adoption will be waiting, ready to undermine everything you've accomplished. For e-learning to succeed, employees need to use what you've built; more than use, they have to adopt it as a new way of working that is capable of creating a fundamental shift in learning. So what can you do to defuse the adoption land mine? The single most effective action you can take is to think of your learners as customers, to look at everything you build from their perspective. Is your e-learning offering ergonomic, in other words, is it easy to use? Does it make effective use of learners' time? Does it deliver what they need when they need it? Does it look attractive and feel comfortable? Successful adoption hinges on the answers to those questions.

There's a distinction to be made here. Your learners are your only customers but they are not your only stakeholders. Build an e-learning application that delights management but no one uses and you fail management and the learner. Build an e-learning application that delights the learner but does not meet the needs of management and you just plain miss the point. Like any business, the needs of customers *and* other stakeholders need to be met.

Building e-learning around the learner — that is, having a learner-centric approach to e-learning — is a recurring theme in this book and a critical success factor for your implementation. While learner-centric learning has become a commonplace aspiration for e-learning practitioners, its roots lie elsewhere. Some understanding of the development of learner-centric learning might provide an insight into what it is and how to build it into your e-learning initiative. It begins with the American psychotherapist Carl Rogers who as early as 1940 was developing the concept of "non-directive counselling" for individual and group therapy. Later, Rogers began to call his work "client-centred therapy" to emphasize that it was clients who were at the centre of the process not techniques or methods. Fifty years ago Rogers encapsulated his thinking about a client-centric approach in an *if–then* statement that can readily be applied to e-learning:

If the individual or group is faced by a problem;
If a catalyst-leader provides a permissive atmosphere;
If responsibility is genuinely placed with the individual or group;
If there is basic respect for the capacity of the individual or group;
Then, responsible and adequate analysis of the problem is made; responsible self-direction occurs; the creativity, productivity, quality of product exhibited are superior to results of other comparable methods; individual and group morale and confidence develop.[14]

Client-centred therapy proved a dramatic success. A university professor as well as a practising therapist, Rogers wondered if the principles underlying client-centric therapy could be transplanted to the university classroom. It turned out they could and "learner-centric learning" enjoyed notable success. In the

1980s Rogers moved his humanistic people-centred approach again—this time to primary and secondary schools as "child-centred education".

In the learning environment, Rogers' goal was "significant learning"; this is how he described it: "*It has a quality of personal involvement*—the whole person in both feeling and cognitive aspects being in the learning event. It is *self-initiated*. Even when the impetus or stimulus comes from the outside, the sense of discovery, of reaching out, of grasping and comprehending, comes from within. It is *pervasive*. It makes a difference in the behavior, the attitudes, perhaps even the personality of the learner. *It is evaluated by the learner*. She knows whether it is meeting her need, whether it leads toward what she *wants* to know, whether it illuminates the dark area of ignorance she is experiencing."[15] Significant learning is what e-learning strives to deliver. On p. 28 we look at how to apply Rogers' vision as learner-centred e-learning.

The learning value chain

There is an often-expressed fear that technology will replace teachers. I can say emphatically and unequivocally, IT WON'T. The information highway won't replace or devalue any of the human educational talent needed for the challenges ahead ... However, technology will be pivotal in the future role of teachers. Bill Gates[16]

There has been a shift from e-learning as a pure e-learning solution to what people call *blended learning*, that is, using a range of Internet-based and traditional media—in the broadest sense—to deliver learning. In practice, the blend often turns out be traditional instructor-led classes alongside synchronous and asynchronous e-learning. While the expression blended learning has become established, many people I know dislike it. I find it more helpful to talk about an enterprise's learning value chain—of which e-learning is a part. A value chain can be described as a group of activities whose output is a product or a service delivered to a customer. It isn't far-fetched to think about learning as a service delivered by an enterprise to employees, partners, suppliers, sales channels and customers. In this context, learning can be seen as a private vertical e-market place, in other words, a value chain (see Figure 1.4).

It's fair to ask why we're having a discussion about instructor-led classes in a book about e-learning. After all, it wasn't that long ago that Trace Urdan and Cornelia Weggen were warning us that "... live classroom-based training is becoming too costly and cumbersome. Even if employees had the time to attend all the courses and seminars and to read all the books and reports they should to remain up-to-date in their area of work, the cost of such learning would be prohibitive. The need to transform how organizations learn points to a more modern, efficient, and flexible alternative: e-learning. The mission of corporate e-learning is to supply the workforce with an up-to-date and cost-effective program that yields motivated, skilled, and loyal knowledge workers."[17] What happened to flip the enterprise's view of the classroom from expensive and

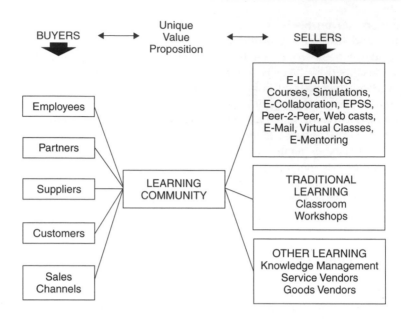

Figure 1.4 — Enterprise learning value chain

inflexible to essential? I believe two different influences account for the adoption of blended learning.

The first is a very human influence: fear. Buoyed with the enthusiasm of the dot-com boom, some enterprises latched on to e-learning the way a child might climb a tree. It's a great adventure until the child feels the branches get flimsier—and looks down. "Oops. How did I get here?" A retreat to firmer footing follows. I think that some early adopters of e-learning have asked the same question—how did I get here?—and, in their efforts to get comfortable, have either reversed their move away from the classroom or slowed it down. We also need to acknowledge that e-learning has turned out to be more revolutionary in its impact and, it follows, harder to implement successfully than it first appeared. In taking a sideways step to blended learning, in restoring the role of the classroom, some enterprises have been giving themselves—and their learners—the chance to catch their breath in the race to transformation.

E-learning author and IBM consultant Margaret Driscoll puts the case this way: "Blended learning allows organizations to gradually move learners from traditional classrooms to e-learning in small steps making change easier to accept. Working in a blended environment enabled instructors and instructional designers to develop the skills needed for e-learning in small increments. Training professionals can move small sections online as they develop the needed e-learning skills."[18] While Driscoll puts a positive spin on blended learning, my concern is that it lacks the transformational power of e-learning, satisfying itself with incremental change instead. Yes, blended learning provides an opportunity to re-evaluate work to date in e-learning and to reflect on the knowledge that the revolution might be more difficult than anyone thought. Is that enough, I wonder, to convince leadership that something fundamentally different is going on in learning? If it isn't, leadership's impatience with incremental change in a dynamic business environment will be understandable.

The second influence behind the adoption of blended learning is highly practical: people believe it works. I'm dragging my feet here because it's early days yet; by mid-2002 only one survey provided evidence of its effectiveness. That survey needs to be seen in the context of literally hundreds of other surveys elegantly if conservatively summarized by Michael Moore and Greg Kearsley, both with a deep understanding and experience of distance learning: "Comparing the achievement of learners (as measured by grades, test scores, retention, job performance) who are taught at a distance and those taught in face-to-face classes is a line of research going back more than 50 years. The usual finding in these comparison studies is that there are no significant differences between learning in the two different environments, regardless of the nature of the content, the educational level of the students, or the media involved ... [it is] reasonable to conclude (1) there is sufficient evidence to support the idea that classroom instruction is the optimum delivery method; (2) instruction at a distance can be as effective in bringing about learning as classroom instruction; (3) the absence of face-to-face contact is not in itself detrimental to the learning process; and (4) what makes any course good or poor is a consequence of how well it is designed, delivered, and conducted, not whether the students are face-to-face or at a distance."[19] In fact, there is a second significant body of research that demonstrates that e-learning is not only as effective but more effective than classroom learning—see Chapter 2 for a fuller discussion of whether e-learning works.

Based on what we know, it's easy to assume that blended learning will prove as least as effective as pure e-learning. NETg, an e-learning content and services vendor, wanted more than assumptions; the company wanted to know:

- How learners would perform using a new blended learning model.
- What the ideal blended learning model should look like.
- How much performance improvement, if any, would occur as a result of moving from e-learning to blended learning.

To find out NetG ran an experimental study called *Job Impact Study: Measuring Competitive Advantage*.[20] Organizations who participated included Lockheed-Martin, National Cash Register, Utah State University, University of Limerick in Ireland, Anoka-Ramsey Community College in Minnesota and Executive Service Corp. The study looked at three groups, each learning to use Microsoft Excel:

- An e-learning group that utilized off-the-shelf NetG learning objects supported—following the NetG e-learning model—by access to live mentoring.

- A blended learning group whose learning included a distinguishing feature — scenario-based exercises (SBEs) designed to provide a real-world context in which to learn.
- A control group who received no learning.

The performance of the groups on real-world tasks was compared. The blended learning performed with 30% more accuracy than the e-learning group and 159% more accuracy than the control group. In turn, the e-learning group performed 99% more accurately than the control group.

The presence of David Merrill, a Professor at Utah State University and leading instructional design authority, as Principal External Investigator lends weight to the study. That said, I have reservations about the outcomes based on at least one critical difference between the e-learning and blended learning designs. That difference, in my opinion, was arbitrary; if I'm right the study was not comparing like with like. By the way, this is the most common criticism of studies that compare distance and face-to-face learning. The SBEs taken by the blended learning group provided learners with access to the full Excel application; this turned out to be an important success factor in making the scenarios "real" and gave the group an edge in the subsequent real-world tasks. The availability of the full application is not an inherent differentiator. If scenario-based exercises worked for blended learning, the lesson to draw is not that blended learning is better but that the design of e-learning should be changed to include the same exercises. There is no reason why e-learning cannot adopt an EPSS (electronic performance support system) design that integrates learning with the full application.

E-learning for adults needs to authentic, solution-centred, relevant and integrated with the learner's work. Without those qualities — and others — e-learning *and* blended learning are bound to fail. (For more about the qualities of e-learning, see p. 29.) The study appears to set higher design standards for blended learning than for e-learning and then to arrive at the inevitable conclusion that higher standards result in higher performance levels.

There are circumstances when sandwiching a classroom event with e-learning has advantages. Here's a straightforward example. Learner feedback on instructor-led courses often reveals an impatience to get to the heart of the matter. "It got interesting on the third day," is a typical comment. The instructor on the other hand feels obliged to set the scene so everyone in the room is on a level playing field. A blended learning solution can meet everyone's needs by prerequiring all learners to assimilate the introductory material through e-learning. Those who already know the material can gallop through it, those who don't can canter or walk. From the start of the first classroom session, the instructor can assume with confidence that all learners are ready for the interesting stuff. Following up the classroom event with online exercises, evaluations and collaborations can help embed the learning. This is exactly the approach taken by IBM in its Basic Blue programme taken by 5000 managers each year. Twenty-six weeks of self-paced e-learning culminates in a 5-day instructor-led session; if managers feel the need, they can follow up the face-to-face event with online peer-to-peer collaboration. (To learn more about Basic Blue, see p. 65.)

There is no such thing as a shrink-wrapped solution to e-learning. If a blended solution meets your business requirements, use it. However, in the long run, I believe it will turn out to be a small levelling off in an unstoppable upward curve. The blend will shift from classroom and e-learning to synchronous and asynchronous e-learning.

How far has e-learning come?

To understand how far e-learning has come first you need to understand that it is a moving target. E-learning is a collection of technologies, products, services and processes — all in a state of constant evolution hurried along by the forces of competition. While some aspects of e-learning — like Learning Management Systems — display maturity and stability, the leading edge — simulations, for example — remains steadfastly on the move. That's not going to change; it's symptomatic of today's technology based markets. What's important is that you no longer have to invest in Version 1.0 of a product — unless you want to; many LMSs have already reached Version 5 or 6 and display the stability you'd expect from a mature application. On the other hand, if you're a visionary and want to work with companies at the leading edge, there are new products and services designed to capture your imagination (see Figure 1.5).

One important indicator of how far e-learning has come is the number of success stories out there — in many sectors, on many scales, with many configurations, and meeting many business needs. Implemented correctly, e-learning works; if it's not working, you're not doing it right. As playwright David Mamet is fond of saying, "Just because you're lost, don't think your compass is broken." Industries whose learning demand is high and constant — for example, those bound by compliance requirements or legislation — have been quick to realize the benefits of e-learning. (See the case study of the Dow Chemical Company in Chapter 21.) Financial services, aerospace and automotive are sectors where e-learning has enjoyed wide and successful adoption for other reasons. Because there are real success stories to point to, the hype surrounding e-learning has diminished but not disappeared. The better informed the buyer, the better they will be able to make the critical distinction between a vendor's aspirations and a vendor's products.

E-learning standards is an area where there has been steady progress. The US Department of Defense's Advanced Distributed Learning initiative has successfully focused the efforts of all e-learning standards bodies on a single integrated model. Even though the publication of a full set of internationally agreed standards is still a while off, the future evolution of draft standards is well signposted and that is already protecting investments in e-learning. So far, development work has been on standards for asynchronous self-paced courses built from learning

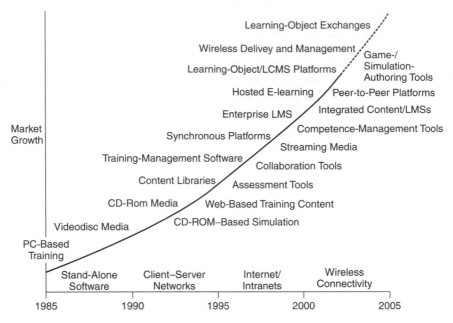

LCMS = Learning-content–management systems; LMS = learning-management systems; CD-ROM = compact-disc read-only memory.

Figure 1.5 — Technology evolution in e-learning[21]
Reproduced by permission of SRI Consulting Business Intelligence

objects; ahead lies the dual challenge of developing compatible standards for synchronous e-learning and simulations.

Is there a downside?

If you're determined to implement e-learning successfully be prepared to (1) work hard, and (2) climb a steep learning curve. A successful implementation also hinges on making the right judgements about a number of key business considerations. The best way to do that is to make the development of rigorously thought out e-learning strategy your first priority. Be prepared to invest serious time and energy in that project. (See Chapter 6 for more about developing a strategy.) Here are some up-front considerations that some people might consider downsides but which I believe a good strategy can eliminate or mitigate.

Cost

While you can expect e-learning to deliver an attractive return on investment, start-up costs for an enterprise-wide implementation are significant, and so is the cost of developing custom content. Large enterprises need the full support of leadership to get sign-off on the budget and, as importantly, to protect it during implementation. Smaller businesses with learner bases of less than 2500 might have to manage ROI expectations or take a longer-term view of payback. Cost issues can be mitigated, for example, by a phased implementation, using a hosted e-learning application instead of building one inside the firewall, developing a curriculum based on generic content with only a limited number of essential custom-built courses. By taking just such an approach, BMW North America have developed a very successful e-learning initiative for a learner base of less than 1200 spread across 15 locations. Costs were controlled with a phased implementation initially based around Thinq's hosted LMS and generic courses. Later, virtual classroom and collaboration functionality were added using a Centra hosted solution.

Integration

Integration is about making (1) e-learning applications work together, for example, an LMS and a synchronous collaborative application, and (2) e-learning applications work with other applications, for example, an LMS and an HR application like PeopleSoft. If integration is planned for and thought through in detail, it can be straightforward; if it's an afterthought, chances are there will be a price to pay in time, money and frustration. The devil is in the detail. While a vendor might tell you that a specific version of their application integrates easily with a specific version of another application, some enterprises learn too late that there is no guarantee any versions of the two applications can be integrated. Vendors themselves might not realize that the latest version of their application won't integrate in circumstances where earlier versions did. Don't be a pioneer when it comes to integration. Get all the details on the table in advance and mitigate risk with careful planning.

The elusive end-to-end solution

Most observers expected at least one enterprise level software vendor to deliver a world class end-to-end e-learning solution that would dominate the market. Companies like Cisco, Microsoft, PeopleSoft, SAP and Sun have all demonstrated a commitment to e-learning but so far expectations of a killer e-learning solution have not been met. That doesn't mean it won't happen, just that so far it hasn't.

The absence of a dominant e-learning vendor disadvantages the e-learning industry and means that even the largest enterprises have to work with a network of small vendors to build the solution they need. It's a fact of life that large enterprises like to do business with other large enterprises — with good reason. Someone with responsibility for e-learning in a Fortune 500 company recently told me he was uneasy with records representing millions of hours of compliance learning being committed to a system developed by a vendor with a total head count of 35. The absence of a dominant vendor also means that no one has had the market clout to enforce *de facto* e-learning standards for the industry to rally round.

These kinds of issues are not unique to e-learning and most enterprises have the project management skills to integrate the products and services of a number of software vendors. The absence of an end-to-end solution might inhibit the adoption of e-learning but it shouldn't prevent it.

Supply-driven market

> So, if you want to sell to me, come into my office with a demonstrated solution to a problem I've got ... That means you've got to understand my business, how I make my money and what my problems are. Roger Krone, Vice-President and General Manager, Boeing Rotorcraf [22]

Historically e-learning has been a supply-driven rather than needs-driven market. It is vendors who have shaped the market and its offerings. It's not hard to understand how this happened. In a new market, vendors had two goals — to stimulate the market, then educate buyers. On the not unreasonable assumption that potential customers don't know what they don't know, vendors told them. After all, none of us knew we wanted portable music players until Sony told us we wanted Walkmans. Unfortunately, telling the market what it needs is a tough habit to break and vendors kept at it when they should have started listening to what their customers needed. This shortcoming led to the view that e-learning was a solution in search of a problem. Customers found themselves choosing from a menu of products none of which really met their needs. Because they weren't listening carefully, vendors also tended to over-promise and under-deliver. They under-delivered usually not through any lack of willingness but when they got closer to their customer's business requirements they discovered too late what they should have known much earlier — the challenge was tougher than it looked.

As the level of understanding about e-learning increases, the market has begun to talk less and listen more. At the same time, potential customers have learned to ask tougher questions. The table has been turned; customers have begun to educate their vendors — and that points to a market better able to deliver the right learning solutions to real business needs.

Content: quantity and expediency versus quality

> ... dull content — no matter how it is delivered — is not an effective way to teach people. Fortune Magazine[23]

Enterprises making a commitment to e-learning face the challenge of developing a full online curriculum in a short period of time. The typical response is to turn to the large generic content publishers and license hundreds of courses with a single purchase order. A mono diet of generic content might not be the best way to capture the imagination, attention and loyalty of learners during an e-learning launch. It's not just off-the-shelf content that can leave learners with an appetite for more. Too much custom content turns out to be dull — exercises in reading from a screen with no attempt to exploit the possibilities for interaction that e-learning offers. "What are the major challenges to e-learning use?" *e-learning Magazine* asked in a User Survey. "Lack of interaction" said 39% of respondents.[24]

There are so many issues to manage in the course of an e-learning implementation — infrastructure, standards, integration, interface design, browser versions, plug-ins, etc — that too often the notion of a quality audit for content becomes lost. All content is not created equal. One content provider or developer is not as good as the next. One course is not as good as the next. The quality of content cannot be sacrificed as a matter of routine to the conflicting demands of speed and cost. There will always be exigencies that demand speed of delivery above all else — the ability to expedite lies at the heart of the e-learning offering — however, enterprises also need continuously to exercise discrimination about the content they deliver to their learners or accept the consequences as reflected in *e-learning Magazine's* survey.

Canada's Committee on Broadcasting began its 1965 Report with these words: "The only thing that really matters in broadcasting is program content; all the rest is housekeeping."[25] E-learning could engage learners more effectively and earn their loyalty more readily by adopting as unequivocal a position about content.

Skills

E-learning is no different from any other area where expertise is required — the best people are in great demand. E-learning is different from some other areas because it is still a relatively new discipline and there are only a limited number of people with skills and experience. Some technology-based skills can be ported from other areas with a minimum of adjustment, for example, graphics designers, developers, system architects, system integrators and programmers, typically with experience in Visual Basic, Java, JavaScript, C and Perl. Finding good people with experience in developing and executing e-learning strategies is much harder; so is finding instructional designers with experience in e-learning.

Most enterprises will have to look externally in order to recruit a project team with the set of skills required to deliver and operate a full implementation. (More about building a project team in Chapter 7.)

Infrastructure

Inevitably, e-learning adds traffic to the corporate infrastructure. The greater the adoption of e-learning, the greater the load it imposes. Even when the e-learning application and content are hosted externally, learners will add to traffic levels inside the firewall. One of the most important lessons of past implementations is to get the enterprise IT department actively involved in any e-learning initiative from day one. It's the only way to evaluate and mitigate potential risks to the infrastructure.

What you need to do

Turn push into pull

What does turning push into pull mean and why do it? It is about the devolution of training from a centralized to a distributed model. Historically, the training model has been based on a centralized repository of knowledge from which trainers pushed out courses to trainees on both a need-to-know and just-in-case basis. Courses didn't have to be pushed very far — trainees travelled to classrooms located in a centralized training facility. Everyone in the classroom was treated as co-equal — the same content was covered in the same time frame even though some trainees struggled to keep up while others two seats away fidgeted in boredom. Just-in-case training was driven by conformity and meant the enterprise made a high-risk investment in learning that might never pay off while at the same time incurring substantial opportunity costs. Look back at Reigeluth's key markers for the Industrial Age in Figure 1.1. They are synonymous with the push model of training.

In the Information Age where change is constant, where knowledge is in flux, where employees change jobs regularly, where technology offers a more customized approach to learning, the push model is no longer appropriate. It's wrong to suggest that no one ever learned anything in the classroom. There were many rich learning experiences; there still are. However, what the centralized classroom can't deliver is fast changing skills and knowledge to everyone in the enterprise. The need for learning will only increase and the classroom doesn't scale well.

E-learning provides the opportunity to change the model from push to pull. Instead of the learning department, place the learner with her shifting learning needs and shrinking lead times at the centre. Give her the responsibility for her own performance. Let the learner draw on the enterprise learning value chain to pull in the content she needs when she needs it and using the channel that suits her (see Figure 1.7).

Think of the push model at one end of a learning continuum and pull at the other. Leverage the power and flexibility of e-learning to move your business along the continuum from a hierarchical state characterized by *training attendance* to a participatory state characterized by *learning engagement* (see Figure 1.8).

The transformation from push to pull shifts both costs and responsibility from enterprise to employee. Savings in travel and instructors' salaries are really made by employees who agree to instruct themselves at their own desks. Neither the cost nor the responsibility go away, they just move. No enterprise can expect employees to take up their new learning responsibilities unless and until the

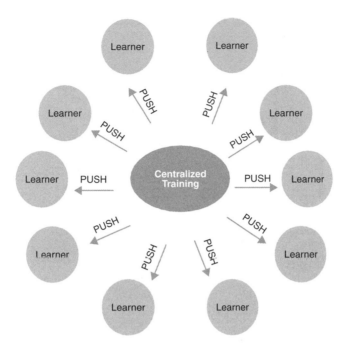

Figure 1.6—Push model of training

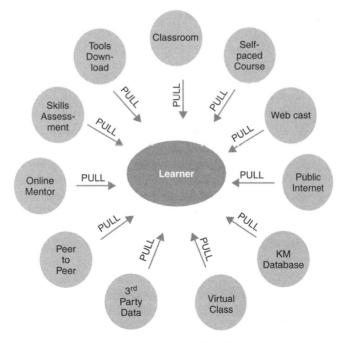

Figure 1.7—Pull model of learning

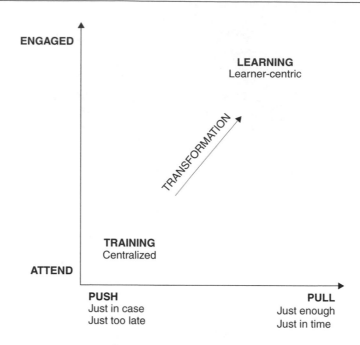

Figure 1.8 — Push model to pull model

leadership give a clear signal that the model has changed, so it's essential that the transformation is supported by an effective communications programme that begins early enough to allow employees time to adjust their behaviours. Like any change programme, the clarity of leadership's signal needs to be reflected by real change at all levels of management. For example, there is no point signalling a transformation in learning if line managers don't allow employees an opportunity to carry out their new responsibilities. In practice, that means allowing them the time to learn in the workplace. A surprising number of e-learning initiatives have stalled and even failed because this didn't happen. Line managers also need to reward employees for taking on the new responsibility. If employees do not see a personal benefit, they will shift cost and responsibility back to the enterprise by turning their backs on e-learning.

Enabling the pull model of learning is more than implementing the technology that supports it — that's the easy part. It requires a new way of thinking about learning in the enterprise.

Create learner-centred content

Learners in the enterprise are adults with the self-motivation to maximize their performance by keeping themselves informed. To support that motivation the enterprise needs to provide content that is designed and delivered with a focus

personalized	engaging
fresh	interactive
just-in-time	granular
authentic	integrated with their work
solution-centred	self-paced
relevant	self-directed
rich	downloadable

Figure 1.9—Qualities of learner-centred learning

on learners' needs. Learners want content that is available anytime, anywhere, increasingly, on any device—and with the qualities listed in Figure 1.9.

Personalized learning

The Internet is the biggest library in the world. It's always open, you never have to return what you borrow, and, unlike its physical counterpart, borrowing a book or document doesn't stop other people from reading it. What the Internet is not personalized. There is no Dewey decimal system to help visitors find what they want. In the absence of an overarching index system, it's up to every visitor to devise their own search and acquire methods. In the world's biggest library, it's every visitor for himself.

Compartments of the Internet, however, are very personalized. Take Amazon.com—when I logon to the US site, among the tabs that let me navigate to specialist shops, there's one labelled "Don's Shop". The first time I saw it, I wondered where it came from. The short answer is, Amazon built it for me—by tracking my interests through my searches and purchases. Look in Don's Shop and you get a pretty good idea of the books, music and technology I—and my family and friends—like. Of course, building my virtual shop is a completely hands-off continuous process. Software does all the work but the outcome is no less personal, no less useful and no less endearing.

My Yahoo is another very personalized pocket of the Internet but Yahoo go about personalization in a different way from Amazon. Yahoo helps me build a highly personalized portal by providing a structure and easy-to-use online tools. My Yahoo portal contains links to the news, weather and sport I'm interested in, a Web search function, a collection of my Web bookmarks, the latest prices of shares I track, a currency converter, local television listings, a place to store and share files online, Instant Messaging, e-mail, a calculator and—this is impressive—the complete contents of my Outlook Contacts so I can access that data from any computer in the world that has an Internet connection. I can add as many pages to my portal as I like and customize their layout and colour scheme.

A vision of e-learning that limits itself to making self-paced content available online turns its back on the Internet's power to customize learning and, in so doing, build learner loyalty by engaging learners in a whole new way. How can we make e-learning personal? Figure 1.10 shows some of the ways customization can be introduced at different levels within the e-learning experience.

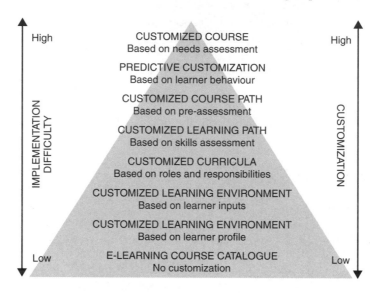

Figure 1.10 — Hierarchy of customization

Use learner profiles to automatically create a localized learning environment that reflects the country and city where the learner works, the business unit and department they work for, and where appropriate the customers they serve. News, information and knowledge management content related to all those customization points can be displayed automatically on the learner's home page. Following Yahoo's lead, give learners the tools to tweak and enhance their personalized learning environment more accurately to reflect individual needs and interests.

Design curricula specific to roles and responsibilities in the business, for example, a project manager's curriculum, a line manager's curriculum, an electrical engineer's curriculum, a call centre agent's curriculum, a security guard's curriculum, and so on. Provide skills and competencies assessments that, first, help the learner determine where their learning gaps lie and, secondly, use the outputs of the assessments to create a personal learning path designed to close the gaps. In self-paced courses, design pre-assessments whose outputs customize the course to reflect what the learner already knows and needs to learn. Skip modules based on knowledge the learner already has. Give each learner at least one e-mentor — manager, supervisor, subject matter expert — who takes a personal interest in the learner's progress. Through online collaboration, the e-mentor challenges and nurtures, manages and monitors. The e mentor also has access to the record generated by the Learning Management System for each learner, so she can track the progress of her mentees. Use automatically generated e-mails to (1) remind learners about virtual classes, online collaborations and instructor-led classes they're registered for, and (2) inform them about new courses and upcoming Web casts.

Follow the lead of Amazon.com and develop smart, predictive personalization — by tracking behaviours — that offers learners what they need before they ask for it, even before they know they need it. A close study of Amazon's features and functions will be rewarded with plenty of food for thought. Provide a list of courses that are relevant to the learner's clients or business sector, or to software applications associated with the learner's job. Provide peer content and virtual class reviews backed up with a rating system — at first, reviews might put content developers' noses out of joint but (1) they'll get used to it, even come to see it as a challenge, and (2) remember whose interests you're looking after — learners' not developers'. Look after both developers and learners with a feature that displays a list of courses developed by same subject matter expert, business unit or development team as the one the learner has just registered for or completed. Introduce the feature with copy along the lines of, "Learners who took this course also registered for these courses."

Plan for deeper levels of customization through dynamic course creation where a unique course is created on the fly — from a repository of learning objects — to meet a learner's specific needs. To achieve this level of customization requires a commitment to the continuous development of reusable learning objects.

Fresh learning

> *... we have a moral obligation to try to give people the tools to meet tough goals. I think it's totally wrong if you don't give employees the tools to succeed, then punish them when they fail.* Steve Kerr, Chief Learning Officer, GE [26]

In the connected economy, only employees working with the latest information can help the enterprise compete effectively. Superseded data may have historical value but when it's passed off as current data, it has negative value. E-learning technologies and processes let enterprises provide learners with the latest corporate strategies, product features, thought leadership, processes, tools, changes in legislation, competitor news and market developments. Use that power to keep employees equipped with fresh learning content — and fully prepared to compete.

In e-learning terms, fresh is relative. Some content changes constantly — technology, for example. If your employees need to know about the leading edge of technology, expect to update technology courses continuously. Other content changes much less frequently. Courses about project management, quality management, using PowerPoint, or interpersonal skills, for example, are unlikely to change monthly or even annually.

Historically, distribution has been a barrier to fresh learning, especially for enterprises with global operations. Dell Computers was an early adopter of e-learning and remains committed to it. At Dell, every course is assumed to be obsolete after one year. Two weeks before the year is up, the content owner is asked whether the content should be kept. If there aren't sound business reasons for keeping it, the course is deleted from the e-learning servers. You don't have to follow Dell's example to the letter but it is important to establish a refresh cycle for all the content you develop or license.

Just-in-time learning

Fresh learning is about keeping content current. Just-in-time learning is about making sure current content is available just when learners need it. There is no point in keeping content fresh if it is delivered just too late. Historically, the process of duplicating, packaging and distributing CD-ROMs often took so long that at least some of the training content was out of date before the shrink wrapping was removed. E-learning eliminates the distribution lag associated with older learning channels. Content can be replicated regionally, nationally or globally in just hours.

One of the shortcomings of the old training model was the practice of delivering learning just in case. The trouble with just-in-case training — no matter how important the content — is that its relevance is unlikely to be recognized. In other words, it's *way too soon* learning. Adult learners don't engage with content that has no obvious application. E-learning allows learners to access learning not only according to a centrally determined schedule but at the very moment the learner needs it most. That's when it is most relevant and most likely to be assimilated.

There are some practical considerations to just-in-time learning. First, it requires foresight and, secondly, good project management. Foresight is required because the learning department needs advance warning of what learners will need to know. Is there a new product or tool being developed? An important new customer coming on stream? New legislation coming into force? In all these examples, learners will need new knowledge at a specific time in the future. There needs to be a rolling process for delivering new requirements and raw content to the learning department early. Where lead times are short by necessity, rapid development methods need to be adopted — or live virtual classes and Web casts used instead. Project management is important to just-in-time learning because content — whether for self-paced courses or live virtual classes — cannot be delivered late. With just-in-time learning, missing the deadline isn't an option.

Authentic learning

Years ago, while developing an interactive video training course for British Airways, I had a short sharp lesson in the importance of authentic learning. The course was designed to change the behaviour of BA staff working on what's known as the ramp—that part of an airport where aircraft are parked, loaded, fuelled and boarded. My approach was to present a realistic dramatization of how even casual abuse of ramp equipment could trigger a domino effect of operational delays that cost the airline money and, by inconveniencing BA's passengers, put future earnings at risk.

One day we were crammed into the flight deck of a 747 to film an exchange between a pilot, played by a real BA pilot and a flight dispatcher, played by an actor. According to the script the pilot was furious that his full load of passengers was being delayed simply because six meals catering for special diets hadn't arrived. At the time, this kind of delay was common. The way I had imagined the scene, the pilot would give the flight dispatcher a stinging reprimand. The chastened dispatcher would scuttle away to castigate the next person down the pecking order. In the first take, the pilot played the scene differently. "Do you have a radio?" he asked the dispatcher in understated tones. The answer came back, "Yes." "Then use it," ordered the pilot quietly. I was disappointed. Where was the stinging reprimand? I reminded the pilot of his situation: behind him 400 delayed passengers, his take-off slot lost—both consequences of a dispatcher not paying enough attention to detail. I asked the pilot to express the full force of his anger. Patiently and in the same understated tone, the pilot explained, "I just did. I humiliated the dispatcher in front of the flight crew."

Given the choice between taking my subject matter expert's advice or forcing him to behave in an unrealistic way to satisfy my appetite for drama, I had the sense to choose the former. Had I done otherwise the exchange would have lost the ring of authenticity for its audience and, as a result, BA would have lost the chance of making its point.

The BA story isn't typical. Authenticity—presenting real issues realistically—is usually a much subtler quality but it is these authentic subtleties that cause learners to accept or reject messages. Learning content needs to reflect the reality of the work environment in form and content. That does not rule out aspirational messages—providing the aspirations are achievable. If learning content commends best practices that can't be put into practice for reasons beyond the learner's control, the learner will reject them. If learners are told to espouse corporate values not practised leadership, the learner will decide that actions speak louder than words and follow management's example. Authenticity is about respect, about not trying to pull the wool over a learner's eyes. Every time you don't treat a learner with respect you lose an opportunity to improve their performance.

Solution-centred learning

Most adult learners earn a living by solving problems for their employers. You can engage and motivate learners by making learning solution-centred. Deliver solutions to real problems that employees are grappling with every day. Deliver tools that employees can keep on using long after the learning event has finished. The power of tools in e-learning shouldn't be underestimated. In *Living on Thin Air*, Charles Leadbeater explains why: "Humans became markedly more intelligent when they learned how to make tools, because tools store and transfer intelligence . . . The most important stores of intelligence are not physical tools but words and books and especially recipes."[27] In a business environment, recipes can mean something as simple as a checklist, a formula, a process or a template. It can mean simulations and electronic performance support tools (EPSS). E-learning consultant Elliott Masie talks about "multiple shots at learning" — that's what tools deliver. You start to learn by familiarizing yourself with a tool in the context of formal learning but the learning continues every time you use the tool to solve a problem. The better the tool, the more often employees will use it; the more often they use it, the more they learn.

Make solutions to real business needs the focus of all learning. Wherever possible embed skills, knowledge and information in tools.

Relevant learning

The notion of relevance figures in a number of the characteristics of learner-centred learning we have already looked at. Giving it a place of its own underlines its importance to the adult learner, first, because it is relevance that engages the mind. So many students sleepwalk through their education because they cannot see the relevance of what they are told to learn. It's a problem you can't afford to reproduce in the enterprise. What learners are asked to learn must have immediate relevance to them. Secondly, relevance is critical because no employee has time or attention to spare. They can only find time to learn what it essential to their work. Asking an employee to learn something that isn't essential to their work is counterproductive since it takes time away from essential tasks.

Relevance can be achieved only through a close working relationship between the learning department and business units. Subject matter experts from business units bring to content development an insight into what is important to their colleagues. Before content is published that insight needs to be double-checked through rigorous user acceptance testing.

Rich learning

Richness is the characteristic that determines the quality of the learning experience. Somehow rich content has become synonymous with media-rich content, that is, content full of audio, video and animations. In fact, multimedia is only one aspect of richness — and the one that requires the most time and resources to develop. To be attractive to learners, content needs to be rich in all these aspects:

- Value
- Features
- Functions
- Interactivity
- Presentation styles
- Media

Rich learning costs time and money to develop and as a result some people believe it does not support fresh learning and just-in-time learning. This tension between rich and fast is one that generates a lot of discussion among practitioners of e-learning. At one extreme, some people hold the view that speed is everything and if that means e-learning content is a collection of Web-enabled PowerPoint presentations, so be it. At the other extreme are those who believe that only a fully-featured course qualifies as e-learning. The answer, it should come as no surprise, lies somewhere in the middle.

Rich cannot be an absolute standard. E-learning content rushed out, perhaps overnight, to a small audience to meet a critical business requirement should not be judged by the same standard of richness as a course with a shelf-life of two years and aimed at a large audience. We've talked about freshness itself being relative, how some content has a longer shelf-life than others. Richness and freshness are co-determined. How much richness you invest in a course must be related to its shelf-life. Practically, there simply won't be enough time to develop exigent content with the same level of richness as content with a longer development cycle. The time-critical content rushed out overnight is very attractive to its small audience because it is rich in value even though its presentation is straightforward.

One of the mitigating factors in the rich versus fast debate is the intensive use of templates in development. Imagine a content-free course sitting on a shelf. The screen layouts are there, so are the colour schemes, the navigation interface, even the assessments. All that's missing is the content. With careful planning, template-driven development can ensure that even content developed in 24 hours can display richness of presentation styles, interactivity, features and functions. Templates also mean that none of those 24 hours will be wasted reinventing the wheel. This is a publishing model. Newspapers, whether printed or online, do not redesign their publication everyday. They create a number of styles and templates, set a number of presentation rules and focus their everyday efforts on creating new content to pour in the mould.

In the real world, an enterprise's e-learning offerings will have varying degrees of richness reflecting the different circumstances in which content was developed. What is important is that learners are not offered a steady diet of thin content. It might reduce development costs but if no one is engaged with the content, if no one's performance improves as a result of it, you need to ask, At what learning cost are development savings being made?

Engaging content

Empathy with the learner is the key to creating engaging content. Never forget that someone has to invest their valuable time and attention in the content you develop, so bring creativity to the development process. Creativity doesn't have to mean off the wall, out of the box thinking. In fact, that style of creativity can be insulting to learners whose challenges and problems are firmly rooted in reality. Daniel Libeskind, a hugely creative architect who is leading a renaissance in museum design, offers a valuable insight into marrying a creative process and empathy with the end user: "The main creative lesson I've learnt building museums is to never give up and to always believe in the public. Never be cynical, never believe that the public doesn't know, never speak down to people and think they don't understand. They do understand very, very well and they do care ... I feel a tremendous responsibility to the people who will use these museums. I don't want them to feel, "now I'm being educated, now I'm enjoying myself, now I'm going to look at something I wanted to see, now I'm seeing something unexpected". I want to create a seamlessness and a feeling that they are being appreciated, that this is for them."[28] E-learning practitioners need to believe in learners the way Libeskind believes in the public.

You've seen how templates can be a powerful tool in the development of rich learning. At structural and presentation levels, templates work. Template thinking, on the other hand, produces unusable learning content. As part of bringing creativity to the development process, take care to choose the right instructional design model and build in all the qualities of learner-centred learning described here. (For more about instructional design see Chapter 16.)

User acceptance testing will tell you if your content is engaging, so will Kirkpatrick's Level 1 and 3 evaluations. (See p. 59 for more about Kirkpatrick's Levels of Evaluation.)

Interactive learning

E-learning offers both the content designer and the learner the possibility of creating interactive learning. There is, in fact, an expectation of interaction on the learner's part. When that expectation is not met or met poorly, the learner has a sense of being excluded from content rather than engaged with it. Interactive learning stimulates and motivates the learner to acquire new knowledge and skills.

Build interactive content that empowers your learners by allowing them to influence their learning in all the ways given in Figure 1.11.

Granular learning

Granular learning is about presenting content in small compact packets in order to make learning flexible and assimilable. Flexible because the learner can take

Assess their competencies	Design their curriculum
Browse the content	Prioritize their needs
Arrange the sequence	Skip the inessential
Regulate the flow	Study the context
Download the tools	Steer the simulations
Save their notes	Check their understanding
React to feedback	Revisit the perplexing
Record their progress	Collaborate with peers
Consult with experts	Customize their environment

Figure 1.11 — How learners can interact

advantage of even short periods of free time to learn and not have to clear one or two hours. Flexible, too, because a granular approach allows learners to skim or skip easily over content they know and focus their efforts on content they don't.

Granular learning is easier to assimilate than large blocks. Psychologically, most learners would prefer to climb a series of steps than one wall. Learners will confidently attack — and master — a 15-minute module; chances are they will baulk at a 2-hour monolith.

From the enterprise perspective, granular learning is in keeping with an object oriented approach to content development. By building a repository of small learning objects, content can be reused to build conventional courses or to build personalized courses on the fly.

Learning integrated with work

This quality describes an approach to learning content that views learning as an aspect of work, not a separate activity. Content that blurs the line between learning and work is attractive to learners because it supports the process of lifelong learning — which is essential if learners are to remain fit to compete — and implies a number of the qualities we have already discussed: relevant, solution-centred, just-in-time and authentic.

Self-paced learning

There are two aspects to self-paced learning. First, it allows learners to schedule their learning at a time and place convenient to them and not constrained by the schedule of a centralized training department. Secondly, it allows learners to move through learning content at a pace they find comfortable. Self-paced learning places the emphasis on the quality of the learning experience and not the speed. What some people learn in half an hour, others might take 2 hours to master. Different learners display different approaches to content. Some like to surf through a whole course before returning to specific areas for concentrated study. Some like to jump from one eye-catching title to the next. Others prefer a methodical progression from beginning to end. Self-paced learning caters to all these approaches. This is important to adult learners who are self-directed and expect to take responsibility for their own learning decisions.

Course structure and navigation need to be designed with self-paced learning in mind, providing learners with both control and flexibility.

Downloadable learning

Even in large enterprises with highly developed infrastructures, learners do not have continuous access to the Internet. Travel can be a barrier. The learner may be on a long flight or train journey. The country they are visiting may have limited connectivity. When working at a client site for extended periods, a learner's attempt to access learning content via the Internet may be thwarted by settings on the local firewall. When working from home learners may not be prepared to tie up the family phone line for extended periods in order to access learning content. Even when access is available, network congestion can sometimes make learning online uncomfortable.

To get round all these issues and to provide as much learning flexibility as possible, learners need to be able to download learning content and work with it offline. The download function needs to be granular — learners should be able to download whole courses or only the parts they want. The offline learning experience should be indistinguishable from the online and there should be no disincentives to offline learning. Learners' progress through content and the results of any assessments they take should be stored locally and uploaded to their personal record in the Learning Management System the next time they logon.

References

1   *The Power of the Internet for Learning: Moving from Promise to Practice* (2000) Report of the Web-based Education Commission to the President and the Congress of the United States [Internet] Available from <http://interact.hpcnet.org/webcommission/index.htm> Accessed 20 Sep 2001.

2   *A Digital Future for European Learning* (2001) [Report] European eLearning Summit, Brussels, 10–11 May 2001.

3   Reigeluth (1996) CM *ITForum Paper #17: What Is the New Paradigm of Instructional Theory* Indiana University [Internet] Available from <http://itech1.coe.uga.edu/itforum/paper17/paper17.html> Accessed 24 June 2002.

4   Longman PJ (997) *Software expands white-collar competition for jobs — The Janitor Stole My Job* [Abstract] [Internet] Usnews.com Available from <http://www.usnews.com/usnews/issue/971201/> Accessed 9 Apr 2002.

5   Knowles M et al (1984) *Andragogy in Action. Applying modern principles of adult education* San Francisco, Jossey Bass In [Internet] Clark D (1999) *Malcolm Knowles* Big Dog's HRD Page Available from <http://www.nwlink.com/~donclark/hrd/history/knowles.html> Accessed 28 Mar 2002.

6   Botkin J (1999) *Smart Business—How Knowledge Communities Can Revolutionize Your Company* New York, The Free Press p 40.

7   *The 2001 Linkage, Inc E-learning Survey* (April 2001) Linkage Incorporated. <http://www.linkageinc.com>.

8   De Cagna J (2000) *Exploring Common Knowledge: An Interview with Nancy Dixon* [Internet] Information Outlook Online. Special Libraries Association. Available from <http://www.sla.org/sla-learning/dixon1.html> Accessed 22 Sep 2001.

9   Hodgins HW (2000) *Into the Future—A Vision Paper* [Report] Commission on Technology & Adult Learning [Internet] Available from <http://www.learnativity.com/into_the_future2000.html> Accessed 21 Sep 2001 p 16.

10 Muoio A (2000) *Cisco's Quick Study* FastCompany Issue 39 [Internet] Available from <http://www.fastcompany.com/online/39/quickstudy.html#> Accessed 9 Apr 2002 Issue 39 p 286.

11 Fletcher JD (1996) *Does This Stuff Work? Some Findings from Applications of Technology to Education and Training* Proceedings of Conference on Teacher Education and the Use of Technology Based Learning Systems. Warrenton VA, Society for Applied Learning Technology[Internet] Available from <http://www.hi.is/~joner/eaps/wh_stuff.htm> Accessed 1 Apr 2002.

12 *Worldwide Corporate eLearning Market Forecast and Analysis, 1999–2004* (2001) IDC [Bulletin] IDC #B23904. In IDG.com [Internet] Available from <http://idg.com/www/pr.nsf/webPRForm?OpenForm&unid=F2420187B8E8FBE988256A000058B5F3> Accessed 16 Nov 2001.

13 *Worldwide Corporate eLearning Market Forecast and Analysis, 1999–2004* (2001) IDC [Bulletin] IDC #B23904. In IDG.com [Internet] Available from <http://idg.com/www/pr.nsf/webPRForm?OpenForm&unid=F2420187B8E8FBE988256A000058B5F3> Accessed 16 Nov 2001.

14 Rogers CR (1984) *Client-Centered Therapy* London, Constable and Company Limited pp 63–4.

15 Rogers CR (1983) *Freedom to Learn for the 80s* Columbus, Charles E. Merrill Publishing Company p 20.

16 Gates B et al (1995) *The Road Ahead* New York, Viking Penguin p 185.

17 Urdan TA and Weggen CC (2000 Mar) *Corporate E-Learning: Exploring A New Frontier* [Report] WR Hambrecht + Co p 6.

18 Driscoll M (2002) *Blended Learning: Let's Get Beyond the Hype* IBM [White paper] [Internet] Available from <http://www-3.ibm.com/software/mindspan/distlrng.nsf/wdocs/20630EC43B8DBB4985256B810060561E?OpenDocument> Accessed 1 Jun 2002.

19 Moore M and Kearsley G (1966) *Distance Education: A Systems View* Belmont, Wadsworth Publishing Company. In Dannenberg RB and Capell P (1997) *Are Just-In-Time Lectures Effective At Teaching?* School of Computer Science, Carnegie Mellon University [Internet] Available from <www.jitl.cs.cmu.edu/effectiv.pdf> Accessed 30 Mar 2002.

20 *Job Impact Study of a Blended Learning Model* (2002) [Report] NETg, Inc. February–March 2002 [Internet] Available from <http://www.netg.com/DemosAndDownloads/> Accessed 25 Mar 2002.

21 Barron T (2002) *Evolving Business Models in eLearning* [Report] SRI Consulting Business Intelligence [Internet] Available from <http://www.sric-bi.com/LoD/summaries/EvolvBizModelsSum.pdf> Accessed 31 May 2002.

22   Lay P (2002) *Under the Buzz— Back to Basics in e-Business* Chasm Group [Newsletter] Vol 3 No 7 [Internet] Available from <http://www.chasmgroup.com/underthebuzz_archives.htm> Accessed 10 Jul 2002.

23   *Online Learning: E-Learning Strategies for Executive Education and Corporate Training* (2000) [Section] Fortune Magazine [Internet] Available from <www.docent.com/misc/wp_strategies.pdf> Accessed 4 Apr 2002.

24   *2001 E-learning User Survey* (2001) E-Learning Magazine [Internet] Available at <http://www.elearningmag.com/elearning/article/articleList.jsp?categoryId=774> Accessed 9 Apr 2002.

25   Fowler RM Lalonde M and Steele GGE (1965) *1965 Report of the Committee on Broadcasting* Ottawa, Queen's Printer p 3.

26   Sherman S and Kerr S (1995) *Stretch Goals: The Dark Side Of Asking For Miracles* Fortune Magazine. In [Internet] The College of St Scholastica. Available from <http://www.css.edu/users/dswenson/web/335artic/stretch.htm> Accessed 5 Apr 2002.

27   Leadbeater C (2000) *Living on Thin Air— The New Economy* 2nd edition London, Penguin Group p 91.

28   Elwes A ed (2000) *Creativity Works* London, Profile Books Ltd. pp 107–8.

2

The new learning landscape: e-learning is here to stay

Internet-based learning experiences hold revolutionary potential—the chance to provide global audiences with critical information and skills, to open the myriad pathways that reach experts and tap their knowledge, simulate experience and allow collaboration in ways never before imagined. E-learning has the potential to be the engine that harnesses the combined power of classrooms, chat rooms, video games, knowledge management, XML, artificial intelligence, the world's largest resource library and what some are calling the new semantic Web. Leslie Freeman, Chief Learning Officer, Morgan Stanley[1]

To think that the new economy is over is like somebody in London in 1830 saying the entire industrial revolution is over because some textile manufacturers in Manchester went broke. Alvin Toffler[2]

What you need to know

Most people buying or selling or thinking about buying or selling e-learning were working in training or HR long before e-learning demanded their attention. For some, especially those uncomfortable with change, there must be a temptation to wait for the e-learning storm to blow over then get back to business as usual. Trouble is, like nostalgia, business as usual isn't what it used to be. Every day, the Internet makes sure of that—and no one I know of has any plans to disconnect the Internet or its progeny, the corporate intranet, any more than anyone has plans to disconnect the telephone network. The notion of interconnectedness which is the essence of the Net is, at the very least, here to stay and likely to develop so intensively that today's Internet will look like a back of an envelope sketch. In fact, when you remember that the genesis of Arpanet—which begat the Internet as we know it—was just such a sketch, there's an inevitability about a second generation SuperNet (see Figure 2.1).

E-learning is an offspring of the Internet—enabled by its technologies, leveraging its interconnectedness and delivered across the public Internet and private intranets. Whether or not we're comfortable with the idea, the Internet has changed the way we think about learning. In 387 BC when Plato established a school of philosophy in the Athens suburb of Academy, he created an enduring model of the university staffed by great teachers as a centre of excellence. A student who wishes to know what the teachers know has to travel to the

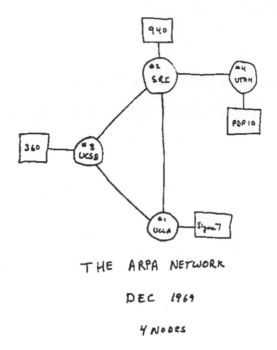

Figure 2.1 — Early Arpanet sketch[3]
Reproduced by permission of Alexander McKenzie

university where knowledge is shared through face-to-face lectures. By bringing the best thinking to learners whenever they need it, wherever they happen to be, e-learning flips the ancient model on its head.

It's not just theory. At the University of Twente in the Netherlands, the Faculty of Educational Science and Technology decided that people already in full-time employment could enrol alongside traditional full-time students. To create a level playing field for both groups, the faculty adopted a multi-channel learning delivery system with the emphasis on e-learning. They even took the decision to stop lecturing on the grounds that lectures are inflexible. It is no longer practical, Twente's professors believe, to gather all students together physically in one room at the same time. As a result, they've decided that no more than three lectures are allowed in any 6-month period.

In *Small Pieces Loosely Joined*, David Weinberger talks about the real impact of the Internet: "The Web will have its deepest effect as an idea. Ideas don't explode; they subvert. They take their time. And because they change the way we think, they are less visible than a newly paved national highway or the advent of wall-sized television screens. After a while, someone notices that we're not thinking about things the way our parents did."[4] Almost 40 years ago Marshall McLuhan told us the same thing when he announced that the medium is the message. McLuhan was warning us that the medium of television would change society forever regardless of what content it broadcast. Weinberger goes on to argue that the message at the heart of the Internet is, matter doesn't matter—the Net overcomes the physical world. This idea, too, has sound provenance. For years, MIT's Nicholas Negroponte has been entreating us to work more effectively by moving bits instead of atoms. Send an e-mail not a letter, publish a PDF not a brochure, arrange a conference call not a meeting. attend a virtual class not a classroom.

I don't believe we can un-invent e-learning. It isn't a storm to be weathered but a new way of going about lifelong learning. We still talk about the phenomenon of e-learning but the day when learners stop seeing the delivery channel and see only the content it delivers—as we do with television—is getting closer. Of course, there is a financial as well as cultural aspect to this. Historically, it's been a given that training is one of the first casualties when enterprise budgets need to be cut. In the information economy, hopefully enlightened HR directors and CIOs will see to it that this will happen less but until the learning department has established its credentials as a profit centre, it remains vulnerable. That's why enterprises who believe e-learning is nice-to-have need to feel good about the economy before green-lighting an initiative. Enterprises with a deep insight into the benefits e-learning can deliver in all financial conditions will be more comfortable signing off the significant start-up costs, even when the feel good factor is missing. Realistically, the question of whether e-learning is here to stay can be rephrased as: can e-learning weather economic uncertainty? Already, tremors from three global events have been felt by e-learning buyers and vendors: the end of the dot-com boom, the events of September 11, and the chain of accounting transgressions that began with Enron.

E-learning after the dot-coms

> *The once over-hyped and now restructuring Internet economy should not dissuade businesses from hearing two clear messages. First, while many "dot-coms" failed financially, they did prove that the new technologies are here to stay. And second, one of the residual effects of the past few years is acceleration in the amount of knowledge that's now made available through new technological platforms—knowledge that must be better managed.* DiamondCluster International[5]

E-learning rode on the tails of the dot-com boom. Dot-com dreams, promises and hype were the dreams, promises and hype of e-learning. E-learning vendors convinced themselves and set about convincing would-be customers that overnight all learning would become e-learning, that e-learning would sweep across the corporate world like re-engineering and Enterprise Resource Planning before it. So when the dot-com sector dropped like a stone, conventional wisdom informed us e-learning was bound to follow.

IDC (International Data Corporation) offered e-learning an alternative scenario: "With the collapse of the Internet stock bubble, the conventional wisdom is that the so-called New Economy and the impetus for e-business have collapsed as well. But is conventional wisdom correct? Before the crash, IDC recognized that the dot-com sector was over-heated, but it also understood that it represented just a small part of overall investment in Internet technologies and services. More than 90% of that spending came from brick-and-mortar companies."[6] It's those brick-and-mortar companies—often faced with the challenges of intense global competition, geographically dispersed work forces, serial mergers and acquisitions, and the relentless advance of technology—that form the natural client-base for e-learning.

It gets better. One of the more questionable hypes of the dot-com days turned out to be, well, true. E-learning vendors boasted that of all the e-applications for which the drum was being banged, e-learning was the one with the greatest staying power—because, unlike most e-offerings, it was not a solution in search of a problem. E-learning addresses a real business need. If you want proof about that, take a hard look at the e-learning vendor market. Bryan Chapman, e-learning analyst at Brandon-Hall, did and discovered that only about 3% of e-learning vendors go out of business.[7] E-learning, as they say, has legs. According to Cisco Systems, over 70 million people did their learning online in 2000. That year, the e-learning market was worth $2.3 billion. By the end of 2006, it's set to be worth almost $29 billion.[8]

While the business climate post the dot-com debacle has been testing, particularly for technology-related businesses, smart e-learning vendors and buyers know the best is yet to come. IDC agrees: "... we have four times as much opportunity between now and 2005 as we had from 1997 to 2000. If e-businesses stick to business fundamentals, adopt global orientations and world-class technologies, partner aggressively, and focus on customer needs, opportunities may expand even faster than we foresee."[9]

Harvard Business School's Michael Porter sees something positive in the shakeout: "Many companies now are in a classical cyclical downturn where everybody's afraid. They just aren't sure when revenue will pick up again, so people have cut back on systems investments. But there's also a new rigor in insisting that a business case be made for Internet deployment. That is very healthy."[10]

E-learning vendors and buyers know Porter is right. Despite the savings and benefits e-learning has proven it can deliver, it doesn't merit a free ticket to ride. In a post dot-com market, every implementation should be underpinned by a thorough and watertight business case. (For more about business cases and ROI, see Chapter 3.)

E-learning after September 11

If any single day could have focused the business world's attention on the benefits of moving bits not atoms, it was 11 September. Reducing travel costs and time away from work have always been important benefits of e-learning. Now with employee security a significant consideration, e-learning's ability to reduce all learning-related travel has been brought into sharp focus. Businesses will turn increasingly to e-learning's virtual classrooms, peer-to-peer collaboration, e-mentoring and self-paced courses as travel-free cost-saving solutions to keeping employees in a state of readiness to compete.

E-learning after Enron et al.

It will take time for investors' confidence in corporate probity to return. Instead of just waiting, publicly quoted corporations and their auditors should act to earn back that confidence. Since everyone has been tarred by the same brush, even businesses that operate with integrity need to be proactive.

Post Enron uncertainty and low share prices will have halted the countdown for some e-learning initiatives sitting on the launch pad and delayed the expansion of those already operational. That's not smart. Rather than putting the brakes on e-learning, this kind of crisis should accelerate it. In times of corporate crisis, management needs a fast, responsive, global channel to deliver critical learning messages.

Business leaders who want to demonstrate a commitment to high ethical standards — to their employees and the market — need to call for the immediate development and delivery of new business ethics courses tailored to specific roles and responsibilities in the enterprise. The courses should be mandatory and form a key part of future induction programmes. Generic content publishers should be smart enough to recognize an opportunity and work overtime to add new ethics courses to their catalogues. Enron and crises like it are opportunities for e-learning. All it takes is the vision to recognize them and the commitment to act on them.

In view of market conditions and a general clampdown on IT investments during 2002, what was surprising was that e-learning activity grew. When e-learning consultants Brandon-Hall surveyed 600 enterprises, they learned that 60% were delivering learning through e-learning channels. That's a 49% increase on the previous year.[11]

The new learning landscape

Enterprises are making a commitment to e-learning. A SkillSoft survey indicated that 43% of US businesses had implemented or were in the process of implementing e-learning.[12] An ASTD survey indicated that 42% of respondents were either beginning implementation or had been using e-learning for some time.[13] In the UK, a Xebec McGraw-Hill survey showed a similar level of commitment. Twenty-eight per cent of companies with intranets were using them to deliver e-learning; 54% said they had plans to deliver e-learning within one to three years.[14] Each year e-learning becomes a more common feature on the learning landscape. For enterprises turning their backs on e-learning that creates a risk.

Will their employees be able to compete effectively with competitors' employees who already enjoy the benefits of e-learning?

Some businesses have justified standing on the sidelines of e-learning by pointing to the absence of standards. That position makes less sense every day. While there won't be a full set of e-learning standards for a while yet, the development path is clearly signposted and what risks the absence of standards once posed have all but disappeared. A sound e-learning strategy and due diligence in the selection process will protect your investment.

Does it work?

Does e-learning improve learner performance? To earn a place in the enterprise, it has to. No effort has been spared in the search for an answer. Hundreds of surveys have compared the effectiveness of learning delivered face-to-face in a classroom with learning delivered at a distance. Many focused specifically on e-learning; others pre-date e-learning as it's defined in this book and compared classroom learning with *technology-based learning*.

Only a very small percentage of surveys found that technology-based learning disadvantages the learner. What differentiates learning that works from learning that doesn't is not the delivery channel. Barbara B. Lockee, Assistant Professor of Instructional Technology at Virginia Polytechnic Institute and State University, has had first-hand experience: "The delivery mode we know for a fact does not impact the learning. It's the design of the instruction that impacts the learning ... Instead of comparing, say, our online multimedia-authoring course to the face-to-face course, we would look to see that our distance learners are achieving our intended outcomes no matter how they're getting it. That's the question that we need to answer ..."[15]

In what must have been a labour of love, Thomas L. Russell, Director Emeritus of Instructional Telecommunications at North Carolina State University, has compiled a bibliography of 355 surveys, none of which found any significant difference between technology-based and classroom learning. Russell calls his collection *The No Significant Difference Phenomenon*.[16] The current edition covers the years from 1928 to 2001. "The good news," declares Russell, "is that these no significant difference (NSD) studies provide substantial evidence that technology does not denigrate instruction."[17]

Bill Orr, a researcher in the Vocational-Adult Education Department at Auburn University in Alabama, goes further. He believes all the surveys in Russell's bibliography skew the outcome because they are quantitative and according to Orr that ensures technology-based learning cannot perform significantly better in a survey than face-to-face learning. He maintains that only qualitative research can deliver a true analysis of the learning benefits of technology. To prove the point, Orr has compiled his own bibliography of some 60 qualitative surveys made between 1988 and 1999; each indicates that technology-based learning does deliver a significant difference in performance improvement over face-to-face learning.[18]

E-learning reduces the cost of instruction by about one-third and either reduces instruction time by about one-third or increases the effectiveness of instruction by about one-third. It's a claim that should make any CIO or HR director sit up and take notice. Surprisingly, it didn't emanate from a marketing department but from the Institute for Defense Analyses (IDA). In business since 1947, IDA is an American non-profit corporation "whose primary mission is to assist the Office of the Secretary of Defense, the Joint Staff, the unified commands and defense agencies in addressing important national security issues, particularly those requiring scientific and technical expertise".[19] Dexter Fletcher, an IDA researcher, came up with "the thirds" by extrapolating the results of five meta-studies of technology-based learning (see Figure 2.2). Fletcher explained the importance of using meta-studies: "... current practice suggests that no single evaluation study, no matter how carefully done, is conclusive, that we must combine the results of many evaluation studies to draw a cumulative picture of what we've learned".[20]

Averaging the reductions in learning time across 93 studies allowed Fletcher and those following in his footsteps to claim with justification that e-learning reduces instruction time by about one-third or increases the effectiveness of instruction by about one-third. Fletcher justified his claim for about one-third cost-savings in a similar way.

A more recent survey received a lot of attention when it demonstrated the benefit of e-learning over traditional classroom learning; it also illustrated some of the difficulties facing researchers. In the autumn of 1996, Jerald G. Schutte, a sociology professor at California State University at Northridge, randomly divided 33 of his social statistics students into two groups. He taught a group of 17 students in a traditional classroom; the other group, with e-learning. "The motivation for doing this was to provide some hard, experimental evidence that didn't seem to exist anywhere," Schutte explained.[27] There were no statistically significant differences between the groups in terms of sex, age, computer literacy or attitude toward the subject. Here's how Schutte described his procedure: "The traditional class met every Saturday during the next 14 weeks as scheduled from 9:00 am to 1:30 pm. The virtual class met only twice after the first two weeks — during the 7th and 14th week to take the midterm and final examination. The traditional class solved common weekly problem assignments submitting them in each week. The virtual class had four assignments each week: 1) e-mail collaboration among randomly assigned groups of three students in which they generated weekly statistical reports and sent them to the instructor using e-mail; 2) hypernews discussion in which a weekly discussion topic was responded to twice a week by each student; 3) forms input via the WWW which allowed for student submission of the same homework problems being solved by the traditional class; and 4) a weekly moderated Internet relay chat (mIRC) in which student discussion and dialogue were carried out in real time in the virtual presence of the professor."[28] Both groups were given identical tests under the same conditions. Care was taken to ensure course content was standardized across both groups though Schutte's own

Meta-study	Year	Sub-studies (#)	Learning time reduction (%)
Orlansky, S. and String, J. *Cost-Effectiveness of Computer-Based Education in Military Training*[21]	1979	32	30
Kulik, J.A. *Meta-Analytic Studies of Findings on Computer-Based Instruction—Higher Education*[22]	1994	17	34
Kulik, J.A. *Meta-Analytic Studies of Findings on Computer-Based Instruction—Adult Education*[23]	1994	15	24
Fletcher, Dexter. *Effectiveness and Cost of Interactive Videodisc Instruction in Defense Training and Education.* Institute for Defense Analyses[24]	1990	6	31
Johnston, B.R. and Fletcher, J.D. *Effectiveness of Computer Based Instruction in Military Training.* Institute for Defense Analyses[25]	1995	23	28

Figure 2.2—Dexter Fletcher's meta-analysis[26]

description reveals the two groups' noticeably different modus operandi—and this has led to some criticism of the design and methodology of the study.

Against expectations, the e-learning group scored an average of 20% higher than the traditional class in both mid-term and final examinations. Compared with the traditional class, post-test results indicated that the e-learning class demonstrated a significantly higher level of (1) interaction with their peers, (2) time spent on class work, and (3) flexibility and understanding of course content—as well as displaying a better attitude to their professor, their class, computers and maths. "The students formed peer groups online as compensation for not having time in class to talk," Schutte said of the e-learning group. "I believe that as much of the results can be explained by collaboration as the technology."[29] If spontaneous peer-to-peer collaboration was both encouraged and enabled by the technology, it seems to me to be a fair development within a comparison between e-learning and classroom learning. It's a view supported by Dexter Fletcher: "The technologies by themselves do not guarantee this impact, but the functionalities they support with their applications do."[30] There was, after all, nothing to stop the classroom group from collaborating on a face-to-face basis — and enjoying the same benefits as the e-learning group.

So, does e-learning work? According to research, the worst case scenario is that e-learning is as effective as traditional face-to-face classroom learning; the best case scenario, that e-learning delivers significant advantages to the learner — both in the quality of learning and the level of performance that results.

References

1   Freeman L (Jul 2001) *E-Learning: An Open Door Policy* The Education Industry Reports Issue 26 July 2001 [Internet] Available from <http://www.eduventures.com/news/education_industry_report/corpTraining/printCorpTrain.cfm> Accessed 26 Jul 2001.

2   Useem J (2001) *And Then, Just When You Thought the "New Economy" Was Dead ...* Business 2.0 August 2001 [Internet] Available from <http://www.business2.com/articles/mag/0, 1640, 16684|8,FF.html> Accessed 3 Aug 2002.

3   McKenzie A (1969) *The ARPA Network* [Online image] Available from <http://www.cybergeography.org/atlas/arpanet2_small.gif> Accessed 4 Apr 2002.

4   Weinberger D (2002) *Small Pieces Loosely Joined — A Unified Theory of the Web* Cambridge MA, Perseus Publishing pp 174–5.

5   *Building A Knowledge-Powered Company* (2001) DiamondCluster White Paper [Internet] Available from <http://www.diamondcluster.com/Work/WPapers/WPKnowledgeMgmt.asp> Accessed 28 Apr 2002.

6   Gantz J (2001) *Perception Versus Reality* IDC White Paper [Internet] Available from <http://www.idc.com.au/promotions/pdf_files/Whitepaper.pdf> Accessed 5 Sep 2001 p 1.

7   Chapman B (5–6 Mar 2002) *State of the Industry* [Conference proceedings] London, Online Learning 2002 Europe Conference and Expo.

8   *While Corporate Training Markets Will Not Live up to Earlier Forecasts, IDC Suggests Reasons for Optimism, Particularly eLearning* (2002) IDC [Press Release] [Internet] Available from <http://www.idc.com/getdoc.jhtml?containerId=pr2002_09_17_150550> Accessed 6 Jan 2003.

9   Gantz J (2001) *Perception Versus Reality* IDC White Paper [Internet] Available from <http://www.idc.com.au/promotions/pdf_files/Whitepaper.pdf.> Accessed 5 Sep 2001 p 13.

10 Byrne JA (2001) *Q&A: Caught in the Net* BusinessWeek Online [Internet] Available from <http://www.businessweek.com/magazine/content/01_35/b3746630.htm> Accessed 22 Oct 2001.

11 Pack T (2002) *Corporate Learning Gets Digital* EContent Magazine July 2002 [Internet] Available from <http://www.econtentmag.com/bs1/2002/pack7_02.html> Accessed 31 Jul 2002.

12 *e-Learning in USA & Canada Benchmark Survey* (2001) Taylor Nelson Sofres Commissioned by SkillSoft [Internet] Available from <http://www.skillsoft.com/elearning/white_papers/index.asp> Accessed 29 Apr 2002.

13   Schafter A ed (2001) *E-Learning Survey* ASTD [Internet] Available from <http://www.learningcircuits.com/2001/oct2001/survey.html> Accessed 29 Apr 2002.

14   *Corporate E-Learning ... Realizing the Potential* (2001) Xebec McGraw-Hill [Internet] Available from <http://www.nln.ac.uk/delg/keydocuments/DELG%2001%20007.pdf> Accessed 29 Apr 2002.

15   Carnevale D (2001) *What Matters in Judging Distance Teaching? Not How Much It's Like a Classroom Course* The Chronicle of Higher Education [Internet] Available from <http://chronicle.com/free/2001/02/2001022101u.htm> Accessed 30 Mar 2002.

16   Russell TL (2001) *No Significant Difference Phenomenon* [Study] [Internet] Available from <http://teleeducation.nb.ca/nosignificantdifference> Accessed 29 Apr 2002.

17   Russell TL (1999) *No Significant Difference Phenomenon* Raleigh, North Carolina State University p xiii.

18   Orr B (1999) *A Significant Difference* [Study] [Internet] Available from <http://teleeducation.nb.ca/content/articles/A-Significant-Difference.html> Accessed 29 Apr 2002.

19   IDA [Internet] Available from <http://www.ida.org/IDAnew/Welcome/history.html> Accessed 12 Jul 2002.

20   Fletcher JD (1996) *Does This Stuff Work? Some Findings from Applications of Technology to Education and Training* [Conference proceedings] Teacher Education and the Use of Technology Based Learning Systems. Warrenton, VA: Society for Applied Learning Technology [Internet] Available from <http://www.hi.is/~joner/eaps/wh_stuff.htm> Accessed 29 Apr 2002.

21   Olansky S and String J (1979) *Cost-Effectiveness of Computer-Based Education in Military Training* [Report] Arlington, Institute for Defence Analysis—Science, and Technical Division.

22   Kulik JA (1994) *Meta-Analytic Studies of Findings on Computer-Based Instruction—Higher Education* In Baker EL and O'Neil HF *Technology Assessment in Education and Training* Hillsdale, LEA Publisher.

23   Kulik JA *Meta-Analytic Studies of Findings on Computer-Based Instruction—Adult Education* In Baker EL and O'Neil HF *Technology Assessment in Education and Training* Hillsdale, LEA Publishers.

24   Fletcher D (1990) *Effectiveness and Cost of Interactive Videodisc Instruction in Defense Training and Education Alexandria*, Institute for Defense Analyses.

25   Johnston BR and Fletcher JD (1995) *Effectiveness of Computer Based Instruction in Military Training* Alexandria, Institute for Defense Analyses.

26   Fletcher JD (1996) *Does This Stuff Work? Some Findings from Applications of Technology to Education and Training* [Conference proceedings] Teacher Education and the Use of Technology Based Learning Systems. Warrenton, VA: Society for Applied Learning Technology [Internet] Available from <http://www.hi.is/~joner/eaps/wh_stuff.htm> Accessed 29 Apr 2002.

27   Schutte JG (1996) *Virtual Teaching in Higher Education: The New Intellectual Superhighway or Just Another Traffic Jam?* Northridge, California State University [Abstract] [Internet] Available from <http://www.csun.edu/sociology/virexp.htm> Accessed 30 Mar 2002.

28   Schutte JG (1996) *Virtual Teaching in Higher Education: The New Intellectual Superhighway or Just Another Traffic Jam?* Northridge, California State University [Abstract] [Internet] Available from <http://www.csun.edu/sociology/virexp.htm> Accessed 30 Mar 2002.

29　*Online students fare better* (1997) CNET [Internet] Available from <http://news.com.com/2100-1023-263035.html?legacy> Accessed 30 Mar 2002.

30　Fletcher JD (1996) *Does This Stuff Work? Some Findings from Applications of Technology to Education and Training* [Conference proceedings] Teacher Education and the Use of Technology Based Learning Systems. Warrenton, VA: Society for Applied Learning Technology [Internet] Available from <http://www.hi.is/~joner/eaps/wh_stuff.htm> Accessed 29 Apr 2002.

ROI, metrics and evaluation: how can we tell if we're getting it right?

3

... the business world is not about learning. It is about doing business. This means producing, marketing, and ultimately getting customers to use goods and services. If e-learning can make people better at producing and marketing goods and services, and help customers get better use out of them, fine. E-learning supports business processes; it's not a process unto itself. Mark Cavender, The Chasm Group[1]

... once you're clear about what it is you want to measure, you can then go out and measure it. It's not rocket science. The equation's pretty simple. It's perceived customer value over investment; that's ROI. Edward Trolley, The Forum Corporation[2]

What you need to know

Human capital

Ask any executive what his enterprise's most valuable asset is and his answer will be: "Our people." Why? Because of what they know—their human capital. In the knowledge economy there has been a phenomenal growth in the value of human capital:

- Strategically, because as Thomas A. Stewart explained in *Intellectual Capital*, "Information and knowledge are the thermonuclear competitive weapons of our time. Knowledge is more valuable and more powerful than natural resources, big factories, or fat bankrolls."[3]
- Financially, because as Charles Leadbeater notes in *Living on Thin Air*, "Only about 7 per cent of Microsoft's stock-market value at that time [May 1997] was accounted for by traditional, tangible assets—land, buildings, machinery, equipment—recorded on its formal balance sheet. The missing 93 per cent of the company's value was due to intangible assets which accountants do not measure: brands, research and development, and people."[4]

From an investment perspective the problem with human capital and the knowledge it embodies is that neither can be owned. When an enterprise hires an employee in effect it is licensing that person's knowledge, experience and skills. Invest in a plant and the result turns up on your balance sheet as an asset.

Invest in staff and the result turns up on the wrong side of the balance sheet as a cost. Laurie Bassi and Daniel McMurrer, respectively Chair of the Board and Chief Research Officer at Knowledge Asset Management, Inc., explain how that leads to under-investment in learning: ". . . because training and education are treated on a firm's books as costs, not as investments, those firms that make such investments must do so in spite of the pressures of the market (to reduce costs) rather than because of them (as might be the case if the market had the information necessary to recognize such expenditures as worthy investments). This leads to a collective tendency to under-invest in human capital — more inefficiency that affects society as a whole. It's bad for stockholders and firms, and it's bad for the people who work in them, since research has found that workplace training is an important determinant of workers' future earnings capacity."[5]

Manage an investment in human capital properly and the benefits are increased competitiveness, shareholder value, efficiency, customer satisfaction, peak performance, and so on. No right-thinking executive can dismiss these returns. Even so, investing in staff does not match up to the traditional accounting concept of investment. Even the tools available for evaluating the investment — the ROI — are left over from the industrial era. As a result, accountants frequently deliver misleading results about human capital costs, recording the known costs but lacking the tools to uncover the deeper more significant costs *and* benefits. Accountants resort to measuring *efficiency* which is concerned only with input variables when what is needed is a measure of *effectiveness* which takes account of both input and outcome. Everybody knows that just because someone is busy doesn't guarantee they're accomplishing anything.

Human capital costs cannot be ignored; they can account for 70% of a business's operating costs. To understand what a business gets in return for those costs and how the results can be measured, we first need to understand the human capital value chain which, according to Bassi, works like this:

- "In addition to being fairly compensated, people place high value on:

    - being in an environment where they can grow and learn and advance
    - the managerial skills/abilities of their immediate supervisor
    - being treated fairly, appreciated and acknowledged
    - doing work that makes a contribution

- These determinants of employee satisfaction drive employee retention.
- The retention rate among key employees drives customer satisfaction.
- Customer satisfaction drives customer retention.
- Customer retention drives profitability and other measures of financial performance including total stockholder return."[6]

What is interesting here is how much is driven by employees' own assessment of the enterprise that employs them. Learning plays a significant role in these assessments. Not many enterprises have the tools or the will to make a connection, for example, between an increase in learning spend and an increase in staff retention. Most of the time, a manager only discovers during an exit interview that learning opportunities were too sparse or too poor. By then the employee is walking out the door taking her human capital with her. Money considered "saved" by not investing in learning ends up being spent to recruit a replacement and make them performance ready. What could have been invested in increasing employee satisfaction is spent to maintain the status quo. The Royal Bank of Scotland learned from exit interviews that disappointment in training was one of the top two reasons employees were leaving; turning that round became a driver for e-learning. (To learn more about the bank's e-learning, see the case study in Chapter 20.)

Bassi and McMurrer's interest in the impact of human capital investments led them to research the performance of 500 publicly-traded US companies. What they uncovered was more dramatic than employee satisfaction: "In general, we found a clear relationship between training expenditures per employee and financial performance in the following year. Almost all financial measures (stock performance, income per employee, gross profit margin, market value per employee) are significantly higher for those companies that spend an above-average amount per employee on training . . . a firm's current training investments are the single most important statistical predictor of its total stockholder return (stock price change plus dividend yield) for the following year—more telling than other key investments that are publicly-reported, such as R&D."[7] The pair are so convinced of the significance of their findings that they've set up an investment management business based on the principle of investing in companies that invest in people.

If it is true that in the knowledge economy, human capital is a business's most important asset—and you would be hard-pressed to find an expert who argues otherwise—businesses need to face up to the challenge of measuring the return on investment in people even if their first toolsets and results are imperfect.

The metrics challenge

What I like about Edward Trolley's observation—at the start of this chapter—about ROI as it applies to learning is how elegantly he leaps over the mess in a single bound: ". . . once you're clear about what it is you want to measure . . .". For many enterprises, achieving clarity and agreement about what needs measuring has proved a challenge. Deciding what needs to be measured usually means making a choice between an old and a new business model—and between old push-training and new pull-learning. That decision is one reason for the difficulty. People attached to one model aren't easily persuaded to give it up in favour of another.

Dot-com proselytizers labelled the two models "bricks" and "clicks". The bricks model emanates from the mindset of the industrial economy where what matters is tangible—plant, machinery, raw materials—and can be recorded in the company books; the clicks model, from the mindset of the knowledge economy where what matters is intangible — the knowledge in people's heads — for which there is no recognized notation.

The object of the ROI exercise is, first, to predict and, later, to validate the monetary value of learning to the enterprise. Both value and learning are intangibles. That's why applying a model designed to value in bottom line terms what can be loaded onto a freight train to measure what employees carry around in their heads is not, on the face of it, a very helpful proposition.

ROE

One school of thought argues there's no point even trying to use the old measuring tools; a new set of knowledge and performance metrics is required for e-learning. These are not expressed in monetary terms because e-learning ROI is not about monetary value, it is about the value of knowledge. This school is much more comfortable with ROE — return on expectation — an approach developed originally by William Trochim, a professor at Cornell University. Here's how Trochim rationalizes it: "Doing ROI analysis is expensive and tricky. Put simply, *the ROI of doing ROI well is usually too low to justify the effort and expense*. It's smarter to focus instead on doing a good up-front job laying out what you are trying to do, establishing consensus, and tracking that initial vision all the way through the project to measures of performance and change. Then you evaluate the project based on how close it came to the original expectations. This "Return on Expectation" (ROE) is quite different from traditional "Return on Investment" analysis."[8]

That's OK — as far as it goes. What we really need to ask is whether ROE goes far enough. It's easy to argue that knowledge is the oxygen of the new economy and, it follows, learning does not need a business case made for it. What we lose through this soft approach, however, is the ability to discriminate. As long as expectations are largely met, we've succeeded. ROE ducks questions like: could the same effect have been achieved sooner, faster, cheaper? Could we have achieved a better effect in the same time and for the same cost? Ultimately, ROE is subjective.

Bricks with clicks

Post the dot-coms, peace has broken out in the battle between bricks and clicks. Harvard Business School's Michael Porter believes a lack of understanding led to polarization in the first place: "Too often, people confuse change with disruption. What disruption means is that it invalidates or makes substantially less important the advantages of incumbents. The Internet didn't invalidate the importance of the product, the brand, the distribution system, or even physical locations like stores and warehouses ... There was no inconsistency between having online ordering and having stores. You could do both together."[9]

That the old model and the new are not mutually exclusive is a lesson e-learning practitioners are learning, too. You can apply the metrics of the knowledge economy *and* establish monetary values for ROI even — or especially — for elusive soft skills. Working with the old model and the new isn't easy, which is why most learning departments don't. On the other hand, if a financial ROI is what's standing between your learning department and an e-learning implementation or next year's e-learning budget, it's time to face up to the challenge. The reward is a win–win situation that benefits the business, the learning department, and the learner.

ROI

ROI can be predictive or historical. The best predictive ROI will draw on historical ROI data. Sometimes no data is available, for example, when you're building a business case for an e-learning implementation — or implementing an e-learning course for new hires. In both cases new ground is being broken and you can't put your hand on your heart and promise a specific return on investment. What you can do is research the experience of other businesses in similar situations, take advice from e-learning consultants and vendors, factor in your experience of ROI in traditional learning environments and make a conservative prediction of ROI. The credibility of your business case will be enhanced by these efforts especially if your figures are conservative — extravagant ROI predictions undermine your proposal and your long-term credibility in the board room.

Six months to a year after your business case has been signed off, you should validate your predictive ROI with historical data. If a learning department can consistently validate predictive ROI, learning proposals will be treated with respect and enjoy an easier passage through the sign-off process.

A commitment to full learning evaluation remains the exception rather than the rule. In practice, learning departments have equated ROI with illustrating that the delivery of e-learning is cheaper per learner than the delivery of instructor led classroom learning. It's an easy case to make. There can be dramatic savings in travel expenses, accommodation and opportunity costs.

However, as Cisco's Tom Kelly points out, savings associated with a shift in delivery channels are usually an unrepeatable offer: "There are some fantastic cost savings, but only for one year — you can't keep saving over time. If I can save a company $5 million in training-related travel this year, how much would they save next year? Nothing, because they'd take it out of the budget. You can't do it just on cost savings. The ROI is based on business impact. Can we, for example, demonstrate that salespeople who are great consumers of e-learning training products have better customer satisfaction and sales achievement? That requires looking at departmental metrics and tying company performance to increased knowledge sharing and increased skill development."[10]

It is only ongoing ROI that can prove the true worth of learning but it takes commitment.

Performance is the metric that matters

It's time that training be accountable for much more than high instructor ratings. Management can and should expect T&D to produce tangible, calculable value with every training dollar, euro, or rupee. Just as a projected new factory must promise a positive return to justify the funds to build it, training too must demonstrate and deliver real value. High-quality training is not cheap, and it must pay for itself with tangible results. It doesn't seem too much to ask, does it? David van Adelsberg, Edward A. Trolley[11]

Metrics that are easy to measure get measured even if they don't tell us what we need to know; too often, metrics that are hard to measure are avoided. With e-learning, it's easy to measure course registrations, course completions, module completions, pages visited, hours of learning, assessment scores—so they get measured even though the resulting data doesn't tell us whether e-learning is doing its job.

Imagine you're a learning manager and you've just parked your car in the company car park. As you walk to the building you cross paths with the CEO who is also on his way to the building. After the usual exchange of pleasantries, you calculate that you have the CEO's undivided attention for 90 seconds. You decide to use that time to share a learning success story. The day before, you read a report about the learning metrics for the previous quarter and it brought a smile to your face. You want to see the same smile on your CEO's face, so you give him your best shot, "I had some good news yesterday. In the last quarter, e-learning course completions were up from 46 to 66%!"

Truthfully, what kind of reaction do you think you'd get? Is it far-fetched to assume your CEO might reply, "Impressive numbers. By the way, Laura—it is Laura, isn't it?—what are "course completions"?"

Take two: You give him your best shot. "You might be interested to know that last quarter our new courses meant sales teams in every market got up to speed on three new products in half the time it used to take—and for half the cost." "Impressive numbers," your CEO replies and means it. You're talking about business results and in a language senior managers understand.

What lesson can we draw from this imaginary encounter?

The only metric that matters is performance. All the rest is housekeeping.

I am not saying that tracking learner inputs shouldn't be done. It should. I am saying that tracking learner inputs isn't enough. Look at what Cisco tracks under the heading of Penetration and Usage:

- "Number of e-learning offerings each learner utilized and total offerings utilized organization-wide (i.e. each learner utilized five offerings and a total of 1000 offerings were utilized organizational-wide)
- Number of training offerings assigned, enrolled-in, completed, passed
- Number of logins per course, per learner (i.e. how often did learner visit a given e-learning offering)

- Learner overall usage of available course offerings (i.e. how many offerings did learner utilize)
- Length of attendance per session
- Total hours logged per month for individual learners
- Number of target audiences that used course offerings
- Percentage of learner's (curriculum) roadmap completed
- Type of delivery utilized (e.g. CiscoCast, VOD, Cisco/IPTV, VC, ILT, CD, WBT, or book)
- Geography by theatre, country and region as applicable
- Per cent of offering "touched" by learner, per learner
- Number of learners within a job role — with management reporting relationships, per offering".[12]

In addition, Cisco measures Satisfaction, Effectiveness, Relevance and Cost under 21 separate headings. One Effectiveness measurement focuses solely on performance: "Offering's direct effect on: decreasing cost, increasing productivity, increasing profitability, enhancing employee retention (as defined by quantitative and qualitative evaluation data)."[13]

You can learn a lot from learner inputs and demographics but if they are all you track, you will not understand e-learning's impact on your business. For impact read change, for example, an increase in the size and frequency of orders, a reduction is wastage, increased repeat business, shorter time to market, lower inventory levels, lower cost of new hires.

You are what you measure

Every enterprise needs to improve its performance somewhere. To pay its way, e-learning needs to be a key part of the enterprise's performance-improvement strategy. In other words, e-learning needs to be about outcomes not inputs.

A record of the number of hours of e-learning that took place in a month is a record of input. So many people spent so long doing something — but what about the outcome of their action? Did their knowledge increase? Is that increase reflected in an increase in productivity? Did less work have to be re-done? How much less? Would more learning have produced a better outcome? Would better learning have produced a better outcome? Would less learning have produced the same outcome?

Most enterprises don't ask these performance-related questions. Is that because the learning department lacks conviction? Or lacks the tools to prove it is having a positive effect on performance? In practice, there are four major barriers to evaluating learning:

- "Senior management does not ask for it.
- Training managers do not know how to do it.

- Training managers do not know what to measure and evaluate.
- The effort may be both costly and risky."[14]

Whatever the reason, the effect is the same: the learning department is marginalized. In how many enterprises does the head of learning carry the same weight in the board room as the head of production? With or without justification, senior executives perceive production as mission-critical and learning as mission-trivial. Only when the learning department holds itself as accountable for the performance of the enterprise as sales, marketing and production can its status change. That leads us back to metrics.

What a learning department measures tells us something about what it believes important. If it measures only inputs that tells us it believes efficiency is important, in other words, good housekeeping. When it measures both inputs and outputs that tells us that it believes effectiveness is important, that is, business performance. That's why metrics are so important — you are what you measure. If you want to change the focus of a learning department, start by changing what it measures.

Kirkpatrick: an evergreen evaluation model

Nineteen fifty-nine. Charles De Gaulle became President of the Fifth Republic in France. Soviet space probe Luna 2 became the first man-made object to reach the moon. Motown Records was launched. Fidel Castro took control of Cuba. The Ho Chi Minh Trail between North and South Vietnam opened. So did a Broadway musical called "The Sound of Music".

Meanwhile at the University of Wisconsin, Donald Kirkpatrick, a professor of marketing, was designing a model for the evaluation of learning. He did a good job. Though not without critics, Kirkpatrick's model has pervaded the global learning community, turning up again and again in books, articles and White Papers. In 1997, according to ASTD (American Society for Training and Development), 67% of American organizations that conducted training evaluations used the Kirkpatrick Model. Its levels have become a recognized taxonomy of learning evaluation and as such serve as a shorthand for learning managers and designers.

- *Level 1* Reaction: a measure of learner satisfaction.
- *Level 2* Learning: a measure of learning.
- *Level 3* Behaviour: a measure of behaviour change.
- *Level 4* Results: a measure of results.

Typically, learning managers apply the model by answering a series of questions associated with each level (see Figure 3.1).

Is the model relevant to e-learning? Kirkpatrick thinks so. He views the Web as another learning channel, subject to the same constraints and rules as other

Level	Questions
1 Reaction	• Did the learners like it? • What do they plan to do with what they've learned?
2 Learning	• Did the learners get it? • Have their skills, knowledge or attitudes changed as a result? • How much have they changed?
3 Behaviour	• Can the learners go out and do it? • Has their behaviour changed as a result of learning?
4 Results	• Do the learners use what they've learned? • Does the change in their behaviour have a positive and measurable impact on the business?

Figure 3.1 — Questions for each Kirkpatrick level

media. "I think my levels of evaluation apply however you might want to measure it," Kirkpatrick explains. "I don't care whether you are talking about technical training or soft training, we have to measure skills. Are the people learning the skills we are training? It doesn't make any difference what kind of organization it is, people want to know: "Are we getting our money's worth out of our training budget?"" [15]

Kirkpatrick's model is characterized by four levels of evaluation that taken together embody a holistic, coherent process. The model allows for a lot of flexibility in its implementation. For that reason some people view the four levels as a framework or a taxonomy rather than a model. Others interpret the four levels as a menu from which they can evaluate à la carte.

Jack Phillips, considered to be the father of ROI in the US training industry, understands that the complexity of the model can lead to a selective approach. "Some organizations attempt to manage the process by setting targets for each level. A target is the percentage of training programs measured at that level. For example, at Level 4, where it is difficult to measure, organizations have a low level of activity — usually less than 20 per cent." [16] Other enterprises adopt a phased approach to the model, implementing Level 1 in year one, Level 2 in year two, etc. According to ASTD most courses are evaluated at Level 1, almost none at Level 4 (see Figure 3.2). Kirkpatrick's levels appear to suffer a high rate of attrition during a phased implementation.

Neither targeting nor phasing levels gets Kirkpatrick's blessing. "None of the levels should be bypassed simply to get to the level that the trainer considers the most important." [17] The model is an all or nothing process; a partial implementation only thwarts its purpose. You can't extrapolate success in Level 1 across the other three levels. It's like testing your car's brakes and because they pass assuming the whole car — steering, tyres, headlights — is safe (see Figure 3.3).

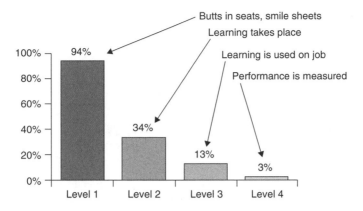

Figure 3.2—Percentage of courses evaluated at each level[18]
Source: ASTD

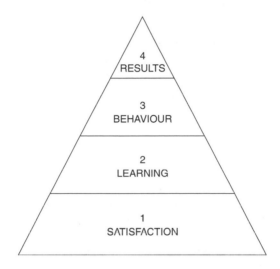

Figure 3.3—Hierarchy of Kirkpatrick's model

Collecting data for Kirkpatrick

Because the model is cumulative, data from each level is carried forward to the next. At each subsequent level, collecting fresh data becomes more time-consuming and expensive. Implementing Kirkpatrick's model requires commitment and perseverance but it does pay off. Most learning managers are familiar with Level 1 data collection even if they aren't familiar with Kirkpatrick. At the end of a course or a session each learner completes a simple questionnaire or in learning vernacular a "smile sheet". The purpose of the smile sheet is to find out if learners enjoyed the learning experience and whether they believe it is relevant. A typical relevancy question might be: "Will your work performance improve over the next 12 months as a result of this learning experience?" (see Figure 3.4).

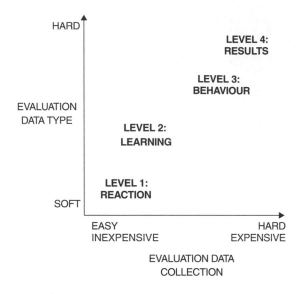

Figure 3.4—Data characteristics associated with each level

Smile sheets elicit subjective data. There's a danger that they reflect a body of learner opinion unconnected to the performance-related course objectives. Dr Bill Lee, Director of Measurement and Performance Analysis at American Airlines Corporate FlagShip University, advocates a move away from smile sheets based on open questions to an objectives-based survey. Of course, you can only do that if course designers have built the content around performance objectives based on desired outcomes in the first place. Assuming they have, the survey becomes a way of checking whether learners believe the course they have taken will help them meet known objectives.

Lee looks for accurate diagnostic information but doesn't believe smile sheets deliver it. "The answer to the survey question typically found on smiley sheets, "The course met my expectations," is of little use unless you first specifically ask the respondents what their expectations are. If their expectations match the intent of the course, then their response to this question might be accurate. However, what if their expectations were different from those intended and you neglected to ask specifically what their expectations are? What would it tell you if this survey item was rated low? Not much, I would suggest. But you might think the course was of little value and redesign or discontinue it if you get a large number of similar responses. What was really needed in this case was to rewrite the course description so potential participants understood the intended outcomes before they registered for the course."[19]

Data for Level 2 evaluations are usually collected by analysing pre- and post-course assessments. Level 3 marks an escalation in the amount of time it takes to collect data. Sources include line managers' observations, follow-up interviews with learners, and 360° evaluations.

Level 4 data measure impact on performance, for example, larger orders, increased cross-selling, reduced absenteeism. (For a comprehensive list of performance outcomes, see p. 70.) In answering the question, Does the change in learners' behaviour have a positive and measurable impact on the business?, Level 4 provides a measure of Return on Expectation. If the key driver for a course is to reduce time to proficiency, ROE should be expressed as a percentage reduction in learning time, for example: The course delivered an average reduction in time to proficiency of 25% or 5 days.

Often Level 4 data is recorded by normal business processes that are independent from the evaluation processes. The challenge for learning evaluators is to find effective means of harvesting the data from the appropriate business systems *before and after* learning interventions and to make meaningful comparisons of the data sets. Bear in mind that the impact of learning on performance sometimes becomes apparent only after 6 months or a year, and schedule data collection at meaningful intervals.

Kirkpatrick acknowledges the challenge of collecting data and makes an important distinction about what the data is capable of delivering: "As we look at the evaluation of reaction, learning, behavior, and results, we can see that evidence is much easier to obtain than proof. In some cases, proof is impractical and almost impossible to get."[20]

The old model gets an upgrade

Many HR practitioners consider a training evaluation complete when they can link business results to the program. But for the ultimate level of evaluation — return-on-investment — the process isn't complete until the results have been converted to monetary values and compared with the cost of the program. This shows the true contribution of training. Jack J. Phillips[21]

As evergreen as Kirkpatrick's model has turned out to be, it could not have foreseen the scale of change that has taken place in the business environment since 1959 when the integrated circuit had only just been invented and each one sold for $1000. All-seeing, all-knowing management information systems tell executives more about what their businesses are spending and earning, and what works and doesn't work faster and better than anyone could have imagined 20 years before the personal computer was invented. Faced with the sweeping effects of change and competition, senior executives are turning to learning as a way of increasing productivity among employees and cutting costs — and expect to see a bottom-line result. They believe — and it's hard to argue otherwise — that the same rigorous performance criteria applied to R&D, production, sales and marketing, and distribution should apply to learning.

In 1996 Jack Phillips updated Kirkpatrick's model by adding a fifth level of evaluation — return on investment. The new level poses the question: "Did the monetary value of the results exceed the cost of the training?" If a Level 4 evaluation proves a positive change in performance but the subsequent Level 5 evaluation indicates the cost of the positive change exceeds its value, what's the point? All that's happening is one part of the business is buying success for another. Positive results from evaluations at Levels 1, 2, 3 and 4 become irrelevant when a learning initiative falls at the final hurdle — ROI in Level 5. Learning managers shouldn't expect management to invest in a cure that is more expensive than the disease.

Moving a learning department from an efficiency model (measure input) to an effectiveness model (measure input and outputs) with a measurable ROI can leave learning managers feeling overworked and unappreciated — and that human response needs to be taken account of. However, adding ROI to the evaluation process delivers benefits that can't be ignored both to the business and the learning department.

Delivering good ROI on a regular basis protects the learning department's budget against cutbacks during economic downturns. More than that, consistent ROI gives the learning department an irrefutable business case for growing its budget — and influence across the enterprise — year on year. Some enterprises have implemented an investment control process that includes a minimum level of ROI that investment proposals must meet before they become eligible for consideration. If the learning department is the only one without a track record of ROI, its investment proposals are more likely to be rejected than those from departments which regularly justify the investments made in them.

That's why it is hard to understand why some people argue that not every learning initiative needs an ROI analysis. For example, if an enterprise has decided to implement SAP, it's obvious that an enterprise-wide learning programme is required — and because it's obvious, why bother with predictive ROI? The need for SAP itself was probably just as obvious to senior management but it's unlikely they gave that project the green light without a rigorous ROI analysis. It's just a normal part of due diligence. Besides, if the need for learning is so obvious, the ROI should be very dramatic, making a good impression and helping the learning department to raise its overall ROI for the year.

No matter how you look at it, not to make the calculation is to miss an opportunity. Ultimately, the objective of Level 5 is to prove that the learning department is a profit not a cost centre. Which raises a pertinent question.

Can e-learning deliver a ROI?

Again and again the answer comes back, Yes. Yet this remains a tricky area for the understandable reason that enterprises are happy to beat the drum for their learning successes — maybe even to enhance them a little — but fast to bury their failures. Other enterprises, whether their learning initiatives are successes or failures, are simply not comfortable sharing what they consider confidential information with strangers and competitors.

Here's a case study of exceptional ROI from a household name enterprise. Each year IBM trains 5000 new managers; historically, they attended a 5-day learning event which covered the basics of IBM culture, strategy and management. As IBM's business became more complex it became clear that 5 days wasn't long time to induct new managers effectively. Only an ongoing learning process could make and keep managers fit to compete. After a careful study of the options, Nancy Lewis, Director of IBM Management Development, adopted an e-learning solution delivered through Mindspan, one of IBM's own products. Lewis's team developed *Basic Blue for Managers*, based around IBM's four-tier multi-channel learning model that takes advantage of self-paced e-learning courses, virtual collaborative tools, content libraries and simulations to complement instructor-led learning. Each manager participates in a 26-week programme of self-paced courses. Issues that arise over this period are handled using peer-to-peer online collaboration.

In 2001 Nucleus Research conducted an independent analysis of *Basic Blue* and came to the striking conclusion that IBM had achieved a 2284% return on its investment over a 2-week payback period. Nucleus's calculations are displayed in Figure 3.5.

See the case studies of the Royal Bank of Scotland in Chapter 20 and the Dow Chemical Company in Chapter 21 for other examples of e-learning ROI.

Defining cost

To answer the question: "Did the monetary value of the results exceed the cost of the training?" we need to know three things:

- The cost of both developing and delivering e-learning.
- The return or benefits.
- The period over which benefits accrue.

Laurie Bassi, President of Human Capital Dynamics and a Saba Fellow, analyses learning development and delivery costs under three headings: direct, indirect and opportunity.

Direct costs

Here is how Bassi breaks down the direct cost of learning (see Figure 3.6):

Notice that Bassi does not include infrastructure costs under e-learning but assumes that a network capable of delivering e-learning is in place and paid for out of a separate budget. This is almost always the case. The cost of the network is a historical cost and not charged to e-learning.

IBM Basic Blue

Summary	
Project:	**Mindspan elearning**
Annual Return On Investment (ROI)	**2284%**
Payback Period (Years)	**0.04**
Net Present Value (NPV)	**31,496,564**
Average Yearly Cost of Ownership	**1,676,571**

Annual Benefits	Initial	Year 1	Year 2	Year 3
Direct	0	18,574,487	18,574,487	18,574,487
Indirect	0	10,820,513	10,820,513	10,820,513
Total Benefits Per Period	0	29,395,000	29,395,000	29,395,000

Depreciation Schedule	Initial	Year 1	Year 2	Year 3
Software	0	0	0	0
Hardware	0	0	0	0
Total Per Period	0	0	0	0

Expensed Costs	Initial	Year 1	Year 2	Year 3
All expensed costs	1,231,712	1,266,000	1,266,000	1,266,000
Total Per Period	1,231,712	1,266,000	1,266,000	1,266,000

Financial Analysis	Results	Year 1	Year 2	Year 3
Net cash flow before taxes		28,129,000	28,129,000	28,129,000
Net cash flow after taxes		14,064,500	14,064,500	14,064,500
Annual ROI - direct and indirect benefits		2284%	2284%	**2284%**
Annual ROI - direct benefits only		1405%	1405%	1405%
Net Present Value (NPV)		11,614,144	22,248,927	**31,496,564**
Payback (Years)	0.04			
Average Cost of Ownership (TCO/Years)		2,497,712	1,881,856	1,676,571
3-Year Cumulative ROI	5214%			
3-Year IRR	2284%			

Basic Financial Assumptions		
All Government Taxes	50%	All calculations are based on Nucleus Research's independent analysis of the expected costs and
Discount Rate	15%	benefits associated with the application profiled in the accompanying case.

Figure 3.5—IBM Basic Blue ROI[22]
Reproduced by permission of Nucleus Research

Direct Learning Costs

Classroom	E-learning
• wages and salaries of trainers • payments to outside vendors • facilities expenses • development • production and distribution of materials • travel expenses • administrative and support costs	• development • purchase and/or licensing of materials • hardware for delivery

Figure 3.6—A breakdown and comparison of learning costs[23]

Indirect costs

Indirect costs are defined by Bassi as: "... compensation — the wages and benefits paid to learners while they are learning — as well as the overhead costs associated with both the direct and indirect costs".[24] She points out a relationship between direct and indirect costs and in so doing signposts the cost advantage of e-learning over classroom learning: "The available evidence suggests that the indirect, compensation costs of traditional learning are typically at least as great as the direct costs. When overhead (which also applies against the direct cost) is added in, the indirect costs of traditional learning are likely to be twice the direct costs ... a conservative estimate of the total cost of typical, classroom learning is that it is at least three and perhaps up to five times the direct costs. And that is one of the major attractions of e-learning; it holds the promise of reducing all three categories of costs, but perhaps most significantly, the indirect and opportunity costs of learning. Under some circumstances, firms have estimated the total cost of e-learning to be less than half the costs of traditional learning."[25]

Opportunity costs

Opportunity costs are business opportunities lost because employees are busy learning and not available for other responsibilities. A conservative estimate of opportunity costs is that they are equal to indirect costs. They can turn out to be dramatically higher, especially when the learner works in sales and marketing. The US Navy Postgraduate School makes an interesting distinction; it believes the ratio of opportunity cost to salary is 1.5:1 for a civilian and 1:1 for military personnel.

Because e-learning (1) is so time-effective, and (2) avoids learning-related travel, it incurs much lower opportunity costs than classroom learning. That said, all learning incurs some opportunity cost. There's another question about opportunity costs that doesn't often get asked but should: Are the opportunity costs associated with not learning greater than those associated with learning?

The fixed cost of learning includes content development, that is, intellectual property development and licences, instructional design, studio costs and programming costs. Whether the content is used by 20 or 20 000 learners does not have an inherent effect on development costs. Occasionally, e-learning fixed costs will include extending or upgrading the network. These occasional costs should not be carried by one course but spread across a number of courses that all benefit from an improved infrastructure. Fixed costs for e-learning are significantly higher than for classroom learning — reflecting the higher number and value of resources required to author an e-learning course compared with a classroom course.

The variable or marginal costs of learning delivered in a classroom are significantly impacted by the number of learners. In contrast, the variable costs of e-learning are negligible. Classrooms are subject to what a Canadian study called *stepped costs*: "We differentiate between costs which relate to number of students and course deliveries, because depending on the circumstances and method of delivery, these factors will have a different impact on the analysis. That is because certain cost items will remain *fixed* for a given course delivery regardless of the number of students, up to the delivery capacity of that item. Beyond that point, an additional cost would be incurred by adding a student to the course."[26] For example, if an instructor books a classroom that holds 15 learners, whether one learner or 15 register, the variable cost remains the same—of course, indirect costs will vary. However if 20 learners register, the cost of delivering the course doubles because two classrooms are required with an instructor in each.

So long as the overall size of a workforce remains constant, e-learning is not usually subject to stepped costs. An acquisition, on the other hand, could generate stepped indirect costs for e-learning, for example, distributed content management and server upgrades. Large virtual classes can also generate stepped costs. One instructor to 20 learners is the rule of thumb for keeping virtual classes effective and interactive. With larger classes, adding one assistant instructor for each additional 20 learners maintains effectiveness and interactivity. The assistants vet and prioritize questions from the "floor" leaving the instructor free to concentrate on the quality of the class and the interactions. This stepped cost shouldn't be seen as a deterrent to large virtual classes. The cost of assistants is more than balanced by savings in travel and opportunity costs for 200 learners.

What you need to do

Start by making a commitment to evaluation. Adopt Kirkpatrick's Four Level Model enhanced with Phillip's Fifth Level of ROI and you can be confident that you are building a process for holistic, coherent evaluation. If you have already implemented e-learning in your enterprise, it's a question of implementing Kirkpatrick's model. Figure 3.7 sets out Kirkpatrick's own implementation guidelines level by level.

After e-learning has been implemented, you need to validate your predictive ROI and implement Kirkpatrick-plus-Phillips to ensure ongoing ROI analysis in a cycle of prediction and validation.

If you are building a business case for e-learning, you need to calculate a predictive return on investment. Usually that means demonstrating that e-learning is more cost-effective than classroom learning. Laurie Bassi has an approach you might like to follow (see p. 72).

The right thing to measure

Performance is the right thing to measure, in other words, Kirkpatrick's Level 4. And the only way to measure it accurately is to measure Levels 1, 2 and 3 first.

The specific performance benefits your business case—whether for an enterprise-wide or business unit implementation, or a individual course—promised

Implementation Guidelines for the Four Levels of Evaluation By Donald L. Kirkpatrick	
Level	**Guidelines**
1 Reaction	• Determine what you want to find out. • Design a form that will quantify reactions. • Encourage written comments and suggestions. Attain an immediate response rate of 100 per cent. • Seek honest reactions. • Develop acceptable standards. • Measure reactions against the standards and take appropriate action. • Communicate the reactions as appropriate.
2 Learning	• Use a control group, if feasible. • Evaluate knowledge, skills or attitudes both before and after the training. • Attain a response rate of 100 per cent. • Use the results of the evaluation to take appropriate action.
3 Behaviour	• Use a control group, if feasible. • Allow enough time for a change in behaviour to take place. • Survey or interview one or more of the following groups: trainees, their bosses, their subordinates, and others who often observe trainees' behaviour on the job. • Choose 100 trainees or an appropriate sampling. • Repeat the evaluation at appropriate times. • Consider the cost of evaluation versus the potential benefits.
4 Results	• Use a control group, if feasible. • Allow enough time for results to be achieved. • Measure both before and after training, if feasible. • Repeat the measurement at appropriate times. • Consider the cost of evaluation versus the potential benefits. • Be satisfied with the evidence if absolute proof isn't possible to attain.

Figure 3.7 — Kirkpatrick's implementation guidelines[27]

to deliver are the ones you need to measure, for example, increase staff retention or reduce the amount of rework. Since each course has been designed to achieve a different outcome, course level measurements will almost always vary from course to course.

Figure 3.8 provides a comprehensive taxonomy of performance outcomes. Developed by the Australian National Training Authority, the analysis suggests the scope of what's possible when the power of e-learning is applied correctly.

A Taxonomy of Possible Training Outcome Indicators	
Productivity and Efficiency	• production costs per unit • productivity targets met/exceeded • production/completion time per unit (e.g. forms, loans, clients, projects) • output (per worked hour, per shift, per machine, or per annum) • equipment/facility/asset utilization (e.g. down time due to machine stoppages, shift change over time) • equipment maintenance (costs or repair time), or replacement costs • response time (e.g. to service calls or orders) • capacity of staff to solve routine and non-routine problems (e.g. supervision time required) • staffing requirements and workforce flexibility (e.g. dependence on casual/contract labour) • overtime (quantity, cost) • improved innovation in products/services • induction time for new employees • productivity of new employees
Sales and Profitability	• overhead costs • operating costs • operating costs as a percentage of total costs/revenue • value of contracts won, loans processed • revenue/income/sales (monthly, annually, per employee, per team, per branch or store) • market share (number of customers, dollars spent, unit volume sold) • sales to new customers • group operating profit • profit per employee • stock market performance (i.e., shareholder return)
Quality of Products and Services	• on-time provision of products/services • wastage, reject, error or rework rates • conformance record with quality specifications (e.g. batch yields, throughput of invoices) • achievement/maintenance of quality rating • compliance with quality, legal and/or ethical requirements • achievement of quality award • company image and reputation • compliance with the Investors in People national quality standard

Figure 3.8 — Taxonomy of training outcomes[28]
Reproduced by permission of Janelle Moy and Rod McDonald

Customer Service and Satisfaction	• customer satisfaction levels (with timeliness, availability, quality and price of goods and services) • customer relationships and experiences • repeat business (customer retention or loyalty) • new business resulting from client referrals • more/new customers or markets (e.g., contracts won, loans processed, funding awarded) • lost business • number of complaints
Occupational Health and Safety	• accidents or injuries (number, time lost, compensation costs, premium cost/rating) • safety critical incidents (number, cost) • compliance with safety and health requirements (e.g., hygiene testing results) • violation of safety rules • improved response to crises
Organizational Learning and Development	• performance appraisal ratings • achievement of organizational competency profile requirements (e.g., to meet accreditation or licensing requirements, new operating environments or facilitate organizational expansion) • number/percentage of employees with nationally recognized qualifications • internal promotions resulting from employee competence and performance • training awards received • employee perceptions of training and development opportunities • alignment with human resources, business and strategic planning
Organizational Climate, Culture and Practices	• employee retention/turnover/recruitment (e.g., numbers, costs) • absenteeism • disputes/grievances (number, cost or time lost) • number of employee suggestions (submitted or implemented) • employee satisfaction and motivation • interpersonal relationships and commitment to team goals • participation in teams and committees • team performance • internal communication and information systems • implementation of new work practices • standardization of work practices • implementation/maintenance of a service culture • contribution to re-engineering and refocusing of enterprise

Figure 3.8 — (*continued*)

Basic ROI — classroom learning versus e-learning

Like any comparison, this one is meaningful only when apples are compared with apples. For example, one hour of instructor-led classroom learning does not have the same value as one hour of self-paced e-learning. It turns out that e-learning is between 25% and 60% more time effective. Because the learner learns more in less time, you need to work with equivalencies. If you assume e-learning is about 30% more efficient than classroom learning, the cost of 8 hours of e-learning should be compared with the cost of 10.5 hours of classroom learning.

Laurie Bassi has developed a useful worksheet for comparing classroom learning with e-learning (see Figure 3.9). The asterisks indicate where costs are likely to be insignificant — or as Bassi puts it, can be made to appear insignificant. It's obvious from the number of asterisks on the e-learning side that it has a good chance of coming out on top in the comparison. What gives e-learning a savings advantage are travel expenses, learners' compensation and opportunity cost. It's important to remember that marginal costs — some people call them variable costs — vary according to the number of learners; fixed costs don't. That explains why Bassi shows the marginal costs for "Materials, Development" as insignificant: more e-learners do not equal more development costs. In practice, you might decide to invest more in a course with a large learner base and less in a course with a small one but that's a choice not a given.

	Traditional Learning		E-Learning	
	Fixed Cost	Marginal Costs	Fixed Cost	Marginal Costs
Direct Cost				
Trainers' compensation			*	*
Outside vendors				
Materials, development				*
Materials, production			*	*
Materials, distribution			*	*
Hardware	*	*		
Software	*	*		
Travel expenses			*	*
Administrative/support				
Indirect Cost				
Learners' compensation			*	*
Overhead				
Opportunity Cost			*	*

Figure 3.9 — Classroom and e-learning cost comparison form[29]
Reproduced by permission of Learning in the New Economy eMagazine (Linezine.com)
and the author, Laurie Bassi Ph.D.

One of the challenges of using this deceptively simple form is accessing the data. In most cases, you'll need to be prepared to do some aggressive data mining.

Formulas for ROI calculations

To calculate return on investment, you need to know the total cost of an e-learning initiative or event. The formula for that calculation is:

$$\text{Total cost} = \text{all fixed costs} + (\text{number of learners} \times \text{variable cost})$$

The basic formula for calculating ROI as a benefit-to-cost ratio is:

$$\frac{\text{Customer defined value}}{\text{Total cost}} = \text{Return on investment}[30]$$

There are many ways to represent the cost–benefit ratio. What I like about this one is how it expresses one of the two input values in this formula as *Customer defined value*. It's a useful reminder that at the heart of ROI lie the customer's business requirements.

When ROI needs to be expressed as a percentage use this formula which substitutes *Net monetary benefits* for *Customer defined value*:

$$\frac{\text{Net monetary benefits}}{\text{Costs}} \times 100 = \text{ROI(\%)}$$

By expanding *Net monetary benefits*, we can take this generic formula and make it learning-specific:

$$\frac{\text{Monetary benefits} - \text{Total cost of learning}}{\text{Total cost of learning}} \times 100 = \text{ROI(\%)}$$

(To find out what formula the Royal Bank of Scotland used to calculate its predictive ROI, see p. 339.)
In additional to a cost–benefit ratio and percentage, time can be introduced into the equation and ROI expressed as time to break even — in other words, how long it takes for the investment in learning to be covered by benefits the learning helped to generate. This is the formula:

$$\frac{\text{Cost}}{\text{Benefit}} \times \text{Period} = \text{Time to break even}$$

Here's an example of how these formulas might be applied. An enterprise in financial services has developed a portfolio of new products that are radically different from anything it's offered before. To everyone's surprise the launch of the portfolio is a failure. It turns out that the sales channels are struggling to explain the benefits of the new products to potential customers. The portfolio's novelty is proving more of a handicap than an attraction. The learning department is asked to develop a 1-hour virtual class and a 3-hour self-paced e-learning course to familiarize sales channels with the new products and their unique benefits.

The cost of developing content for the virtual class is $10 000. The cost of developing content for the self-paced courses is $30 000 per hour, giving us a total of $90 000. The total cost of content development is $100 000. Because the content is about new proprietary products there was no opportunity to buy content off the shelf; it had to be developed from scratch.

We'll assume that the enterprise infrastructure is already being used to support synchronous and asynchronous learning, so there are no significant costs for hosting and delivering the content.

Let's also assume that the virtual classroom event which kicks off the learning has been scheduled for very first thing in the morning—and that learners are encouraged to take the self-paced course in six half-hour sessions, again, first thing in the morning. The timing has been designed to minimize opportunity costs. In practice, meetings with clients are seldom scheduled before mid-morning. Telephone calls to and from clients are uncommon before that time.

In our scenario, the new product re-launch turns out to be the success everyone had expected in the first place. After 6 months the half-year profit target of $15 million has been reached. It's time to calculate the historical ROI for this learning initiative. Figure 3.10 shows how senior management and the project team analysed business factors that contributed to the success.

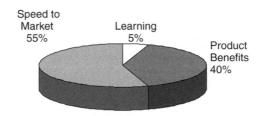

Figure 3.10—Success factors in new product launch

Since we know learning was believed accountable for 5% of the success of the product launch, we can calculate its historical ROI using this formula:

$$\frac{(15\,000\,000 \times 5\%) - 100\,000}{100\,000} \times 100 = 650\%$$

A 650% historical ROI means that after all learning costs have been recovered from income, the enterprise received $6.50 for each learning dollar it invested. One of the lessons in this example is that learning shouldn't take all the credit for any success—many other often interacting factors make important contributions. In the same way that making extravagant ROI predictions will undermine your business case, making extravagant claims about learning's contribution to historical business success will undermine your future credibility. Take the advice of

Bob Woodruff, former chairman of Coca-Cola: "There is no limit to what a man can achieve as long as he doesn't care who gets the credit."

Six hundred and fifty per cent ROI is very respectable but let's say senior executives also need to know the time to break-even. Here's how it works out for the 6 months after re-launch:

$$\frac{100\,000}{(15\,000\,000 \times 5\%)} \times 6 \text{ months} = 0.1333 \times 6 \text{ months} = 0.799 \text{ months} = 24 \text{ days}$$

So 24 days after the new products were re-launched, the learning had paid for itself.

Let's look at what might happen in the year 2 — the year after the new portfolio of financial products was launched. The business predicts that the portfolio will contribute profits of $20 million. The learning department is allocated a budget of $30\,000 to maintain and upgrade the content, and to run virtual classes for new joiners to the sales channels. This year only 1% of the anticipated success of the products will be attributed to learning — down from 5% in year one. Here's how to calculate the predictive ROI for year two:

$$\frac{(20\,000\,000 \times 1\%) - 30\,000}{30\,000} \times 100 = 567\%$$

This is the formula for time to break-even in year two:

$$\frac{30\,000}{(20\,000\,000 \times 1\%)} \times 12 \text{ months} = 0.15 \times 12 \text{ months} = 1.8 \text{ months} = 54 \text{ days}$$

The challenge of calculating ROI for soft skills

In the example of selling financial services products, the learning output was increased product knowledge and selling skills in sales channels. Usually an improvement or introduction of skills will produce measurable benefits, that is, hard data. The benefit to our imaginary enterprise was measurable: income and profit.

Sometimes the learning output is a skill that addresses a critical business need but which does not produce easily measurable benefits, for example, an enterprise might recognize the need to improve its writing skills for proposals and presentation. It's a challenge to establish a cause and effect relationship between soft skills like improved writing skills or problem solving and an increase in business won, income or profit. The temptation is to stop short of ROI and simply list benefits as non-monetary, for example, more compelling proposals and presentations — in other words, to stop evaluation at Level 4. The temptation should be resisted.

Dr Harold Stolovich is a professor emeritus at Université de Montréal, a clinical professor of Human Performance Technology at University of Southern California and head of a Canadian performance consulting practice. With Jean-Gabriel

Maurice, Stolovich developed a seven-step model that produces meaningful ROI figures for learning investments even where returns are in soft performance areas (see Figure 3.11). This is how to use it.

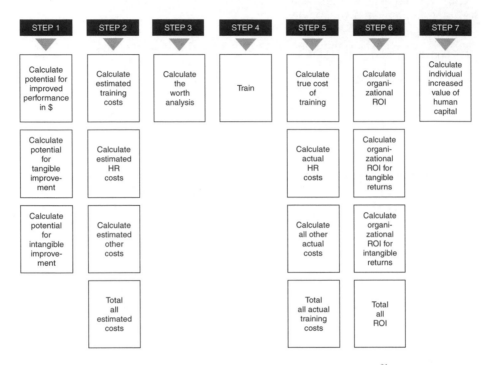

Figure 3.11 — Seven-step soft skills ROI — overview[31]
Reproduced by permission of Performance Improvement

Step 1: Calculate the potential for improved performance

According to Stolovich and Maurice, the starting point for the calculation is always a front-end analysis that determines the nature of the performance gap and whether learning has the potential to close it. The most fundamental of questions hangs over all enterprise learning activity: Does learning work? The answer is, Yes! — but not when one or more of these conditions produces a performance gap:

- A deficient work environment.
- Lack of motivation on the part of the staff.
- Inadequate, inappropriate or counterproductive incentives.

It's a fact of life that developing and delivering an e-learning course is easier and faster than tackling root causes. Changing established processes, introducing new tools, recruiting new staff and re-designing incentives are all daunting projects for busy managers. Without a rigorous front-end analysis, there's a danger the learning department will be asked to cure a problem that exists outside its circle of influence and, ultimately, will end up owning another department's shortcoming.

Let's assume the front-end analysis points to a performance gap that can be addressed by learning. Stolovich and Maurice next establish performance targets for soft skills. There are two approaches; one is straightforward, the other more involved.

The straightforward approach is based on the work of Thomas F. Gilbert, a self-described engineer, behaviourist and philosopher, who in 1978 published *Human Competence: Engineering Worth Performance*. In his book Gilbert tackled the question of establishing performance targets with his Second Leisurely Theorem and the notion of "performance improvement potential" or PIP which he measured with the formula:

$$PIP = \frac{Worth_{exemplary}}{Worth_{typical}}$$

Let's apply it to the marketing department of our enterprise with an appetite for sharper writing skills. Exemplary performers in the department are responsible for annual sales of $2 million while typical performers' figures are around $500 000. Applying the formula we can see that in this case the PIP is four. In other words, transforming every typical performer into an exemplary performer will increase sales by a factor of four.

If Gilbert's PIP doesn't do the job, Stolovich and Maurice prescribe a four-part process.

Step 1: Part 1

List the competencies of learners in the target audience including those the proposed e-learning intervention will cover. Next calculate the percentage of learners' work associated with each competency. When you're finished the list will look something like Figure 3.12.

Competency	% of work
Effective use of human resources	25
Budget administration	10
Management and evaluation of work	10
Planning	15
Work coordination	25
Problem-solving	15
Total	100

Figure 3.12 — Part 1 competency analysis

Step 1: Part 2

Further analyse each competency on the list so that it is broken down into between five and eight "critical performance" requirements. Work with line managers and the learners themselves to identify requirements. Under "Problem-solving" you might list requirements like: "Rigorously identify, analyse, prioritize and monitor risks before they become problems."

Next, rate each critical performance for Gilbert's exemplary and typical worth using a scale of one to nine. You might specify a typical worth of four and an exemplary worth of eight. Sometimes you will have to use aspirational values for some exemplary ratings — usually because no one is yet performing to an exemplary level. When you've assigned worth values to every critical performance, add up all the typical values and all the exemplary values for each competency. Apply the PIP formula to the sums. Here's a typical result.

$$PIP = \frac{Worth_{exemplary}}{Worth_{typical}} = \frac{96_{exemplary}}{28_{typical}} = 3.4$$

In this example, Part 2 has demonstrated a performance gap of 3.4 for "Problem-solving". There is the potential to more than treble learners' performance for this requirement.

Step 1: Part 3

The objective here is to place a monetary value against each competency in the list. Go back to the output of Part 1 and apply the percentages established there against the learners' salary. Let's assume the learners are junior managers and that their annual base salary is $65 000. Using a base salary produces a conservative potential for improved performance; using a fully-loaded salary will produce a much higher potential, one that might be more representative of the true impact of learning (see Figure 3.13).

Competency	% of work	Salary value ($)
Effective use of human resources	25	16 250
Budget administration	10	6 500
Management and evaluation of work	10	6 500
Planning	15	9 750
Work coordination	25	16 250
Problem-solving	15	9 750
Total	100	65 000

Figure 3.13 — Part 3 competency value analysis

Step 1: Part 4

Remember, the objective is to calculate the potential for improved performance in monetary values. Start by calculating the monetary value of each competency for all learners. If we assume there are 500 junior managers in our audience then the monetary value of their work in "Problem-solving", for example, is:

$$500 \times 15\% \times \$65\,000 = \$4\,875\,000$$

Part 2 demonstrated that the PIP for our hypothetical learners is 3.4. That means the current return the business is getting from an annual spend of $\$4\,875\,000$ on "Problem-solving" is:

$$3.4x = \$4\,875\,000$$

$$x = \$1\,433\,824$$

If the current return is $\$1\,433\,824$, the scope for improvement is:

$$\$4\,875\,000 - \$1\,433\,824 = \$3\,441\,176$$

Part 4 has demonstrated that an investment in learning designed to create a positive change in "Problem-solving" performance has a potential value of $\$3\,441\,176$.

Step 2: Calculate estimated learning costs

To estimate learning costs, apply the formula for total learning costs using predictive data:

Total cost = all fixed costs + (number of learners × variable cost)

Stolovich and Maurice recommend that administrative and HR costs are calculated fully-loaded which, using a rule of thumb, means three times base salary.

Step 3: Calculate the worth of the performance interventions

Stolovich and Maurice tell us that the worth of a performance intervention (WPI) equals the potential value (V) of reaching exemplary levels of performance divided by the costs (C) of the learning intervention — which we calculated in Stage 2. This produces the formula:

$$\text{WPI} = \frac{V}{C}$$

It turns out to be the same formula for ROI as a cost-to-benefit ratio — see p. 73:

$$\frac{\text{Customer defined value}}{\text{Total cost}} = \text{Return on investment}$$

Step 4: Develop and implement learning interventions

This step does not involve any ROI calculations.

Step 5: Calculate the true cost of learning

Repeat Step 2 using historical rather than predictive data. For our "Problem-solving" example, we'll assume that the true cost of developing learning for 500 junior managers is $185 000.

If the learning content has a long shelf-life, it's important to include content maintenance costs along with development and delivery costs.

Step 6: Calculate organizational ROI for intangible improvement

Step 5 substitutes historical cost data for cost predictions. Similarly, Step 6 substitutes historical performance data for performance predictions — and converts performance data into monetary value. Since our example is "Problem-solving", the data might reflect productivity gains, improvements in meeting delivery dates and reductions in unplanned spend. After studying all relevant data, again rate each critical performance under "Problem-solving" for Gilbert's typical worth using a scale of one to nine. There are no rules about when this step should happen, although experience has shown it can take 6 months to a year for a learning intervention to impact on performance in a measurable way.

Step 1 Part 2 showed a typical example of estimated performance improvement potential:

$$PIP = \frac{Worth_{exemplary}}{Worth_{typical}} = \frac{96_{exemplary}}{28_{typical}} = 3.4$$

Let's assume that the learning intervention delivered to junior managers was successful and the value of a typical "Problem-solving" performance rose from 28 to 56. That gives us a new PIP:

$$PIP = \frac{Worth_{exemplary}}{Worth_{typical}} = \frac{96_{exemplary}}{56_{typical}} = 1.7$$

PIP can also be expressed as a per centage of exemplary performance. Before the learning intervention, junior managers' typical "Problem-solving" efforts were running at 29% of potential, now they're running at 58%. We can calculate the monetary value of that positive change by referring back to the competency value analysis we made in Part 3 which showed us that $9750 of junior managers' salaries could attributed to Problem-solving. So:

$$Before = 29\% \text{ performance} \times \$9750 = \$2827$$

$$After = 58\% \text{ performance} \times \$9750 = \$5655$$

The financial value of the performance improvement is $2828 per junior manager — or $1 414 000 for the whole target audience. In Step 5, we assumed that the historical cost of the learning intervention was $185 000. With these facts, we can establish the ROI of a soft skill:

$$\frac{\text{Benefits}}{\text{Cost}} = \text{ROI}$$

$$\frac{\$1\,414\,000}{\$185\,000} = 7.6 : 1$$

Step 7: Calculate individual increased value of human capital

Calculating the return on investments in human capital should serve employees as well as the enterprise. In Stolovich and Maurice's vision, each employee should have their own human capital account which reflects their contribution to the business. The account is opened as soon as an employee joins the enterprise. The opening balance is equal to their base salary—which represents their value to the business.

Technically, new hires with no sector experience or who join straight from school or university have less value to the business than their base salary indicates. However, in the expectation that their value will soon equal what they're paid, their opening balance is equal to their base salary.

As the value of an employee's competencies increases, so does the balance in their account—by the amount learning interventions contribute. Because the enterprise bears the risk of the investment in human capital and because learning is not the only contributor to an increase in competency, it would not be fair for the employee to receive the full value of these increases.

The main purpose of the account is to track the value of an employee's human capital, so not every contribution to the account should immediately be paid out in salary or bonuses. But what happens if the balance of an employee's human capital account becomes significantly higher than the employee's salary and benefits? Most employees will recognize the moment when they become worth more to the business than they are being paid. Rather than risk losing human capital in which it has made an investment, the smart enterprise will increase the employee's salary and/or benefits to an amount which equals the value of their capital account.

Final word

As important as evaluation and ROI are, it's critical you put the horse before the cart. If your resources are so limited that conducting ongoing evaluation will mean a reduction in the amount of e-learning delivered across the enterprise, focus your limited resources on learning not evaluation. You won't be alone. General Electric Company boasts Six Sigma quality levels but an approach to learning that excludes ROI. The emphasis is on learning not evaluation. Surveys help GE keep learning aligned with business needs and career development. That's as far as evaluation goes.

References

1   Cavender M (2000) *eLearning SchmeeLearning* LineZine Fall 2000 [Internet] Available from <http://www.linezine.com/2.1/features/mces.htm> Accessed 13 Sep 2001.
2   *SmartForce Roundtable Discussion on ROI* (2000) The Forum Corporation [Report] [Internet] Available from <http://www.forum.com/publications/smartforce.pdf> Accessed 25 Mar 2002.
3   Stewart TA (1997) *Intellectual Capital: The New Wealth of Organizations* Doubleday.
4   Leadbeater C (2000) *Living on Thin Air—The New Economy* 2nd edition London, Penguin Group p 47.
5   Bassi LJ and McMurrer DP (2002) *Investing in Companies that Invest in People* HR.com [Internet] Available from <http://www.knowledgeam.com/downloads/Article_hr.com.pdf> Accessed 2 Aug 2002.
6   Bassi L (2001) *Human Capital Advantage: Developing Metrics for the Knowledge Era* LineZine Spring 2001 [Internet] Available from <http://www.linezine.com/4.2/articles/lbhca.htm> Accessed 30 Oct 2001.
7   Bassi LJ and McMurrer DP (2002) *Investing in Companies that Invest in People* HR.com [Internet] Available from <http://www.knowledgeam.com/downloads/Article_hr.com.pdf> Accessed 2 Aug 2002.
8   Trochim W (2001) *Forget ROI: Measure "Return on Expectations"* Concept Systems Incorporated [Internet] Available from <http://www.conceptsystems.com/papers/whitepapers/forget_roi/Forget%20ROI%20Whitepaper.html> Accessed 14 Mar 2002.
9   *Q&A: Caught in the Net* (2001) Business Week Online 27 August 2001 [Internet] Available from <http://www.businessweek.com/magazine/content/01_35/b3746630.htm> Accessed 22 Oct 2001.
10 Stewart S (2001) *Tom Kelly: Myths and Realities of E-Learning* Cisco Systems IQ 13 September 2001 [Internet] Available from <http://resources.cisco.com/app/tree.taf?asset_id=68789&section_id=44748&level=two&public_view=true> Accessed 24 Sep 2001.
11 van Adelsberg D and Trolley EA (1999) *Running Training Like a Business—Delivering Unmistakable Value* Berrett-Koehler Publishers Inc [Executive summary] [Internet] Available from <http://www.forum.com/RTLBexec/main-reports-rtlab2.html> Accessed 16 May 2001.
12 *Global E-Learning Evaluation Systems—Overview and Requirements* (2000) Cisco E-Learning Metrics Task Force 2000 [Report] [Internet] Available from <www.cisco.com/warp/public/10/wwtraining/elearning/educate/cisco_e-learning_metrics.pdf> Accessed 16 May 2002.
13 *Global E-Learning Evaluation Systems—Overview and Requirements* (2000) Cisco E-Learning Metrics Task Force 2000 [Report] [Internet] Available from <www.cisco.com/warp/public/10/wwtraining/elearning/educate/cisco_e-learning_metrics.pdf> Accessed 16 May 2002.
14 Grove DA and Ostroff C (1990) *Training Program Evaluation* In Stolovitch HD and Maurice J-G (1998) *Calculating The Return on Investment in Training: A Critical Analysis and a Case Study* Performance Improvement Vol 37 No 8 pp 9–20.
15 *Training in a Distributed World* (1998) Government Technology—Education [Internet] Available from <http://www.govtech.net/publications/gt/1998/june/education3/education3.phtml> Accessed 12 Mar 2002.

16   Phillips JJ (1996) *Measuring ROI: The Fifth Level of Evaluation* Technical & Skills Training April 1996 [Internet] Available from <http://www.astd.org/virtual_community/comm_evaluation/phillips.pdf> Accessed 25 Mar 2002.

17   Kirkpatrick DL (1996) *Evaluating Training Programs: The Four Levels* Berrett-Koehler Publishers Inc In Yu S (1999) *Return On Investment (ROI): What We Know and Still Need to Know* The Pennsylvania State University [Final paper] [Internet] Available from <http://www.personal.psu.edu/staff/z/x/zxy113/Papers/ROI.html> Accessed 13 Nov 2001.

18   Peters R (2000) *The Training-Performance Connection: ASTD Helps You Make the Case for Training* [Presentation] [Internet] Available from <http://www.astdbr.org/pd/peters/connection.pdf> Accessed 5 May 2002.

19   Lee B (2001) *In Defense of Surveys* [Newsletter] ASTD TechKnowledge® E-Learning Tips 15 November 2001.

20   Abernathy DJ (2000) *Thinking Differently About Training Evaluation* Career Journal from The Wall Street Journal [Internet] Available from <http://www.careerjournal.com/hrcenter/astd/primer/20000428-abernathy.html> Accessed 25 Mar 2002.

21   Phillips JJ (1996) *How Much Is the Training Worth?* Training and Development Vol 50 No 4 pp 20–24 [Internet] Available from <http://www.astd.org/CMS/templates/index.html?template_id=1&articleid=11019> Accessed 30 Oct 2001.

22   *ROI Profile: IBM Mindspan Solutions* (2001) Nucleus Research Inc [Case study] [Internet] Available from <http://www.nucleusresearch.com/research/b19.pdf> Accessed 5 May 2002.

23   Bassi L (2000) *Making Sense of E-Learning* Saba Software Inc [White paper].

24   Bassi L (2000) *Making Sense of E-Learning* Saba Software Inc [White paper].

25   Bassi L (2000) *Making Sense of E-Learning* Saba Software Inc [White paper].

26   *Effectiveness of Learning Technologies: The Costs and Effectiveness of Technology-Based Approaches to Teaching and Learning* (1998) Office for Partnership for Advanced Skills [Report] [Internet] Available from <http://www.opas-partnerships.com/research_reports/REPORTS/learn_techs.pdf> Accessed 18 May 2002.

27   Kirkpatrick DL (1996) *Implementation Guidelines for the Four Levels of Evaluation* ASTD [Internet] Available from <http://www.astd.org/CMS/templates/index.html?template_id=1&articleid=20842> Accessed 18 May 2002.

28   Moy J and McDonald R (2000) *Analyzing Enterprise Returns on Training* Australian National Training Authority [Report] [Internet] Available from <http://www.ncver.edu.au/research/proj/nr8012.pdf> Accessed 18 May 2002.

29   Bassi L (2000) *How much does eLearning Cost?* LineZine Fall 2000 [Internet] Available from <http://www.linezine.com/2.1/features/lbhmec.htm> Accessed 29 Oct 2001.

30   *Return on Investment: The Measurement Conundrum* (1999) Institute for the Future 4 November 1999 [Report].

31   Stolovitch HD and Maurice J-G (1998) *Calculating The Return on Investment in Training: A Critical Analysis and a Case Study* Performance Improvement Vol 37 No 8 pp 9–20.

The e-learning cycle: once is not enough

4

... we live in an on-going circular environment ... in which each action is based on current conditions, such actions affect conditions, and the changed conditions become the basis for future action. There is no beginning or end to the process. People are interconnected. Many such loops are intertwined. Jay W. Forrester[1]

What you need to know

An enterprise-wide e-learning implementation looms large in both our imaginations and project plans. As a result, it tends to block our view of something more important: the continuous delivery of e-learning. This emphasis on implementation is understandable but misinformed — we implement once but deliver many times. Continuous delivery of e-learning is an evolutionary process in which output is converted to input over and over. People talk about "the e-learning cycle"; in fact, the continuous delivery process consists of a number of related cycles. Examine them closely and you'll discover that like fractals they have self-similarity.

The largest cycle is what Jay W. Forrester, a pioneer in system dynamics and senior lecturer at MIT, calls a closed-loop structure (see Figure 4.1). Its design allows dynamic feedback to be incorporated into any cycle. With neither a beginning nor an end, a closed-loop structure is self-correcting and self-improving — what some people call a virtuous circle.

The Learnativity Spiral

Knowledge carried by an individual only realizes its commercial potential when it is replicated by an organization and it becomes organizational knowledge ... The most successful companies of the future will be designed to make this process of knowledge generation and appropriation flow as powerfully as possible. Charles Leadbeater[2]

Describing the effect of the closed-loop structure, Forrester says: "Through long cascaded chains of action, each person is continually reacting to the echo of that person's past actions as well as to the past actions of others."[3] It makes for a good description of the e-learning process. Some people portray this never-ending story as a spiral — emphasizing a Darwinian evolution. Wayne Hodgins, Director of

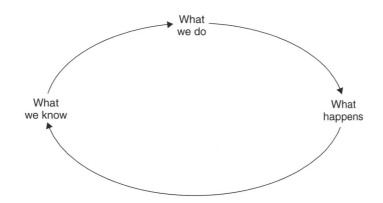

Figure 4.1 — Closed-loop structure

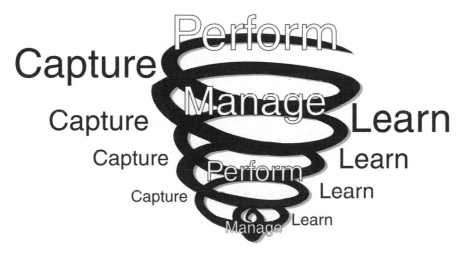

Figure 4.2 — The Learnativity Spiral[4]
Reproduced by permission of H. Wayne Hodgins

Worldwide Learning Strategies at Autodesk Inc, developed the Learnativity Spiral to illustrate what happens at the highest level of e-learning. It maps almost directly to Forrester's closed-loop structure (see Figure 4.2).

The simple spiral offers a vision of the learning enterprise. Hodgins makes the vision clear in his definition of Learnativity: "... knowledge in action, a continuous spiralling conversion of tacit knowledge (such as know-how and experience) into explicit knowledge that can be captured, shared with others, diffused within groups, and turned back into new tacit knowledge gained from learning by doing. Learnativity is a way of continuously creating new, actionable knowledge. The key is to see this as a single state ...".[5] In Hodgins's closed loop, tacit knowledge creates explicit knowledge which—having been assimilated and applied—creates new tacit knowledge.

Learnativity was inspired by the work of Japanese academics Ikujiro Nonaka and Hirotaka Takeuchi who, writing in *The Knowledge-Creating Company*, describe a knowledge spiral: "Tacit knowledge of individuals is the basis of organizational knowledge creation. The organization has to mobilize tacit knowledge created and accumulated at the individual level. The mobilized tacit knowledge is "organizationally" amplified through four modes of knowledge conversion and crystallized at higher ontological levels. We call this the "knowledge spiral", in which the interaction between tacit knowledge and explicit knowledge will become larger in scale as it moves up the ontological levels. Thus, organizational knowledge creation is a spiral process, starting at the individual level and moving up through expanding communities of interaction, that crosses sectional, departmental, divisional, and organization boundaries."[6]

Figure 4.3 shows the high level activities that take place at each stage of Learnativity.

Stage	Activity
Capture	Understand the tacit knowledge of subject matter experts. Document it in explicit forms—for example, the written and spoken word, illustrations, animations, videos, models and simulations—so understanding can be shared. In other words, develop learning content.
Manage	Convert explicit knowledge into complex and valuable combinations of ideas, insights and experiences that can be shared. In practice, this means developing curricula and learning paths, delivering virtual classes and self-paced learning, and facilitating peer-to-peer collaborations across the corporate infrastructure.
Learn	Draw on all learning resources that have been made available through all learning channels—individually, socially, formally and informally. Embrace know-how, know-what and know-why by taking shared explicit knowledge and internalizing it through observation, reading, practice and reflective thought.
Perform	Achieve continuous peak performance by integrating and applying what has been learned to solve problems—at all levels: individual, team and enterprise. Convert explicit knowledge into tacit knowledge by using it continuously and successfully. Peak performance needs to be achieved by individuals, teams and the enterprise.

Figure 4.3—Learnativity stages and activities

Opening the closed loop

If the ultimate benefit delivered by learning is to transform the way the enterprise learns through a bottom-up process, the transformation cannot be achieved if e-learning cycles in the process have a closed single-loop structure. Yes, the closed loop is self-correcting and self-improving—but it is also self-limiting. As Figure 4.4 illustrates, the closed loop does not interact with its governing programme—its mandate.

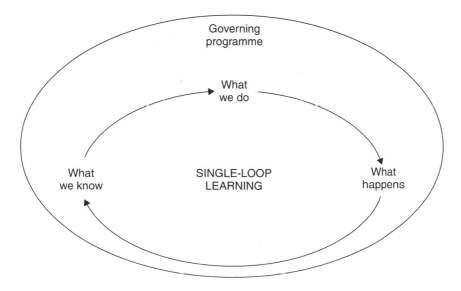

Figure 4.4—Closed single-loop learning

To break out of the closed-loop structure, e-learning cycles need to be implemented as what Christopher Argyris, Professor Emeritus of Education and Organizational Behavior at the Graduate School of Business at Harvard University, calls *double-loop learning*. The defining characteristic of double-loop learning is a reference back to the master programmes that control a process with the aim of Darwinian evolution and long-term success. Double-loop learning has the responsibility of questioning and influencing the underlying values of the process and in so doing to create a new framework for learning (Figure 4.5). Contrast that with single-loop learning which refers back only to actions arising from itself.

You can only have a learning department if you are willing and able to re-visit and revise the original business case for a specific e-learning intervention in light of what you learn by implementing the intervention. If the business plan is inherently flawed, for example, if it mandates e-learning to close a performance gap that is the direct result of a broken salary and benefits package, no amount

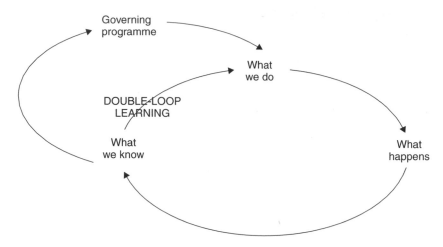

Figure 4.5 — Double-loop learning

of correction within the single-loop cycle can make the learning do what's asked of it. Revising course content, for example, whether the navigation controls, the copy, the graphics or the inflection in the voice-over is just rearranging deckchairs on the Titanic. On a much broader scale, you can only have a learning organization if you are willing and able to re-visit and revise the original business drivers for implementing enterprise-wide e-learning in light of what you learn from the implementation — and, of course, in response to changes in strategy at enterprise level.

Are these challenging, long-term undertakings? Yes. Are they essential? Not if you see e-learning as a quick fix. Yes, if you see it as a tool for transforming an enterprise.

Two domains

An organization's commitment and capacity for learning can be no greater than that of its members. Peter Senge[7]

I believe that learning in the enterprise takes place in two domains: the Business Domain and the Learner Domain. Two Learnativity stages — Capture and Manage — occur in the Business Domain, the other two — Learn and Perform — in the Learner Domain. The domains represent an important notion in e-learning. The Business Domain is responsible for providing the context, the bulk of e-learning content and the delivery channels, but that isn't the whole story. The learner has a responsibility, too — above all to learn but also:

- To provide content — for example, knowledge, experience, questions — in real-time learning events and through peer-to-peer channels.

- To provide feedback and evaluation.
- When asked to act as subject matter expert.

This responsibility is met in the Learner Domain which is outside the control and reach of the Business Domain. Management can't enforce learning; it can only support and facilitate it. To be effective across the enterprise e-learning must be successful in both domains—and at least some people on the e-learning team need to be aware both domains exist each with different but related cycles.

Business Domain Cycles

What happens in this domain is the responsibility of the business and the learning department. The learner is not involved except for contributions to evaluation (see Figure 4.6).

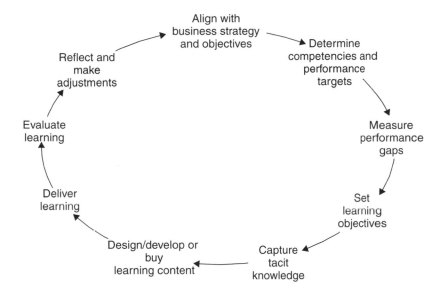

Figure 4.6—Business Domain E-learning Cycle

Align with business strategy and objectives: The objective of e-learning is unambiguous: to support the strategy and the objectives of the business by ensuring that individuals and teams across the enterprise work continuously at peak performance. It follows that the e-learning cycle in the business domain always starts by aligning learning with the business. In the connected economy, strategy and objectives can change overnight. The e-learning cycle you develop for your enterprise must be nimble enough to react in lockstep with the agenda of senior executives.

Establish competencies and performance targets: Determine what competencies and levels of performance are needed for each role in the enterprise to be able to support business objectives.

Measure performance gaps: Once you know what you need, the next stage is to quantify what you already have and to measure any performance gaps you discover. This can be done on a predictive basis by having employees perform competency and activity assessments. Some Learning Management Systems have competency modules that allow these assessments to made online with the resulting data gathered and analysed automatically. Performance gaps can also be observed operationally by managers in business units whose teams are failing to achieve the required results.

Set learning objectives: Once you've quantified performance gaps you need to set learning objectives for learning paths and individual courses designed to close the gaps.

Capture tacit knowledge: If the knowledge required to meet learning objectives resides within the enterprise, the next stage is to capture it from subject matter experts. When that knowledge is not available internally, consult external subject matter experts or buy the knowledge from third parties. If there's a

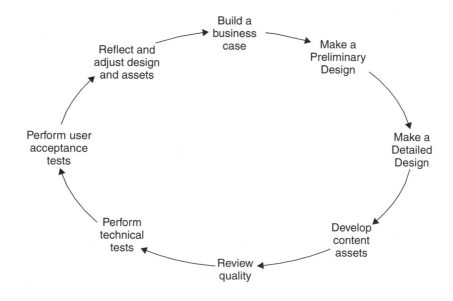

Figure 4.7 — Content development cycle

Knowledge Management programme in your enterprise, it might have knowledge capture tools and resources you can use. If there isn't, it's normal for the Instructional Design team to work with subject matter experts to capture tacit knowledge.

Design/develop or buy learning content: Once learning objectives have been set and the required knowledge captured, you're ready to start designing and developing learning content. If the knowledge isn't proprietary, you might be able to save time and money by buying off-the-shelf content. Content development has its own cycle (see Figure 4.7).

Deliver learning: Leverage the whole learning value chain. Delivering self-paced courses, models, simulations, archived Web casts and peer-to-peer platforms is a hands-off process. Virtual classes, mentoring, live Web casts, and classroom-based learning require management.

Evaluate learning: In Chapter 3, the learning evaluation process is explored in detail. What is important in terms of the Business Domain E-learning Cycle is that the output of evaluation is one of the key inputs to the next stage in the Business Domain Cycle.

Reflect and make adjustments: This is a critical stage — the one that makes the cycle a closed-loop structure. There are no rules about how to manage reflection or what adjustments to make; there are too many variables to consider at each stage of the cycle. For example, in *Design/develop or buy learning content*, user acceptance testing could indicate that the Preliminary Design specified the wrong instructional design model, or the wrong mix of delivery channels; the Detailed Design — the script for animations, graphics, and so on — might have failed to convey learning points clearly; more prosaically, course navigation could have confused learners. However, unless you reflect on what you've learned and apply it to the next cycle, opportunities for self-correction and self-improvement — which lie at the heart of the closed-loop process — will be lost.

Learner Domain Cycles

While the Business Domain provides context, infrastructure and content, the Learner Domain is where learning happens. That might be in a classroom, an aircraft, the learner's office, the factory floor, a client site or a hotel room. Often real learning happens after the learning event — when the learner assimilates content by applying it in a work context. Where learning is instructor led — either a virtual or physical class, for example — the Business Domain has some control over events in the Learner Domain. With most e-learning channels, it doesn't. That's one of the fundamental differences between traditional learning and e-learning.

Kolb and Fry

In 1975, American psychologist David Kolb and his associate Roger Fry built a four-stage model to represent the cycle of experiential learning. It remains a seminal point of reference. Kolb was interested in exploring the processes of making sense of concrete experiences—and the different styles of learning that might be involved. Kolb and Fry maintain that the learning cycle can begin at any one of the four stages though typically it begins with a concrete experience. They also believe it should be seen as an endless spiral (see Figure 4.8).

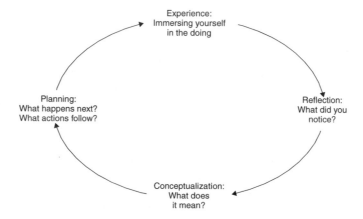

Figure 4.8—Kolb and Fry's Learning Cycle[8]
Reproduced by permission of David A. Kolb

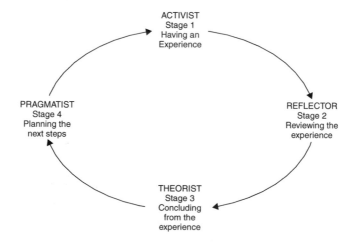

Figure 4.9—Honey and Mumford's Learning Cycle[9]
Reproduced by permission of Peter Honey Publications Ltd

Honey and Mumford

Leading British psychologist Dr Peter Honey and his colleague Professor Alan Mumford noticed different people in their classes displaying different behaviours. Some were forthcoming; others, reticent. Some were quick to volunteer as presenter or syndicate chairman; others kept a low profile. Some were cheerful and laughed a lot; others, serious and earnest. Some were prepared to take a risk with spontaneous ideas; others needed thorough preparation. Honey and Mumford also noticed that these behaviours had a direct effect on the way people learned. The pair drew on these observations when in 1982 they adapted Kolb's learning cycle with a new focus on how different people demonstrate a preference for different stages of the learning cycle (see Figure 4.9).

These preferences are for what's called a *learning style*. The strengths and weaknesses inherent in a learner's personality can sometimes be reflected in their preference for a particular learning style. Despite a preference for one of the stages, in order to learn every learner has to adopt *every* role — at different times in the learning cycle, to be an activist, a reflector, a theorist and a pragmatist (see Figure 4.10).

A Double-loop Cycle

Both cycles in the Learner Domain — Kolb and Fry's, and Honey and Mumford's — are single-loop processes. If learning fails — if an employee's performance does not improve as a result of learning experiences — neither of these cycles can help the learner nor the business to diagnose the failure. Neither cycle makes reference back to the controlling programme, in effect, the Business Domain. Both assume the learner is motivated and the content fit for purpose, that is, relevant, authentic, fresh, etc. These are critical success factors for adult learning; if they're not present, there needs to be a process in the Learner Domain for influencing the Business Domain to ensure they are. With that crossover in mind, I'm suggesting a new e-learning cycle for the Learner Domain, built on Honey and Mumford's foundations, aware of the context of the Business Domain, and supporting double-loop learning (see Figure 4.11).

Four new stages and roles support double-loop learning. These are the attitudes associated with the new roles (see Figure 4.12).

The Performer-learner experiences a business performance problem creating both a business context and a personal motivation to learn. When the Collaborator-learner shares ideas and reactions with peers, a closed-loop structure is created and supported. By contributing feedback about learning experiences with the business (Kirkpatrick Levels 1 and 2), the Contributor-learner supports a double-loop structure that crosses from the Learner to the Business Domain. By helping to answer the questions, "Was my performance

Style	Attitude	Learn best from activities where ...
Activist	What's new? I'm game for anything.	There are new experiences/problems/ opportunities from which to learn. They can engross themselves in short 'here and now' activities, e.g. business games, competitive tasks, role-playing exercises. They have a lot of the limelight/high visibility. They are thrown in at the deep end with a task which they think is difficult.
Reflector	I'd like time to think about this.	They are encouraged to watch/think/chew over activities. They are allowed to think before acting, to assimilate before commenting. They have the opportunity to review what has happened, what they have learnt. They can reach a decision in their own time without pressure and tight deadlines.
Theorist	How does this relate to that?	They have time to explore methodically the associations and interrelationships between ideas, events and situations. They are in structured situations with clear purposes. They have the chance to question and probe the basic methodology, assumptions or logic behind something. They are intellectually stretched.
Pragmatist	How can I apply this in practice?	There is an obvious link between subject matter and a problem or opportunity on the job. They are shown techniques for doing things with obvious practical advantages currently applicable to their own job. They have the chance to try out and practise techniques with coaching/feedback from a credible expert. They can concentrate on practical issues.

Figure 4.10 — Honey and Mumford's Learning Preferences[10]

improved by learning? Was the business's?" (Kirkpatrick Levels 3 and 4), the Stakeholder-learner becomes part of the Business Domain's evaluation process and again supports double-loop learning. In this new e-learning cycle, all learners adopt all roles, typically experiencing greater comfort and success with some than others. Roles are not necessarily sequential; for example, a learner is both a Collaborator and a Reflector when he reviews a learning experience with peers.

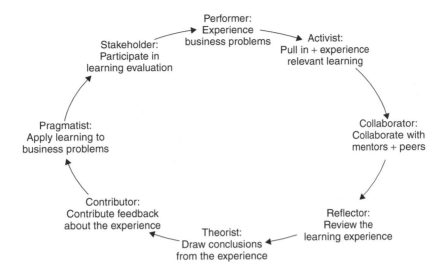

Figure 4.11 — Learner Domain E-learning Cycle

Style	Attitude
Performer	I do what it takes to optimize my work performance.
Collaborator	Let's share our thoughts about what we're learning.
Contributor	Here's what I thought about the learning content. Here's how I plan to use it. Here's what I've learned.
Stakeholder	Learning is critical to the success of the business. I'll do whatever I can to help the business make it better.

Figure 4.12 — New learner styles

References

1   Forrester JW (1991) *System Dynamics and the Lessons of 35 Years* Sloan School of Management [Internet] Available from <http://sysdyn.mit.edu/sdep/papers/D-4224-4.pdf> Accessed 6 May 2002.

2   Leadbeater C (2000) *Living on Thin Air — The New Economy* 2nd edition London, Penguin Group p 71.

3   Forrester JW (1991) *System Dynamics and the Lessons of 35 Years* Sloan School of Management [Internet] Available from <http://sysdyn.mit.edu/sdep/papers/D-4224-4.pdf> Accessed 6 May 2002.

4   Hodgins HW (2000) *Into the Future — A Vision Paper* [Report] Commission on Technology & Adult Learning [Internet] Available from <http://www.learnativity.com/into_the_future2000.html> Accessed 21 Sep 2001 p 16.

5 Hodgins HW (2000) *Into the Future— A Vision Paper* [Report] Commission on Technology & Adult Learning [Internet] Available from <http://www.learnativity.com/into_the_future2000.html> Accessed 21 Sep 2001 p 16.

6 Nonaka I and Takeuchi H (1995) *The Knowledge-Creating Company* New York, Oxford University Press p 72.

7 Senge PM (1990) *The Fifth Discipline The art and practice of the learning organization* New York, Doubleday In *Learning: The Critical Technology* (1996) Wave Technologies International, Inc [White paper] [Internet] Available from <http://www.learnativity.com/download/Learning_Whitepaper96.pdf> Accessed 6 May 2002.

8 Smith MK (2001) *David A. Kolb on Experiential Learning* The Encyclopedia of Informal Education [Internet] Available from <http://www.infed.org/b-explrn.htm> Accessed 27 Mar 2002.

9 Honey P and Mumford A (2000) *The Learning Styles Helper's Guide* Maidenhead, Peter Honey Publications Ltd p 13.

10 Honey P (1998) *Building on Learning Styles* IMC Tutors Guide [Appendix] [Internet] Available from <http://www.mcb.co.uk/services/coursewa/tutguide/tut-010.htm> Accessed 12 Sep 2001.

Part II
Learning Strategy

Business drivers: the real reasons for implementing e-learning

5

There's certainly no arguing the altruistic side of education — that well-trained people are more valuable than untrained people. But that's kind of esoteric. If customer satisfaction goes up because we have a more knowledgeable sales force, that's not esoteric. If technology adoption occurs faster because the sales force is better-trained, we have real business impact that's measurable. That's the real benefit of e-learning. Tom Kelly, Cisco Systems[1]

Trainers need to stop confusing the activity with the goal. People get very locked in on the means, rather than the end. Learning and performance are the goals . . . Gloria Gery[2]

What you need to know

Here's a question I hear asked a lot. What's the difference between information and knowledge? Nancy Dixon, author of *Common Knowledge: How Companies Thrive by Sharing What They Know*, provides an answer: "The way I think about that distinction is that knowledge is actionable. Knowledge is something you can actually do something with, and that may mean that it is procedural in nature or that may mean that it is "how to" in nature, but it's of that kind."[3] The goal of e-learning is to improve individual and enterprise performance; it needs to deliver knowledge not information. Knowledge has two aspects: "know why" and "know how". To take effective action that improves their performance learners need both.

Many training departments measure success in terms of training activity. Budgets are justified by the number of employees who take courses. The greater the number, the more successful the department. The impact of training on performance gets left out of the equation. The separation of training from performance is captured in the trainer's cynical adage "spray and pray". E-learning forces training departments to change their focus from delivering courses to improving business performance.

This shift is difficult in enterprises where the learning department is funded by charging business units on the basis of course registrations. Since every registration generates income, the training department comes to believe it's in the business of attracting registrations. Training departments funded this way like the idea of e-learning because Learning Management Systems automate course registration and simplify the process of raising internal charges. In other words, they think e-learning is about housekeeping. You also have to question the motives of the business units in this scenario. Why are they prepared to pay for learning as a commodity? Is it a habit they've fallen into? Are internal charges taken less seriously than external ones? Or do the business units have such low expectations of learning's impact they don't bother to look for measurable outcomes?

Drivers for e-learning aren't fixed. They vary according to where an enterprise is in its business cycle. A critical driver for e-learning one year might not figure the next. That's an important feature of e-learning: it can change direction in lockstep with corporate strategy. When building a business case for e-learning you need to establish the *initial* drivers, those current high-priority business requirements for which e-learning can deliver a solution. Because e-learning is a response to specific and changing business requirements, there is no such thing as a shrink-wrapped, one-size-fits-all solution. You can learn a lot by studying how other enterprises have implemented e-learning but don't copy blindly. An e-learning system designed to meet someone else's business requirements won't meet yours.

Common e-learning drivers

An *E-Learning Magazine* survey reveals the most common drivers for e-learning in the USA. Ninety-nine per cent of respondents had already implemented e-learning in their organizations. The three largest groupings of respondents were (1) corporations and companies who accounted for 53% of responses; (2) government and military, for 19%; and (3) higher education, for 12%. The three highest ranked drivers were "availability anytime" with a score of 79%, "cost savings" with 59%, and "self-paced learning" also with 59%.

The survey results for the three key groups are summarized in Figure 5.1. With one exception, the value of self-paced learning to the US Government and Military, the results are surprisingly consistent across the groups. Notice that increasing training activity doesn't figure in the survey. It's not on senior management's radar and it shouldn't be in your business case.

The Masie Center's E-Learning Consortium is a collaboration of major corporations, government agencies and e-learning providers who share an interest in the future of e-learning. When the Center asked Consortium members, "Why is your organization considering e-learning?" responses from 80 organizations reflected a similar set of drivers to the ones in *E-Learning Magazine's* survey but different priorities (see Figure 5.2).

Where e-learning stakeholders sit in the enterprise colours their understanding of what constitutes a valid business driver. Figure 5.3 illustrates how the drivers at Cisco Systems reflect the concerns of a broad range of stakeholders.

Driver	Corporate (%)	Government and Military (%)	Higher Education (%)
Available anytime, anywhere	80	75	80
Cost savings	65	57	65
Allows for self-paced learning	57	75	57
Provides just-in-time learning	52	52	52
Ease-of-use	44	44	44
Content can be altered easily	42	42	42
Fast distribution	32	32	32
Improves instructor availability	25	25	25

Figure 5.1 — *E-Learning Magazine's* business drivers ranking[4]

Driver	Responses (%)
Geography To reach people that we could not otherwise access	76
Time To shift time, accommodate schedules, save time	66
Frequency To train people more frequently, just-in-time	60
Expense Management To decrease our training budget, development time	46
Revenue Growth To increase sales	24
Instructional Design Accommodate varied learning styles, personalize training	23

Figure 5.2 — Masie Center E-Learning Consortium business drivers ranking[5]

Drivers for senior executives

Competitive advantage accrues to those who invest more than their competitors to connect to more people and share knowledge faster and farther. Dr Jim Botkin[6]

DRIVERS OF CISCO'S LEARNING AND TRAINING NEEDS

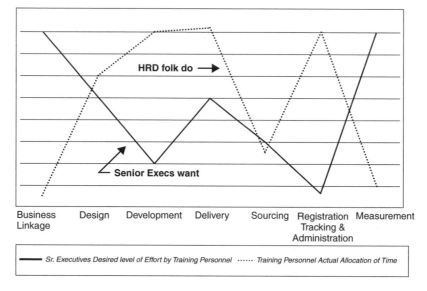

The Objectives
* Fast, Effective Deployment of Mission-Critical Knowledge
* Well-Trained and Up-to-Date Workforce
* Lower-Cost Learning

The Challenges
* Geographically Dispersed Learners
* Phenomenal Growth
* Difficult/Expensive Training Logistics
* Need for Knowledge on Demand

The Pressures
* Relentless Competition
* Constantly Changing Technology
* Shorter Product Cycles
* Shorter Time to Market

Source: Cisco Systems

Figure 5.3 — Cisco's drivers reflect all stakeholders[7]

HRD folk do ➞

Senior Execs want

Business Linkage   Design   Development   Delivery   Sourcing   Registration Tracking & Administration   Measurement

▬▬▬ Sr. Executives Desired level of Effort by Training Personnel   ······ Training Personnel Actual Allocation of Time

Figure 5.4 — Training actions and values mismatch[8]
Source: ASTD

When Linkage, Inc asked senior and mid-level managers how committed key stakeholders were to their enterprise's e-learning initiative, only 22% said their key stakeholders were fully committed. Six per cent said key stakeholders were positively not committed. When asked what specific business needs prompted an interest in e-learning, only 27% replied that demand from senior executives was the driver.[9] Too often there's a striking mismatch between what training departments and senior executives believe are the key drivers for learning — as Figure 5.4 illustrates.

The full support of senior executives is critical to the success of an e-learning implementation. If the drivers in your business case don't reflect their needs, you won't get their support. It's that simple. So what drivers are important to senior executives?

Transform the business

Every executive understands that his business can only deliver shareholder value if it can compete effectively. To achieve a competitive edge in the flux of the connected economy means transforming the way a business learns. Here's how Jack Welch, former chief executive of GE, described the process: "... inspiring people to learn because the excitement and the energy they get from that learning is so enormous ... [that's] how you energize an organization. By making it curious, by making it say "Wow!", by finding "wows" all of the time, by creating new learning. That is what making an organization win is all about."[10] Welch was describing a bottom-up process. Only by changing the way individuals learn can an executive change the way a business learns. E-learning is a powerful tool for making that transformation. Properly implemented, it has the power to bring staff to a state of readiness to compete quickly and cost-effectively — and to remain there whatever challenges are thrown up by vortical markets.

Support strategic change

Keeping the enterprise nimble is a challenge for every executive. An enterprise with the momentum of an oil tanker where the captain's decision to change direction only takes effect 20 km later is an enterprise that can't compete. A smart management team can make fast changes in strategy and direction but unless those changes permeate the business quickly and effectively, the advantage is lost. E-learning can deliver clear, consistent messages about strategic change across time zones and continents immediately. By leveraging learner profiles, e-learning has the flexibility to deliver strategic messages to specific audiences defined, for example, by role and geographic location, and to contextualize a global message with local content.

Harmonize mergers and acquisitions

E-learning can be a powerful tool for streamlining harmonization after a merger or acquisition. Too often the process of harmonization drags on for months or years. Synchronous e-learning — virtual classes, Web casts, peer-to-peer collaboration — and asynchronous learning — self-paced courses, archived virtual classes and Web casts — deliver clear consistent messages about the new entity without delay. Because time and distance don't pose barriers to learning, the business benefits from a new shared corporate culture that emerges within weeks. Knowledge about shared product and service lines can be exchanged almost immediately and new catalogues operationalized with the least possible delay. Because the combined knowledge of both businesses is harnessed faster and more effectively, launching new products which reflect the strengths of the merged organization happens sooner and more efficiently.

It's not only knowledge about client-facing activities that can be exchanged quickly. E-learning helps staff get up to speed on internal systems and applications faster, too. A full e-learning implementation will also be able to measure competencies and skills—and determine where gaps exists. This functionality helps executives understand the competencies of the acquired workforce and how these can be integrated into the new organization.

Support constant innovation

Constant innovation is a challenge in every sector but particularly those like financial services and pharmaceuticals where new products are rolled out continuously. By leveraging rapid content development and overnight publishing, e-learning gives executives the opportunity to significantly reduce time to market. Not only staff but partners, suppliers, sales channels and customers all get the message about new products and services faster than they ever could in a traditional classroom setting. Michael Dell, CEO of Dell Computer Corporation, understands that the value chain is only as strong as its weakest link and argues that the enterprise should be "a knowledge broker between customers and suppliers". E-learning can be the engine of that brokerage. Instead of training getting tagged on to the end of the development cycle, e-learning enables learning to take place in parallel with the development process. "Time-to-understanding" and "time to performance" are minimized, so are the opportunity costs historically associated with training.

Support enterprise initiatives

Constant innovation needs to take place inside the enterprise as well as in its client-facing activities. The timely delivery of enterprise-wide solutions like e-procurement, CRM and data warehousing can have a make or break impact on an enterprise. In the same way that e-learning can help executives reduce cycle time for products and services, it can reduce cycle time and time to performance for the delivery of key enterprise solutions.

From the employee's point of view, understanding a new enterprise solution hinges on getting the answers to two questions. One, why are we changing? If that question isn't answered to employees' satisfaction, senior executives won't get the buy-in they need. Two, how does this change affect me? If that question isn't answered satisfactorily, even people who've bought into the need for change won't know how to leverage it. E-learning can help answer the first question through live and archived Web casts by senior executives, through discussion forums moderated by subject matter experts, and through white papers and self-paced courses that position the change. The second question—how does this affect me?—raises operational issues. E-learning can help answer it by delivering local virtual classes led by line managers, the people in the best position to explain to learners how new solutions affect business units, departments and individuals. E-learning can also provide online simulations of new applications enabling learners to get hands-on experience in a safe environment.

Meet certification and compliance regulations

There isn't a country or an industry where levels of regulation are decreasing. More and more employees have to meet certification and compliance requirements before they can carry out their responsibilities. Some industries are more regulated than others. Health and safety, for example, is a high priority in transport, energy, chemicals, healthcare, manufacture and the military. E-learning can deliver certification, compliance learning and evaluation cost- and time-effectively. It can automate certification tracking and compliance management by maintaining up-to-date records for employees and managers. These records enable senior managers and compliance officers to cross-reference compliance requirements with group and individual roles and responsibilities quickly and accurately.

Companies using e-learning to deliver compliance and safety training include 3Com, American Airlines, Compaq, IBM and Intel. (To learn how the Dow Chemical Company uses e-learning to meet its compliance requirements see Chapter 21.)

Hunt talent

No enterprise can compete effectively without the best people. In an up cycle, enterprises need to compete for them. A down cycle, when people with talent are more readily available, gives smart enterprises the opportunity to strengthen their teams in preparation for the next up cycle. In both cycles unequivocal management commitment to an e-learning initiative can help attract the best people; a programme of continuous learning can help retain them.

The kind of people senior executives want are those focused not on a job for life but on continuous professional development. Corporate futurist Thornton May sets out new rules for talent hunting: "Executives of the future must design workplaces that foster fast learning. Members of the new workforce will not tolerate a work environment in which their skills do not expand as a by-product of their labour. Their motto: "Make me smart and make me rich, or colour me gone"."[11] E-learning is a tool designed to help executives meet the challenge of fast learning.

Leverage IT investment

The cost of doing business in the connected economy is significant. Executives have watched their IT capital expenditure and operating costs grow annually.

Because e-learning runs on the existing corporate infrastructure and intranet, it gives executives an opportunity to leverage their historical investment in IT.

Educate customers

Executives understand the value of CRM (Customer Relationship Management) strategies and systems in building brand loyalty and establishing lifelong relationships with customers. E-learning can be an important part of CRM, driving customers to B2C e-channels and generating additional revenue. It's become clear that from the consumer's point of view, physical and virtual channels are not an either-or choice. The brand loyalty that results from engaging consumers in e-learning can also drive them to higher-value physical channels.

Educating customers works for B2B relationships, too. Imagine an enterprise that's made the decision to upgrade its desktop to Windows XP and Office XP. In order to be compatible with the new operating system, all desktop and laptop systems need to be upgraded. As part of the hardware and software deal, the vendor gives the enterprise's staff free access to e-learning courses about Windows and Office XP. The vendor's status is enhanced because he's offering a real technology solution and not just shifting boxes. A relationship between the vendor and enterprise staff develops. The enterprise's IT support staff benefit because an informed user base means less demand for support. The enterprise-wide upgrade initiative benefits because the question, "How's this going to affect me?" is answered.

Accelerate new hires into performance

Senior executives understand new hires are an opportunity cost. Time to understand and time to perform describe a period when wage, benefit, overhead and learning costs are going out of the enterprise with no opportunity for generating income. Accelerating new hires into performance creates a double benefit — a reduction in both learning and opportunity costs. Even a reduction of 4 or 6 weeks in time to perform will create dramatic savings when annualized across all new hires. Learning managers can use e-learning to assess the knowledge and competencies of new hires as soon as they join, then create customized induction learning paths to close the gaps. Customized self-paced learning means new hires with previous industry experience or who are fast learners aren't held back by slower learners or learners coming straight from schools and universities.

E-learning can help enterprises manage the expectations of new joiners, too. A global financial services business was losing new sales recruits because they weren't realizing their first sale — and their first commission — quickly enough. Working with the Cisco Internet Business Solutions Group, the business conducted a study to find out whether e-learning could help. New hires were split into two groups. One group took traditional instructor-led classroom training; the other, a series of short e-learning courses. The e-learning group made their first sale 25% faster — and the value of the first sale was twice as high as the other group's. For the e-learning group, the disillusionment factor melted away. The business benefited from both reduced learning costs and earlier productivity.

Save costs

Everyone wants more for less. So why aren't cost savings at the top of e-learning drivers for senior executives? Because experience has shown that many executives have little idea of how much they spend on learning. When you tell the board you can reduce learning costs by 30%, they don't know the value of the reduction. When you tell them you can reduce learning costs by $30 million, they don't know whether it's a significant or marginal saving. Don't rule out cost savings as a driver for senior executives but do some research before positioning it as a key driver. If executives want to cut costs across the board, naturally it should be one of your drivers. The guiding principle is, as far as cost savings are concerned, look before you leap.

Drivers for line managers

In a world where project teams are continuously forming and reforming, it becomes critical to be able to form them rapidly, bring the members together into cohesive groups, elicit their peak performance to complete the projects, and then dissolve them so the individuals can move on to new teams. Wayne Hodgins[12]

Line managers work where the rubber meets the road. That's where the drivers that interest them operate.

Meet targets

Line managers have targets to meet — sales, production, service and delivery. Their success or failure in meeting those targets depends on how well their teams perform. E-learning competency and performance management systems help managers recruit strong teams from the best qualified staff. Once the team is assembled, continuous customized learning ensures that each individual works at peak performance. The right teams working the best way help line managers achieve — and surpass — targets.

Satisfy customers

In highly competitive markets, delivering customer satisfaction can often be best achieved through proactive behaviour — anticipating issues whenever possible and, when it's not, devising solutions to issues as soon as they arise. Managers can leverage e-learning's speed and flexibility to support proactivity by keeping their teams up to date with competitive intelligence, industry information, corporate strategies and the progress of product cycles. This just-in-time learning helps teams realize competitive advantage by building customer satisfaction, growing customer loyalty and increasing market share as a result.

Drivers for learning and HR departments

We like saving money and a quick payback but that's not why we did this. We did it for the effectiveness of our managers around the globe. Nancy Lewis, Director Management Development, IBM[13]

The success of e-learning should be measured in business terms not in training terms, but that doesn't mean that HR managers can't benefit from e-learning.

Save costs

Cost saving is an important driver for e-learning. The enterprise and business units benefit from most of the savings, for example, in opportunity, travel and accommodation costs. What learning and HR managers benefit most from are savings in delivery costs through scalability. Once a self-paced e-learning content has been developed, there's virtually no difference in the cost of delivering it to 100, 1000 or even 10 000 learners. Contrast that with classroom content where the cost difference between delivering a course to 100 and 10 000 learners is dramatic.

Increase learning effectiveness

E-learning delivers more learning in less time. Enterprises that implement e-learning often benefit from a 30–60 effect: either employees learn 30% to 60% more in a comparable period of time — or they learn the same but in 30% to 60% less time. A reduction in learning time not only means more effective learning but it also produces a reduction in opportunity costs.

Support self-paced learning

E-learning supports learning that is self-initiated, self-directed and self-paced. Learning managers understand that self-paced learning is more effective learning. Learners don't have to sit through content they already know. Fast learners are not held back by slow classes. Slower learners are not rushed along by faster learners. Everyone has an opportunity to learn at the pace that suits them best. Self-paced learning also means learners are not tied to centrally arranged schedules but work at times that suit them.

Centralize learning management

While e-learning decentralizes learning, it centralizes learning management to provide learning managers with flexible control over global and local content, budgets and delivery. Costs and resources can be saved by eliminating

(1) messages duplicated globally and locally, and (2) competing learning initiatives in different business units.

Measure and manage continuously

The lifecycle of a competency in the knowledge economy is often measured in months where once it was measured in years, even decades. If competencies and skills are redefined continuously, skills and performance gaps need to be measured continuously. E-learning provides learning managers with tools to measure and manage continuously — and to close gaps that appear with learning customized (1) at the curriculum level for specific roles and responsibilities, and (2) at the learning path level for individual learners. As a result learners benefit from relevant content delivered just in time.

Deliver quality content

When an enterprise sends a signal to its employees that learning is a critical part of what they do, expectations about the quality of learning content naturally increase. If senior executives really are committed to transforming the way the enterprise learns, the signal needs to be backed up with high-quality learner-centric content. E-learning provides learning managers with tools and processes to develop and deliver learning that engages and motivates employees because it is fresh, rich, relevant, granular and available just when it's needed.

Make learning easy

Whether it's a new mobile phone, a new PDA, or e-learning, every technology-based solution comes with a learning curve. What matters is the steepness of the curve. Because e learning is Web based, and because more and more employees have personal and work experience of the Web, learning managers benefit from a shallow learning curve that requires little support. Providing the design of the user interface is friendly, intuitive and fit for purpose, there's no reason for new e learners to struggle with the mechanics of e-learning.

Automate housekeeping

Like cost-saving, easier housekeeping should never be the *raison d'être* of e-learning, however, it comes as part of the e-learning package and is a clear benefit for learning managers. E-learning automates the recording of (1) learner and course registration, (2) individual learners' progress through their learning path and specific courses, (3) assessment results, (4) certification and compliance commencement and expiry dates, (5) course usage levels, (6) the number of concurrent users in the system throughout the day. Not only does automation reduce administrative overheads, the information that results can help managers plan for system upgrades and make a valuable contribution to aspects of the evaluation process including ROI.

What you need to do

You need to work with representatives of all stakeholders to establish and prioritize key business drivers across the enterprise. You'll need a champion at board level to help you understand current thinking about short-, medium-, and long-term strategy. Work with your e-learning team — and experienced vendors — to discover how e-learning can support enterprise business drivers. Study how other enterprises have benefited from e-learning but don't mimic what they've done unless you're certain your enterprise has the same business requirements.

The more stakeholders you can demonstrate benefits to, the more buy-in you'll get but never forget that without senior executives' support your e-learning initiative will fail. Ensure your priorities reflect senior management's. The more your e-learning proposal is seen to be driven by business needs, the more seriously it will be taken in the board room.

Because familiarity breeds contempt, your proposal can be disadvantaged because it's internal. Adopt the mindset of an external supplier; it will give your work a more businesslike approach and help you avoid dangerous assumptions. Work with external vendors and consultants to (1) take advantage of their experience, and (2) test your thinking. Combining your inside knowledge with their third-party perspective will sharpen your focus on the real business drivers for e-learning in your enterprise.

There is another way of approaching e-learning business drivers — "start small". Instead of working at enterprise level, look for one specific performance issue in a business unit or central service. Focus all your efforts on devising an e-learning solution to that issue and present it to the person who owns the problem. If you can win over the problem owner and convince them to support your solution, you have an instant e-learning pilot. Do whatever it takes to make the pilot a success. If it is, e-learning will begin to benefit from good word of mouth. With one success story behind you, your work at enterprise level will be taken more seriously.

References

1   Muoio A (Oct 2000) *Cisco's Quick Study* FastCompany Issue 39 [Internet] Available from <http://www.fastcompany.com/online/39/quickstudy.html> Accessed 9 Apr 2002 p 286.

2   *Online Learning News* (2000) [Internet] Available at <http://www.vnulearning.com/archive.htm> Accessed 29 Oct 2001 Vol 2 No 42.

3   De Cagna J (2000) *Exploring Common Knowledge: An Interview with Nancy Dixon* [Internet] Information Outlook Online. Special Libraries Association. Available from <http://www.sla.org/sla-learning/dixon1.html> Accessed 22 Sep 2001.

4   *2001 E-learning User Survey* (2001) E-Learning Magazine [Internet] Available at <http://www.elearningmag.com/elearning/article/articleList.jsp?categoryId=774> Accessed 9 Apr 2002.

5   *Benchmarking & Networking Analysis* (2001) The Masie Center [Report] [Internet] Available from <http://cons2001.masie.com/2001/cf/baselinesurvey_summary.cfm> Accessed 12 Mar 2001.

6   Botkin J (1999) *Smart Business— How Knowledge Communities Can Revolutionize Your Company* New York, The Free Press p 49.

7   *Learning On Demand: A Strategic Perspective* (1999) SRI Consulting [Report] p 23.

8   Peters R (2000) *The Training-Performance Connection: ASTD Helps You Make the Case for Training* [Presentation] [Internet] Available from <http://www.astdbr.org/pd/peters/connection.pdf> Accessed 5 May 2002.

9   *The 2001 Linkage, Inc E-learning Survey* (April 2001) Linkage Incorporated. <http://www.linkageinc.com>.

10 Masie E (2001) *The Business Case for Learning, Training, and Technology: An Interview with Jack Welch* [Presentation] TechLearn Orlando, October 2001 [Internet] Available from <http://www.techlearn.net/intranet2001/results/sessions/299/jackwelchtranscript.htm> Accessed 13 Nov 2001.

11 May T (2001) *The Promise of Fast Education* Fast Company Learning [Internet] Available from <http://www.fastcompany.com/learning/braintrust/tmay.html> Accessed 11 Mar 2002.

12 Hodgins HW (2000) *Into the Future— A Vision Paper* [Report] Commission on Technology & Adult Learning [Internet] Available from <http://www.learnativity.com/into_the_future2000.html> Accessed 21 Sep 2001 p 14.

13 *ROI Profile: IBM Mindspan Solutions* (2001) [Case Study] Nucleus Research Inc [Internet] Available from <http://www.nucleusresearch.com/research/b19.pdf> Accessed 5 May 2002.

E-learning strategy: dramatically improve your chance of success

6

Our plans miscarry because they have no aim. When you don't know what harbour you're aiming for, no wind is the right wind. Seneca

Technology strategy used to be, What do I buy, and how much do I have to spend on it? Now it's, What do I deliver, and how should it be designed? Thornton A. May[1]

What you need to know

As a limbering up exercise, consider Figure 6.1. I believe these facts but I can't make sense of them. Fact 1, we have no map. Fact 2, without a map we find it very difficult to get where we need to go. Fact 3, we're not sure where we need to go. Fact 4, we're going anyway. Fact 5, we know the absence of a map will continue to make journeys difficult. Why would anyone want to approach e-learning with that mindset? Isn't the answer as simple as getting a map? It might not be an easy solution — it takes time and effort — but it is a simple one. Here's another fact:

Ultimately, the success or failure of your e-learning initiative is in direct proportion to the quality of strategic thinking that underpins it.

Fact #1	69% of senior managers admit their enterprises have no e-learning strategy[2]
Fact #2	56% of senior managers say the absence of a defined e-learning strategy is a barrier to successful e-learning — no other barrier is ranked higher[2]
Fact #3	0% of senior managers say business requirements form part of their current e-learning strategy[2]
Fact #4	58% of senior managers say their businesses implemented e-learning without a formal strategy signed off at board level[3]
Fact #5	76% of senior managers admit their current e-learning strategy is not adequate for meeting their future e-learning needs[2]

Figure 6.1 — The facts about e-learning strategies

What and why

An enterprise e-learning strategy provides a vision and a framework to inform the implementation process. The vision needs to be compelling. Doing the same things better isn't enough; the vision should present a picture of doing what you've never been able to do before.

The framework isn't a project plan; it's an analysis of everything that impacts on an e-learning implementation. The analysis results in a series of guiding principles for the dimensions of e-learning (see Figure 6.2):

- The driver of change: business needs.
- The enabler of change: technology.
- The agent of change: content.
- The arena of change: corporate culture.

An e-learning strategy operates at micro and macro levels. There are hundreds of detailed questions to consider; each is an aspect of larger questions, like: What are the business reasons for doing this? What's the right way for us to do this? What is the financial impact of doing this? It's important not to confuse strategic thinking — what your e-learning strategy is about — with strategic planning. Henry Mintzberg, Professor of Strategy and Organization at McGill University, makes a clear distinction between the two: "Planning has always been about analysis — about breaking down a goal or set of intentions into steps, formalizing those steps so that they can be implemented almost automatically, and articulating the anticipated consequences or results of each step ... Strategic thinking, in contrast, is about synthesis. It involves intuition and creativity. The outcome of strategic thinking is an integrated perspective of the enterprise, a not-too-precisely articulated vision of direction."[4] Because e-learning demands such high levels of system integration, detailed planning is essential during the implementation phase but that's the "how"; Mintzberg's strategic "thinking" is the "why".

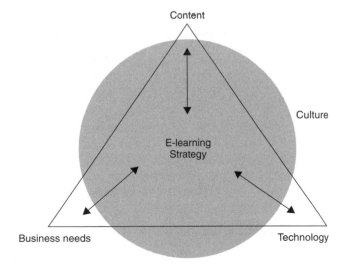

Figure 6.2 — The dimensions of strategy

It's no secret that not every enterprise gets e-learning right first time. Failure to manage technology effectively is one reason; failure to keep e-learning aligned with the changing needs of the business is another. An e-learning strategy needs the flexibility to respond quickly to changes in business requirements — and to developments in e-learning products, services and technology. There's no point implementing e-learning with a strategy that's out of date. The way to avoid that is through iteration; be prepared to re-visit every aspect of the strategy in light of internal and external changes. That means your strategy should not be built around a specific e-learning vendor or solution.

There are many stakeholders in an e-learning implementation. If they're all pulling in different directions, you will either fail to implement e-learning or what you implement will fail. An e-learning strategy ensures that there is a shared vision for e-learning across the enterprise, one the implementation can be judged against later. Experience has shown that a coherent strategy also supports funding. A proposal supported by a well thought through strategy is more likely to get budget sign-off than one without one. The absence of an enterprise e-learning strategy precipitates complications, for example, business units or regions faced with learning challenges will be tempted to develop their own strategies and initiatives. This leads to competing initiatives that duplicate effort, dilute funding and muddy issues in the minds of senior executives.

An important exception to the strategize-before-implementation rule is when there's a pain point in the enterprise and e-learning is seen as a potential solution. Whether the pain is being felt at enterprise level or in a business unit, the objective is to eliminate it fast. Much of the value of an e-learning strategy is to achieve consensus about what needs to be done. In fire-fighting situations, you know exactly what needs to be done — resolve a very well-defined problem with a rapid e-learning implementation. The danger comes later, for example, if you rolled out the same solution across the enterprise without going back to question whether it's the one for all business needs.

Alignment

Strategies help an enterprise focus on how to achieve its objectives in the environment in which it operates. The interests of the enterprise are not served when conflicting strategies pull it in different directions. Your e-learning strategy needs to be aligned with other key strategies already in place. The way to ensure alignment is to consult the owners of the other strategies or engage them as stakeholders.

Business Strategy: The key alignment is with the business strategy that sets out the goals of the enterprise, how it intends to compete for market share, and how it plans to drive value into the business and increase its share price. This strategy drives all others.

E-Business Strategy: Most enterprises are still transitioning from business to e-business and have an e-business strategy in place to guide the process. Typically, the strategy defines an infrastructure, processes and priorities for connecting everything to everything. In some enterprises, e-learning is seen as an aspect of e-business and the e-business group owns the e-learning initiative. This situation should make strategic alignment between e-business and e-learning straightforward. Even when this isn't the case, e-learning should not be at odds with e-business.

Human Resources Strategy: The e-learning strategy should be aligned with the HR strategy which sets out how the enterprise's investment in human capital can be leveraged better to execute its business strategy. There is a natural alignment between HR and learning; it should not be hard to ensure that e-learning has the same strategic objectives as HR.

Knowledge Management: At the highest level, both Knowledge Management and e-learning are about capturing tacit expert knowledge and transforming it into explicit common knowledge. They are natural partners and their strategies should be easily aligned. This alignment might later develop into a formal integration programme.

IT Strategy: The technology that underpins e-learning should not be at odds with the technology that underpins other business processes. E-learning can impacted by IT strategy at a number of levels — for example, approved technology vendors and infrastructure evolution.

E-learning is one of the channels an enterprise has at its disposal for the delivery of learning. There should never be a conflict between learning and e-learning — both share the aim of raising the performance level of employees. At a practical level, an e-learning strategy might address technology, instructional design and development issues unique to itself and be developed at a different time than the learning strategy but their aims should be the same — improving the performance of the enterprise by improving the performance of the individual. In enterprises where there is no learning strategy, the development of an e-learning strategy must take all learning requirements and channels into account.

Barrier #1: The e-learning industry

The nature of the e-learning industry can work against strategic thinking. Although there are no true end-to-end solution vendors, large Learning Management System vendors go a long way to meeting most enterprise needs. The attraction of a large packaged solution from a high profile vendor can distract from the need for a strategy. Marketing messages will give the clear impression that the solution delivers everything you need and more. Maybe it does, maybe it doesn't. The only way to know for certain is to have a clear, shared understanding of everything you need before going shopping. Where is your business headed? What is its geographic spread? Is that likely to increase as a result of mergers and acquisitions? Are staffing levels likely to rise significantly? Is staff turnover too high? Are product cycles getting shorter? Is competition heating up? Is there increasing emphasis on outsourcing? Cost reduction? Without real insights into these kinds of questions, you're just guessing about the kind of e-learning system you need.

Barrier #2: Time

Pressure of time seems to present the perfect excuse for not developing a coherent e-learning strategy. Experience says it isn't. Issues not addressed or resolved in the course of developing a strategy don't go away, they get deferred. Here's an example. One way of opening a dialogue with e-learning vendors and learning what they can bring to your implementation is to issue a Request for Information (RFI) document. If a vendor's response makes you think you might like to do business with them, add their name to a shortlist. When it's time to buy products and services, send shortlisted vendors a Request for Purchase (RFP) document. The better your strategy, the better your RFI and RFP — because you have a clear idea of what you need and the critical evaluation factors on which to base your selection. The better your RFI and RFP, the better the responses you'll receive.

Without a strategy in place, you'll spend too long developing the RFI and RFP and even then the documents lack focus because your thinking lacks focus. More than facilitating the initial selection process, your e-learning strategy will help you (1) develop effective long-term relationships with vendors, and (2) negotiate advantageous contracts — because you know exactly what you need and what you don't. An e-learning strategy will help you expedite relationships internally, too, with line managers and learners. You'll get buy-in faster and with deeper commitment because you can easily and confidently share agreed outcomes. That way everyone knows what's in it for them — and what's expected of them.

Far from wasting time, developing a strategy streamlines the implementation process by eliminating the stop–start development pattern that results from having to refer questions to different parts of the enterprise as they crop up. With a well developed strategy, all key questions are answered in advance.

What you need to do

A strategic plan provides the training and development function, its funders and clients, and management with a shared understanding of learning's role and value.

It outlines the accountability of the training function, milestones, and how training will be designed, developed, and delivered. Margaret Driscoll[5]

Your e-learning strategy does not need to provide a definitive answer to every question it encounters. Instead, it should inform the implementation process with context, requirements, priorities and best practice. Your strategy will probably need to address most of these topics which are covered later in the chapter:

Vision	Content
Senior Executive Support	Culture
Business Case	Transition
Success Criteria	Risk Register
Stakeholders	Roll Out and Communications
Learning Value Chain	Human Resources
Technology	Schedules, Milestones

Getting started

Establish an e-learning group whose members have an interest and possibly experience in e-learning. The more the group is representative of the enterprise, the more effective it will be. It limits the scope of discussion and influence if most members are from the learning department, for example. Use the group to ferret out any knowledge of e-learning across the enterprise. There's probably more there than you think.

Use formal or informal surveys to gain an understanding of opinion about e-learning at all levels of the enterprise. If opinion is positive, build on it; if it's negative, start educating people. Find out if anyone has had personal experience of e-learning in another enterprise, at university, or on the Internet. What's their opinion of the experience? If it's positive, recruit them as e-learning champions. Find out if there have been any local e-learning initiatives in business units or regions. Were they a success or a failure? Find out why. Are they still operational? The objective of these activities is to capture the current state of e-learning across the enterprise. Learn from outside the enterprise, too. Study the implementations of your competitors and learn from their successes and failures.

Involve stakeholders

There are many stakeholders to involve and influence. Titles and numbers will vary from business to business but stakeholders will usually include:

- senior management
- e-learning steering group (when it forms)
- IT department

- e-business department
- Knowledge Management department
- learning department managers and staff
- e-learning implementation team (when it forms)
- local e-learning initiatives
- internal and external certification and compliance regulators
- internal clients
- subject matter experts
- coaches and tutors
- line managers
- learners
- learning technology, services and content vendors
- internal communications department
- partners
- sales channels
- suppliers
- customers

A strategy needs to be informed by the business and learning requirements of all stakeholders and to coalesce their support for e-learning by educating and guiding them. In the course of developing a coherent strategy all stakeholders need to become clear in their own minds about the benefits of e-learning. A strategy cannot be imposed on stakeholders. At the heart of strategizing lies a process of discovery and dialogue—that's what's important. The strategy document that gets signed off by the board and actioned by the e-learning build team is simply a record of how an enterprise got smart about e-learning.

SWOT

Wherever possible, do a SWOT analysis under each strategy heading and sub-heading. The acronym is an abbreviation of Strengths, Weaknesses, Opportunities and Threats. The goal of the analysis is to identify critical strategic factors—and then to:

- Build on core strengths.
- Eliminate undermining weaknesses.
- Take quick advantage of significant opportunities.
- Circumnavigate or mitigate threats.

There's no point to a half-hearted or cosmetic SWOT analysis; that only reinforces the status quo. SWOT is a tool for questioning assumptions and thinking outside the box. A SWOT analysis of your learners might look like this:

	SWOT analysis: learners
Strengths	• Over 90% are computer literate. The technology of e-learning will not present a barrier.
	• Learners are highly competitive and will see e-learning as a tool for improving their personal performance.
	• Increasingly, new joiners will have used e-learning during their formal education, will appreciate its benefits, and have high expectations of what it can deliver.
Weaknesses	• There have been a number of poorly implemented local e-learning initiatives that have left learners cynical.
	• Learners' desktop configurations vary from business unit to business unit. Learning content might not "behave" or "look" the same to all learners.
	• Post-engagement/exit interviews indicate that learners are disappointed in the volume and freshness of learning provided—and blame the training department.
Opportunities	• The business has a global spread. E-learning can deliver consistent learning content to every learner no matter where they are.
	• E-learning technology allows us to create global learning communities in which best practices can be shared.
	• E-learning allows us to bring our partners, suppliers and customers into these learning communities.
	• Some learners spend extended periods away from the office. E-learning allows them to continue training during these absences.
	• There is an unacceptably high level of no-shows for classroom training events—usually the result of conflicting commitments. The flexibility of self-paced, self-scheduled e-learning can break down this barrier to learning.
Threats	• There is some evidence that line managers do not support desktop learning which they see as a distraction from real work. If line managers do not provide incentives for adopting e-learning, it will fail.
	• Learners working in customers' premises are embarrassed to use desktop learning because they believe it undermines their authority by making them appear unqualified.

SWOT analysis: learners (*continued*)

Threats	• Learners interpret the implementation of e-learning strictly as a cost-saving exercise instead of a commitment to the provision of lifelong learning. Adoption rates suffer as a result. • Managers fail to see benefits of e-learning and do not give it a high priority. As a result, potential subject matter experts and coaches/tutors are not freed up to make contributions.

If you subject your senior executives to a SWOT analysis, the result might look like this:

SWOT analysis: the senior executive

Strengths	• Senior executives have a track record of leveraging technology to meet business requirements. • Senior executives see speed-to-market as a critical business driver. • Senior executives are committed to retaining the best staff.
Weaknesses	• Traditionally senior executives have not placed a high value on training, which most view as a cost centre. • Senior executives have a reputation for not honouring commitments to annual training budgets which are subject to cuts whenever cost savings are required. • The senior executive rarely makes itself available to the training department. • The senior executive does not include any members from the training department.
Opportunities	• The HR director has shown a genuine interest in e-learning, especially if it can interface with existing HR systems to support enterprise-wide competencies management and project recruitment. • Two of our competitors have implemented e-learning providing dramatic success stories to attract the senior executive's attention. • The senior executive is committed to a programme of mergers and acquisitions. E-learning has a proven record of accelerating post M&A coalescence.

SWOT analysis: the senior executive (*continued*)

	• The senior executive is committed to an ongoing program of cost savings. E-learning can demonstrate impressive ROI — and not just in headline items like travel and accommodation.
Threats	• There is evidence of factional clashes in the boardroom. E-learning could become subject to one of those clashes — or different factions could support different e-learning initiatives.
	• The senior executive is committed to a programme of mergers and acquisitions, any of which could disrupt an e-learning implementation by changing leadership's priorities.
	• The senior executive has a reputation for impatience and might not give the e-learning initiative enough time to start delivering benefits.

SWOT analysis is a tool and the analyses themselves don't need to appear in your strategy document unless there's a good reason for including them. However, threats revealed by a SWOT analysis should be carried forward to the Risk Register section of your strategy.

What you need to cover

This is a guide to the kinds of topics and issues that should be covered in an e-learning strategy.

Vision

In the early days of e-learning there was probably too much emphasis on vision at the expense of substance. The pendulum has swung the other way. The e-learning industry is focused on delivery, which is what the market said it wanted, but it seems to me what we need is substance *and* vision, not substance *instead of* vision. That applies to your strategy, too; it needs to face up to hard questions about infrastructure, bandwidth, cost, regional variations, etc., but it also needs to offer a vision — a helicopter view of the major transformations covered in your strategy — as a rallying point for leaders and followers.

The way to start developing a vision of e-learning is to focus on the outcomes you want, for example:

- performance- not activity-driven metrics
- proven, measurable ROI

- dramatic reductions in time to perform, producing marked reductions in time to market
- employees rewarded for sharing knowledge
- fresh, relevant and compelling learning content delivered just-in-time
- learning as integrated into daily work as e-mail
- every employee working at peak performance all the time
- educating the value chain not just the employee
- retaining of the best talent
- prospective employees seeing your enterprise as the employer of choice

Senior executive support

Your strategy needs to identify e-learning ownership and leadership. It should make recommendations about governance and where e-learning will fit in the organization's structure. Who does e-learning report to — learning, HR, e-business, or IT? Provide a rationale for your recommendation.

Your strategy should propose a steering committee to whom the e-learning initiative will be accountable during the build phase.

Business case

Explain the business drivers for e-learning emphasizing those that meet the needs of senior managers. Provide details of the investment required. Make your ROI case.

Talk about business models. What are your strategies for financing e-learning? Is it funded centrally or do business units own their learning budgets — or a combination of both? Once e-learning is operationalized, how will ongoing learning budgets be determined? Some e-learning initiatives have found it useful to spread costs across a number of departments if only to cushion against future budget cuts. Should you negotiate with IT or HR to finance the purchase and support of the Learning Management System — the largest single budget item in most implementations — on your behalf?

Will all e-learning activity be outsourced? This isn't common but some enterprises outsource all HR activity so there is a model to follow. Outsourcing does not have to be an all or nothing option. You can outsource hosting, Learning Management System services, and content design and development. The more you outsource the lower the capital investment. Whether or not you believe outsourcing is right for your situation, it is a box that needs ticking.

With content and applications that are licensed, what works best for your enterprise: site licences that place no constraints on usage or licences based on head counts or numbers of concurrent users?

If you intend to do a lot of work with a few key suppliers, is there an advantage to investing in those companies for financial gain and to oversee their future direction?

Success criteria

Success criteria help to answer the question, How will we know if we've succeeded in what we set out to do? Success criteria flow naturally out of business drivers and ROI calculations. Analyse those and make some decisions about what you're going to measure. Let's say one business driver is to reduce the time to performance for new hires. If exceptional new hires are ready to perform in 6 weeks even though the current induction course lasts 10 weeks, you have the makings of a success criterion. When the introduction of a 6-week e-learning induction programme maintains or, better still, improves performance outcomes, you have demonstrated that e-learning enables all new hires to achieve performance-readiness in the same time frame as exceptional ones.

Stakeholders

Your learning strategy should identify all stakeholders—internal and external—and describe what's at stake for each. Learners are a key stakeholder group. Describe learner demographics and the different audiences within the learner group. Will e-learning be available to all audiences? For example, is the senior executive an audience? Are line managers? Describe the incentives for adopting e-learning. Is it simply the kudos of being part of the early-adopter group? Or will a commitment to e-learning be recognized formally in a learner's annual review? Can learners meet compliance requirements through e-learning? Use a SWOT analysis to challenge assumptions about the learner base in your business.

Partners are another key stakeholder group. They can be internal or external. The IT department is an internal partner. Again, use a SWOT analysis to reveal the kind of partner IT is likely to be and how best to manage the partnership. Is the department well resourced? Does the IT department have enterprise-wide responsibility or is IT run regionally or by business unit? Is IT already over-committed to mission-critical projects? Is IT outsourced? Does IT have a strategic relationship with an enterprise vendor who has an e-learning offering, for example, Cisco, HP, IBM Lotus, SAP or Sun? Can the relationship be leveraged? Will corporate or IT policy force your e-learning initiative to work with the same vendor? Does IT have its own learning requirements?

Learning value chain

The learning value chain is a critical element of your learning strategy. Identify all the learning channels currently in your enterprise and those that need to be added. Here is a list of typical learning channels—few enterprises will have them all:

Instructor-led scheduled classroom events	Web casts
Moderated workshops	Online coaching and mentoring
Self-paced e-learning courses	Simulations
Virtual classrooms	Electronic performance support systems (EPSS)
Moderated online forums	Knowledge Management databases
Ad hoc and scheduled collaborations	Knowledge leadership, for example, white papers

Do a SWOT analysis of each channel to help understand how it supports business and learning requirements. Describe the relationship between channels, for example, do self-paced e-learning courses replace or support classroom courses? Is the content of the KM database integrated with e-learning? When and how? Do online collaborations need to be moderated? When should virtual classrooms be used instead of self-paced courses? Instead of classroom courses? Does it depend on content or timing?

Do the learning channels you propose form a hierarchy? IBM talks in terms of a Four Tier Learning Model which associates learning objectives with channels of learning delivery (see Figure 6.3). Tiers One, Two and Three are prerequisites to Tier Four. This particular model might not address your enterprise's learning

Tier	Goal	Learn from	Channel
1	• Knowledge • Awareness	• Information	• Performance support • Reference materials
2	• Application	• Interaction • Understanding • Beginning of practice	• Self-paced e-learning • Interactive learning • Simulations • Gaming

3	• Applied skill	• Collaboration	• Online collaboration:
			  • Virtual classrooms
			  • E-labs
			  • Live conferences
			  • Teaming–learning communities

4	• Mastery	• Collocation
		• Experience-based Learning
			• Face-to-face:
			  • Classroom mentoring
			  • Role-playing
			  • Coaching
			  • Case studies

Figure 6.3 — IBM Four Tier Learning Model[6]

requirements but a description of the relationships within your proposed learning value chain belongs in your strategy.

Infrastructure and technology

Do a rigorous SWOT analysis of the corporate infrastructure; it will probably overlap with your SWOT analysis of the IT department; they're different sides of the same coin. Here are some of the questions you need to ask about infrastructure:

- Is it stable or in transition? At the micro level, all infrastructures are always in transition. What you're trying to learn is whether imminent enterprise-wide changes will make infrastructure a moving target throughout implementation? For example, is infrastructure about to be outsourced? Or undergo a major upgrade?
- Is the infrastructure consistent globally or are there regional and/or business unit variations? Do all learners in all regions and business units have Internet and intranet access? Surprisingly, the answer is often, No. Different cultures view Internet access differently.
- Few networks have spare capacity. How congested is the network? Can it handle the additional traffic that will be generated by a successful e-learning implementation? The IT department won't compromise the transmission of e-mail and financial data by launching a new enterprise application like e-learning without rigorous load testing. Use your strategy to get infrastructure issues on the table early; they can take longer to resolve than you expect.
- How is the firewall configured? Does it support streaming media and collaborative applications? If not, is this a security issue or because there has been no demand in the past?
- How is security configured? Will learners logging on from outside the firewall be able to access e-learning content inside the firewall? Does the infrastructure support unified logon, or will learners have to logon a second time to access the learning portal? Experience has shown multiple logons to be a big disincentive for learners.
- Does the infrastructure support a mix of server operating systems or only one, that is, UNIX, NT, 2000 or Linux? This will impact on your choice of e-learning applications.

If the infrastructure looks like constraining the implementation to an unacceptable degree, you need to do a SWOT analysis of hosting e-learning outside the firewall with one of the specialist application service providers (ASP). The ASP model is not issue-free — security, for example, can be a consideration — but it might allow you to implement e-learning faster. It can also been seen as Phase One of implementation buying time for a parallel upgrade of the infrastructure.

Ask the same kind of questions about the enterprise desktop:

- Is there a global desktop configuration or does it vary according to region or business unit?
- Does every desktop and laptop system run the same version of the same operating system? If not, what versions of what operating systems are installed?
- Does every desktop and laptop system run the same version of the same Web browser? If not, which versions of which browsers are installed? Do any browser plug-ins, for example, Flash or Real, come as part of the desktop configuration?
- Can e-learning afford to support all versions of all installed operating systems? Can it afford to support all versions of all installed Web browsers?

Here are some other infrastructure and technology questions to think about:

- Will the e-learning application be integrated with other enterprise applications, for example, financial, HR, KM, Procurement and e-mail? What are the benefits and implications?
- Will e-learning support mobile learning, or m-learning as some people call it? How do you define m-learning — laptops, PDAs, WAP devices? Handheld devices can be a cost-effective learning solution for employees who work shifts, who are seldom in the same place for very long, or who have little or no access to networked computers but still need just-in-time learning. Is there a learner group in your business who would benefit from m-learning? If interactions are limited to stylus taps, even typing skills aren't a prerequisite. Is it a Phase One requirement — or can it be added later?

Content

Your content strategy needs to support and be aligned with the characteristics of learner-centred content and your learning value chain. Organize your thinking under these headings:

- sources
- learning objects
- standards
- development technologies and tools

Sources

Where will content come from? It is a question that every e-learning strategy needs to address. The short answer is, you will either build it or buy it. The content you buy will be either generic or industry-specific. Enterprises who have made a success of e-learning tend to have a mix of sources. Whether you intend to use one source or a mix, you need a strategy to inform your choice: When is it right to build? When is it right to buy? (See Figure 6.4.)

When you buy, will it only be from approved vendors? When you build, will development be outsourced or in-house? If it's outsourced, will you establish a network of preferred vendors?

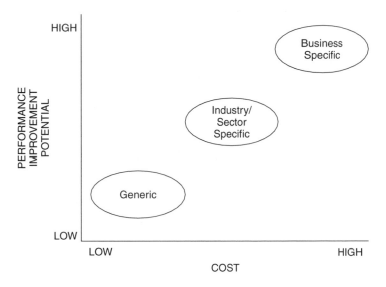

Figure 6.4—Hierarchy of content sources

Learning objects

By creating movable type in the 15th century, Johann Guttenberg changed forever the way knowledge is shared. Movable type was probably the first example of object-oriented thinking. Instead of carving whole words or pages, Guttenberg had the idea of carving individual character objects which could be combined endlessly to make up any word, sentence and, ultimately, thought.

Knowledge objects work the same way. Instead of developing monolithic courses, the trend is to develop small, interchangeable knowledge objects that can be combined endlessly to make up custom learning experiences. Your strategy needs to address the question of whether you will follow the lead of businesses like American Express, Cisco, Dow and Honeywell and adopt an object-oriented approach to e-learning. The decision impacts on your choice of Learning Management System, instructional design strategies, e-learning standards and content development tools.

To benefit from learning objects means making a global, long-term commitment to them: global because running one system for content based on learning objects and one for traditionally structured content is hard to justify in cost and management terms; long term because the benefits of learning objects only kick in when you have amassed a large repository of objects that can be used over and over to create new content. Until you reach the tipping point, developing content based on learning objects will tend to cost more than conventionally developed content.

At the strategic level, here are some of the questions you need to answer about learning objects:

- Will you take an object-oriented approach to learning?
- How do you define a learning object?
- What industry standard supports your definition of a learning object?
- Are you content to support interoperability and real-time assembly at a technology level — or do you want to support it at an instructional design level, too?
- If you want an instructional design solution for learning objects, which one best meets your requirements?

There's a certain though not absolute inevitability about learning objects. There is also room for manoeuvre in the degree to which you commit to them. You could choose to work with content templates and a CMS to accelerate development, or make a total commitment to reusability and customized course creation. What you shouldn't do is duck the question.

Standards

The strategic question about e-learning standards is, what is driving you to (1) adhere to any standard, and (2) choose a specific standard to adhere to? Here are the kinds of answers you might come up with:

- One publisher of e-learning content meets all our business and learning needs. We will use that publisher's content exclusively. The content adheres to standard x, so we will adhere to standard x.
- One Learning Management System meets all our business and learning needs. It adheres to standard y, so all our content whether built or bought will adhere to standard y.
- We intend to outsource all our content development to two specific developers. They both prefer to work with standard z, so our Learning Management System and any generic content we buy will have to adhere to standard z.
- We intend to implement fully learning objects and believe the SCORM reference model offers the best way of doing that, so our Learning Management System, our development tools, our development partners and any generic content we buy has to adhere to SCORM.
- We do not need a Learning Management System and see no benefit in implementing learning objects, so we are standards agnostic.

There are variations on these themes and they're all equally valid. The point is, there isn't a best e-learning standard; there is only a best standard in a specific context. Identify the context and the choice — or rejection — of standards becomes straightforward.

Content development technologies and tools

Your strategy should provide a rationale for choosing between open technologies and tools, and proprietary ones — and between native Windows technologies and third party ones.

A proprietary approach delivers benefits in terms of shallow learning curves, ease of use, rapid development and automatic standards adherence. That needs to be balanced against lock in — you can only edit the content using the same tools you built it with, limited authoring freedom and a smaller installed base than open tools. The size of the installed base matters for peer-to-peer support which developers rely on.

If you use streaming audio and video, Microsoft's WMF (Windows Media File) format is native to Windows and automatically supported by it. If you choose Real or QuickTime for streaming media, each require a plug-in to be installed in the Web browser. Macromedia Flash is a popular tool for animation development and delivery; it requires a plug-in too. Find out whether any of these plug-ins are part of the corporate desktop.

Culture

> *Organizations know how to build or purchase the right technical solution to their business problems or opportunities. Where they tend to fail is in that space where technology and corporate culture intersect. When a new system requires people to think, behave, or believe in a significantly different manner from what they have done in the past, technology's ROI is often in jeopardy.* ODR, Inc[7]

E-learning implementation will impact on corporate culture and vice versa. To be successful, an e-learning implementation needs a strategy for managing these impacts by anticipating their effects and where necessary, creating mitigations. Implementers also need to recognize the difficulty of changing the behaviours of learners and their managers; it can be as difficult to change the behaviours of people working in the learning department.

At the strategic level, a SWOT analysis is a useful tool for drawing out cultural issues: it is as important to build on existing strengths and leverage opportunities as it is to mitigate weaknesses and threats. Here are some of the cultural issues that turn up on a regular basis:

- Learners see the travel associated with visits to training centres or out of town workshops as a benefit; they resist giving it up in favour of desktop learning.
- Learners see face-to-face learning events as valuable opportunities to build personal networks and advance their careers. They resist the loss of these opportunities.

- Line managers and colleagues are not prepared to give learners the time and space to engage with desktop learning.
- Learners lack the confidence and/or skills to take on self-paced, self-directed learning. Instead of feeling empowered, they yearn for an instructor to tell them what to do.
- Line managers do not value learning and resist committing subject matter experts — usually their best-performing employees — to support the development of learning content.
- Subject matter experts know that sharing their knowledge through the development of learning content will not earn positive recognition from their managers and peers and so resist becoming involved. No reward, no buy in.
- Subject matter experts believe that knowledge is power. They resist sharing what they know and diluting their power.
- Employees are comfortable with their own style of sharing knowledge — buddy networks, for example — and resist the shift to knowledge sharing through e-learning.
- Business units are accustomed to thinking vertically and resist sharing knowledge on an enterprise-wide basis.
- Regional units do not believe that enterprise-wide e-learning can overcome cultural and language barriers. Instead of buying in, they create competing e-learning initiatives.
- Line managers do not place a high enough value on learning and neglect to support operational changes that should result from what has been learned by their staff. The result: what has been learned is implemented half-heartedly.
- E-learning becomes associated with other failed enterprise initiatives and is received with cynicism, even hostility.
- The e-learning implementation team fail to appreciate the importance of internal communications. In the absence of positive information about e-learning, employees' reception is lukewarm.
- There is a failure to coordinate and focus communications across the enterprise. Key messages and strategies become confused. A typical response to lack of focus is lack of attention.
- Your employees span three generations. Each generation responds to e-learning differently but the differences aren't acknowledged or acted on.
- Employees who have been with the enterprise a long time find the idea of yet another change to the way things are done overwhelming. They resist e-learning even though they are the ones who will benefit most.
- Employees in the learning department see e-learning as a threat to their self-esteem and job security. They either actively undermine it or simply fail to promote it.
- Employees in the learning department say they are prepared to give e-learning a chance but cannot break free from the classroom paradigm. They fail to see a new model of learning with new benefits and see a pale imitation of the classroom instead. They resist the "imitation".

- Employees in the learning department cannot break free from the support service model they have followed for so long and fail to engage with business requirements.
- The learning department is bureaucracy-driven. It imposes overly complex registration processes that create a barrier to adoption.
- The IT department is security-driven. It imposes overly rigid security measures that create a barrier to adoption.

At least some of these cultural issues will apply to your implementation. You need to set out strategic responses to them.

Transition

Your strategy should include a plan for the transition from where the enterprise's learning is now to where you want it to be.

Will you introduce e-learning with a full implementation, a pilot programme, or the middle path: precision-bombing e-learning into a small number of business units to address carefully chosen performance issues? Are your stakeholders comfortable with the *launch and learn* mentality that a full implementation implies, or do they need the reassurances that a *learn and launch* phased approach provides? Time is a critical factor; a phased approach takes longer to reach the whole enterprise but it can benefit from momentum and good word of mouth. From a pragmatic perspective, there is a danger with pilots and phased roll-outs: they can be cancelled by senior managers more easily than a full implementation.

Based on your conclusions about the type and scale of implementation, document the roles and responsibilities of the e-learning implementation team. Describe your recruitment strategy. What is your transition strategy for the learning department itself — potentially, there will be a significant drop in classroom attendance. What will happen to traditional instructors? Can they make a contribution to the e-learning initiative? Do they need re-skilling? If they do, what is your *train the trainers* strategy?

What is your strategy for developing relationships with the business units — your internal customers? How will you help your customers make a smooth transition from classroom learning to e-learning? How will the change impact on business units? Will there be a domino effect? How might operations and career development, for example, be impacted? If anticipated change is positive, how can you leverage it? If anticipated change is negative, how can you mitigate it?

Implementing e-learning isn't flipping a switch. Learners and their managers need to learn new ways of doing things. Your strategy needs to anticipate the impact of transition and to provide the information, tools, processes and support to ensure the smooth enthusiastic adoption of e-learning.

Risk register

All threats which emerge from SWOT analyses and other thinking should be recorded in a risk register. This isn't the full risk register you will use later during implementation but an acknowledgement that risks exist and a demonstration that they can be mitigated by the right strategies. What enterprises are finding is that it's often unexpected barriers that hamper the fast adoption of e-learning. That should serve as fillip to spare no effort in uncovering potential risks.

Linkage, Inc's survey of US senior and mid-level managers revealed these top 10 barriers to successful e-learning implementation listed in order of frequency:

- No defined strategy.
- Technical difficulties.
- Lack of human touch.
- Associated added costs.
- Motivational difficulties.
- Learners don't want to train "off the clock".
- Quality of courseware and content.
- Lack of executive buy in.
- Lack of IT support.[8]

When building your risk register, be sure to consider these barriers. Here are other risks that you need to consider:

- What happens if our business is acquired by or merges with another business? Can our knowledge and learning assets be combined with those of the other business? In other words, is our implementation merger-ready?
- Is a change in leadership likely? How might that impact on the e-learning initiative?
- What happens if we lose our project champion(s) at senior executive level? Can the initiative survive that loss of support? Can we recruit replacements?
- Are there other e-learning initiatives within the enterprise that can overtake or undermine ours?
- Will project funding be secure? Can the initiative survive a reduction in funding? How large a reduction can it survive?
- Can we recruit the right skills to implement and operate e-learning?
- What happens if we fail to meet the projected ROI?
- What happens if our pilot projects fail to achieve the outcomes we expect?
- What happens if we are too successful? What happens when too many concurrent users logon and the infrastructure can't cope? How do we build for success?
- Are our partners' and vendors' businesses sound? What happens if a partner or vendor closes or is acquired by another business?

Roll out and communications

Have you developed a high-level communications programme to ensure that all stakeholders understand your objectives, your progress and key dates? Are you competing with other enterprise initiatives for the attention of employees? What can be done about that? Do you have a strategy for an ongoing marketing programme to promote new courses, course upgrades, times and dates of special Web casts, new learning features and functions?

Human resources

E-learning has the potential to bridge performance gaps across the enterprise — but that can happen only if you work with HR to develop new or incorporate existing competency models into your learning strategy alongside skills and knowledge requirements. Do you have a strategy for determining which competencies are best addressed by e-learning and which by other channels in the learning value chain?

Schedules, milestones

Have you developed a high-level schedule setting out all key milestones? Does your schedule take account of other enterprise initiatives, the financial year and the impact of holidays? All three can de-rail your project. What happens if you miss the launch date even if it's through no fault of your own? What happens if the senior executive makes project sign-off conditional on markedly shorter lead times? Do you have a contingency plan? Can you move faster?

References

1   LaBarre P ed (2002) *Essay Question 2: Technology Meets Strategy* [Internet] Fast-Company. Available from: <http://www.fastcompany.com/ftalk/nyc2/essay2.html> Accessed 16 Apr 2002.
2   *The 2001 Linkage, Inc E-learning Survey* (April 2001) Linkage Incorporated <http://www.linkageinc.com>.
3   *Click2Learn Research — Executive Summary* (June 2001) Click2Learn <click2learn.com>.
4   Mintzberg H (1994) *The Fall and Rise of Strategic Planning* Harvard Business Review January–February 1994 p 107 In Boyett JH and Boyett JT (1998) *The Guru Guide* New York, John Wiley & Sons Inc.
5   Driscoll M (2001) *Strategic Plans from Scratch* ASTD Learning Circuits [Internet] Available from: <http://www.learningcircuits.org/2001/aug2001/driscoll.html> Accessed 17 Sep 2001.
6   *E-learning: Implementing the 4-Tier Blended Learning Model from IBM* (2001) IBM [White paper] [Internet] Available from: <http://www-3.ibm.com/software/mindspan/

distlrng.nsf/wdocs/e4e36aa7c520bcd185256b12005c6c55?OpenDocument&ExpandSection=1#_Section1> Accessed 24 Apr 2002.

7 *Installation vs Realization* (2000) ODR, Inc [Internet] Available from <http://www.odrinc.com/new/odr_researchFindings.htm> Accessed 12 Apr 2002.

8 *The 2001 Linkage, Inc E-learning Survey* (April 2001) Linkage Incorporated <http://www.linkageinc.com>.

Part III
Implementation

7   The project team: who you need ... what they do ...

Ideas won't keep. Something must be done about them. When the idea is new its custodians have fervour, live for it, and, if need be, die for it. Alfred North Whitehead

While it lacks the simplicity of a functional team composed of, for example, six engineers all reporting to the engineering manager, a cross-functional team has a greater chance of realizing the potential of that old axiom, The whole is greater than the sum of its parts. This group of allies, enemies, and strangers can weave together a cross-functional design that is an amalgam of many cultures. Glenn M. Parker[1]

What you need to know

Some business requirements can be met with a totally outsourced e-learning solution. At the other end of the spectrum, some can only be met with a custom solution built by integrating a suite of applications from different vendors, and hosting the hybrid application behind the enterprise firewall. The two approaches require different teams in terms of both skills and scale. There's no off-the-shelf e-learning solution and no off-the-shelf team. The roles and responsibilities described in this chapter should provide a team template that you can customize to the scale and complexity of your implementation. You might want to think about some of the roles as logical and combine them into a single job description.

It can be helpful to think in terms of two teams even though in practice there could be overlap between them. The first is the *build team* with responsibility for building an e-learning application and platform. The second is the *delivery team* with responsibility for the continuous delivery of e-learning once the application has been operationalized. Some build team members will transition to the delivery team in similar roles; some, in new roles.

The methodology for designing e-learning teams is straightforward:

- Analyse *build* and *deliver* as a collection of processes.
- Determine the nature of the skills needed to operate the processes.
- Calculate the number of people with each skill needed to meet workloads and deadlines.

Steering group

Don't forget the steering group; it's not a team you have to recruit but it is one you need to think about—it has ultimate responsibility for your e-learning initiative. The steering group needs to include at least one sponsor from the ranks of senior management who (1) commands the attention of other senior managers, (2) acts as e-learning champion in the board room, and (3) has your initiative's best interests at heart. According to a survey by Linkage Inc, in about 75% of cases the sponsor has to be recruited, educated, cultivated and motivated.[2] You can't count on the board room to volunteer a sponsor from its ranks.

While a management-level sponsor is of critical importance, every member of the steering group is important to your success. It's unlikely you will be able to manage the make-up of the steering group but you might be able to influence it. The group should contain one member with enterprise level responsibility for each key element of your project. These are typical members of an e-learning steering group:

- Senior Management Sponsor
- Strategy/Planning Director
- IT Director
- Finance/Investment Director
- HR Director
- Learning/Training Director
- Knowledge Management Director
- E-Learning Project Leader
- Business Unit Leader(s)
- Supplier Representative
- Customer Representative

Business units are likely to be your largest customer and learner base. They should be represented in the group in order to have sight of what you're doing and to provide feedback on how well it meets their learning requirements. You need business units to buy into e-learning; the sooner they're involved, the more likely it is they will. Some e-learning will focus on the needs of centralized support groups; their interests are represented by the presence of Finance, IT, HR, Planning and Knowledge Management. If you plan to use e-learning to educate suppliers and customers, there should be a representative of both those communities on the steering group.

Build team: roles and responsibilities

E-learning is still relatively new and there are a limited number of people who have hands-on experience. That means you'll probably need to look outside the

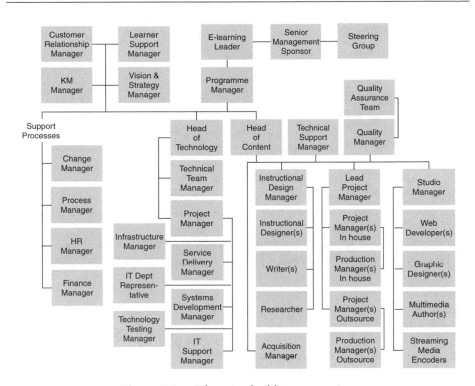

Figure 7.1 — E-learning build team overview

enterprise for at least some of the skills you require. That takes time, so start recruiting as soon as possible (see Figure 7.1).

Here are the key processes the build team needs to put into action, with a description of the team member responsible for each.

Manage the initiative

The team member who owns the responsibility for managing the initiative is usually the enterprise's *e-learning leader* or *manager*. The leader will have management and leadership skills, and experience in enterprise-wide projects. Often the leader is the person driving e-learning into the enterprise. It's common for the leader to come from an HR or training background, although some come from IT. The leader can also be recruited externally in order to benefit from their experience of implementing e-learning in other enterprises. It's likely the leader will have been appointed or approved by the steering group. The leader owns the relationship with the steering group and is responsible for it. The leader needs to be a member of the steering group if only to monitor senior management support for the initiative. It would be normal for the leader to transition to the delivery team which they would also lead.

Manage the vision and strategy

In small to medium implementations this role can be taken by the e-learning leader. In large implementations, the leader's time will be taken up with administration, so a dedicated *vision and strategy manager* is required. A vision for e-learning will be part procedural, part technical, part political and part inspirational. The vision and strategy manager needs to have knowledge of and a feel for each of those areas. They must understand the leading edge of e-learning and not be afraid to set a vision and strategy that is revolutionary enough to test the implementers but which does not frighten off either the steering group or the learners. Vision and strategy need to offer a future that is clearly and demonstrably better than the way things are done today. Presentation is a key part of this process — to the steering group, the build team, business unit leaders and learners.

   While the vision and strategy are themselves a team effort, assigning responsibility for them to one person prevents too many cooks from spoiling the broth. That said, adjustment to accommodate business requirements, technology, vendors' offerings, and so on is inevitable.

Manage the programme

According to the Project Management Institute, "... a program is a group of projects managed in a coordinated way to obtain benefits not available from managing them individually".[3] It's a good high level description of the work of the build team. While there are a number of separate projects in the build, they are all interrelated so it makes sense to coordinate them through one person. It's the responsibility of the *programme manager* to work with all project managers to track their progress against programme milestones, to ensure coordination of effort, to guard against robbing Peter to pay Paul — whether in time, money or resources, to ensure awareness of project dependencies, and to prevent each project team from reinventing the wheel. The programme manager should be experienced in the management of enterprise-wide initiatives.

Manage the finances

The build needs a *finance manager* who owns the overall budget, tracks the spend of each project, manages cash flow, prepares whatever financial reports are required by the team leader and the steering group, and owns the relationship with the source of funding.

Manage the technology

When senior managers were asked to identify the barriers to a successful e-learning implementation, 37% answered "technical difficulties".[4] Technology needs to be managed.

Head of Technology: In a large implementation, you need a number of technology managers, each working in specialized areas and responsible to the Head of Technology with overall responsibility for (1) technology at a strategic level, (2) awarding contracts to technology vendors, (3) the output of the technology team, and (4) the recruitment of technology managers. It is important that the leader has a good knowledge of e-learning vendors and, if possible, existing relationships with them.

IT Department Representative: E-learning is delivered across the enterprise infrastructure and used by learners on the enterprise desktop. It needs to be as secure as any other application running on the enterprise network. For these reasons and others, it is essential that the build team works closely with the enterprise IT department. The earlier this collaboration begins, the better. One way to facilitate the relationship with IT is to second someone from the department onto the technology team even if they're only available on a part-time basis.

Infrastructure Manager: Whether you decide to outsource the hosting of your e-learning application or keep it inside the enterprise firewall, infrastructure is so multi-faceted an issue and so important to the successful delivery of e-learning that it needs to be the sole focus of attention for one person — the infrastructure manager. The person filling this role should have previous experience of enterprise infrastructures.

Systems Development Manager: Every e-learning implementation works with at least one technology vendor. Even non-technology vendors like generic content providers bring technology issues to the table. To build a unified application from the offerings of external vendors and internal resources, all vendors' technologies need to work in harmony. Facilitating this close collaboration is the responsibility of the Systems Development Manager who should have previous experience of managing systems development at enterprise level.

Testing Manager: It is hard to overstate the importance of testing during the build phase. Technology testing occurs at platform, application, course and unit levels. Even user acceptance testing has a technology aspect. The testing manager owns the responsibility for the strategies, resourcing, scheduling, collaboration and reporting associated with all levels of testing. Testing can be outsourced. In that case, the testing manager owns the relationship with the test services provider and retains ultimate responsibility for the scheduling and effectiveness of all testing.

Service Delivery Manager: Whether funded centrally or by the enterprise's business units and service groups, e-learning is a service delivered to customers. That service should be defined in a service level agreement (SLA) between the learning department and its customers. The service delivery manager is responsible for ensuring that the technology that underpins the SLA is implemented and operational so what was promised can be delivered. The manager also has a role in defining what service levels are achievable in what parts of the enterprise — it will vary according to the quality of local infrastructure and policy—and in understanding the service needs of customers.

Technology Project Manager: There are many streams of activity within the technology team. The technology project manager owns the responsibility for managing the interdependencies of those streams, for ensuring that milestones are met—and consequences mitigated when they aren't—and for ensuring that the technology team is aware of and supports the dependencies of other teams.

Technology Team Manager: Depending on the scale of the e-learning initiative and the number of vendors involved, there can be a need for a technology team manager with administrative responsibility for day-to-day operations.

IT Support Manager: The e-learning team tends to use systems and applications not found elsewhere in the enterprise. Content development tools are one example. The content development team also tends to run a number of development servers that have non-standard configurations. Testing is another area where non-standard tools and configurations are used. Central IT support might be unable or unwilling to support this software and hardware; in this circumstance, it falls to the IT team to provide technical support to the whole e-learning team. The manager with this responsibility should have the skills to support the e-learning team's desktop applications and administer its servers.

Manage customers

Since the build phase includes the development or purchase of the first tranche of content, a dialogue need to be established between the e-learning team and its customers—business units and central support groups. Through this dialogue the e-learning team learns in detail about customers' business needs. The *customer relationship manager* owns the responsibility for opening and maintaining the dialogue. The role will almost always be recruited internally since it requires understanding and experience of the structure, operations and management of the enterprise. Depending on the size of the enterprise, a number of customer relationship managers might be required, for example, one assigned to each territory or business unit.

Manage content

Managing content is a complex process that requires a wide range of skills. The process changes little between the build and delivery phases.

Head of Content: The Head of Content has the administrative responsibilities you would expect: planning, recruiting, overall ownership of development schedules and budgets, and ownership of acquisition budgets. This person also works closely with the customer relationship manager to track content development requirements in the pipeline. Most importantly, the Head of Content is responsible for delivering content that meets the enterprise's business needs.

Subject Matter Expert: The development of custom content requires the input of a subject matter expert usually referred to by the acronym SME, sometimes pronounced smee. Normal practice is to second an SME from a business unit for the duration of development. It would be unusual for SMEs to be permanent members of the content team. Sometimes SMEs are recruited externally.

Instructional Design Manager: Instructional design can be defined as, "... the systematic development of instructional specifications using learning and instructional theory to ensure the quality of instruction".[5] The Instructional Designer Manager owns the responsibility for the instructional design process, sets preferred instructional design approaches, oversees instructional design for custom content, and sets standards for instructional design in acquired generic content. Each course will have a design team; all teams answer to the Instructional Design Manager. The teams include:

> *Instructional Designer*: Each course has a lead instructional designer. Large courses can require a number of instructional designers all working to the lead designer. The essence of the instructional designer's task is to (1) work with a business unit to gain an understanding of a performance gap or learning need, (2) work with a subject matter expert to gain an understanding of the skill or knowledge that needs to be learned or enhanced, (3) choose the appropriate instructional strategy, and (4) develop the design documents that specify content development. In the UK there is an undersupply of instructional designers with e-learning experience. Faced with that shortage, developers tend to recruit designers with experience in computer-based training or directly from colleges and universities with instructional design courses.

> *Writer*: Small courses can be designed and written by the same person. With large courses, time can be saved by splitting the design and writing processes with one or more writers working within the framework of the instructional design.

> *Researcher*: Normally the SME will bring all required knowledge and information to a course, however, there will be circumstances when it is either necessary or expedient to bring in a researcher to work with the SME, the instructional designer, and the writer.

Quality Assurance Manager: Developing e-learning content involves a series of key documents which are eventually transformed into Web content and media assets. The manager owns the responsibility for quality assurance throughout the development process. That includes copy editing and proofreading design documents, and ensuring that the Web content and media assets accurately reflect the signed-off design documents. The QA Manager works closely with the Testing Manager on the technology team.

Acquisition Manager: Where an enterprise regularly licenses generic content from third-party publishers in order to meet some of its learning needs, there is a role for an acquisition manager. This person owns the business relationship with all vendors of generic content, is familiar with their catalogues, tracks new titles, understands the instructional design approach used by each vendor and understands whether their content interoperates or can be made to interoperate with the enterprise's e-learning application.

Project Manager: Every content development project requires a Project Manager who carries out all the tasks you would associate with project management—budgeting, scheduling, tracking milestones and spend, ensuring that the agreed design specification is realized without compromise. If development is outsourced, the Project Manager owns the business and operational relationship with the vendor; if development is in house, the relationship with the studio. If a large number of courses are being developed concurrently, a requirement for a lead project manager is likely to emerge to ensure efforts are coordinated and duplicate effort avoided.

Production Manager: Large content development projects, whether outsourced or in house, can benefit from the contribution of a Production Manager who works to the project manager and who owns responsibility for day-to-day operations and processes, and the managements of assets. The quantity of assets in even a medium sized course can be huge: code, text, graphics and multimedia files; each needs to be reviewed, tested, signed off and archived. Even when a Content Management System or Learning Content Management System is used for workflow and content storage, the Production Manager ensures that the system is leveraged. Where assets fail to achieve customer sign-off or fail unit or integration tests, the Production Manager sees to it they are fixed without compromising the schedule.

Studio Manager: Learning departments that intend to develop e-learning in house on a regular basis need a studio resource and a Studio Manager with responsibility for it. The Studio Manager's key tasks include (1) recruitment, (2) resource scheduling, (3) adherence to budgets and schedules, (4) assembling the right teams for each project, and (5) implementing e-learning standards. A Studio Manager will have had previous experience in Web development and, ideally, in e-learning content development. People who work in the studio under the manager's supervision include:

> *Web Developer*: Developers bring programming skills in languages commonly used on the Web to content development, for example, HTML, DHTML, XML, Java, JavaScript, Visual Basic and Perl. Some developers specialize in database development usually working with Oracle, Sequel and Informix. Some also have graphics and multimedia skills.

> *Graphics Designer*: Graphics designers are responsible for creating screen layouts, user interfaces and graphical elements like illustrations, diagrams,

logos, buttons and icons. They work with a variety of software tools, frequently with Adobe's Photoshop and Illustrator. Some graphics designers have skills in multimedia authoring. As long as they are sympathetic to the needs of the learner, a good graphics designer can move into e-learning from any Web design background.

Multimedia Author: Multimedia authors work with video, audio and animations. Having dedicated multimedia authors only makes sense where there is a large volume of media to handle. Otherwise multiskilled Web developers and graphic designers can author multimedia assets.

Streaming Media Encoder: Audio and video files need to be encoded before they can be streamed over the Web as e-learning content. If there is enough multimedia content, a dedicated resource in the studio can prove effective. Another option is to outsource encoding.

Technical Support Manager: This member of the content team is responsible for providing technical support to both third-party developers and the in-house studio — with the aim of ensuring that all learning content conforms to (1) guidelines for presentation styles and navigation, and (2) the e-learning standards that have been adopted. Technical support takes the form of consultancy and a software development kit (SDK) which provides developers with the approved frameset, page templates, sample code and documentation. Some people believe that the Technical Support Manager should be part of a technology team. Practically, it makes little difference; what is important is that technical support is available to developers.

Manage Knowledge Management

As e-learning and Knowledge Management (KM) converge, there is an increasing requirement to integrate e-learning content with content from KM databases. While the benefits of convergence are clear, there's little if any "best practices" available and there are no standards to support interoperability between e-learning and KM applications. If your e-learning strategy points to convergence, you need a *KM Manager* on your build team. The person will have previous experience of Knowledge Management and will bring an understanding of both the logical and technological issues involved in making the integration of content a reality.

Manage learner support

Support is used here in the sense of helping learners to use e-learning, not helping them to acquire knowledge or skills. The *Learner Support Manager* has responsibility for (1) the development and delivery of online help, and (2) designing, building and manning help desks that in global enterprises need to accommodate time zone and language variations. When e-learning content doesn't work the way the learner expects it to, the problem can lie with the application, the learner's desktop or the infrastructure. To resolve these issues painlessly, the support manager needs to arrange close collaboration between the e-learning help desk and the enterprise IT support desk. E-learning help desks can be outsourced; where they are, the learner support manager owns the relationship with the service provider.

Manage processes

The build team doesn't just build an application, it builds processes for the continuous delivery of e-learning. The processes need to be integrated and documented. This work is the responsibility of the *Process Manager* who works with each process owner to establish policy, best practice, workflow and interworkings. Depending on the scale of the e-learning initiative, the process manager might need to be supported by process consultants.

Manage change

Properly implemented, e-learning represents significant change across the enterprise. To succeed, that change needs to be accepted. Achieving acceptance is the responsibility of the *Change Manager*. Change management is a top-down process and senior executives have a critical role to play; part of the change manager's responsibility is to work with senior executives to ensure they understand their role. Communicating the vision for e-learning to stakeholders and staff is another key task. At a practical level, the change manager issues regular bulletins to keep staff in touch with build progress and launch dates. This role should be filled by someone with previous experience in change management; that might mean an external consultant.

Manage human resources

The *HR Manager* owns the responsibility for resourcing the build and delivery teams, recruiting both inside and outside the enterprise. The HR manager also works with the central HR department to establish a pay and benefits structure for the new roles e-learning will establish within the enterprise. The HR manager should have previous experience of e-learning or e-business to ensure they understand the roles and responsibilities associated with Web development and delivery.

Delivery team: roles and responsibilities

Moving the initiative from build into delivery brings some clear changes. E-learning is operationalized and has a place in the enterprise structure, typically, inside the learning department, HR, or occasionally IT. There is no longer a need for a steering group. The build process called *Manage the Initiative* transitions into *Manage E-Learning*; the incumbent *e-learning leader* is well-positioned

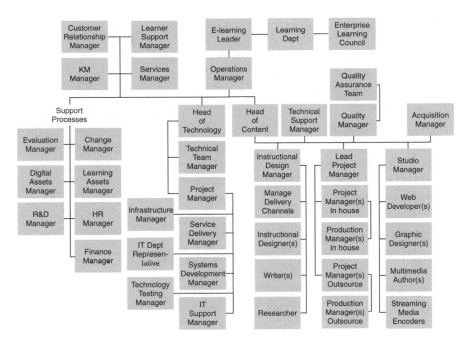

Figure 7.2 — E-learning delivery team overview

to transition to a new operational role. *Manage the Programme* transitions into *Manage Operations* with very similar responsibilities; the programme manager is well-positioned to become operations manager. By definition *Manage Processes* is no longer required since its output — documented processes — has already formed the basis for the delivery team's operations; a much smaller requirement for ongoing process review remains. *Manage Change* should not be a permanent process within e-learning but it should transition into delivery and remain for as long as it is required. *Manage the Technology* remains a valid role though with a much smaller team. An exception is where implementation is phased and the technology team move straight from building phase one into building phase two. With minor adjustments, the other processes transition to delivery while six new processes are introduced (see Figure 7.2).

Manage services

Manage the Vision and Strategy transitions into a process called *Manage Services*. With e-learning operationalized, the vision and strategy are being delivered as a series of services or, in a phased implementation, as the first phase of the service offering. The *Service Manager* is responsible for the ongoing development of services that over time will extend the original service vision. The service manager also maintains the e-learning strategy which needs to remain in lockstep with changes in corporate strategy. To ensure that services reflect real business requirements, the service manager works closely with customer relationship managers and business units. To ensure that services leverage the latest developments in the e-learning industry, the service manager works closely with the R&D manager and the service delivery manager.

Manage evaluation

To deliver e-learning that improves performance, to earn respect at board level, to protect and grow its budget, to increase its influence and value across the enterprise, e-learning needs to operate a continuous, coherent evaluation programme. Designing and operating that programme is the responsibility of the *Evaluation Manager*.

Manage delivery channels

E-learning adds a number of channels to the enterprise's existing learning value chain, for example, self-paced learning, virtual classrooms, Web casts, online collaboration, online mentoring and coaching, and simulations. Learning departments need to develop skills and processes for developing mixed-channel solutions that leverage the strengths of particular channels to meet learning requirements. The development and application of those skills and processes is the responsibility of the *Delivery Channel Designer*. An experienced instructional designer is likely to have the most appropriate skill set to bring to the task. Logically the delivery channel designer works with the customer relationship manager and subject matter expert but is part of the content development team and answerable to the lead instructional designer.

Manage digital assets

At the lowest level of granularity, digital assets are files: instructional design documents; graphics in file formats like PSD, GIF, JPG and BMP; multimedia in file format like AVI, WAV and WMF. Moving up through a hierarchy of granularity, digital assets can also be pages, learning objects, modules and courses. Digital assets represent a substantial investment by the enterprise; it needs to be protected and leveraged through the process of digital asset management. The *Asset Manager* owns those responsibilities. Asset management leverages the investment by making assets readily available for reuse — whether as part of a formal learning objects approach to development or simply through an assets library. Good asset management protects the continuous 24/7 delivery of e-learning by making back-ups readily available when hardware and software failures occur. The implementation of a Content Management System is the best way of supporting digital asset management.

When enterprises license generic content from third-party publishers and host it on their own servers, taking delivery of and loading these digital assets also needs to be managed.

Manage learning assets

Every learning department owns a back catalogue of operational and dormant learning assets — classroom courses, CD-ROMs, PowerPoint presentations, videos, print material. Once e-learning has gone live, it's a good idea to audit this content with a view of jettisoning superseded items, and refreshing and recycling in an e-learning format what remains relevant. This is an occasional activity rather than a continuous process. It is the responsibility of a part-time *Learning Assets Manager* who works closely with customer relationship managers and instructional designers to assess the value and relevance of existing learning assets.

Manage research and development

E-learning products, services and technologies develop continuously. To assess and leverage developments, you need an R&D programme that tracks new product and service launches and evaluates those with a potential application in your enterprise. New versions of all the applications you use — from the Learning Management System to authoring tools — need to be assessed in order to decide if and when to upgrade. Relationships with vendors need to be cultivated to learn what's in their development pipeline before it comes to market. You need to be an active participant in industry and vendor user groups and standards committees to influence the future shape of e-learning so that it meets your business requirements. You need to push the boundaries of your content development techniques searching for ways to deliver better content faster. All these tasks are the responsibility of the *R&D Manager* who is part of the technology team. The R&D manager's own team is virtual, seconded from the technology and content teams.

References

1   Parker GM (1994) *Cross-Functional Teams: Working With Allies, Enemies, and Other Strangers* San Francisco, Jossey-Bass p 5.
2   *The 2001 Linkage, Inc E-learning Survey* (2001) Linkage Incorporated <http://www. linkageinc.com>.
3   *A Guide to the Project Management Body of Knowledge* (2000) Project Management Institute [Internet] Available from <http://www.pmi.org/publictn/download/2000welcome. htm> Accessed 23 Jan 2001 p 24.
4   *The 2001 Linkage, Inc E-learning Survey* (2001) Linkage Incorporated. <http://www. linkageinc.com>.
5   *Definitions of Instructional Design* Applied Research Laboratory, Penn State University [Internet] Available from <http://quark.arl.psu.edu/training/def-inst.html> Accessed 11 Apr 2002.

Infrastructure: denial isn't an option

8

Introducing technological change that might threaten the overall speed of the network in a company that generates 90% of its revenue over the Web is no laughing matter. People don't want to get an email telling them that they're responsible for slowing down the network. Tom Kelly, Cisco Systems[1]

What you need to know

A Learning Management System vendor told me that as much as 60% of the time and effort he spends on e-learning implementation was taken up by infrastructure issues. If you're involved in an implementation, infrastructure is going to take up a lot of your time too. So what is infrastructure and why is it central to e-learning? What follows isn't a technical guide; it's a primer to help you to understand the issues and ask the right questions.

Here's how Whatis.com defines infrastructure: "In information technology and on the Internet, infrastructure is the physical hardware used to interconnect computers and users. Infrastructure includes the transmission media, including telephone lines, cable television lines, and satellites and antennas, and also the routers, aggregators, repeaters, and other devices that control transmission paths. Infrastructure also includes the software used to send, receive, and manage the signals that are transmitted ... to some information technology users, infrastructure is viewed as everything that supports the flow and processing of information."[2] Infrastructures aren't static. IT departments are constantly upgrading their networks — adding connectivity, bandwidth, servers, processors, memory and routers.

When talking about infrastructure, it's helpful to think about the e-learning platform you're building as an application. The platform might consist of several component applications, for example, a Learning Management System, a virtual classroom, a message board and Instant Messaging. Taken as a whole these components form the application that runs on servers connected to the corporate infrastructure. It is important to remember that your application is not the only one running on the infrastructure. Some, like e-mail, are mission-critical. In most cases, your e-learning application will be fighting for a share of scarce infrastructure resources (see Figure 8.1).

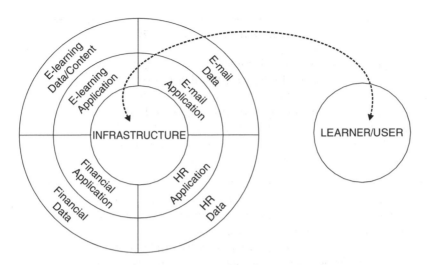

Figure 8.1 — Application + Data → Infrastructure → Learner

Infrastructure upgrade

If you learn that the corporate infrastructure won't support your design for an e-learning application, in principle, upgrading the infrastructure is an option. In practice, you will probably find the time it takes to implement an enterprise-wide upgrade will cause an unacceptable delay to your e-learning implementation. You will probably also find the cost of the upgrade completely undermines your ROI analysis. One of the reasons that e-learning delivers such a good return on investment is that the analysis almost always assumes learning will be delivered through the existing infrastructure; if it needs a fresh investment in infrastructure, the ROI picture can change dramatically.

Once e-learning is established and has demonstrated attractive ROI, increases in the number of learners or the complexity of content — real-time simulations, for example, consume a lot of bandwidth — might make a strong case for upgrading the infrastructure. Upgrading during implementation is unlikely. In most cases, infrastructure is a given. Denial isn't an option; you have to work with what's there. Addressing infrastructure issues early and realistically can significantly reduce risk and implementation timescales.

Outsourcing: good news, bad news

Outsourcing elements of e-learning can provide a solution to a number of infrastructure issues. Busy IT departments might not be able to add servers across all regions fast enough to meet your implementation schedule. The infrastructure might be in the middle of an upgrade and the IT department not in a position to install and support your application. You might find a Learning Management

System or virtual classroom application that meets all your needs but runs only on, say, Server 200n when your infrastructure supports UNIX. The speed at which you need to implement e-learning across your business could mean that an ASP (Application Service Provider) model is the only viable solution. Companies like THINQ, KnowledgePlanet and Docent provide hosting and Learning Management System services.

Outsourcing doesn't make bandwidth issues go away. Even though your application and content reside on third-party servers outside your infrastructure, there is no separate, direct connection between the learner and content; in the end, it all comes through the infrastructure and competes for bandwidth with data from other corporate applications. Only when learners logon remotely — from home, a hotel, a client site — does an ASP model deliver a bandwidth advantage. In most businesses, remote learners are the exception rather than the rule, so the overall reduction in traffic is small.

Some enterprises outsource their infrastructure. It makes little difference to an e-learning implementation. The implementation team simply find themselves dealing with an external IT department rather than an internal one. The infrastructure provider's customer is the enterprise IT director, so any change to the infrastructure required by an e-learning implementation will only happen when he signs the purchase order.

Don't confuse global with uniform

Some infrastructures are global, some multinational, more regional. Almost none have been built from scratch to a common specification. Most are patchworks sewn together over time, often as the result of mergers and acquisitions. The newest parts of the infrastructure are usually state of the art and enjoy comfortable amounts of bandwidth; older parts tend to creak.

Some variations are not technical but the result of local policy. For example, some country or regional IT managers might take a conservative view of security and close the firewall to multimedia content, or have high security settings for Web browsers. You might even find areas where employees don't have Web or intranet access and Internet use is restricted to e-mail.

These differences raise challenges for enterprise-wide e-learning implementations. You can only design and build one application, but it has to run on what amounts to different networks. If you design to the lowest common denominator, you run the risk of creating an application that looks dated and disappoints most learners in terms of impact and interactivity. If you design to the highest infrastructure specification, you run the risk of creating an application that won't work the way it should for many learners. One way forward is to prioritize. If giving the most learners the best learning experience is important, work to the network that has the greatest number of learners. If uniformity is important, work to the lowest common denominator. If innovation is important, work to the highest specified network.

Using learner profiles to shape content is another way of dealing with uneven infrastructures. For example, if one country doesn't support streaming media, create a content template for that country that substitutes graphics for audio and video. When a learner launches a course, the system looks at the learner's profile; if they work in the specified country, the system uses the template with no multimedia. The downside to this approach is extra work for content developers who need to create scripts to query the learner profile and to create, test and maintain a number of templates for each course.

Scalability

Scalability is an important concept to grasp when implementing e-learning. Richard Winter, a specialist in large database technology and implementation, defines scalability as: "The ability to grow your system smoothly and economically as your requirements increase."[3] Winter explains the benefits of scalability as: "Being able to increase the capacity of your system at an acceptable incremental cost per capacity unit without encountering limits that would force you either to implement a disruptive system upgrade or replacement, or to compromise on your requirements."[4]

In e-learning terms that might mean being able to accommodate 25% more learners or doubling the number of self-paced courses in the catalogue simply by plugging *proportionately* more servers into the existing infrastructure or by adding *proportionately* more processing power to the existing servers. If you have to re-design your system to accommodate more users or more content, it's not scalable. However, no matter how well designed, no system is infinitely scalable — despite what vendors might tell you. Realistically, you need to set parameters around scalability. You might say that your e-learning system needs to be able to scale for growth over 3 years, or to x registered learners, y concurrent learners and z volume of content.

There are four dimensions of scalability: data size, speed, workload and transaction cost. Scalability delivers *linear* incremental increases in all dimensions. In a scalable e-learning application if you increase the size of your catalogue from xGB to $3x$GB without upgrading hardware, you can expect a catalogue search to take three times longer. Conversely, if learner activity increases from y transaction per hour to $5y$, providing you increase processing power from z to $5z$, a scalable e-learning application will show no performance degradation in tracking learner activity. What you want to avoid is a system that requires an increase in processing power of x to $10x$ to maintain performance when transactions have only increased from y to $2y$.

Scalability is about cost. Management does not want an e-learning implementation that penalizes success by demanding disproportionate investments in hardware or bandwidth just to maintain the same levels of performance. However, if your e-learning initiative grows continuously, sooner or later you will move onto a new plateau where the old scalability no longer applies and you will have to upgrade both the quality and quantity of servers, routers, bandwidth or whatever infrastructure elements you've outgrown.

Security

Security has never been higher up the enterprise agenda. Your existing infrastructure is already as secure as the IT department can make it. What your e-learning application cannot do is reduce security. There is no inherent reason why it should, although getting security right can take a lot of detailed work by the e-learning implementation team, the IT department and external suppliers.

Learner logon is a key element of security. Enterprises with unified logon — that is, where a single network logon validates the user for any application on the network — will have the least issues. Where a separate logon is needed to access the e-learning application, there will be more issues. In these cases the question arises, what is the learner's logon being validated against? Is it the enterprise's register of employees? If it is, you'll need to create a secure dialogue between the e-learning application and the register. Or is the logon validated against an e-learner's register? That appears attractive because it poses fewer security challenges but since almost everyone in the enterprise is an e-learner, you will end up with two virtually identical registers. Who maintains the register of e-learners and how is it synchronized with the enterprise register which will almost certainly be owned by HR? Every time someone joins or leaves the enterprise, the e-learner's register has to be updated. That's likely to mean a daily update on a global basis — not a trivial task. Since e-learning should form a key part of new joiners' learning, the last thing you want is a lag between additions to the enterprise register and replicating those additions on the e-learning register.

Understandably, IT departments exercise great caution when dealing with the security of the infrastructure. That means nothing gets rushed. Make sure security issues are raised early so there is enough time to deal with them.

Latency and replication

If your e-learning application is going to be accessed globally or across wide geographic areas, you need to think about latency and replication. Latency is the time delay encountered by data packets travelling between source and destination; it can be caused by the quality of the transmission medium and processing en route. Because of its global reach, latency is inherent in the Internet. One of the remedies is replication, the process of copying the content of one Web server onto a second server called a mirror site. The mirror site is an exact replica of the parent site. Replication and mirror sites are used to improve performance by reducing the physical distance between the learner and e-learning content.

If all your servers are in the USA and some of your learners are in Australia, it's likely Australian learners are going to experience lower levels of performance than American learners. By installing mirror content servers in or close to Australia all learners enjoy the same levels of performance. It's not necessary to replicate the e-learning application because the amounts of data that move between the learner and application are small.

Here's how it works. The learner logs onto to the central e-learning server thousands of miles away and requests a course from the Learning Management System. The LMS launches the course content from a mirror server just a few hundred miles away from the learner. As the learner works their way through the course, activity tracking data and assessment results are posted back to the central server. Because the large volumes of data — graphics, streaming video and audio, animations — are travelling relatively short distances, the learner enjoys high performance levels. The use of mirror content servers is transparent to the learner who doesn't need to know that logon is a dialogue with one server while content is pulled down from another.

The advantage of keeping the application in one place is that learner profiles and tracking data — which can both change by the minute — do not have to be replicated. Only content — which changes less often — is replicated. This is how KnowledgePlanet, an LMS provider with an ASP model, serves its European customers. Content servers are, in Europe, close to learners, but the LMS launching and tracking courses resides on servers in KnowledgePlanet's US server farm where it is easy to maintain the application and backup tracking data.

You need a replication strategy; for example, is it scheduled once a day or conditional on new content being loaded onto the central servers? Ideally, content is replicated when the least number of learners is likely to be accessing the mirror sites, usually in the middle of the night. In most cases, replication is a hands-off operation which happens under the control of software scripts.

Content Delivery Networks

A Content Delivery Network (CDN) formalizes and adds intelligence to the concept of mirror sites. Here's how Webopedia describes a CDN: ". . . a network of servers that delivers a Web page to a user based on the geographic locations of the user, the origin of the Web page and a content delivery server. A CDN copies the pages of a Web site to a network of servers that are dispersed at geographically different locations, caching the contents of the page. When a user requests a Web page that is part of a CDN, the CDN will redirect the request from the originating site's server to a server in the CDN that is closest to the user and deliver the cached content."[5]

A CDN does not replace your existing network but is layered on top of it. For global enterprises, a CDN can improve the performance of self-paced e-learning courses as well as archived virtual classes and Web casts — any learning content, in fact, that is media rich. Cisco Systems was an early adopter: "Cisco understood the benefits of having a distributed-server CDN for its rich media content from the start. Moving high-bandwidth content to the edge of the network, as close to the learner as possible, enabled a highly interactive, engaging experience at the desktop without the bandwidth constraints or Quality of Service (QoS) limitations associated with an Internet connection."[6]

Think about a CDN if (1) you are delivering content across a wide geographic area, (2) the content is media rich, and (3) performance testing of your e-learning application shows disappointing results. Generally, CDNs are outsourced to specialist providers like Akama and Volera.

Bandwidth

Here's how Whatis.com defines bandwidth: "Bandwidth (the width of a band of electromagnetic frequencies) is used to mean how fast data flows on a given transmission path ... Generally speaking, bandwidth is directly proportional to the amount of data transmitted or received per unit time ... For example, it takes more bandwidth to download a photograph in one second than it takes to download a page of text in one second. Large sound files, computer programs and animated videos require still more bandwidth for acceptable system performance. Virtual reality (VR) and full-length three-dimensional audio/visual presentations require the most bandwidth of all."[7]

Bandwidth is a zero-sum game; bandwidth used by one user is unavailable to others. It's like a road network. The speed at which vehicles travel on the network depends on how many there are; the more vehicles, the greater the congestion, the slower the speed. Data on an infrastructure behaves the same way. More traffic equals more congestion. Another way people express bandwidth is to talk about infrastructure in terms of "pipes". "Thick pipes" or "big pipes" have more bandwidth and can move large volumes of data quickly.

Your learners will connect with the e-learning application in different ways. Different connections deliver amounts of bandwidth. Learners connecting through the corporate intranet usually benefit from much more bandwidth than learners dialling up. Bandwidth can vary during a learning session, either improving or degrading. You need to scale the media richness of your content to available bandwidth or run the risk of frustrating learners with inconsistent performance, but that's not something you can do on the fly. Only by conducting tests in all parts of the infrastructure can you draw a conclusion about the optimal quantity and quality of multimedia for courses. You can adjust multimedia content, trading off sound and picture quality against efficient delivery.

E-learning has a reputation with IT departments for making large demands on infrastructure because its multimedia content consumes more bandwidth than most network applications. The reputation is not always deserved. All learners do not access audio and video content all the time or at the same time; during a session, some learners might not access any. On the other hand, any learner watching a Web cast or participating in a virtual classroom is continuously pulling down streaming audio and video.

Concurrent users

Concurrent users describes the number of learners logged onto the e-learning application at the same time — as distinct from the number of learners registered to use the system. There might be 20 000 registered learners across the enterprise but at any given time a maximum of 300 learners might be logged on. There is a more refined definition of concurrent users: the number of learners actively requesting and retrieving data at the same time. So of the 300 learners logged on simultaneously perhaps 250 are reading static content or completing an assessment while only 50 are actively pulling content down from the server. Bear in mind that you might have two distinct concurrent learner groups: (1) those concurrently engaged in self-paced e-learning, and (2) those engaged in one or more virtual classes.

Establishing numbers of concurrent learners isn't about limiting the number of employees who can e-learn simultaneously. It's a way of measuring the load on a system. There are three reasons for establishing an upper limit of concurrent users.

Investment: The more concurrent learners, the more robust your e-learning application needs to be; the more robust it is, the more it will cost to build. There is no point investing in a platform with more capacity than you need, besides a well designed e-learning application can always be upgraded if demand begins to outstrip resources.

Performance: There's no point building a platform with less capacity than demand. If there are more concurrent learners than the application was designed to handle, sluggish performance will undermine the learning experience and eventually drive learners away.

Software Licences: Some software vendors — LMS providers and generic content publishers, for example — base their charges on the number of concurrent users. To ensure that you're paying the right price, you need to know how many learners will be using the applications or content concurrently.

Numbers of concurrent learners is part of the technical specification required by your LMS vendor, systems integrator and IT department. There is no magic formula for establishing numbers of concurrent users in advance of your e-learning application going live. You'll need to make some assumptions taking into account the overall learner base, time zones where e-learning is available and regional staff numbers. Because e-learning is available to all learners 24/7, you also need to make allowances for learners logging on outside local business hours. Your IT department can help by sharing their knowledge of general traffic patterns on the infrastructure and the numbers of concurrent users across the enterprise. Vendors can help too by drawing on their knowledge of other customers with a similar number of employees. Some vendors claim they can scale to 3500 concurrent learners engaged in self-paced courses and 10 000 in a virtual classroom. In practice, there are few enterprises with more than 500 concurrent learners accessing self-paced courses.

What you need to do

Gather information

In practice, infrastructure is a given. You might not be able to change it but you do have to learn about it. You can only do that with the help of the IT department. Be prepared for IT being less than forthcoming with details. There are few enterprises in which the infrastructure is as good as it could be; even though shortcomings might not be the fault of the IT department, you could find it adopts a defensive posture. IT departments are often under-resourced — that can also account for their reticence about sharing information or getting too involved in your initiative.

   Here are some of the things you will need to learn:

Infrastructure: Is the infrastructure controlled and maintained centrally? Or are there regional IT departments who will need to be involved? Is the infrastructure or any part of it outsourced? If it is, to whom? Find out if servers are running Server 200*n*, Windows NT, Linux or one of the many flavours of UNIX. Is there a mix of server operating systems? Your choice of e-learning applications might be constrained by the IT department's reluctance to support or integrate an additional operating system. Find out about regional variations in your infrastructure.

Bandwidth: Find out the bandwidth parameters across the infrastructure. That might be a country by country or region by region analysis. Establish the connection speed in a typical enterprise premise and off site using dial-up. Are there different styles of dial-up, for example, RAS and VPN? Are the connection speeds different? Estimate the learner population associated with each connection speed.

Desktop: Is there a standard desktop across the enterprise? What operating system and applications does it support? Find out the versions too, for example, is it Internet Explorer 5.0, 5.5 or 6.0? For Microsoft products, find out what Service Packs have been installed. Are versions and Service Packs consistent across the enterprise? Pay special attention to the Web browser. Is it Internet Explorer or Netscape? Are any plug-ins installed as part of the desktop: Flash, Shockwave, Real, QuickTime, Acrobat Reader, a VRML viewer (interactive 3-D modelling)? What is the policy about desktop upgrades? Some desktops are so locked down, upgrades can only be made through a network-controlled installation; if learners install applications or plug-ins independently, the additions are automatically uninstalled the next time the learner boots up their system.

Under these circumstances, you'll have to involve IT whenever learners need a new application, plug-in, or version installed.

Security: Find out whether unified logon is supported and what logon is validated against.

Upgrade Schedules: Find out whether any upgrades are scheduled, for example, from one version of a browser to another, from Windows 2000 to Windows XP, from Windows NT to Server 200*n*, or from Windows to UNIX or vice versa. Significant upgrades can impact on your implementation schedule.

Resources: Does the IT department have the resources to host and support your application on the infrastructure? Where the infrastructure is outsourced, can the service provider look after your hosting and support requirements? Does the IT department have the resources to host and support your content development and test environments? Can the IT department install mirror sites and support replication? Does it have a relationship with a CDN provider? Resources that aren't available from the existing infrastructure will have to be built and supported by your e-learning initiative or purchased externally.

Test

To understand the enterprise infrastructure and the impact it will have on your e-learning application and vice versa, there is no substitute for real-world testing. Work with volunteers in every geographic region where you will deliver e-learning to test the impact of bandwidth, latency and local variations. Work with the IT department to test the load your e-learning application will put on the infrastructure.

Plan for success

Whether you buy or build your e-learning infrastructure, make sure it is scaled for success. During the first few weeks or even months, the novelty factor—stimulated by your communications programme—will drive learners to your learning portal. Don't disappoint them with servers that can't cope and performance that makes learning online feel like hard work.

To a degree, you can control initial demand by launching on a region by region or business unit by business unit basis. Roll out e-learning over a period of weeks or months rather than with one big bang. With a controlled roll out you can make improvements as you go along. If your corporate infrastructure supports it, you can simply make the site available to one defined group, then another, and so on. If your infrastructure makes that difficult, target your communications programme at one defined group at a time—but remember, e-mail messages and URLs are easily shared so expect some leakage in your targeted communications.

References

1   Muoio A (2000) *Cisco's Quick Study* FastCompany [Internet] Available from <http://
    www.fastcompany.com/online/39/quickstudy.html> Accessed 9 Apr 2002 Issue 39
    p 286.
2   Whatis.com [Internet] <http://www.whatis.com>.
3   Winter R (1999) *Lexicology of Scale* Intelligent Enterprise Vol 2 No 3 [Internet] Available
    from   <http://www.intelligententerprise.com/db_area/archives/1999/991602/scalable.
    shtml?scalability> Accessed 25 Apr 2002.
4   Winter R (1999) *Lexicology of Scale* Intelligent Enterprise Vol 2 No 3 [Internet] Available
    from   <http://www.intelligententerprise.com/db_area/archives/1999/991602/scalable.
    shtml?scalability> Accessed 25 Apr 2002.
5   Webopedia [Internet] <http://webopedia.lycos.com>.
6   *The Cisco Internal Implementation of an Enterprise Content Delivery Network to Support
    E-Learning* (2001) Cisco White Paper [Internet] Available from <http://www.cisco.com/
    warp/public/10/wwtraining/elearning/implement/cdn_white_paper.pdf> Accessed 25
    Apr 2002.
7   Whatis.com [Internet] <http://www.whatis.com>.

9

Vendor relationships: good partners help you learn and move fast

The secret to a great relationship: You stick to your core competencies and let your partner (or partners) stick to theirs. Stan Davis, Christopher Meyer[1]

What you need to know

In the context of an e-learning implementation, your core competency is your knowledge of your enterprise: its learning needs aligned to its business needs, its culture, its strengths and its foibles. To move your initiative fast and to deepen your understanding of e-learning, you need to form partnerships with one or more e-learning vendors. To derive the maximum benefit from vendors, you need to share your understanding of your business with them — once confidentiality agreements are in place. To deliver the most effective learning solutions, your vendors need to apply their knowledge and experience in the context of your requirements. This is where an e-learning strategy starts to deliver a return on investment. Because all your requirements have been articulated and documented there, the strategy facilitates sharing.

Single or multiple vendors

To deliver a solution you will need to buy or license e-learning technology, content and services. One of the first questions you need to address is whether you're going to buy it all from one vendor — or buy the best of breed from multiple vendors. The advantage to a single vendor is simplicity — one contract, one contact point, one specification document. The reality is, at the time of writing there is no single end-to-end e-learning vendor. Even vendors, like Kevin Oakes, CEO of Click2Learn, acknowledge this creates issues: "The single biggest problem we see in e-learning is companies being forced to make disparate technologies work together to provide a complete solution."[2]

For most implementations, the question is not whether to work with a single vendor or multiple vendors but whether you want to manage multiple vendors yourself or have a vendor do it for you. The answer to that comes down to convenience, available project management resources, corporate culture, even procurement policy. If it suits your needs, large business consultancies and enterprise software and hardware vendors can deliver turnkey e-learning solutions.

What you might be trading off is speed and flexibility. A group of smaller vendors might be prepared to deliver more faster, even for less cost providing you're prepared to manage the integration of their efforts, products and services. There is no right answer to vendor selection, only the right answer for you. That will emerge from your requirements and your dialogue with vendors.

About e-learning vendors

Most leading e-learning vendors are US companies. This is especially true of Learning Management System and virtual classroom vendors, and publishers of generic content. They're used to working with customers outside the USA. Many have a sales presence in Europe; some have small operational offices. If you're not US-based, make sure the vendor appreciates that despite the distance, you're looking for an ongoing commitment to the success of your project at all levels and not just a technical implementation by a team flown in for the job. Custom content development is a much more dispersed activity; there are highly skilled development communities in the USA, the UK, Ireland, Canada, Germany and India. E-learning vendors come in different sizes and shapes — and operate in one or more of three market areas.

Technology

The Technology sector is dominated by Learning Management System (LMS) vendors. An LMS is usually the single largest and most visible purchase associated with e-learning; implementation can be complex especially when the LMS needs to be integrated with other e-learning and enterprise applications. There are a surprising number of LMSs to choose from. Vendors include Click2Learn, Docent, IBM, Saba and THINQ. As content and content development become more sophisticated, Content Management Systems (CMS), while not dedicated e-learning applications, have an increasingly important role to play — especially if you are taking an object-oriented approach to content. CMS vendors with e-learning experience include Broadvision, MediaSurface and Vignette. A number of technology vendors have taken the notion of an LMS and added it to the notion of a CMS to create a Learning Content Management System. (To find out more about LMSs and LCMSs, see Chapter 10.)

Virtual classroom applications are another important offering in the technology area. Vendors include Blackboard, Centra, EpicLearning, HP, IBM and InterWise. On the development side, there is a wide range of authoring environments and tools to support content creation, as well as plug-ins to enhance the functionality of Web browsers.

As Knowledge Management and e-learning converge, KM applications like Autonomy will have an increasing presence in e-learning's technology sector. In fact, companies with their roots in other markets are already important e-learning players. Collaboration tools are one example of business applications regularly integrated with e-learning. Applications include eRoom, IBM Lotus QuickPlace and SameTime, and WebEx. AvantGo, the content portal for Palm users, is working with Harvard Medical School, the Ohio State University Medical Center and UCLA School of Medicine to deliver learning directly to medical students' PDAs. Hardware vendors also have a place in the technology sector—either providing proprietary hardware solutions for development and distribution or desktop solutions for learners. Large hardware vendors like Dell, HP, Microsoft and Sun all have e-learning offerings that extend beyond hardware into services and applications.

Content

Some of the largest e-learning vendors are generic content providers who author and publish intellectual property that is licensed by enterprises to meet broad training needs. (To put "largest" in context, remember that no single e-learning vendor owns even 5% of the e-learning market; in 2001, for example, SmartForce, which was then the world's largest e-learning company, had revenues of $261 million.[3]) Some content publishers have broadened their offering by supplementing content with services like these: custom curriculum design, skills assessment and testing, strategy and development consulting, programme implementation and integration support, coaching and mentoring, training effectiveness analysis and hosting.

Custom content developers—generally, much smaller businesses—author content based on IP provided and owned by enterprise customers. Custom content developers tend to specialize in one form of custom content—self-paced courses, media-rich content, simulations, re-usable learning objects, localization and translation, Flash animations, or content for hand-held devices. Other developers specialize in authoring assessments or content designed for virtual classes.

A number of content, LMS and service vendors have set themselves up as "content aggregators", that is, one-stop shops for content from a network of generic publishers. Their proposition was hassle-free access to thousands of courses through a single contract. At the time, content aggregation didn't resonate with either the market or content publishers. But in a reminder that the e-learning market never stops trying, IBM has started offering its Learning Management System bundled with content packages from A-list content providers like Harvard Business School.

Services

The service sector is dominated by ASPs (Application Service Providers) who, in effect, rent space on their proprietary LMSs to enterprises. There are many advantages to using a third-party LMS and external hosting—some technical, some financial, some to do with speed and ease of implementation. Collaboration and virtual classroom applications are also available using an ASP model.

If you decide to build your e-learning application inside the enterprise firewall, you might need the services of a systems integrator, a company that specializes in building complete systems by making software components from different vendors talk and work together. Many enterprises have their own system integrators but these resources tend to be in high demand, so having an external resource experienced in e-learning systems can be crucial when facing tough deadlines. Not surprisingly, most LMS vendors provide system integration services or have partners who do.

The important area of learner support and mentoring can be outsourced to specialist service providers. Some content development teams outsource the encoding of streaming media because it is time-consuming specialist work; some enterprises outsource the hosting of streaming media because it can put a heavy load on enterprise servers and shifting that load to dedicated third-party servers makes sense.

By bringing their experience and knowledge to bear, e-learning consultants can help enterprises devise the right e-learning strategy, then build the right e-learning application to realize the strategy. Some consultants have specific skills like vendor selection or learning needs assessment. Again, as Knowledge Management and e-learning converge, third-party knowledge and data providers will play increasingly large roles in the e-learning service market.

Figure 9.1 provides a high-level logical view of how elements from the three areas of the e-learning industry come together to form an enterprise e-learning application. Notice how the LMS sits at the centre and interconnects the other elements.

Even though e-learning is a relatively young industry, it has developed quickly and now offers a wide range of products and services. It's unlikely that you have an e-learning requirement for which someone hasn't developed a solution. In

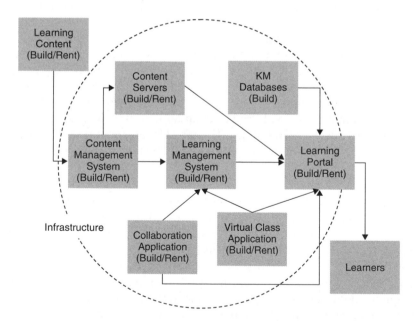

Figure 9.1—Logical view of e-learning application

fact, the range of products and services can be bewildering. Corporate University Xchange's survey of 65 learning organizations reflected the importance of finding the right e-learning partners: "Corporate learning practitioners are conducting extensive market research to determine whether potential e-learning partners meet specific criteria. What factors are important during the vendor selection process? When asked to rate a list of 23 factors, corporate learning professionals rated the following criteria as highly important:

- Compatibility of vendor with existing technology infrastructure
- Quality of programs
- Competency and expertise of staff
- Willingness to understand their business
- Scalability of products
- Interestingly, price has not dominated purchasing decisions.

Organizations will invest in quality products that align with the education needs of the organization and will not necessarily turn away products based solely on costs."[4]

Getting to know vendors

There is no shortage of ways to get to know e-learning vendors. E-learning conferences, workshops and expos provide a good introduction to what's available, and the industry is well served in this area. Some of the better known events are organized by:

- ASTD
- *E-Learning Magazine*
- The Masie Center
- VNU Business Media

The E-Learning Centre maintains a comprehensive online list of e-learning events around the world. E-learning newsletters from consultants, vendors and industry groups can help you develop a feel for what's happening in the industry and how particular vendors are regarded in the market. (See Appendix 1 for a list of newsletters.) ASTD provides a free online searchable Buyer's Guide to e-learning products and services — with an American flavour. The *European eLearning Directory* provides details of around 150 European vendors.

Webinars — Web-based seminars — are another way to get to know vendors and learn more about e-learning without having to leave your office. Industry groups and leading vendors regularly schedule Webinars, delivered through collaboration tools like Webex and Centra, and led by e-learning authorities. You can find out about upcoming Webinars through the organizers' newsletters and Web sites. Sessions are recorded, so you can watch archived Webinars too. Some are free; some have an "entrance fee" — there are even "group rates". Book a conference room with a Web connection and a projector and invite your whole implementation team along.

The largest barrier to establishing relationships with vendors is time. It's a slow process to research vendors, make contact with them, and take a demonstration of their offerings. E-learning consultants can speed up the process. Brandon-Hall publishes an impressive range of "how to" guides and reports on e-learning technology vendors. Hall is probably best known for his annual review of Learning Management Systems. Reports can be downloaded from the Brandon-Hall Web site for a fee; usually a free executive summary is available. Lguide is an e-learning consultancy best known for its online reviews of generic course content. It also provides a useful collection of articles with analysis and advice on current e-learning issues. Access to LGuide is by annual subscription.

In addition to online resources, there is a broad range of consultants offering expertise in vendor selection. Some of these consultancies are part of organizations that are also e-learning vendors or have partnerships with e-learning vendors. E-learning has become an accepted feature of the business landscape so almost every business consultancy offers e-learning services. If your enterprise has a relationship with a business consultant, there's something to be said for using the same organization to help with e-learning vendor selection since they should already have a good understanding of your business requirements

Don't forget your personal network. Is there anyone you know who has had experience of implementing e-learning and has relationships with vendors? Have there been any other e-learning initiatives in your business—perhaps a project limited to one business unit or product line? Could the initiative owners provide information about their vendors? Have any of your customers implemented e-learning? Would they be prepared to share their knowledge of vendors with you?

What you need to do

The vendor selection process

To help you manage vendor selection, here is a 10-step process. The Learning Management System vendor is the most taxing to select. You can use this process for LMS vendors. Not every selection requires all 10 steps; adjust the process according to circumstances.

Step #1—Nail Down Business Requirements: If you've been smart and set your e-learning strategy before doing anything else, you can skip this step because the work is done. If you don't have an e-learning strategy, now's the time to focus on and document the business requirements driving your e-learning implementation.

Step #2—Get to Know as Many Vendors as Possible: Create a vendor selection team that reflects a range of knowledge and experience. If you're looking at generic content, aim to have someone who understands instructional design, someone who understands e-learning interoperability standards, and someone with subject matter expertise. Use the team to cover as many vendors as possible. It can be an advantage to recruit a outside consultant onto your team (1) to provide expertise that would otherwise be missing, or (2) to bring a fresh eye to evaluation.

Step #3—Develop an RFI for a Limited Number of Vendors: RFI stands for "Request for Information"—the first key documents in this process. The RFI gives vendors a chance to tell you something about themselves by answering a series of questions. A model RFI is given on p. 169.

Step #4— Visit Vendors for Presentations and Demonstrations: Once the RFI responses are in, try to visit as many of the vendors as possible to take in presentations and demonstrations. Spending a little time on the vendors' premises will give you insights into the company that you don't gain if presentations happen on your premises. Don't ignore touchy-feely reactions to vendors—they're relevant. If you feel good about a vendor, mark it in their favour; if you have a bad reaction to a vendor the first time you visit their premises that tells you something, too.

Step #5—Document Requirements: At this stage, you should be able to document your high level product or service requirements which are a reflection of your (1) business requirements, (2) functional requirements—the features and functions learners and e-learning managers need, and (3) system requirements—technical specifications and performance parameters. For example, if compliance training is a key business driver for e-learning, keeping an accurate record of each employee's e-learning is critical; generating tracking data and posting it to the LMS becomes a functional requirement of content.

Step #6—Make Your First Shortlist: Make sure the team puts aside enough time to evaluate RFI responses. Create a scorecard based on your requirements. Using the scorecard, each team member ranks vendors based on the information they provided. Combine the team's rankings to create an overall score. Decide on a cut-off point and eliminate the vendors below it.

Step #7—Develop an RFP for the Shortlisted Vendors: RFP is an abbreviation of "Request for Proposal"—the second key document in the process. RFP is part of best practice in IT procurement; it delivers these benefits:

- Makes vendor comparison easier.
- Ensures objectivity and a level playing field.
- Encourages focused responses.
- Sharpens price competition among vendors.
- Reduces risk for buyers and vendors.
- Minimizes complaints from vendors who fail.
- Helps project team justify costs internally.
- In case of a contract dispute or scope change, provides a clear point of reference for both vendee and vendor.

A typical RFP is made up of these components:

- *Introduction*: This sets out the housekeeping — when proposals are required, where to submit them, and a point of contact for questions. It also describes the background to the project including the high level drivers, for example, "A series of recent acquisitions has created a need for employees to work regularly in virtual teams. In turn that has created a need for employees to rapidly improve their skills with online collaboration tools."

- *Directions*: This explains what to include and the evaluation process. Sometimes it specifies the format of the proposal, maybe a Word file or an attached form.

- *T&Cs*: This provides the vendor with your standard terms and conditions including purchasing policies, invoicing terms, transaction currency, etc.

- *Statement of work*: This is the heart of the document where requirements are described in as much detail as vendors need to make a meaningful response. In some cases, the work required will already be understood in detail; in others, only the symptoms of a problem will be known and vendors are expected to propose solutions as part of their response.

- *Credentials and References*: This is where you ask vendors to tell you about work they've done in the past that qualifies them to work on your implementation. It's also where you ask for references. While it's true that referees will always be chosen to reflect a vendor's best work and most successful client relationships, do not underestimate their value in helping you form an opinion. If you speak to three referees, a pattern should emerge. If it doesn't, the smart thing to do is to ask the vendor why. In this section, you should also ask the vendor about their approach to best practice.

- *Culture*: The most successful working relationships occur between businesses with compatible cultures. If you have a vendee with a very hierarchical structure and a vendor with a flat structure, the difference will militate against a comfortable working relationship. One party will have to act out of character to accommodate the other and over time that creates stress. During your visit to the vendor's premises, in your written and verbal communications with them, you will be making your own judgements about cultural fit but this section of the RFP gives you the opportunity to ask for the vendor's own view of their culture.

- *Pricing*: This is where you ask the vendor to set out their pricing policy and practices and, of course, to cost the work.

Step #8—Make Your Second Shortlist: Narrow your candidate vendors down to three or four. Responses to RFPs can run into hundreds of pages, so make sure the team has set aside enough time to evaluate them properly. Again, use a scorecard. Be wary of eliminating candidates on price alone. If a vendor has everything right but cost, remember (1) you can always negotiate, (2) the vendor's experience might be leading them to the right price for the work and you will need to make budget adjustments, and (3) perhaps some of your less important requirements are driving up the price—you need to align costs with priorities.

Step #9— Meet Shortlisted Vendors, Make Up your Mind: Tell each vendor whether or not they made the cut. Try not to close the door on vendors who did not make the shortlist. You need to maintain relationships with vendors who might be right for future work. Take a presentation from all shortlisted vendors—this time on your premises. Carefully prepare a list of questions arising out of the RFP responses. You can always ask follow-up questions by phone or e-mail but this is your last opportunity for face-to-face information gathering. Make sure your whole team attends the presentations. Develop a final scorecard; this one should be more specific than the previous two because by now you will have a clear understanding of the deciding issues. Evaluate, discuss, decide.

Step #10— Negotiate the Contract: There is usually a final round of financial discussions to take account of ongoing changes in the scope of work, or to change the scope of work to get the price right. There are often last-minute cost negotiations, too. If the decision-making process has taken longer than expected, the start date and delivery dates might need to be adjusted.

An RFI model

The model is based on an RFI for custom content developers. It can easily be adapted for other types of vendors.

[Cover Page]

<COMPANY NAME AND LOGO>

REQUEST FOR INFORMATION
FROM
E-LEARNING CUSTOM CONTENT DEVELOPERS

Date

[First Page]

Continued on page 170

Continued from page 169

INTRODUCTION

The Company

\<Provide a brief overview of your enterprise. You can include the URL of the corporate Web site.\>

Project Background

\<Provide an overview of the project and the stage you're at. Has e-learning been implemented? If it has, how long have you been delivering e-learning? Set out the high level drivers for e-learning in your enterprise. Define the size of the learner base and the its geographical spread. Set out the technology parameters of the learning environment:

- desktop applications including versions
- browser including version and plug-ins
- LMS, LCMS, CMS
- the draft standards you use for tracking and content interoperability
- sample templates if available

Explain other content standards: preferred instructional design strategies, evaluation requirements, etc.\>

RFI Background

\<Explain why you are requesting information. Are you developing a network of preferred suppliers? Are you looking to establish partnerships? Do you foresee the need for high volume content development? Are you looking for development specializations — in learning objects, simulations, media-rich content? Are you looking for experience in developing content for your sector?

Ensure the vendor understands that all you're asking for is information and no work will awarded as a direct result of a response.\>

INSTRUCTIONS

\<Make clear any conditions which affect how vendors respond. Is there a mandatory non-disclosure agreement? Are there other legal conditions? Are attachments required — like the vendor's annual accounts? You might require every question to be answered or explanations provided for omissions.

Are there formatting requirements? You might say that only files created using Microsoft Office will be accepted or that the authors' names need to be on each document. Do you require hard and soft copies?

Continued on page 171

Continued from page 170

Explain your evaluation process. What are the critical factors? Instructional design skills? Technology? Service? Price? Process? These should be evident from the questions you ask but if some factors are more important than others, it helps to say so.

Most RFI responses are developed at the vendor's expense. If that's the case, say so; if there are exceptions, spell them out.

Be clear about the submission date and whether it's flexible. Be clear about where responses should be sent: provide an e-mail and/or postal address. If you are prepared to discuss the RFI before submission, provide a point of contact. Commit yourself to providing feedback to responses by a specific date.>

REQUIRED INFORMATION

Company: Provide the following details:

- Name
- Public or Private — if public, provide details
- Year established
- Part of a group — if yes, provide group details
- Registered office details

Revenue: Provide details of your company's gross revenue for the last three years — and analysed by:

- The development of e-learning content.
- The development of learning content.
- Non-learning activities.

Customer Base: Provide details of the size of your customer base and the number of active contracts. Who are your largest customers and what percentage of your turnover do they account for?

References: Provide the names and points of contact for three current clients who are prepared to discuss the work you have done for them.

Staff: How many staff are employed in each office? What is your annual staff turnover as a percentage?

Project Team: Provide details of the project team who would work on our account. We require names, roles, a summary of relevant experience. We expect one senior management figure to head the project team.

Resource Management: Explain your resourcing policy. What if any work do you outsource? What is the ratio of full-time staff to contract workers? How do you manage fluctuating demands on resources?

Continued on page 172

Continued from page 171

Partnerships and Joint Ventures: Provide details of any partnerships and joint ventures of which your company is a part including the names of other participants, what you and they bring to the relationship, what territories are covered by the agreement.

Multiple Vendor Contracts: Provide details of any work performed under multiple vendor contracts. State whether or not you were the lead vendor. Describe the risks and mitigations associated with multiple vendor contracts.

Core Competencies: Describe your company's core competencies. How would describe your brand strengths and ability to execute?

Products and Services: Provide details of the products and services you offer.

Industry Experience: Provide details of any work you are doing or have done for other companies in <your industry>.

Documentation: Is your company ISO accredited? If so, provide details and the date of accreditation. If not, do your processes conform to ISO standards?

Processes: Describe in detail your process for content development and quality assurance. What is the typical lifecycle of a content development project? What are the key documents in your processes?

Testing: Describe your approach to testing and any in-house testing resources you have.

Content Maintenance: Describe your approach to content maintenance. Include cost implications.

Critical Success Factors: Describe your critical success factors for content development projects.

Industry Standards: What draft industry standards (AICC, IMS, SCORM) does your content support? What resources can you bring to the integration of your content with our e-learning system?

Instructional Design: Describe your approach to instructional design. Do you have instructional designers on staff?

Assessments: Describe your approach to assessments in terms of (1) instructional design, (2) authoring, (3) tracking, and (4) learner interactions.

E-learning: In your view, what does a successful e-learning implementation look like?

Localization: Describe the resources you can apply to our localization requirements. Can you provide local management and support? <Provide the vendor with a brief description of the countries where learning will be used and into

Continued on page 173

Continued from page 172

which languages it will be translated. Include a description of any difficult cultural issues.>

Intellectual Property: Describe your IP policy.

Content Hosting: Do you provide a hosting service? Do you have partnerships with third-party hosting vendors? Describe projects in which your content was hosted on third-party servers.

Pricing: Provide details of prices and pricing models for each product and service you offer.

Authorized Point of Contact: Provide an authorized point of contact for any communications regarding this RFI.

_____
Signature of authorized contact

_____
Company

_____
Date

References

1 Davis S and Meyer C (1998) _Blur— The Speed of Change in the Connected Economy_ Oxford, Capstone Publishing Limited p 227.

2 Hickey E (2002) _New Tricks— The Hard Way_ Ziff Davis Smart Business [Internet] Available from <http://www.smartbusinessmag.com/article/0,3658,s=103&a=25455,00.asp> Accessed 10 May 2002.

3 _SmartForce Signs Agreement to Acquire Centra Software; Reports Strong Fourth Quarter 2001 Financial Results_ (2002) SmartForce PLC [Internet] Available from <http://www.smartforce.com/corp/marketing/about_sf/press_releases_02/jan_16_earnings.htm> Accessed 7 May 2002.

4 Meister JC ed (2002) _Pillars of e-Learning Success_ [Executive Summary] New York, Corporate University Xchange, Inc. [Internet] Available from <http://corppub.iuniverse.com/marketplace/cux/00057.html> Accessed 9 May 2002 p 12.

Learning management systems: the engines of e-learning

10

Enterprises are beginning to realize that a learning management system (LMS) is more than just the administrative part of an e-learning deployment. It can and should be considered the critical application for employee, partner and customer knowledge transfer. Gartner[1]

If you buy the wrong authoring tool, you can always go get another one. Get the wrong LMS and you're going to want to change your business card. Brandon-Hall[2]

What you need to know

In building your e-learning application, you will probably license generic content from more than one publisher; when you outsource custom course development, you will probably work with more than one developer; when you develop content internally, you will probably use authoring tools from more than one vendor. However, you will only select one Learning Management System (LMS). You need to make the right choice. It isn't easy — but that's understandable. You wouldn't expect an application that touches the working life of every employee in an enterprise to be easy to select and implement. Every LMS is rich in functions and features and as a result makes substantial configuration and implementation demands. LMSs also represent a large investment and can impact significantly on people, technology, structure and process. So the first question has to be, do you need an enterprise LMS?

If your enterprise employs more than 2500 employees and has a learning budget equal to at least 1% of employees' loaded salaries, you could be a candidate for an LMS. If you need to deliver e-learning to a geographically dispersed workforce, that adds weight to the case for an LMS. If your staff levels are lower, your financial commitment to learning less and your workforce concentrated on one site, it doesn't mean you can't benefit from an LMS but you might be better off with an Application Service Provider (ASP) model, in effect, leasing space on a third-party LMS rather than running your own.

Defining terms

One of the biggest — and most justifiable — criticisms levelled at the e-learning industry is that it has failed to present a clear picture of its offerings. This is particularly true of LMS vendors. The offerings might be clear in the minds of vendors; in the minds of their prospective customers, there's confusion. Facing up to the LMS challenge will be easier if we define terms.

LMS (Learning Management System)

In the course of some research, I entered a string of key words in Google and clicked on Search; one key word was "LMS". At first I was mildly surprised when the majority of hits were not for Learning Management System but for Library Management System, then it occurred to me that a library management system was an interesting way to start thinking about a Learning Management System. You'd expect a library system to provide a searchable catalogue of every book in the library, a register of all borrowers, and cross-referenced transaction records for every book and every borrower. A more ambitious system might link to other library systems extending the number of books available to the borrower. You would also expect administration functions that allowed new books to be added to the catalogue and redundant ones removed, new borrowers to be added to the register and former borrowers removed. There should be a report that lists every book out on loan and books overdue.

What you wouldn't expect the library management system to know is what pages borrowers read on what days, whether they read cover to cover or browsed, or how well they understood the content. If you swap e-learning courses for books, a Learning Management System does everything you'd expect a Library Management System to do *and* what you wouldn't expect it to.

A Learning Management System is a large Web-based software application — comprising a suite of tools — that centralizes and automates aspects of the learning process through these functions:

- register learners
- maintain learner profiles
- maintain a catalogue of courses
- store and deliver self-paced e-learning courses
- download e-learning modules and tools
- track and record the progress of learners
- assess learners
- track and record assessment results
- provide reports to management

Not all LMSs are not fully Web-based; some administrative functions — like loading a new course — might be executed through desktop applications. Since this limits flexibility, all LMSs should be migrating to fully Web-based implementations.

Some LMSs deliver additional functionality, for example, they can help:

- personalize content
- maintain job-based skills inventories

- identify skills gaps
- match staff to jobs
- manage compliance and certification
- manage classrooms and classroom resources
- track and report learning costs
- integrate Knowledge Management
- integrate live e-learning/virtual classes
- integrate collaboration tools
- support the whole learning value chain
- author content

In the same way that few users take advantage of all a word processor's functions and features, few enterprises implement all the functions and features of an LMS.

TMS (Training Management System)

The TMS was around before the LMS. It's a network application that manages and automates all traditional training activity. Like an LMS, it registers and tracks learners, however, the TMS assumes all learning is face-to-face. It maintains a catalogue of courses and classrooms, classroom resources and classroom events. Its calendar function allows a trainer to book a classroom for a specific number of learners on specific dates — and to book a projector, a flip chart, and any other resources she needs. Learners can then register for the course using an authorization code issued by their manager. The TMS allows the instructor to note in each learner's personal records the sessions they actually attended. Behind the scenes, the TMS uses the authorization code to charge the cost of the course to the learner's business unit.

With the arrival of e-learning, TMS vendors simply added a new module to manage what was to them just another learning resource — online learning. When e-learning became more important, vendors changed the description of their product from TMS to LMS. Meanwhile new dot-com entrepreneurs were developing dedicated Web-based LMS applications that exploited the power of Internet technologies in ways the TMS-based systems couldn't. However, it wasn't long before prospective LMS customers asked the new entrepreneurs how they planned to handle classroom courses. The entrepreneurs simply added a TMS module to their LMS. Customers had to choose between a TMS with an LMS module or an LMS with a TMS module. That kind of confusion has dogged the market ever since.

CMS (Content Management System)

A CMS is not a dedicated e-learning application but it can be closely integrated with an LMS and used to support the effective development and delivery of course content — especially if you are working with learning objects.

The principle underlying a CMS is the separation of content and presentation. Content—text, graphics and multimedia files—is stored in a central database in presentation-neutral formats. Photographs might be stored as BMP files—an uncompressed format; video, as AVI files—another uncompressed format. Separately, a series of templates are developed to reflect (1) a consistent visual interface and style, and (2) an appropriate technical specification. The templates provide the presentation layer. When a user browses to a Web page, its template is displayed and populated with content in real time. Photographs are rendered as Web-optimized JPG files; video, in a streaming file formation like WMF.

An online newspaper is a classic application of CMS technology. While content is updated constantly, the presentation layer is seldom changed. Journalists and picture editors don't have to worry about presentation; they just save content to the CMS. Neither has to have Web authoring skills; the skills and rules for applying them are embedded in the templates. When a user requests a page, content—news, sports, weather—is automatically poured into the associated template. A CMS can manage real-time data, too—like share prices and flight arrivals. Because data is stored in a presentation-neutral format, a CMS can support more than one delivery channel. A newspaper's CMS can deliver the same raw content to templates designed for (1) print, (2) the Web, (3) hand-held devices running the Palm or Windows CE operating systems, and (4) WAP-enabled devices.

This approach can be applied to self-paced course development. Create a series of templates to reflect typical course pages; develop content separately and store it in the CMS in channel-neutral formats. When the learner launches a course and accesses a page, the associated template automatically pulls in the right content on the fly. A CMS supports an object-oriented approach to e-learning content. Because all learning objects are stored in a central CMS, they can be reused by different authors to build different courses. Here are other benefits of CMS-based e-learning content development and publishing:

- When centrally stored content is updated or corrected, every course in which it appears is automatically updated or corrected.
- When the e-learning application is given a facelift—perhaps to reflect new branding, a merger, or an acquisition—only templates need to be redesigned; content, by far the larger of the two elements, is not involved.
- By supporting automated workflow between instructional designers, subject matter experts, media developers and quality assurance, a CMS enables team-based rapid content development.
- Local templates can be developed to accommodate local language and culture.
- Alternatively, templates can be used globally but based on a learner's profile; content is displayed in the local language.
- As enterprises develop more and more channels to deliver the right learning at the right time, a CMS can automate and accelerate the distribution process while reducing development costs.

LCMS (Learning Content Management System)

An LCMS has more to do with a CMS than an LMS. It's a CMS dedicated to learning content and a learning environment. Here is LCMS vendor Robert Koolen's definition: "The most simple definition of a Learning Content Management System is a system that enables the creation, storage, management and deployment of learning content in the form of learning objects to serve the needs of individuals."[3]

The LCMS declared its intention to carve out a space in the e-learning market around November 2000 when a group of vendors, all working on the intelligent storage of learning objects and content, formed a consortium later named the LCMS Vendor Council. It was led by WBT Systems' Michael Thomas. "The goal of the vendor council is to help define what an LCMS is, to distinguish the participants in this segment, and to encourage IDC and other analyst groups to recognize the differences between e-learning content management systems and learning management systems," explained Thomas. "The vendor council is pushing the e-learning industry to view the LCMS product class as a major industry segment, which can be evaluated separately with or without a corresponding LMS."[4]

Generally, an LCMS will provide a content authoring module, an assessment authoring module, a publishing module, an administration module, a server engine, a data repository — and from the learner's perspective, a module that presents personalized adaptive learning in a customized workspace. An LCMS should simplify and accelerate the content authoring process allowing subject matter experts with the appropriate access rights to self-publish. It is this self-publish function that some people believe gives the LCMS the potential to act as a knowledge sharing and Knowledge Management tool. An LCMS can also link to content in knowledge databases inside and outside the enterprise.

An LMS and LCMS are not interchangeable nor are they mutually exclusive. They should work together — as IDC's white paper about LCMSs explains: "When tightly integrated, information from the two systems can be exchanged, ultimately resulting in a richer learning experience for the user and a more comprehensive tool for the learning administrator. An LMS can manage communities of users, allowing each of them to launch the appropriate objects stored and managed by the LCMS. In delivering the content, the LCMS also bookmarks the individual learner's progress, records test scores, and passes them back to the LMS for reporting purposes"[5] (see Figure 10.2).

E-learning consultancy Brandon-Hall has analysed most LMS and LCMS products. Figure 10.1 illustrates how the results distinguish the functionality of the two applications.

In the same way that the functionality of TMSs and LMSs overlapped, most LCMSs offer some LMS functionality — course administration, course catalogue, learner registration and learner tracking, for example. LCMS vendors either claim or have demonstrated interoperability with some LMSs. At the same time,

	LMS	LCMS
Primary target users	Training managers, instructors, administrators	Content developers, instructional designers, project managers
Provides primary management of...	Learners	Learning content
Management of classroom, instructor-led training	Yes (but not always)	No
Performance reporting of training results	Primary focus	Secondary focus
Learner collaboration	Yes	Yes
Keeping learner profile data	Yes	No
Sharing learner data with an ERP system	Yes	No
Event scheduling	Yes	No
Competency mapping–skill gap analysis	Yes	Yes (in some cases)
Content creation capabilities	No	Yes
Organizing reusable content	No	Yes
Creation of test questions and test administration	Yes (73% of all LMS tools have this capability)	Yes (92% of all LCMS tools have this capability)
Dynamic pre-testing and adaptive learning	No	Yes
Workflow tools to manage the content development process	No	Yes
Delivery of content by providing navigational controls and learner interface	No	Yes

Figure 10.1— LMS and LCMS Functionality Comparison[6]
Reproduced by permission of Brandon-Hall

an increasing number of LMS vendors—currently around 30—have their own LCMS offering. Finally, a good LMS supports a personalized learner home page, learner profiling, reusable learning objects and adaptive learning based on skills and pre-course assessments—just like an LCMS.

Business benefits drive everything

When evaluating LMSs, your thought sequence should be:

- These are the business benefits I want to deliver.
- What LMS functions support the benefits?
- What features are supported by these functions?

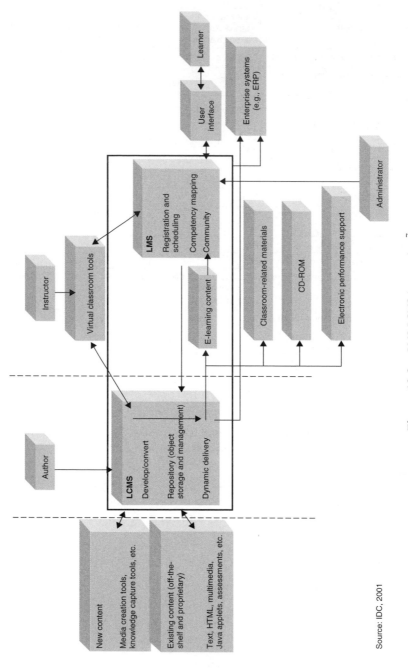

Figure 10.2 — LMS LCMS integration [7]
Reproduced by permission of IDC

Source: IDC, 2001

It's easy to become distracted and move in the opposite direction. This is an interesting feature — I wonder how we could use it? Resist the temptation. The business benefits driving the implementation of e-learning form the most important section of your e-learning strategy. Make sure LMS vendors understand your drivers and design their proposals around them.

A long-term commitment

An LMS represents a long-term commitment on your part — to the application and the vendor. When you don't have an LMS, the process of selecting one and getting it up and running is all consuming — but it's only a first step. Even a savvy learning organization can take years fully to implement its LMS. Most LMS implementations are work in progress. The long-term nature of the relationship impacts on the following:

Strategic Vision: You need to know that your vision for e-learning and your vendor's match up. You will have to realize your vision within the parameters of your LMS. If your vision is taking you in a different direction from your vendor, eventually you will have to choose between (1) compromising your vision, or (2) building expensive customized modules and facing the challenge of integrating them with your LMS.

Future Plans — Your Vendors, Yours: You need to be aware of the future direction of your vendor's business. Will your vendor stay focused on LMS development or could they become distracted by the market for LCMSs and services? Is your vendor giving signals to the industry that they would look favourably on an acquisition or merger offer? If they are, you could end up owning a long-term relationship with a different company — and a different strategic vision — from the one you started with. Does your own business have any plans to reorganize its structure in a way that would impact on learning? Is your vendor able to cope with the changes that would follow? Is your business planning mergers and acquisitions? Is the LMS sufficiently scalable that it could cope with double or treble the number of learners? Is it supported globally? Can it be configured to take account of localization? At the outset of what will be a long journey, you need to know and be comfortable with your travelling partner's plans.

Working Relationship with Vendor: Ask yourself, are these people I would be happy to work with closely month after month, year after year? Are they focused on our needs? Are they proactive, responsive, empathetic, reliable? Is there a good cultural fit? Do they have the depth of resources to look after our long-term needs? Do they deliver the technology resources and information we need? Do they deliver when they say they will? Are communications reliable? These considerations are separate from the quality of the vendor's product — but if you're not completely comfortable working with a vendor during the selection process, it augurs badly for a successful long-term relationship.

User Communities: Customers of well-established software vendors sometimes establish self-help online communities. People who use an application day in, day out often learn things about it even vendors don't know, or do know but aren't prepared to admit. If you have a long-term commitment to an application, it can be comforting and useful to participate in a self-help group. Find out from your LMS vendor if such a community exists; if it doesn't, consider starting one. Smart software vendors will form customer panels to represent the voice of the customer. Panels might meet once or twice a year under the vendor's auspices to provide feedback on current products and suggest direction for future product development. To be an active member of a customer panel takes time but it can pay dividends by (1) enabling you to influence future development, (2) providing a preview of upgrades and new products, (3) supporting a dialogue with other customers.

Integration

The learning value chain describes the channels available for the delivery of learning across the enterprise. Generally, the more channels you have the more you need to integrate your LMS with other vendors' applications. Find out if prospective LMS vendors have integrated their application with others you are already committed to. You might have decided that only one virtual classroom application meets your needs; any LMS you buy needs to integrate with it. Or you might need to integrate your LMS with enterprise applications like JD Edwards, Oracle, PeopleSoft, SAP and Vantive. Have your potential LMS vendors worked successfully with your enterprise applications?

In all systems work, the devil is in the detail. With integration, detail starts with the version numbers of applications. It isn't enough to know that vendor A has successfully integrated their application with vendor B's. You need to know which versions were integrated. Too many implementation teams learn too late that because A's Version 4.2 integrates smoothly with B's Version 3.1 does not guarantee that A's Version 5.0 integrates smoothly with B's Version 4.0. If you're an early adopter of a new version of an LMS, chances are the vendor has had little or no experience integrating it and is basing all claims on what happened with previous versions. Be prepared to ask tough questions about integration.

When you visit vendors' Web sites and read their brochures, you'll soon discover they have anticipated your need to integrate applications by (1) developing their own integrated suites, and (2) forming partnerships with other vendors to close the gaps in their offerings. The arrangements look good on paper. What you need to work out is if the "partnerships" are marketing ploys or the result of having worked together successfully. There's a crucial difference between an LMS and a virtual classroom being a good strategic fit and making the applications work together seamlessly.

Don't confuse configuration with customization

Every LMS comes with a long list of documented variables—sometimes as many as 3000. Some variables must be configured as part of the implementation process; you have to configure system roles and rights to match your business or department structure. Other variables are optional. In Phase 1 of implementation, you could choose to turn off skills assessments. You might not take advantage of all available fields in the employee's profile, or you might remove some features from drop-down menus.

Some configuration is cosmetic. Usually, you can brand the LMS by inserting your company's name and logo, changing the colour scheme and even change fonts. Confusingly, cosmetic configuration is sometimes referred to as customization; people also talk about customizing reports, a relatively simple task often carried out using a third-party report generator integrated with the LMS by the vendor. Don't confuse *configuration* and *customization*. Configuration options are built into the application—most like a series of switches that can be set to different positions. Other configuration options require text inputs, for example, URLs that point to content servers. Configuration is a normal and necessary part of the implementation process; it is not an extra cost.

In contrast, customization happens outside the application, was not anticipated by the application's developers, and requires fresh code to be written—often to enable the LMS to talk to other applications about which it knows little or nothing. Customization is expensive and high-risk. Some LMS customization projects cost more than the LMS itself. It's high-risk because (1) it might not work, and (2) vendors can't guarantee an upgrade path for a customized LMS implementation. Custom code creates a hard-wired link between specific versions of applications; when the LMS vendor—or the vendor of the other application—releases a new version of their application, existing custom code might no longer work. The hard choice then is between (1) getting left further and further behind on the upgrade path, or (2) absorbing the cost of customizing each new version.

Generally, customization isn't recommended, however, don't let that stop you from discussing your needs with LMS vendors. If the application you want to integrate is mainstream, the vendor might decide it's such a good idea that the integration functionality will be part of all future releases. Under those circumstances, you could share customization costs or the vendor might even be prepared to absorb them.

Time and cost

The figures here are guidelines. Costs are bound to change over time and as LMSs mature, speed of implementation should increase. For an accurate indication of costs and implementation schedules, you need to talk to vendors about specific requirements, geographic spread and numbers of learners.

The range of licence costs for LMSs range from $35 000 to $600 000 per year. The higher figure isn't a ceiling since licence costs are based on the number of learners — the more there are, the higher the cost. Surprisingly, LCMS costs can be higher than LMS costs.

Internal costs shouldn't be ignored. In organizations that cross-charge for people's time, there will be costs associated with data migration, process re-engineering and housekeeping. In organizations that don't cross-charge, there will be opportunity costs as people are taken away from their day-to-day responsibilities to work on the implementation.

There are some small LMSs whose vendors claim can be implemented in a matter of days. It's unlikely these will meet enterprise needs. The implementation manager of one enterprise LMS told me that if everything went as planned, implementation could take as little as 6 weeks. One of his clients later told me it was a struggle to get the LMS running in 3 months, then admitted it took another 3 months to fine tune it. Even 6 months is an aggressive implementation schedule. It's not just a question of installing an application. There are staff records to migrate, courses to load, other applications to integrate — and testing. One year from signing a contract to launching e-learning across the enterprise is good going though you might be able to launch pilot programmes with limited functionality and in limited geographic areas sooner. It could take another 6 months to a year to implement all the LMS functions and features you need.

The apparent slow rate of progress can be linked to factors outside the implementation. There can be issues with the infrastructure, security, hosting and the desktop. Technology is not the only external source of delay. There might be things happening elsewhere in the enterprise that preoccupy your steering committee and prevent the implementation from getting the attention and sign-offs it needs. Slow progress can be the fault of the e-learning team too. If you haven't developed a strategy and prepared thoroughly, you can slow down the configuration process because you don't have the answers the vendor needs and don't know where to find them. Your vendor can only move as fast you let them.

The LMS market

In 2002, Brandon-Hall reviewed more than 70 LMSs for its annual report. Some people claim there are as many as 200 LMSs to choose from. But while there is plenty of choice, there is no clear market leader. It's safe to assume that a number of LMS vendors would like to become the market leader and if they can't achieve leadership by growing their sales, they will try to achieve it through merger and acquisition. That means there's likely to be change in what is, after all, an immature market. There are indications that the boutique quality of the LMS market will give way to domination by a handful of enterprise software vendors — who all aim to bring a full function LMS to market — and that the resulting stability will be a good thing for e-learning. It's a credible scenario but so far no dates have been announced. The largest LMS contracts are not being awarded to enterprise software vendors but to small dedicated LMS vendors.

Not surprisingly, vendors whose products have the most mature and stable architecture have attracted the largest client base but that doesn't mean their products are the best; it means their products have been around longest. The choice is between stability and innovation.

Here are some of the better-known LMS vendors:

Click2Learn	<http://click2learn.com>
Docent	<http://www.docent.com>
Hyperwave	<http://www.hyperwave.com>
IBM Lotus	<http://www.ibm.com/mindspan/>
Intellinex	<http://www.intellinex.com>
KnowedgeNet	<http://www.knowledgenet.com>
KnowledgePlanet	<http://www.knowledgeplanet.com>
Learnframe	<http://www.learnframe.com>
Oracle	<http://www.oracle.com>
Pathlore	<http://www.pathlore.com>
Plateau Systems	<http://www.plateau.com>
Saba Software	<http://www.saba.com>
SAP	<http://www.sap.com>
Sun Microsystems	<http://suned.sun.com/US/enterprise/>
TEDS	<http://www.teds.com>
THINQ	<http://www.thinq.com>
WBT Systems	<http://www.wbtsystems.com>

Some businesses have developed their own custom LMSs and used them to support large successful e-learning initiatives—especially where requirements are limited or so specific they're not met by third-party products. Some people have even used Microsoft Access as the engine of their do-it-yourself LMS. Providing you design the data structure properly, data from these applications can later be migrated to a large third-party LMS. Before setting off down this road, do a rigorous buy-build analysis. Include the risks inherent in all software development, and remember that slippage and scope creep in this project could undermine the whole e-learning initiative. Don't underestimate the cost and effort of ongoing maintenance, upgrades and support. There's a real risk, too, this development will take your team's focus away from where it should be—on the need to improve individual and enterprise performance.

What you need to do

E-learning standards

All the important LMS vendors implement the emerging e-learning standards to a greater or lesser degree. You need a clear understanding of (1) the standards their products conform to, (2) the parts of those standards they implement, and (3) their strategy for integrating full standards as they're published. It's also important to learn how involved vendors are in the standards development process. Without involvement and the understanding that comes from it, vendors — and their customers — are vulnerable to the development process obsoleting their products. Find out the specific contributions vendors have made to the development process. Usually a vendor will have an area of special interest and that's where they make contributions. It might be content metadata, content packaging, content sequencing, question and test interoperability, learner profiles, or run-time interactions. Eventually each of these areas will have its own standard. You'll be making an investment in e-learning before these standards have emerged. You can protect that investment by making sure your vendor has a strategy for making their existing products standards conformant and a commitment to working closely with you to implement the strategy.

Evaluation processes and tools

Use the 10-step process in Chapter 9 to help select an LMS vendor. Remember, you are evaluating the vendor as well as their product — if the best product comes from a vendor whose management style, culture, or financial status makes you uncomfortable, think about going with the second-best product. To evaluate an application as complex as an LMS, you will need to use a number of tools, for example:

- RFI/RFP
- evaluation checklist
- visits to vendor site
- vendor presentations
- vendor references
- content integration test
- SWOT analysis
- gap analysis
- scorecard

Some of these tools are covered by the 10-step process; the rest are explained below.

RFP

As THINQ's Vice-President for Business Development, Dave Egan has seen RFPs from the whole spectrum of potential customers pass across his desk. Based on that experience, he offers would-be RFP developers some good advice:

- It's not a checklist, it's a strategy

  - Complex does not equal better
  - More granular does not equal better
  - Bigger does not equal better

- Goal: To find the right one

  - Growth requires a partner for the "long haul"
  - Due diligence requires vision and a clear process

- Get at the root of your need

  - Scenario-based RFPs
  - What are you trying to accomplish
  - Review business-aligned learning objectives
  - Pick the top 10 — the big objectives
  - Create scenarios: demand details on exactly how the objectives will be met by existing technology and services[8]

A vendor's response to your RFP is their first deliverable. It gives you an insight into the way the company goes about things. Was the response delivered on time? Did it deliver everything you asked for in the form you asked for it? Did it over-deliver? Did you feel the over-delivery added value to the response or padded it out? Did you feel the response was template-driven or took full account of your specific business requirements?

Evaluation checklist

Your task is to learn how closely each LMS product matches your business needs and to compare the products in light of what you learn. Here is a checklist of the kind of questions you need to ask. The list is comprehensive but does not take account of your particular requirements, so also think about enterprise-specific questions. Don't ask a question for the sake of one; you'll only get an answer for the sake of one.

Technology

Server requirements

- What back-end platform does the LMS support: Windows NT, Server 200n, UNIX, Linux? What databases does it support: SQL Server, Domino, Oracle, DB2? Does the LMS support the back-end specified by your IT department? Do you expect the vendor to provide servers and back-end operating systems and applications?
- Does the LMS support geographically dispersed servers? Does it support Content Delivery Networks (CDNs)?

- Does the vendor offer an ASP model, that is, outsourced LMS and hosting? Where is the vendor's server farm? Does the vendor have a distributed data network to facilitate global reach? Can the vendor host custom and generic content as well as the LMS application?
- What is the minimum, average and maximum bandwidth required by the LMS? How much bandwidth does it require for 10, 100, 1000 or 10 000 students? Do bandwidth requirements increase linearly with the number of concurrent users?

Support

- Does the LMS vendor offer Professional Services, for example, needs analysis and project planning?
- How long is the warranty? What are the charges for support outside the warranty?
- Does the vendor provide integration and configuration support? Does the vendor have internal resources — or are integration and configuration outsourced? Who owns the project management of integration and configuration?
- What tools are provided to monitor and optimize the operation of the LMS?
- Exactly what support is provided — and is it included in the licence agreement or as an extra cost?
- Does the vendor provide a Service Level Agreement that covers availability, customer support response times, LMS and database repairs, bug fixes, help desk availability, etc?
- Does the contract include maintenance or version update provisions?
- How does the vendor handle "bugs"? How are bugs defined? Is the cost of a bug fix covered in the contract?
- Who is responsible for database maintenance and repair?
- Will the IT department — or whoever is responsible for day-to-day support of the LMS — require training? Does the vendor provide this training? What costs are involved?
- Does the vendor provide a live help desk? For administrators and managers, or learners? What hours is it operational? What languages does it support?

Systems integration

- Is the LMS built on an "open architecture'" to support integration with other enterprise and e-learning applications?
- Is integration with enterprise applications based on batch process updates — say, once a day — or real-time updates?
- What versions of these applications does the LMS support? Can the vendor provide customer references to corroborate successful integrations?
- Does integration result in a common database of learner records for all applications and content integrated with the LMS including generic content stored on publishers' servers, synchronous learning applications and collaboration tools?

- Can the LMS use the enterprise e-mail application to communicate with learners? If your enterprise uses Lotus Notes, find out if or how the LMS integrates with Notes Mail.
- Can the LMS use templates to customize automated e-mail notices about upcoming or cancelled courses, successful accreditation, etc?
- Can the LMS integrate Knowledge Management sources — to deliver information to learners as well as course content?

Security

- What is the LMS's approach to security? What security protocols are in place to protect enterprise and learner data?
- Can LMS security be integrated seamlessly with enterprise network security to avoid multiple log-ins?
- Assuming the LMS is installed behind the corporate firewall, can it deliver content to learners outside the firewall, for example, learners dialling into the intranet from home or a hotel?
- Can the LMS use the corporate extranet to deliver content to customers and suppliers?
- Can data be imported from outside the firewall, for example, to allow third-party content developers to load learning content into the CMS or LCMS?

Scalability

- Can the LMS scale smoothly and quickly to meet growing numbers of learners?
- How many concurrent learners does the LMS support? Can the vendor provide customer references to corroborate the number of concurrent learners the LMS supports?

Multinational operations

- Does the LMS support all international time-date formats?
- Does the LMS understand time zones?
- How does the LMS handle currencies?

Industry standards

- What draft standards does the LMS support? Can the vendor provide customer references to corroborate the implementation of all the standards it supports?
- Is the LMS standards-compliant or standards-certified?

Compatibility

- Does the LMS require a proprietary browser or a thin client? How is the installation of this software handled? How large is the download?
- Does the LMS require proprietary client-side software, typically, browser plug-ins?

- What standard browsers and browser versions does the LMS support—Internet Explorer and Netscape Navigator?
- Does the LMS support all industry standard plug-ins—Flash, Shockwave, RealPlayer, QuickTime? Can the LMS determine what plug-ins are installed on a user's system and automatically install any that are required to run course content?
- Are proprietary plug-ins needed? Does the LMS support them?

Learning content

- What publishers' generic e-learning content does the LMS support? Can the vendor provide customer references to corroborate the successful integration of all generic content the LMS supports?
- Does the LMS support standards-*compliant* content or only standards-*certified* content?
- Does the LMS support content stored on third-party servers, for example, publisher's servers?
- Can the vendor provide or build documented API's to integrate third-party content which is crucial to your plans but which is not standards compliant or certified?

Authoring tools

- Does the LMS support content developed with all authoring tools and authoring systems? Can the vendor provide customer references to corroborate the integration of content developed with all the authoring tools and systems the LMS supports?
- Does the LMS have a suite of integrated authoring tools?
- Does the LMS support metatags?

Content management

- How does the LMS handle content management? Has it been integrated with third-party CMSs and LCMSs?
- Are there restrictions on the kinds of files that can be stored?
- Does the LMS support reusable learning objects?
- How does the LMS handle multiple languages?

Offline and offsite learning

- Does the LMS support offline or disconnected learning with subsequent uploads of tracking data? Is the learning experience the same online and offline? If it isn't, how does it differ?
- Does the LMS support handheld or WAP-enabled devices?

Downloading tools

- Does the LMS support the downloading of tools by learners? Tools usually consist of Word, Excel, Acrobat, text and HTML files — and sometimes executable files.

Administration and management

Cost

- What is the LMS's cost per learner? Ask the vendor to analyse the gross figure under these headings: installation, usage, licensing, maintenance, support, configuration and consulting.

Records

- What is the process for populating the LMS with existing learner records, in other words, data migration?
- Is there a common record for learner activity in e-learning, classroom courses and virtual classroom courses?
- How are learner records maintained — added, deleted, edited? How are duplicate records handled?
- How does the LMS handle suppliers and customers? Can it add, change and suspend them — or convert them to employees? How does the LMS handle guests, that is, any temporary learners not in the enterprise database?
- How many learner records can the LMS support?
- What fields does the learner record support? Are the fields configurable? Are these fields included?

  - Last name
  - First name
  - Role
  - E-mail
  - Telephone
  - Business unit/department
  - Country
  - Region
  - Office
  - Coach/line manager
  - Mentor
  - Competencies
  - Subject matter expertise

Roles

- How does the LMS handle rights for administrators and managers?
- Are access levels pre-defined? Can they be configured?

Registration

- Does the LMS support self-registration for new learners? What is the process?
- What is the process for e-learning course registration?
- What is the process for classroom course registration? Does it support confirmation e-mail, seat allocation, notification e-mail — and a cancellation process?
- Is there a common registration process for e-learning, classroom courses, virtual classrooms?
- Will the LMS flag duplicate or conflicting course enrolments?
- Can the LMS control how many courses a learner can register for within a given period?
- Do registration processes work for learners outside the enterprise — customers and suppliers?
- How does the LMS handle overbooking? What priorities are used to determine who gets in and who gets bumped? Are the priorities configurable? Does it keep a waiting list?
- How does the LMS handle learner cancellations? Will a learner on a waiting list automatically be informed that a place has become available?
- How does the LMS handle group bookings, say, a batch of new joiners who need to take a series of classroom and virtual classroom courses?

Instructor-led classroom courses

- What is the process for inputting a scheduled classroom course? Does it cover instructor, guest speaker, dates, venue booking, resource booking, number of learners?
- Is it an intelligent process, for example, does it use drop-down menus to ensure that only qualified instructors are entered for particular courses, and only venues capable of holding the required number of learners can be booked? Can an event be entered if required fields are blank? Can a cut-off time-date be implemented for learner registration? Is it fixed or configurable for each event?
- Does the LMS flag conflicts — doubled-booked instructors, venues, equipment, etc?
- How does the LMS handle changes to scheduled learning events, for example, changes of instructor, venue, or date and time? Is there an auto e-mail function to inform all participants?
- How does the LMS handled cancelled events? Are all registered learners informed automatically? Are learners automatically offered a new date?

Tracking

- Can the LMS launch self-paced courses and track learners' progress through them? At what level of granularity — modules, sub-modules, screens?

- What information is tracked—start date, progress, completion date?
- Does the LMS track the results of pre- and post-assessments? Can it apply the output of a pre-assessment to adapt the presentation of a self-paced course?
- Does the LMS track the results of skills assessments? Can it apply the output of a skills assessment to create a personal learning path?
- Can the LMS automatically produce reports to show which learners have successfully completed courses and assessments?
- Can the LMS track learning costs per learner and across the enterprise—and export these to enterprise financial systems?
- Does the learning record support courses taken and accreditations received by the learner outside the system?
- Does the LMS support book marking by the learner? At what level of granularity—fox example, module, sub-module, or page? How many bookmarks can be saved?
- Can usage of learning resources be tracked—for example, venues, video players, projectors, laptops, electronic whiteboards, consumables, catering?

Assessments

- How does the LMS handle assessments?
- What question types and interactions are supported: multiple-choice, fill in the blanks, drag and drop, etc? Does the LMS have published APIs to allow customized question types to be tracked?
- Does the LMS support dynamic feedback to questions based on the learner's input? Can feedback be tiered—for example, a hint after the first two wrong inputs, and the right answer after the third wrong input?
- Can learners re-take assessments? If the learner takes an assessment more than once, are there rules about which score is saved to the learning record—the last score, the highest score?
- Are assessment questions always presented in the same sequence or can the order be randomized for learners who take assessments more than once? Or, can assessments be built from a pool of questions to minimize the likelihood of the same questions appearing in consecutive attempts?
- Is the number of questions in an assessment limited in any way?
- Can the LMS use the output of assessment to recommend a remedial study plan where required?
- Can learners "test out" whole courses or parts of courses based on the results of a pre-assessment?
- Does the LMS support accreditation and certification assessment? What is the reporting process that follows a successful attempt?

Reporting

- What reports does the LMS support out of the box—active and inactive courses, number of registered learners, number of concurrent learners, number of study hours? Is there a report that cross-references learners and courses in order to assess operational readiness? Is there a report that gives the status of a classroom event—for example, confirmed venue, resources, instructor and learners?

- What is the process for creating customized reports? Can reports be developed by anyone with basic PC skills or are programming skills required?
- Is training required before administrators and managers can run reports?
- Can reports be associated with security levels, that is, only certain administrators and managers have access to certain reports?
- Can the LMS schedule automate the running and distribution of reports?
- Can reports of individual instructor's weekly or monthly schedules be generated and printed? Can reports of learning event details be generated and printed?

Evaluation

- How does the LMS support the evaluation of learning by the enterprise at Kirkpatrick's levels 1, 2, 3 and 4?

Catalogue

- Is there a common catalogue for custom and third party e-learning courses, classroom courses and virtual classes?
- What search/query functions does the catalogue support—by course name, course code, business unit, product, curriculum, skill, delivery channel, community, geographical location?
- What views does the catalogue support—by course name, course code, business unit, product, curriculum, skill, delivery channel, community, geographical location?
- What is the process for maintaining the catalogue?
- How does the LMS handle a new release of an existing course when some learners are still taking the superseded version? Are both versions listed in the catalogue? Can a course be active without being listed in the catalogue?

Skills, competencies, job matching

- What skills and competencies assessments does the LMS support? What are the processes for configuring, customizing and maintaining both the models and job profiles that underpin these assessments and the assessments themselves?
- Can the LMS use the results of these assessments to generate a personalized learning path?
- Can the LMS use the results of these assessments to match employees with jobs?

Learner experience

Access

- How can learners access self-paced e-learning courses — through the corporate intranet, through the Internet, through dial-up, offline?
- What impact on performance does a dial-up connection have?

Learning interface and environment

- Is the learner interface configurable? Is it customizable? Can this work be done by enterprise staff or only by the vendor? If by enterprise staff, is training necessary? If by the vendor, are there costs involved?
- Is the interface simple, attractive and intuitive?
- Does the learner have a learning home page? How is the home page personalized to reflect the learner's profile? Is the personal learning path displayed? The learner's active courses? Progress through courses?
- Is the learner's home page configurable? What are the variables — font, font size, colours, themes, learner's photograph, nickname?
- Can the learner's home page display notices about new functions and courses, upcoming Web casts, newly archived virtual classes?

Communications

- Does the LMS support collaboration and knowledge communities? How?
- Does the LMS support communications between learner and instructor or coach?
- Does the LMS automatically inform the learner when they have been successfully accredited or certified?
- Can the LMS remind learners by e-mail when their accreditations or certifications are going to expire?

Support

- Does the vendor provide live help desks for the learner? What hours is it operational? What languages does it support?
- Do learners need any training to use the LMS? Does the vendor provide it? What costs are involved?
- Does the LMS support online help files and tutorials?

Vendor references

Make sure you talk to someone who played a key role in the implementation from beginning to end. Check at least two references for each vendor. Don't approach referees on an ad hoc basis. Make an appointment even for a telephone conversation. You want them to know it's important to you. Develop a standard interview to facilitate the comparison of vendor references. Besides, the more focused you are, the more likely you are to elicit a focused response. Here are the kinds of questions you might ask.

Benefits, features, functions

- What were your business drivers?
- Did the vendor achieve an understanding of your business, corporate culture and business requirements?
- Did the LMS deliver the functionality you needed out of the box? If there was a gap, did you fill it by customizing the LMS or by integrating other products?
- Did the LMS impact negatively on existing business processes?

Cost-value proposition

- What was the vendor's cost-value proposition to you? Has it been validated?

Implementation

- What version of the LMS did you implement?
- What percentage of the LMS's functionality was implemented?
- Was the vendor responsible for project managing the implementation? Did the vendor outsource the project management?
- Did the vendor have a documented implementation methodology? Did the vendor's implementation team have the right skills? Did the team have any "heroes" you could name?
- Were you satisfied with the implementation process?
- What was the scale of your implementation — pilot, phased, full?
- How many registered and concurrent learners does the LMS support?
- Do you use the LMS to deliver e-learning to (1) employees, (2) suppliers, (3) customers? Do you use the LMS to manage financial transactions with business units?
- Does the LMS support a learning value chain, that is, self-paced e-learning, instructor-led classroom learning and virtual classes?

Integration

- Did you integrate the LMS with the enterprise

  - e-mail application? Which one?
  - HR system? Which one?
  - financial system? Which one?
  - security system?
  - Knowledge Management sources?

- Was the integration based on real-time or batched data exchange?
- Does the vendor have published APIs? Did you use them?
- What is your opinion of the integration performance?

Ability to execute, performance, service

- Was the implementation clearly scoped? Was what was promised delivered?
- Was implementation delivered on time? How much of the credit or blame lies with the vendor?
- Was implementation delivered within budget? How much of the credit or blame lies with the vendor?
- What was your opinion of the vendor's ability to execute an implementation? Was the vendor proactive in its approach and responsive to your needs?
- Do you have any advice about how to work with and get the most from this vendor?
- Would you work with this vendor on a fresh LMS implementation?

Training, knowledge transfer

- Did the vendor provide any training? Were you satisfied with it?
- Did the contract include knowledge transfer? What form did it take? Were you satisfied with it?

Post-implementation

- Do you have a Service Level Agreement (SLA) to define the nature and quality of service?
- What type of support does the vendor provide? Is it 24/7 or business hours?
- Have you had to use the vendor's service? Were you satisfied with it?
- Have any software upgrades been installed since going live? Did the vendor install the upgrade or was it done internally?
- Was the upgrade process trouble-free? Did it improve performance or fix the bugs it claimed to?
- Is there a user support group? Does the vendor have a customer panel? Are you a member of either? Have you seen benefits from membership?

General

- Was there a single factor in your evaluation that led you choose this vendor? Who else was on your shortlist?
- What was the biggest lesson you learned in the course of the implementation?

Content integration test

If there's custom or generic content you need your LMS to support, provide sample courses to the vendor and ask them to test (1) content loading, (2) course launching and (3) activity tracking. Even if the test does not go smoothly, the vendor should arrive at an understanding of what needs to be done to integrate your content successfully. That information will inform their response to your

RFP. If the vendor already supports generic content from a publisher you plan to license content from, ask for a demonstration.

SWOT analysis

After you receive vendors' responses to your RFP, you need to find ways to compare one with another. A SWOT analysis can be a powerful tool for comparison. Strengths and opportunities work in a vendor's favour; weaknesses and threats, against them. You can develop mitigating strategies for threats associated with a vendor; you can do little about weaknesses. A SWOT doesn't give you a clear winner — the way a scorecard does — but it does help you think through the relative merits of the competitors. Here are some typical headings for a vendor SWOT:

Ability to Execute: Think about speed, experience, resources, technology expertise and project management skills.

Features and Functions: Is what the vendor offers what you need? Is the LMS evolving or static? Is that a strength or a weakness?

Market Position: A leader or a follower? What kind of reputation does the business have with industry analysts and consultants? With its customers?

Vision: Does the vendor know where e-learning is going? Does it know where its business is going?

Business: How stable is the business? What does its order book look like? Is the business big enough to handle your implementation and expectations? Does the vendor deliver value? (See Figure 10.3.)

	S	W	O	T
Ability to Execute				
Features/Functions				
Market Position				
Vision				
Business				

Figure 10.3 — LMS vendor SWOT analysis

Gap analysis

Don't be surprised if none of the vendors' responses score a bull's-eye as far as your requirements are concerned. After all, an LMS is an off-the-shelf application while your requirements are unique. A gap analysis can help you measure what's missing from each vendor's functionality. The form of analysis doesn't have to be sophisticated. List all required functions down the left side of a spreadsheet and all the vendors left to right across the top. Enter a rating against each function for each vendor. You could use a simple Yes–No rating system — or a High–Medium–Low rating accompanied by a brief explanation. If the analysis needs more granular demarcations, use colour codes, or ratings systems like Excellent–Good–Average–Poor–No Opinion and 1 = strongly disagree, 2 = disagree, 3 = neutral, 4 = agree, and 5 = strongly agree.

When the analysis is complete, you might want to eliminate some vendors immediately because the gap is so large. The next step is to think about the best way to close the remaining gaps — by customizing the LMS, or integrating another application. You need to discuss the options with each vendor in order to understand their view of the time and cost impact.

Scorecard

A scorecard provides a different way of assessing the data you looked at in the SWOT analysis. Take the same headings from the SWOT and assign a weighting to each one. Weighting reflects the relative importance of each heading to the project and is usually expressed as points out of 100. If you believe that the most important considerations are (1) getting the job done quickly and efficiently, and (2) the depth and match-up of functions and features, your weighting might look like this:

Ability to Execute	25
Features/Functions	25
Market Position	20
Vision	10
Business	20
Total	100

These headings are too broad to support analytical scoring, so create sub-headings. There are no prescribed numbers of headings or sub-headings — you could have five or six sub-headings under one heading and only two under another. Use whatever it takes to reflect your values and priorities. Under *Ability to Execute* you might list:

- responsiveness
- experience
- resources

- technology expertise
- project management processes
- project management skills

Have the evaluation team enter a score from 1 to 5 for each sub-heading. Calculate the actual *Ability to Execute* score as a percentage of the potential score and apply the percentage to the weighting which is 25.

A scorecard will produce a ranking of LMS candidates. Providing you have chosen headings and sub-headings that reflect your business needs, the ranking should make an important contribution to your evaluation.

The final selection

Let's assume you have developed your RFP with care and economy and those qualities are reflected in the responses. Let's assume you have taken advantage of as many evaluation tools as your team felt necessary. The time comes when you have to make a decision. If you have lingering questions, this is the time to ask them.

At this stage, you need to confirm that you have support for your selection from all stakeholders. If necessary, present the outputs of your evaluation processes to stakeholders. Finally, when you make a decision, select a first, second and third choice LMS. There is no guarantee that contract negotiations with your first choice will go smoothly and no way to ensure the vendor will have the resources you need when you need them.

References

1   Lundy J (2002) *The 2002 E-Learning LMS Magic Quadrant: Who Survives?* Gartner Group [Report] [Internet] Available from <http://www.gartner.com/reprints/saba/104389. htm> Accessed 4 May 2002.
2   Barron T (2000) *The LMS Guess* ASTD Learning Circuits [Internet] Available from <http://www.learningcircuits.org/apr2000/barron.html> Accessed 10 Dec 2001.
3   Koolen R (2001) *Learning Content Management Systems — The Second Wave of eLearning* Knowledge Mechanics [White paper] [Internet] Available from <http://www.knowledgemechanics.com/downloads/lcms2ndwave.pdf> Accessed 13 May 2002.
4   Schelin E (2001) *Corporate: LMS and LCMS!* e-learning Magazine 1 June 2001 [Internet] Available from <http://www.elearningmag.com/elearning/article/articleDetail.jsp?id= 3933> Accessed 14 May 02.
5   Brennan M Funke S and Anderson C (2001) *The Learning Content Management System—A New eLearning Market Segment Emerges* IDC [White paper] [Internet] Available from <http://www.knowledgemechanics.com/downloads/IDCLCMSWhitePaper.pdf> Accessed 13 May 2002.

6   *Learning Management Systems and Learning Content Management Systems Demystified* (2001) Brandon-Hall.com [Internet] Available from <http://www.brandonhall.com/public/resources/lms_lcms/lms_lcms.htm> Accessed 17 Mar 2002.
7   Brennan M Funke S and Anderson C (2001) *The Learning Content Management System— A New eLearning Market Segment Emerges* IDC [White paper] [Internet] Available from <http://www.knowledgemechanics.com/downloads/IDCLCMSWhitePaper.pdf> Accessed 13 May 2002.
8   Egan D (2001) *A New Route to the Right LMS* [Presentation] ASTD TechKnowledge 2002 Las Vegas 7 February 2002 [Internet] Available from <http://www.astd.org/astdtk2003/Handouts_for_Web/Th104.ppt> Accessed 17 May 2002.

Testing: mission-critical, not nice to have

11

The Testing Team's Motto: We are a service organization whose job is to reduce damaging uncertainty about the perceived state of the product. Brian Marick[1]

Validation: Establishing documented evidence which provides a high degree of assurance that a specific process will consistently produce a product meeting its pre-determined specifications and quality attributes. FDA[2]

What you need to know

One of the things that makes e-learning different from all the forms of learning and training that went before is that it is a system in both the logical and technological senses of the word. What is a system? Here is part of *The Oxford English Dictionary's* answer:

- *gen.* A group or set of related or associated material or immaterial things forming a unity or complex whole.
- *Computing.* A group of related or interconnected hardware units or programs or both, esp. when dedicated to a single application.[3]

Building and operating a system is demanding — often in ways that people from a background in training are unlikely to be prepared for. Moving from a classroom learning environment, the production of training videos, even the development of training CD-ROMs to a full e-learning application is not an incremental step, it's a leap. An e-learning system can be complex, often comprised of elements that have to interwork even though they weren't designed to.

What you have to test and how you have to test it depends on the nature and scale of the e-learning application you're building but make no mistake, test you will have to — as Yoda might put it. Some of the tests are highly technical and carried out only by experts but they need managing and their outputs can impact on anyone in the implementation team. Just running tests isn't enough. The sequence of testing is critical, so is the environment in which tests are carried out. Before you run a single test, you need to develop a testing strategy.

System and software testing is a discipline and specialization in its own right. An in-depth guide to testing is beyond the scope of this chapter; instead, it sets out the broad testing issues likely to be unfamiliar to anyone involved in their first e-learning implementation.

Testing strategy

What are the key goals of testing? They fall into three categories:

- *Non-functional Testing*: demonstrate that requirements — business, system and technical — have been met and properly implemented
- *Functional Testing*:
  - validate that the integrated application works as expected
  - identify issues and defects, and ensure they are addressed before going live
  - validate the processes supporting the operation of the application
  - validate the security of the application

- *Service Level Testing*: demonstrate that system performance and availability requirements have been met

A full e-learning application is built from a number of sub-systems and is integrated with a number of external systems (see Figure 11.1). This high level view does not show the databases — applications in their own right — that support most systems in the application. Figure 11.2 provides a different picture, reflecting all hardware and software layers in the system.

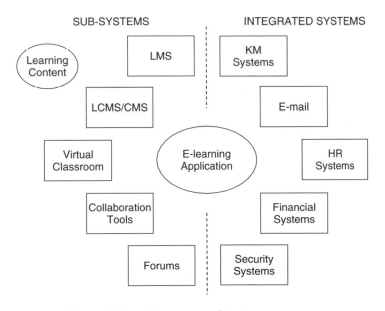

Figure 11.1 — E-learning application components

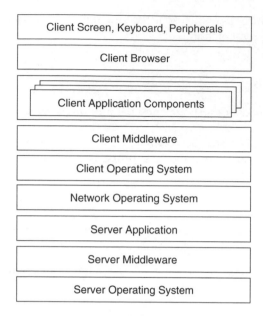

Figure 11.2 — System hardware and software layers

Because there are so many interworking parts, testing needs to tell you not only that there is a problem but *where* and *why*. Here's a simple example: if testing reveals that learner activity tracking data is not being saved to the learner's record in the LMS, does the problem lie with (1) code embedded in the content, (2) the invisible frame in the Web browser that handles tracking data at the learner's end, or (3) within the server that hosts the LMS and its associated database? It could be in any or all of these places. Only when a problem is isolated can it be fixed.

Working in a series of isolated environments will help you isolate problems. During implementation, you need at least three environments: development, testing and production. Because the application and content need to be tested independently, there should be isolated development and testing environments for both. The principle is, only when a component works as designed in one environment is it promoted to the next (see Figure 11.3). That way, when testing shows something isn't working, you can be confident the problem lies in the area which differentiates the previous environment from the current one. So you start by asking the question: What's changed that could impact on what we're testing?

More about environments

The Production Environment is the configuration of servers and infrastructure that will be used to deliver e-learning once the application goes live. Normally, you

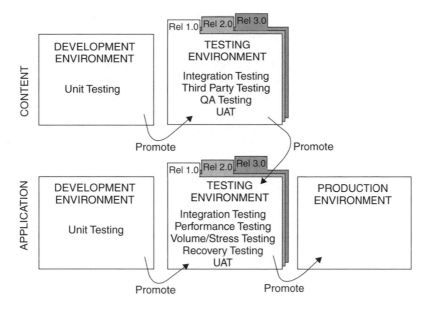

Figure 11.3 — Isolated environments

would only promote an application or content to the Production Environment once you were certain that it worked as intended. During implementation, however, you can use the Production Environment for testing. Before your go-live date, the URL of the Production servers hasn't been made public and, in any event, you can password protect the servers. It's a one-time offer though. Once the system goes live, you should never test in the Production Environment — unless you want to involve all learners in the test.

The Testing Environment should be an exact replica of the Production Environment. In practice, it doesn't make sense to build a Testing Environment on the scale of the enterprise infrastructure. What you do need to replicate is the *functionality* of Production Environment. You want to be confident that if it works as intended in the Testing Environment it will work as intended in the Production Environment. The application Testing Environment is where you integrate all components of the application including content. It's where you will see your application running for the first time. Before this point, you will have seen only aspects of the application running in isolation.

Both the content and application Testing Environments need to include every desktop configurations used across the enterprise. The desktop is a component of your e-learning application. Variations in it can impact on both the presentation and performance of e-learning. Work closely with your IT department to understand the desktop specification. Even enterprises that claim to have a common desktop tend to have subtle regional variations. Your application and content need to be tested with each one.

The Development Environment is not a replica of the Production Environment. It's designed to meet the specific needs of developers. Authoring tools used by content developers often have more demanding system requirements than most in the enterprise. Developers' systems tend to have massive amounts of memory and large displays set at maximum resolution. Prototypes sometimes need special development environments that the released product won't need. What is important is that the outputs of the Development Environment support the Production Environment. The only testing carried out in the Development Environment is Unit Testing.

New releases mean new testing environments

During implementation, you only have Release 1 of the application and Release 1 of the content to test, so all you need is one content and one application Testing Environment. You can continue to use those environments to test service releases of the application and content, that is, releases that don't change functionality. However, when you develop Release 2 of either the application or content with new functionality, you need a new clean Testing Environment. There's a temptation to use the existing Testing Environment and overwrite Release 1 with Release 2. That approach will make it difficult to determine whether problems with Release 2 lie within the new release or are the result of overwriting. Unless a new Release has a "clean" installation, you will be left with too many variables for effective testing.

Best practice is to retain both Testing Environments for Release 1 for as long as the Release 1 application and content are in the Production Environment. That means you need a minimum of two Testing Environments for the application and two for content, used in rotation — see the example in Figure 11.4.

Production Environment	Application Test Environment A	Application Test Environment B
Version 1.0	Version 1.0	Empty
Version 1.0	Version 1.0	Version 2.0
Version 2.0	Version 3.0	Version 2.0
Version 3.0	Version 3.0	Version 4.0

Figure 11.4 — Rotating test environments

Types of testing

Content and application development environments: unit testing

Unit testing is carried out by developers in the development environment. If you outsource development, your contract with the developers should specify that all content is unit tested before delivery. Unit testing content will tell you that a screen, a graphic, or a Flash animation accurately reflects the detailed design that specified it — and that in a standalone environment it works as intended: the screen layout accurately matches the design template, the graphic is legible, the Flash animation plays straight through from beginning to end at a speed that facilitates the assimilation of content. What unit testing cannot tell you is that the unit is free from defects. In practice, unit defects often show up only when the unit interacts with another part of the system. The most unlikely interactions can reveal unit defects: A page renders the way it was designed to in Internet Explorer Version 5.5 but not in Version 6.0 or vice versa; animation text is legible on a desktop display but not on a laptop display — or vice versa.

Unit testing should operate on a standalone pass–fail basis without trying to take account of other sub-systems. When testing a unit that interfaces with an unreliable or unpredictable sub-system, the best practice is to simulate the input–output of the sub-system in order to create predictability in your unit test. For example, if an application module has to send and receive e-mails, unit testing the module should not become distracted by the real-world variable performance of the e-mail sub-system. Instead, the unit test should simulate the input and output of e-mail's POP and SMTP servers. These simulations are both a strength and a weakness: a strength because they bring consistency and efficiency to unit testing; a weakness because they don't tell you how the application will perform in the real world.

Unit testing applies to sub-systems, too. You might have decided that peer-to-peer communication will be supported with an Instant Messaging (IM) sub-system. Before integrating IM with the other sub-systems, you should unit test it; install IM in the application Development Environment to validate that it can do what you expect on a standalone basis. When you're confident it can, integrate it with other sub-systems.

Content testing environment: integration testing

At its simplest, content integration testing is about loading all course elements in your LMS to see whether they interact as intended with (1) the LMS, and (2) each other. In the early stages of implementation, the LMS might not be available so you need other means. If you use an LCMS for development and delivery, you will be able to do integration testing within the LCMS. If you use a CMS to support content development, you can use it for initial integration testing but you'll need to simulate the input–output of the LMS. Some people prefer not to use their LMS for initial integration testing but load course components in a custom-built application that simulates an LMS. Once your LMS has been implemented, integration testing will become routine.

Content testing environment: third-party testing

As the name suggests, third-party testing is not carried out by developers but takes place outside the development environment. The name isn't meant to suggest the testing is outsourced though it could be. Third-party testing takes a top-down approach called *black box testing*: The input–output behaviour of the application is tested from the learner's perspective to demonstrate that each function is fully operational and works as designed. The expression black box tells us the tester makes no attempt to look inside the application to learn why something isn't working. The testers use the same systems and desktop as learners. If there are two laptop and three desktop system configurations in the enterprise, each course needs to be tested five times. To minimize duplicated effort, the five tests should be made by the same person or by a small highly collaborative team — otherwise, issues common to all configurations will be reported five times.

Third-party testing should be scripted. Testers do not work their way through content according to their personal interests and whims but follow a script that has been designed to ensure all course functions and features are covered. Scripts ensure consistency of testing; if the same defect appears under the same scripted conditions on all five systems, you can assume the defect is in the content not in the system. Testing only helps developers if bugs or problems are documented and reproducible. Scripts can't guarantee that a bug is reproducible but they go a long way to ensuring that it is. Providing testers follow the script they don't have to remember the sequence of interactions that revealed a bug; it's already written down for them. Script-driven testing is only as good as the scripts. They should be developed by people who know the course design and feature-function set well.

Finally, third-party testers need to be given some leeway to follow their noses when scripted testing provides a glimpse into issues not covered by the script. When "something funny" happens, a good tester working under a good mandate explores it and documents what he finds.

Content testing environment: quality assurance testing

Quality assurance or QA testing is also carried out by third-party testers. Its objective is to find problems at the presentation layer: typographical errors, spelling mistakes, poor copy editing, and discrepancies between what the Detailed Design Document specifies and what's on the screen.

Objective defects like typos and spelling mistakes should be easy to spot and fix. Subjective issues like the quality of copy writing and the interpretation of instructions in the design document can prove awkward to diagnose and resolve. Template-driven content development and good workflow practices go a long way to minimizing defects at this level.

Content testing environment: UAT

UAT stands for User Acceptance Testing. In e-learning we almost always refer to *users* as *learners*, so perhaps we should start calling this LAT instead. Whatever it's called, it's important. Learners are your consumers; if you're not delivering what they need in the form they need it, they will desert you. UAT needs to be carefully handled. Participants must be representative of the target audience; if they aren't, their reactions can be misleading — what constitutes crucial learning for one group can be irrelevant to another. Even when the testers' demographics are right, the test needs to be designed so that it's clear what testers are responding to. When a learner rejects the objectives of a course, they could be wrong; the business unit leader and SME who set the course objectives might know better. On the other hand, when a tester says they can't understand a graphic or an animation, they are almost certainly right.

Fixing the problems that UAT reveals can be either quick and simple or long and involved. That's why you should try to do some UAT as early as possible; you don't want to find out at the last minute that learners find the navigation system difficult to use, or that some interactions contribute nothing to the learning experience.

During implementation when the learning environment has not been fully developed, running UAT early might mean that testers experience content in a makeshift environment. One solution is to run this initial phase of UAT in controlled conditions, for example, by bringing testers together in moderated panels. In these circumstances, you have an opportunity to put the content in context and to deal immediately with obvious shortcomings — like functions not yet fully implemented. Post implementation, the problem of makeshift environments goes away.

Application testing environment: integration testing

Integration testing is about running integrated sub-systems to see whether they operate and interact as intended. Ultimately, it answers the question: Does the application work as a whole? Integration testing takes a bottom-up approach that is the logical opposite of black box testing. Called *white box testing* or more correctly *glass box testing*, it exercises all the internal components of the system to validate that they perform as intended. It is specialist work carried out by system integrators resourced internally from your IT department or externally, sometimes from the LMS vendor.

Additive testing

Integration testing shouldn't be left until all sub-systems are available but carried out as each new sub-system becomes available. Additive integration testing avoids a log jam at the end and more importantly helps isolate sub-systems that impact negatively on the performance of the application.

Let's say there are five key sub-systems in your application: security, LMS, virtual classroom, moderated forums and Instant Messaging. If no integration testing takes place until all five modules are available and the application performs below expectation, it will be difficult to establish which sub-system is the problem. On the other hand, if you test the integrity of the application as each new sub-system becomes available, it will be clear which sub-system is the culprit — the last one to be integrated.

Regression testing

To be effective, additive integration testing must be supported by regression testing. When you integrate a new sub-system, it's not enough to run tests associated with what's been added, you need to re-test the whole application. This is the only way to be sure that what's been added hasn't broken previously integrated features and functions. Interactions between sub-systems are complex and difficult to predict.

Application testing environment: performance testing

Performance testing determines whether performance specifications are being met. For example, you might have specified that logon should take a maximum of 5 seconds for the round trip from client to server and back, irrespective of connection type or geographic location. Testing from different locations on different connections will establish if that performance is being delivered. You might have also specified that every page accessed by a learner loads within 3 seconds. Again, only testing conducted in all regions on all connections can tell you whether the application meets that specification.

Performance testing only delivers valid results when it is conducted under real-world conditions. You will need to organize a network of testers representing all system types and configurations, and all geographic areas you serve. Exactly what you test for depends on the specific performance parameters you've set.

Application testing environment: volume and stress testing

Even a badly designed application can perform well when there are only a handful of learners logged on. Volume and stress testing are forms of performance testing that validate what happens when large numbers of concurrent learners use the system.

Volume testing

As part of the specification for your e-learning application, you defined a maximum number of concurrent learners. The question volume testing sets out to answer — *before* the application goes live — is: Does the application perform as expected when the maximum number of concurrent learners is logged on? You might have specified 500 or 1000 concurrent learners. Volume testing uses software scripts to simulate the specified level of learner activity. There are companies that specialize in providing volume testing services. It's not unusual to discover that an application performs as expected up to a certain level after which performance degrades gracefully or the application crashes. With a graceful degradation all errors are reported to the learner, all data is saved, all files are closed, and no data is overwritten. Volume testing should reveal no performance degradation when the specified number of concurrent learners is simulated. If there is degradation, you need to find and correct the defect. Failure to perform as expected under normal loads might be the fault of the server architecture or specification, or the way content has been built.

Stress testing

Stress testing tells you how your application performs beyond the specified number of concurrent learners. The aim is to find how large a load the application can bear and still function, and the extreme point at which it breaks. Let's say you've specified 1000 concurrent learners and you've established that your application performs as expected under that load. Now you want to know what happens when 1500 or 2000 learners logon. Stress testing can tell you.

You can use stress testing as a planning tool. You might stress test when there's a possibility of an acquisition that will double your learner base overnight, when there's a critical course that all employees need to take in a short period of time, or to learn about the limits of the e-learning system's scalability. Stress testing is also a risk management tool. It helps you understand the probability and impact of a system crash due to overloading. For example, it will tell you whether data will be lost.

Application testing environment: disaster recovery testing

All systems experience failures — some hardly noticeable, others disastrous. You need a contingency plan for resuming normal operations as soon as possible after failures. The plan should identify vulnerabilities and potential threats, set out containment strategies, identify internal and external redundancy and back-up systems, and prioritize recovery procedures. It should be published in a disaster recovery manual.

All data on your server should be backed up regularly so the application can be restored quickly and effectively. Some sub-systems integrated with your application are outside your direct control; some might even be situated outside your organization. What are your disaster recovery plans for those? Do you have appropriate service level agreements with all vendors?

The worst case scenario is to have to put your disaster recovery plan into operation for the first time after a catastrophic failure, only to find critical gaps or errors in the process. Disaster recovery testing is about developing failure scenarios, simulating them, and implementing the recovery plan under controlled conditions. Schedule a full dress rehearsal before your e-learning application goes live.

Application testing environment: UAT testing

There has already been UAT testing in the content testing environment. UAT in the application testing environment differs in these ways:

- It takes place within the full e-learning application.
- It includes not only learners working with self-paced content, virtual classrooms, collaboration tools, etc., but the whole user community including system administrators and managers.
- It tests processes as well as hardware and software. Does registering for a classroom or self-paced course work as designed? Does the help desk work as designed? If there are mirror sites or a CDN, is content being replicated properly? Are learner records in the LMS being updated when courses stored on remote third-party servers are taken?

Like performance testing, UAT testing here requires a network of testers representing all the geographic areas you serve, and all system types and configurations used by learners.

Schedule testing, then protect the schedule

Because testing tends to happen late in the development process, there is a tendency to "steal" time allocated to testing and spend it somewhere else in the development cycle. It's a bad idea. Going live without adequate testing puts your whole implementation and the credibility of e-learning at risk. Here are three guiding principles for testing:

- Don't skimp.
- Don't procrastinate.
- Expect the unexpected

Ideally, testing should never be scheduled so close to the launch date that there is no time to diagnose the problem, fix it and regression test the application. In practice, testing schedules tend to reflect a best case scenario because working to a worst case scenario makes schedules unworkably long.

What you need to do

Content test environment: third-party testing

These are the kinds of issues that third-party testing of e-learning content should cover:

- Do all functions and features work as designed?
- Does all course navigation work as designed?

- Do all interactions — including feedback — work as designed?
- Assessments are an important type of e-learning interaction — do they work as designed?
- Does what's on the screen accurately reflect the Detailed Design? Are there omissions?
- Do all pages render as designed? Different PCs and desktop configurations can render pages slightly differently. The goal is not pixel for pixel uniformity across all platforms but usability and legibility.
- Do all graphics and multimedia content render as designed?
- Are there typographical errors? Testers should report typographical errors even though there will be a separate Quality Assurance test

Content and application test environments: UAT

Use standard forms so you can see response patterns emerge but leave room on the form for a short subjective evaluation. These are the kinds of topics and questions you should cover:

Identification

- Please provide the following information:

  - Name
  - Role
  - Office
  - Region
  - Country
  - Competency rating (or the local equivalent)

- Which system were you using?

  - Desktop? Which brand/model?
  - Laptop? Which brand/model?

- Which browser/version were you using?

Access evaluation

- Where were when you accessed e-learning content?

  - Which country?
  - Which city?
  - In a company office? Which one?
  - At home?
  - In a hotel?
  - Another location?

- Were you able to access the content on your first try?

  - Yes/No?
  - If "No", do you know why your first attempt failed?

- Across the whole learning session, I found the speed of the connection and the responsiveness of the site acceptable.

N/A	Strongly Disagree		Neutral	Strongly Agree	
0	1	2	3	4	5

- Some areas of the site or pages in the course were unacceptably slow.

N/A	Strongly Disagree		Neutral	Strongly Agree	
0	1	2	3	4	5

  - If you agree, where were the slow parts or pages?

- I was able to access the whole course.

N/A	Strongly Disagree		Neutral	Strongly Agree	
0	1	2	3	4	5

  - If you disagree, what were the parts or pages you couldn't access?

- All of the links to content outside the course worked.

N/A	Strongly Disagree		Neutral	Strongly Agree	
0	1	2	3	4	5

  - If you disagree, what links didn't work?

Content evaluation

All questions are answered using the sliding scale:

N/A	Strongly Disagree		Neutral	Strongly Agree	
0	1	2	3	4	5

- Overall I believe taking the course was worth my time.
- I believe the course's stated objectives are valid.
- I believe the course met its stated objectives.
- The prerequisites were appropriate.
- The content was relevant.
- The level of difficulty was appropriate to the content and my experience.
- The course added to my knowledge and/or skills.
- The course will help me to perform my job better within the next 6 months.
- I found that topics were covered in appropriate breadth and depth.
- The interactive exercises reinforced the content and added value to my learning/understanding.

- The feedback in the evaluations reinforced the content and added value to my learning/understanding.
- The audio sequences reinforced the content and added value to my learning/understanding.
- The video sequences reinforced the content and added value to my learning/understanding.
- The animations reinforced the content and added value to my learning/understanding.
- It was easy to navigate around the course.
- I would recommend this course to my colleagues.
- I would use e-learning on a regular basis.
- I would recommend e-learning to my colleagues.

Feature and function evaluation

List all course features and functions and ask the learner to rate them on the sliding scale. This will help you understand what learners find useful and, it follows, where you should direct your resources. Don't be surprised if the Pareto Principle applies, that is, 80% of learners give a high rating to 20% of the features and functions while only 20% of learners express approval for the rest. If that is the case, you need to decide whether to accept the verdict at face value or whether there are mitigating circumstances to take account of, for example, learners have not had enough time to appreciate the long-term value of some features.

Open questions

- Were you able to finish the course?

  - Yes/No?
  - If "No", why?

- How long did you spend working with the course?
- How do you think the content could be improved?
- How would you describe the experience of using e-learning?
- Please add other comments that you think would help us see this course from a learner's point of view.

How to rate issues

When third-party testing and application integration testing uncovers issues, it is best practice for the tester to rate them in terms of severity and priority. While the IEEE Standard 1044 provides an in-depth explanation of software anomaly classifications including a five-level severity rating, many people prefer to devise their own systems. Here are two samples:

Severity Ranking

1	Catastrophic	A defect that causes disastrous consequences for the system, for example, critical loss of:

- data
- system availability
- security

There is no workaround and testing cannot continue.

2	Severe	A defect that causes disastrous consequences for the system, for example, a sub-system or function is completely broken. There is no workaround and testing of the function cannot continue.
3	Major	A defect that causes significant consequences for the system. It needs to be fixed but there is a workaround.
4	Minor	A defect that causes small or negligible consequences for the system with little or no loss of functionality. The consequence is easy to recover from or workaround — for example: misleading, incorrect or missing error messages and presentation issues like incorrect formatting, fonts or colours. Testing is not affected.
5	No Effect	A slight defect that does not impact on the system or generate incorrect outputs. Examples include typographical errors and unintended screen layouts. (Of course, what has no effect in terms of the application can have a major impact in terms of learning.)

Priority Ranking

1	High	This has a major impact on the implementation and enterprise. It must be fixed immediately.
2	Medium	This has a major impact on the enterprise or learner. It must be fixed before the version of the application currently in development goes live.
3	Low	This has a minor impact on the enterprise or learner. It should be fixed if there is time but can be left until the next service release.

References

1   Marick B (1995) *The Testing Team's Motto* [White paper] [Internet] Available from <http://www.testing.com/writings/purpose-of-testing.htm> Accessed 22 May 2002.
2   Center for Drugs and Biologics and National Center for Devices and Radiological Health (1987) *Guidelines on General Principles of Process Validation* Rockville MD, Food and Drug Administration [Internet] Available from <http://www.fda.gov/cdrh/ode/425.pdf> Accessed 23 Jul 2002.
3   *New Shorter Oxford English Dictionary* (1997) Vers 1.0.03 [Software] Oxford, Oxford University Press.

Part IV
Delivery

Multi-channel delivery: leveraging the learning value chain

12

Today, in the broad space between yesterday's irrational exuberance and today's equally irrational orthodoxy, there is a new frontier of business strategy. Don Tapscott[1]

What you need to know

Every enterprise has a learning value chain, although not everyone thinks of it in that way (see Figure 1.4 on p. 18). Most learning departments already use delivery channels like the classroom, e-mail, distributed PowerPoint presentations, print-based material, CD-ROMs, Knowledge Management, communities of practice, audio and video conferences, and so on. E-learning adds to the value chain channels like self-paced courses, virtual classrooms, e-mentoring, downloadable tools and downloadable content for offline study.

Blended learning

What I call a learning value chain some people call blended learning. However, "blended learning" is being used increasingly to mean not just a mix of delivery channels but a mix of both delivery channels and content that reflects different learning styles and instructional designs. I don't believe dumping every aspect of learning in a bucket and labelling it "blended learning" is helpful. Here is an example: "Blended learning focuses on optimizing achievement of learning objectives by applying the "right" learning technologies to match the "right" personal learning style to transfer the "right" skills to the "right" person at the "right" time."[2] It's not that I don't agree with the authors' goals, I support them entirely. What I don't agree with is calling the process "blended learning". This is simply a description of best practice in enterprise learning. The word "blended" adds nothing.

Some vendors have begun to use "blended learning" when they really mean an end-to-end learning solution. Again, there's nothing wrong with an end-to-end solution but calling it "blended learning" doesn't inform the discussion. The more the term is used to describe different things or diffuse notions, the less value it has. I would be happy to retire it here and now. I'm not alone. Colleagues, clients and well-respected figures in the e-learning industry have all remarked to me that the term doesn't resonate with them.

Channel strategy

Whatever you call it, having more than one way of delivering learning brings with it the responsibility of developing strategies for effective multi-channel delivery. Some enterprises and e-learning vendors aspire to deliver *all content in all channels* with the aim of matching delivery to individual learning and working styles. While feasible, especially with an object-oriented approach to content and a well implemented CMS or LCMS, all content in all channels is very ambitious in terms of time, cost and resources.

Some vendors and enterprises even aspire to *all content in all learning* styles, that is, delivering content personalized to each learner's preferred style of learning. Apart from the effort involved, there is more than one reason why this approach can't be justified. It assumes that preferred learning styles can be determined through online evaluations. This is probably true; Peter Honey offers such assessments. It further assumes that all learning content can be expressed in all styles. This is probably not true. Peter Honey and Alan Mumford, pioneers of the notion of the Learning Cycle and preferred learning styles, make the point that *all* learners must adopt *all* styles at different points in the learning cycle.

Even Howard Gardner, the father of Multiple Intelligences (MI) theory, is guarded about the direct application of MI theory to learning practice: "If one wants to know students well, it is helpful to have a set of categories by which one can describe their strengths and weaknesses, bearing in mind my cautions about labeling. One needs to go well beyond the eight intelligences, because they represent, at the most, a first cut. And one must be prepared to update the descriptions regularly, because, happily, the minds of students—and, indeed, even the minds of their elders—are subject to change."[3] If, as Gardner tells us, a learner's most effective intelligence is a moving target, can learning in the enterprise ever be both dynamic and focused enough to hit it? Moreover, is it realistic to believe the enterprise can use music to teach business and production processes to learners with a musical intelligence?

Dr David Merrill, a leader in instructional design since the early days of CBT (computer-based training) and multimedia, is also sceptical—and puzzled—by the apparent need to cater to learning styles: "So many people talk about them and believe in them, there might be something there. It's just that I grew up with psychologists like Dick Snow and Lee Cronbach, individual-difference experts. I watched these two very respected researchers spend 10 years trying to establish the existence of important aptitude-by-treatment interactions, and they found none. In other words, there is no hard, scientific evidence that if you treat people with different personality attributes differently in the classroom or via technology, there will be significantly different outcomes in their learning. Yet the popular articles persist and the belief persists and the sessions at the training and education association conferences persist."[4]

I'm not sure we can or need to deliver all learning content in all channels and learning styles. Instead, multi-channel delivery — at least with the current generation of e-learning technology and instructional design — should be about leveraging the learning value chain to ensure that learning messages are delivered through the most effective channels.

A dynamic approach to delivery channels

There's no formula for determining the most effective delivery channel. The most important consideration is the business driver for the learning. When an unexpected change in business strategy in a global enterprise needs to be communicated to as many staff as possible in the least amount of time, a series of large virtual classes might be the right solution. Developing content for virtual classes tends to take much less time than developing content for self-paced courses; that means there will be a minimal delay in rolling out the learning. The virtual classes can be recorded for employees unable to "attend" live sessions. However, if the change in strategy looks like becoming a medium- to long-term policy, the content of the virtual class should be redeveloped as self-paced courses. The new courses can reflect any developments in the strategy and its practice, deliver a level of complexity suited to self-paced learning, draw on a range of media to deliver the message, and be available to all new joiners as well as existing staff.

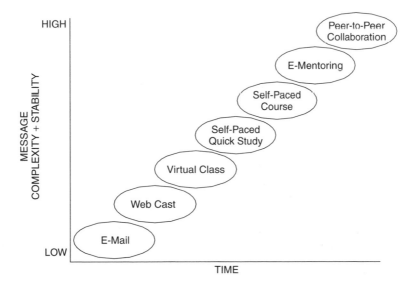

Figure 12.1 — Matching delivery channels to requirements

A learning value chain needs to respond to change within the enterprise. Change, however, seldom emerges fully formed. You might need a strategy that uses different learning channels in sequence in order to deliver a learning message that starts only as an indication of change and ends 6 months later with, say, a new fully developed go to market strategy supported by processes and tools. E-mail might be the right learning channel to signal that change is imminent; live Web casts or virtual classrooms might be the right channels to deliver learning about the next stages in strategy development; ultimately, a large self-paced course might be required to convey all details of the strategy and how to use its new processes and tools; finally, e-mentoring, online collaboration and face-to-face learning might have important roles to play in helping learners become expert with the new strategy and tools (see Figure 12.1).

Challenging assumptions about delivery channels

There is an assumption about delivery channels that I believe should be challenged. It's this. Only face-to-face learning in the classroom can change attitudes; distributed learning is effective only for conveying information. This view places learning types on a continuum that moves from attitudinal skills through psychomotor skills to cognitive skills. The types are sometimes called learning of the heart, learning of the hands and learning of the mind. Delivery channels are placed on a parallel continuum that moves from face-to-face classroom learning, through virtual classrooms, e-mentoring, EPSS, and so on — but always ends with self-paced e-learning courses. At the heart of the assumption is a belief that only by looking someone in the eye can you change their attitudes. I don't buy it. Here's why.

False distinctions

The distinction between learning that changes the learner's attitude and learning that doesn't is false — at least it is in the enterprise. Learning that does not change the attitude of a learner is no learning at all because it cannot improve performance. All learning needs to be attitudinal. It's a common complaint that even employees who know best practice don't follow it. Take security. Why don't staff change their network passwords and back up their data as often as they know they should? They've learned the processes; they recognize the importance. That they're short of time is a given. What's probably lacking is a sense of personal responsibility for security within the enterprise. To be effective, learning about security needs to engage learners' minds, hands and hearts. Knowing isn't enough; learning needs to be realized through doing. In the enterprise, there is no such thing as pure cognitive learning that can be safely assigned to distributed learning.

Ignoring precedents

The physical or virtual presence of an instructor is one way of engaging learners' hearts but by no means the only way. The delivery channel that has had the greatest impact on how people think, feel and act, that has had the power to change history is the humble book — the ultimate asynchronous, distributed, self-paced, self-directed learning channel. There is nothing face-to-face about the book — it does, however, engage the reader both mind to mind and heart to heart. Authors change attitudes and behaviours every day.

When we describe a book as a "page turner", we are complimenting the author on their ability to engage us so deeply we just about lose control of the reading process; ironically, when we describe a self-paced e-learning course as a "page turner", we are censuring its author for delivering an unengaging linear experience. Using the same expression to mean opposite things is a result of contrasting expectations. Learners expect e-learning content to be interactive — but they also expect it to be fresh, just-in-time, authentic, solution-centred, relevant, integrated with their work, and so on.

If the text-based book has the power both to inform and change behaviours, why do we assume that these abilities are beyond e-learning which has an arsenal of presentation tools at its disposal? In the context of learning in the enterprise, why do we assume that only face-to-face learning has the power to engage meaningfully? Here's my answer: we are not good enough yet at developing self-paced, self-directed e-learning content. Different surveys give slightly different results but I think it's accurate to say that in 2002 two-thirds of US enterprises delivered two-thirds of learning using traditional channels, in other words, the classroom. There are many more experienced classroom instructors than there are e-learning instructional designers and developers. Instructional design itself is still coming to terms with learning distributed through Internet technologies.

I'm not saying no one knows how to design and develop effective e-learning; I am saying the people who do are in a small minority. The majority (1) lack the vision and imagination to exploit e-learning's potential, or (2) lack the skills, budgets and possibly support to realize the vision, or (3) reject the vision because it makes them uncomfortable — and maybe that's the most important point. It's a truism that change — especially technology-driven change — is not always comfortable. However, unless we're prepared both to challenge our assumptions about delivery channels and to raise the bar on the quality and nature of e-learning content, we will fail to transform learning in the enterprise.

It isn't easy to develop e-learning content with the power to change attitudes and behaviours. It takes energy, application, subject matter expertise, technical know-how, empathy and creativity. To engage the right and left sides of the learner's brain — another way of talking about cognitive and attitudinal skills — you have to engage both sides of your own. In *Drawing on the Right Side of the Brain*, Betty Edwards explains their roles: "The left hemisphere analyses, abstracts, counts, marks time, plans step-by-step procedures, verbalizes, makes rational statements based on logic ... On the other hand, we have a second way of knowing: the right-hemisphere mode ... We see how things exist in space and how parts go together to make up the whole. Using the right hemisphere, we understand metaphors, we dream, we create new combinations of ideas ... In the right-hemisphere mode of information processing, we use intuition and have leaps of insight—moments when "everything seems to fall into place" without figuring things out in a logical order. When this occurs, people often spontaneously exclaim, "I've got it" ..." [5]

Only when you have fully engaged the learner in this way can you change attitudes and behaviours. That engagement can result from reading a good book or taking a well designed, well executed self-directed self-paced e-learning course. Of course, it can also happen in the classroom but not automatically as many people appear to assume; a bad classroom learning experience isn't inherently better than a good e-learning experience. At this point, it's fair to ask, What is it, if anything, the classroom does better than other delivery channels? It can facilitate face-to-face interaction between learners.

For some kinds of learning, this interaction can be significant. The Dow Chemical Company has discovered real benefits in bringing leaders together for face-to-face learning, so has IBM. Seventy-five per cent of its Basic Blue for Managers course is delivered through e-learning channels, 25% in the classroom where the focus is on building relationships and communities through learning labs, mentoring, role playing, coaching and case studies. (For more about Basic Blue, see p. 65.)

What you need to do

The goal is to design a learning solution that leverages the learning value chain in your enterprise. Make it a team task involving the project leader, a subject matter expert, an instructional designer and, if neither has experience in developing e-learning content, make sure the team includes someone who does. On the one hand you have a number of drivers to consider; on the other hand, a number of channels to choose from. Drivers and chancels don't necessarily map one to one. Many drivers are interrelated, so are some delivery channels. Not every enterprise will have the same delivery channels available. In the end you need to make an informed judgement about whether to deliver through (1) a single channel and which one, or (2) multiple channels and which ones in what sequence (see Figure 12.2).

Speed to market

In the connected economy, the ability to respond quickly is as critical for learning as it is for product development, manufacture and marketing. How

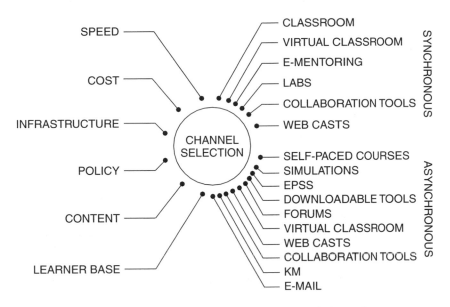

Figure 12.2 — Channel selection: drivers and channels

important is speed to market for the learning solution under consideration? If the learning is related to a merger or acquisition, a new product line, a new go to market strategy, the emergence of a new competitor or competitive product range, speed will be critical. The fastest way to get a simple message to large learner base is through a series of live Web casts or live virtual classes. Both can be recorded and made available 24/7 after the live event. The speed associated with Web casts and virtual classes isn't just about live delivery but also about the speed of content development relative to self-paced e-learning courses.

Cost

Cost can be an upfront constraint on learning solutions. There are two basic costs: (1) content development and (2) content delivery. It turns out that content that is cheap to develop — instructor-led classroom courses — is expensive to deliver, while content that is expensive to develop — self-paced e-learning — is cheap to deliver. Virtual classrooms are not the answer to every learning need but they do deliver content that is inexpensive to develop inexpensively.

Size of learner base is important when assessing the impact of cost on delivery channel selection. Below a certain number of learners, it can prove impossible to justify the cost of developing self-paced e-learning content. Though important, remember that cost might not be the key driver.

Channel selection is one of the first things you need to consider, not an afterthought. Costs associated with delivery channels should form part of every business plan developed in support of learning solutions.

Infrastructure

The effectiveness of e-learning in all its forms makes assumptions about the reach and robustness of an enterprise's infrastructure. Web casts and virtual classes might be the fastest way to deliver a learning message across an enterprise but only if the infrastructure can deliver multimedia content (1) to all learners and (2) to large numbers of concurrent learners. If one-third of your learners are based in a region where intranet bandwidth is limited, you're going to need to find an alternative delivery channel for them. If your infrastructure is already operating at maximum throughput, your IT department is not going to be sympathetic to the idea of large numbers of learners accessing a Web cast concurrently. Using third-party video Web cast services like Yahoo Broadcast Solutions and Real Broadcast Network can reduce the load on a network's servers but doesn't reduce the impact on its bandwidth. If your infrastructure is neither consistent nor robust, you might need to think about using e-mail to deliver learning messages fast, but don't incur the wrath of your IT department — and colleagues — by attaching huge files. The extra load can reduce e-mail traffic to a crawl.

Policies and targets

Learning policies and targets can influence your selection of delivery channels. For example, an enterprise-wide target of delivering 75% of all learning through e-learning channels could change your selection from face-to-face classroom learning to virtual classroom learning. A policy of high-investment in learning that supports accounts with the greatest profit potential might lead you to select high cost, high impact delivery channels even when there are less expensive options available.

Content: Lifecycle

All content has a lifecycle separate from the development lifecycle. Strategies, processes, tools, techniques, approaches and legislation all start as notions and develop over time; eventually, most fall out of fashion, are disproved or superseded. The content lifecycle should be considered when selecting delivery channels. Making an investment in a long self-paced course for content that is embryonic or about to be superseded is counter-productive. Look instead to channels that lend themselves to fast, cost-effective content development.

Self-paced and instructor-led courses are appropriate for stable content with a long lifecycle.

Content: Refresh cycle

The content refresh cycle is related to content lifecycle but is not the same. It describes how frequently content needs to be updated during its lifecycle. A course about project management or safe driving theory will be on a long refresh cycle and, as a result, justify an investment in a large self-paced e-learning course. In contrast, the bulk of courses about fast changing e-business processes might be best confined to virtual classes and mini-courses with inexpensive development costs and fast updates.

Learner base: Size

Small numbers of learners suggest face-to-face or virtual classes; large numbers, Web casts, large virtual classes and self-paced e-learning courses. Very large numbers might indicate a need to cater to differences within the group with focused learning channels like e-mentoring.

   The size of a learner base can be related to the content lifecycle. The longer the lifecycle, the larger the learner base. Five hundred learners in one year might not justify an investment in a self-paced course but if the course has a 5-year lifecycle — for example, a vision and values course for new joiners — the learner base is really 2500.

Learner base: Geographic spread

If your learner base numbers 25 and they all work in the same region, an instructor-led class is the obvious solution. If they all work in the same city, bring the instructor to the learners and pay one set of travel and accommodation expenses instead of 25. If the learners are spread around the world, a virtual class supported by e-mentoring and peer collaboration is a more appropriate solution. If the 25 learners happen to be the senior executives, no matter where they are based the cost of bringing them together for a face-to-face session can be justified. The session might have some prerequisite online learning and be followed up with e-mentoring and online collaboration.

   If your learner base numbers 10 000 spread across all continents, virtual classes and self-paced courses are obvious delivery channels. With a learner base that diverse and dispersed, remember localization. Are translation and cultural adjustments required? You might decide to develop a large self-paced e-learning course in English for all learners but to follow that up with virtual classes in the local language to deal with local issues as simple as different names for job titles and equipment or as complex as religious practice and cultural sensitivities. Build localization costs into your business plan.

Learner base: E-learning experience and access

Consider whether your learner base has had previous experience of e-learning and whether they have easy access to network systems. A lack of previous experience shouldn't stop you from using e-learning channels but might make you consider supporting them with instructor led classes — or introducing self-paced e-learning as part of face-to-face classes.

Be realistic about intranet access. If it's difficult for a group of learners — off-site workers or plant technicians, for example — to get time on network systems, using e-learning delivery channels is a disincentive to learning. Access is unlikely to be improved for just one course; it is usually a constraint that needs to be addressed on a long-term basis. However, critical time-sensitive content — for example, a course that is required learning for all staff in order to comply with new legislation — can be a powerful lever for improving access to the network. Sometimes access has to do with time constraints. Shift workers and sales staff, for example, might be unable to access scheduled face-to-face and virtual classes. For these learners, self-paced courses with 24/7 access are effective.

References

1   Tapscott D (2001) *Rethinking Strategy in a Networked World* Strategy + Business Magazine Third Quarter 2001 [Internet] Available from <http://www.strategy-business.com/media/pdf/01304.pdf> Accessed 31 Jun 2002.
2   Singh H and Reed C (2001) *Achieving Success with Blended Learning* Centra Software [White paper] [Internet] Available from <http://www.centra.com/download/whitepapers/blendedlearning.pdf> Accessed 31 May 2002.
3   Gardner H (1999) *Individually Configured Education: The Key Educational Imperative of Multiple Intelligences* [Excerpt] [Internet] Available from <http://www.angelfire.com/oh/themidasnews/00mar03.html> Accessed 6 Dec 2001.
4   Zemke R (1998) *Wake Up! (And Reclaim Instructional Design)* Training Magazine June 1998 Vol 35 No 6 p 36.
5   Edwards B (1979) *Drawing on the Right Side of the Brain* Los Angeles, JP Tarcher Inc p 35.

13 Learner support: learning with the aid of a safety net

E-learner support is seen as important to the success of e-learning, although nearly one-quarter of e-learning organizations currently do not use any type of support. Not surprisingly over half of these organizations feel that their e-learning is not very or not at all successful. Xebec McGraw-Hill[1]

What you need to know

A well designed e-learning system is completely learner-centric. Every element is there to support learning and the learner. That's why I'm always surprised to find e-mentoring, collaboration tools and peer-to-peer communication described as learner support. They are delivery channels in the learning value chain; they don't support learning, they *are* learning. Learner support is a safety net to catch the learner when interactions between the learner and the system don't go the way the learner or, more accurately, we thought they would. The role of learner support is not to handle learning but exceptions to learning.

One of the things you'll never hear anyone say is that the e-learning initiative failed because there was too much learner support. Learners need and deserve as much support as we can give them. Ultimately, exceptions to learning occur because the learning system we implement is imperfect; it follows that we have a responsibility to help learners when our system fails them.

Learners' difficulties come in different shapes and sizes; support should be designed to match their nature and seriousness. Five levels of support can usually deal with any exception that turns up:

- Level 1: Online help files.
- Level 2: Technology support.
- Level 3: Application support.
- Levels 4 and 5: Content support.

Level 1 support is self-help — all other levels are accessed through a help desk. You might question the need for live support; after all, it's relatively expensive and can pose management challenges. However, the human factor does seem very important to learners as Wired News observed: "Company executives and marketing consultants say over half the calls to US tech support address issues that are already discussed in manuals provided with products. And even though they suspect that no one in the United States has ever read an entire product manual, companies continue to provide them ... "[2] Apparently, users of software information systems—which is what learners are—prefer to resolve difficulties by talking to people, not reading instructions.

What you need to do

Help desk

Ideally, the help desk will be dedicated to e-learning, although in some circumstances it can make sense to share an existing help desk with IT, Human Resources, or Knowledge Management. Outsourcing the help desk has advantages; there are no infrastructure issues to contend with and it might make it easier to provide full-time support. If you're delivering e-learning across time zones or have staff who work flexible hours, you need to think carefully about when support will be available. Global organizations need to decide whether to have a single help desk location operating 24/7 or whether to have a help desk located in each region, for example, one for Europe, the Middle East and Africa, one for the Americas, and one for Asia-Pacific. With a little planning, you can cover the globe with just three help desks and without subjecting help staff to particularly unsocial hours.

To ensure that learners can always contact the help desk, it's a good idea to provide two robust communication options, usually telephone and e-mail. Learners should be able to use the same telephone number and e-mail address no matter which help desk is active. That means employing "intelligent call processing" to connect learners to the active help desk transparently even when it is in a different part of the world. Instant Messaging offers an alternative to e-mail. Some third-party help services use IM to support e-commerce Web sites but its ephemeral nature doesn't facilitate data capture which is an important consideration. By using the intranet for voice communication, VoIP (voice over Internet Protocol) offers an alternative to conventional telephony. It has some weaknesses and one very big benefit. Its weaknesses:

- The quality of the conversation is constrained by bandwidth availability.
- VoIP requires the learner's system to be equipped with a microphone—increasingly, a standard feature on laptops but not yet on desktop systems.
- When the learning portal goes down, VoIP goes down with it.

The big benefit of VoIP is the user-friendliness and immediacy of having a button on every learning page which is labelled: "Click me to talk to the help desk". Many e-commerce Web sites have seen sales and repeat business increase dramatically after implementing VoIP-based support.

If you have been able to integrate your e-learning application with the enterprise e-mail system, it's a good idea to build a feature that launches a pre-addressed e-mail with a single click and incorporates a form designed to help the learner include all pertinent details of their problem.

Ideally, the help desk should be supported by a CRM-style (Customer Relationship Management) application that provides a help "account" for each learner, allows help desk staff easily to enter and store details of problems in the account — either from a telephone call or an e-mail — and to track the progress and resolution of problems. It would be very useful if the application allows agents to access the learning record of learners who contact the help desk to see (1) how experienced an e-learner they are, and (2) what courses they are taking at the time. This information can help the help desk agent tailor their help to the learner's individual needs and experience.

Target response times for each help level should be published and actual response times tracked to monitor whether targets are being met. Every learner who brings a problem to the help desk should be given an estimate of when their question will be answered or problem resolved.

Level 1: Online help files

Like any user-friendly application, your e-learning application should be supported by integrated online help files. Generally these include:

- Getting Started
- IIow To . . . (common tasks)
- Alphabetical listing of Help content
- System Status
- FAQ (Frequently Asked Questions)
- Help desk details

This self-help resource should cover the standard features and functions of both courses and the e-learning application including all sub-systems like virtual classrooms and collaboration tools. If a course has non-standard features and functions, these should be supported by integrated course help files. The FAQ should be a living document updated on a regular basis from the problems and resolutions captured in the CRM system. The initial FAQ can be developed from what has been learned during User Acceptance Testing — and by having help desk agents and the application designers "walk through" likely problem scenarios. The System Status page displays up-to-the-minute system information. If there has been a server or hard drive failure, it is more effective for help desk agents to post the information once on the System Status page along with an estimate of when normal service will be restored than to deal with hundreds of duplicate phone calls and e-mails. Full details about the help desk — operating hours, e-mail address, telephone number, response times, etc. — are another important feature of an online help system.

Level 2: Technology support

The challenge for the e-learning help desk is to distinguish between a genuine technology issue and other issue types which can also prevent a learner from using the e-learning application. For example, if a learner's computer has crashed recently, the operating system, browser or plug-ins might have been corrupted. The result can make it look as if the e-learning application is broken when the problem is specific to the learner's system. Another example of a pure technology problem might be an unexpected shortage of bandwidth across the enterprise. It could leave the e-learning application unusable. When an enterprise-wide technology issue arises, the System Status page should be used to alert learners to the situation. Savvy learners will have a good idea that something's wrong at the infrastructure level because all network applications are likely to be affected.

Technology problems should be escalated to the IT help desk because that's where the expertise and resources to solve technology issues reside. It's important to develop an escalation process and for the two help desks to work together. The last thing you want is a learner caught between e-learning and IT with one side claiming it's a technology issue and the other counter-claiming it's an application issue. Of course, there can be technology issues with the e-learning application. The Support team should work with the IT help desk to develop a triage process: a series of questions designed to establish whether the problem is with the learner's system, the infrastructure or the e-learning application. In some situations, the IT department will be responsible for the maintenance of all three; in others, e-learning vendors or other third parties will be responsible for the maintenance of the application and need to be informed as soon as possible.

Level 3: Application support

Level 3 Support assumes that there are no technology issues involved and the learner is simply having difficulty using the e-learning application. The learner might not be able to register for a self-paced course, or be confused about how to ask a question during a virtual class. Help desk agents should be able to resolve all Level 3 issues themselves. It is important these issues are conscientiously logged in the help desk CRM system since they might reveal defects in the application interface that developers can correct in subsequent releases. Level 3 issues might also reveal shortcomings in the online help files.

Level 4: Content support

Content support is about helping a learner to understand some aspect of content in a self-paced e-learning course. Level 4 Content Support is delivered by help desk agents themselves or in conjunction with the course's instructional designers. It is limited to the content in the course and does not attempt to provide additional content or project-specific advice. Again, Level 4 issues need to be carefully logged since they can reveal defects in instructional design or content presentation.

To deliver Level 4 support effectively, help desk agents need to take each new course and to bring their own queries to the course designers and developers. One way of exposing help desk agents to new content is to include them in all User Acceptance Testing. Not every help desk agent needs to be familiar with every course; agents can share their knowledge of courses.

Level 5: Content support

Level 5 Content Support escalates a learner's query about course content to a subject matter expert. One way of setting up the framework for Level 5 is to have a Service Level Agreement between the learning department and every business unit or central service unit that sponsors a course. The SLA places an obligation on the business unit to support its course by providing subject matter experts for ongoing Level 5 Content Support. It sounds onerous but if it's well organized it needn't be and the alternative — a catalogue of unsupported courses — won't be acceptable to an enterprise that has made a commitment to changing the way its employees learn.

Some subject matter experts can prove reluctant to become involved because they have had negative experiences of becoming locked into extended dialogues with a learner who is really looking for a personal mentor rather than an SME. You can work round this concern by using the help desk as a go-between eliminating direct communication between the learner and the SME. Since all e-mails from the SME are sent to the help desk rather than the learner, this approach has the added advantage of facilitating knowledge capture. The SME's input can be incorporated in a course-specific FAQ for help desk agents engaged in Level 4 Support and built into subsequent versions of the course.

References

1   *Corporate E-Learning ... Realizing the Potential* (2001) Xebec McGraw-Hill [Internet] Available from <http://www.nln.ac.uk/delg/keydocuments/DELG%2001%20007.pdf> Accessed 29 Apr 2002.
2   Delio M (2002) *Read The F***ing Story, Then RTFM* Wired News 4 June 2002 [Internet] Available from <http://www.wired.com/news/culture/0,1284,52901,00.html> Accessed 6 Jun 2002.

Developing curricula: signposted paths to performance improvement

14

If you fail to keep current from a competency point of view, as an individual, the degree of success you can expect to experience in your career will tend to be limited. The risks to an organization are equally severe as we enter the 21st century. You either become a learning organization or lose your competitive edge. Robert L Dilworth[1]

Web-enabled e-learning environments allow for creation of more highly customized and flexible competency-based learning plans than has been possible in the past. Gena Tuso and Warren Longmire[2]

What you need to know

A course catalogue assigns no value to courses; it simply presents what is available. Ideally, it should also support learner-defined searches. Curricula are subsets of the catalogue organized to deliver value as well as information to the learner. Curricula are signposted paths to performance improvement. They can be defined as sets of courses, learning objects and learning events designed to meet known competency and performance requirements within an enterprise. Historically, curricula have been organized around *knowledge* but that doesn't apply in the enterprise — as Jonathon D. Levy, Vice President of E-learning Programs at Harvard Business Online explains: "The desired outcome of the traditional educational process is the retention of knowledge, while the desired outcome of enterprise learning is performance of a task in a manner that increases both individual and corporate competitiveness. In the workplace, learning is about competency."[3]

So, what is competency? In *Learning Without Limits*, Gena Tuso and Warren Longmire offer this definition: "... competency is the qualification and ability to perform a task or job effectively. A more technical and widely used articulation of competencies describes a competency as "a cluster of related knowledge, skills, and attitudes that affects a major part of one's job (a role or responsibility), that correlates with performance on the job, that can be measured against well-accepted standards, and that can be improved via training and development" (Parry, 1996). The key elements of this definition for e-learning implementations are performance, measurement, and improvement."[4]

Levy draws a cause and effect relationship between competency and performance: if you are competent, you will perform. In the cut, thrust and complexity of business, there are many reasons why that assumption is optimistic and needs to be guarded against. What stands between competency and performance is attitude and behaviour: how — or whether — a learner actions a competency. What is true is that knowledge-based curricula do not deliver performance improvements, instead they lead to just-in-case learning when what the learner and the enterprise need is just-in-time learning.

The closer a curriculum matches the roles and responsibilities of a learner, the more effective it is. That is why the qualities of learner-centred learning include: personalized, authentic, relevant and integrated with work. (See p. 29 for more about these qualities.) It is very helpful to learners if the learning value chain and course catalogue are supported by curricula designed for particular roles, responsibilities and career paths. However, a personal curriculum is the best curriculum. "Personal Learning Path" or "Personal Development Plan" are common names for personal curricula. Learning paths can be personalized by different criteria and to different degrees:

Criteria	**Degree**
Job type, for example:	• By course
• executive	• By course module
• manager	• By knowledge object
• performer	
User profile, for example:	
• role	
• theatre of work	
• business unit	
• language	
• clients	
• products	
• technologies	
• career ladder	
Status, for example:	
• entry level	
• experienced	
• top performer	
Competency modelling	
Competency assessment results	
Evaluation, for example, by:	
• line manager	
• coach or mentor	
• peers	

Not all curricula are personal. Some are core, for example, curricula covering corporate vision and values, and new joiner orientation; others are local — often based on legislation governing commercial practice, employment, health and safety, and personal data protection.

Some Learning Management Systems have optional modules designed to help you model and manage competencies, and later to map learning content to competencies to create personal learning paths. These competency and performance modules can sometimes be integrated with an enterprise HR system.

The role of learning objects

A survey conducted by International Data Corporation (IDC) and *Online Learning* Magazine revealed that 77% of companies with e-learning delivery channels use course completions as a measure of learning success. In terms of usage, no other metric even comes close; at 55%, comparing pre- and post-course assessment scores is the second most common metric.[5] It's easy to understand course completion's popularity as a metric: Nothing is easier to track. The LMS or LCMS automatically records completions and dumps the resulting data into a report. What's not so easy to understand is the relationship between course completions and impact on performance, as Harvard Business Online, with over 1.5 million corporate e-learners, discovered: "Last year we learned that one of our largest customers was renewing their contract for a particular program despite the fact that less than 10% of their managers had finished all of the sections required for "completion". It turned out that most managers had no intention of "completing" in the conventional sense, but they employed the learning modules frequently as a performance-support tool to help them succeed in their business initiatives. The course completion metric was useless in determining value."[6]

What's just as useless is delivering content to individual learners that they neither need nor will use; however, if the lowest level of content granularity is a course, over-delivery is inevitable. Course designers don't know the needs of individual learners; they have no choice but to create knowledge-based courses that match the needs of the novice and over-deliver to everyone else. While sophisticated course designs can use the outcome of a pre-assessment to provide the learner with a customized path through course content, the underlying question is, should we be designing and developing courses in the first place? Are they remnants of a pre-digital publishing mindset? In *Small Pieces Loosely Joined*, David Weinberger suggests they are: "The Web ... breaks the traditional publishing model. The older model is about control: a team works on a document, is responsible for its content and format, and releases it to the public when it's been certified as done. Once it's published no one can change it except the original publisher. The Web ditches that model ... The result is a loose federation of documents — many small pieces loosely joined ... It treats tightly bound volumes like a collection of ideas — none longer than can fit on a single screen — that the reader can consult in the order she or he wants, regardless of the author's intentions."[7]

Learning objects are e-learning's small pieces loosely joined. There are many reasons for adopting an object-oriented approach to content; the one that is relevant here is the ability to custom build a course on the fly that exactly meets a learner's needs. The course never existed before the learner's needs demanded it and might never be assembled again — though the learning objects, the building blocks, from which it was built were stored in a central repository. Learning objects pose challenges — in technology, instructional design, content management and ROI. Like so many aspects of e-learning even defining learning objects has been challenging. Here are two definitions that I believe are compatible:

Learning Object Guru David Wiley: "... this study will define a "learning object" as "any digital resource that can be reused to support learning." This definition includes anything that can be delivered across the network on demand, be it large or small. Examples of smaller reusable digital resources include images or photos, live data feeds (like stock tickers), live or prerecorded video or audio snippets, small bits of text, animations, and smaller web-delivered applications, like a Java calculator. Examples of larger reusable digital resources include entire web pages that combine text, images and other media or applications to deliver complete experiences, such as a complete instructional event."[8]

Cisco Systems: Cisco's definition reflects its two-tier approach to learning objects. "Training offerings need to move from large, inflexible "courses" to reusable, granular objects that can be written independent of a delivery media and accessed dynamically through a database. The Reusable Information Object (RIO) Strategy describes how this is being done at Cisco Systems. The RIO Strategy is built upon the Reusable Information Object (RIO). An RIO is granular, reusable chunk of information that is media independent. An RIO can be developed once, and delivered in multiple delivery mediums. Each RIO can stand alone as a collection of content items, practice items and assessment items that are combined based on a single learning objective. Individual RIOs are then combined to form a larger structure called a Reusable Learning Object (RLO)."[9]

Despite the challenges, if the goal of e-learning is to leverage Internet technologies to deliver highly targeted learning that improves individual and corporate performance by closing personal competency gaps, learning objects point to a solution. With personalized competency-driven courses, each learner learns only what they need to learn, not what course designers thought they needed to learn. Neither does a learner have to cover content they already know because courses and learning paths are designed to address specific performance gaps.

What you need to do

Competency model

Populating a learning system with content should begin with the development of a competency model — a definition of the competencies that support each role in the enterprise. If you intend to leverage e-learning across your whole value chain, you'll need to develop a competency model that includes partners, suppliers, sales channels and customers. Such a model might already exist. If it doesn't, there are a number of established methodologies for creating one. Approaches include consulting professional publications, live observations of top performers, and interviews with subject matter experts. Third-party HR vendors and professional associations publish competency models for executives, managers and performers in all businesses. These can form a useful starting point for your own models although they need to be validated by your own top performers and SMEs whose performance the models describe.

Inevitably, you will end up with an unworkably large list of competencies associated with each role. Since you will not be able to include them all in a curriculum, test your top performers in each role to determine the shared competencies that set them apart from the crowd. The subset that emerges will form the curriculum for that role. This isn't a one-off activity. Every 6 months or year, test your top performers again to ensure that competencies are accurately mapped to performance.

Training Magazine ranked Pfizer Inc as the best learning organization in its Training Top 100 of 2002. Pfizer's Capability Continuum, which defines the different levels of skills or competencies that are required within each job family from entry level to the most senior positions, figured large in the magazine's assessment: "In Pfizer's Animal Health Division, where training activities are primarily geared toward the salesforce, the company worked with sales management to develop a set of behaviour-based competencies that each salesperson is measured against on a semiannual basis; the development plan of each salesperson is originated and updated based on these reviews.

As historical data is accumulated, Pfizer cross-references the assessments with the sales results of each individual as compared to their area, region and the nation. This measurement provides Pfizer with answers to two critical questions: Are the behaviours that training is attempting to improve getting better (formative evaluation) and are the improved behaviours making a difference in sales results (summative evaluation)? When combined with management input, Pfizer is quickly able to identify performance issues as well as evaluate the real benefit of the training programmes."[10] This is Kirkpatrick Level 4 evaluation; according to ASTD, only 3% of companies implement it. Based on this report, Pfizer turns out to be one of them.

Courses and curricula

With a competency model in place, you can start designing and developing content to deliver the knowledge — the actionable information — that supports the competencies. Draw on the whole learning value chain in your enterprise. If you have the vision, develop learning objects instead of courses for e-learning delivery channels. Learning objects make a lot of sense with a competency based approach to content because elements of competencies turn up in many roles creating opportunities for reuse of content.

You might be able to license off-the-shelf e-learning courses to support some competencies especially if they involve IT skills. When you have the content in place, develop a curriculum for each role in the enterprise. Because this is a large undertaking, you'll need to prioritize the roles where there is the greatest need for performance improvement. You might also prioritize your effort by roles associated with your highest value clients or most lucrative markets. With role-driven curricula in place, each learner has a learning path to guide them to improved performance.

Personal learning paths

Role-based curricula don't take account of employees' interests and aspirations. Only a personal learning path can do that. At a technology level, the Learning Management System should allow a learner and her line manager to design a personal learning path by adding learning content that reflects her personal and longer term career interests as well as essential role competencies. Figure 18.3 on p. 319 illustrates how PwC Consulting approaches employees' personal learning needs. Ideally, an employee's personal mix of essential and interest-driven content should be established with their line manager as part of regular performance review meetings. Some enterprises might want system rights set so only line managers can input personal learning paths; other enterprises might be comfortable with employees inputting their own. A learner's personal learning path should be accessible from their learning home page and include a display of the learner's progress through the material.

Evaluation

Competency models and curricula are powerful tools that allow an enterprise to focus learning on critical performance areas but they are not magic wands. On their own, competence-based curricula do not guarantee that competency will translate into performance. It's important that curricula are supported by a programme of ongoing evaluation that focuses on the relationship between competency and performance. When competency does not lead to improved performance, you need to ask whether you have chosen the wrong competencies for the role or whether disconnect lies in the learner's behaviour, that is, the effort that turns competency into performance.

References

1 Dilworth RL (1998) *Action Learning in a Nutshell* Performance Improvement Quarterly 1998 11(1) p. 34.

2   Tuso G and Longmire W (2000) *Competency-Based Systems and the Delivery of Learning Content* Learning Without Limits Vol 3 [Internet] Available from <http://www.learnativity.com/download/LwoL3.pdf> Accessed 8 Jun 2002.

3   Levy JD (2001) *Measuring and Maximizing Results through eLearning* Harvard Business Online [White paper] [Internet] Available from <http://www.people.cornell.edu/pages/jl63/Measuring_and_Maximizing_Results102401.doc> Accessed 8 Jun 2002.

4   Tuso G and Longmire W (2000) *Competency-Based Systems and the Delivery of Learning Content* Learning Without Limits Vol 3 [Internet] Available from <http://www.learnativity.com/download/LwoL3.pdf> Accessed 8 Jun 2002.

5   International Data Corporation and Online Learning Magazine (2001) *State of the Industry Report 2001* Online Learning Magazine October 2001 [Internet] Available from <http://www.onlinelearningmag.com/onlinelearning/images/pdf/2001state_of_industry.pdf> Accessed 8 May 2002.

6   Levy JD (2001) *Measuring and Maximizing Results through eLearning* Harvard Business Online [White paper] [Internet] Available from <http://www.people.cornell.edu/pages/jl63/Measuring_and_Maximizing_Results102401.doc> Accessed 8 Jun 2002.

7   Weinberger D (2002) *Small Pieces Loosely Joined—A Unified Theory of the Web* Cambridge MA, Perseus Publishing pp viii–ix.

8   Wiley DA (2000) *Learning Object Design and Sequencing Theory* Brigham Young University [Dissertation] [Internet] Available from <http://wiley.ed.usu.edu/docs/dissertation.pdf> Accessed 9 Jun 2002.

9   Barritt C Lewis D and Wieseler W (1999) *Reusable Information Object Strategy* Cisco Systems [White paper] [Internet] Available from <http://www.cisco.com/warp/public/779/ibs/solutions/learning/whitepapers/el_cisco_rio.pdf> Accessed 9 Jun 2002.

10 Galvin T (2002) *The 2002 Training Top 100* Training Magazine 21 February 2002 [Internet] Available from <http://www.trainingmag.com/training/reports_analysis/feature_display.jsp?vnu_content_id =1350647> Accessed 3 Apr 2002.

E-learning standards: protecting investment and leveraging technology

15

The successful companies select a few standards and enforce them strictly. Bill Gates[1]

We know two things for sure about learning standards and metadata: (1) We have to have them if we are going to see e-learning take off. (2) Initially, they are very confusing to most people. Wayne Hodgins, Director of Worldwide Learning Strategies, Autodesk Inc[2]

What you need to know

You can't buy an LMS or develop e-learning content without first doing battle with the fire-breathing hydra known as e-learning standards. At least that's the conventional wisdom. Correcting misconceptions is a good way to begin a discussion of e-learning standards:

- At the time of writing, there are no e-learning standards. That might not be the impression given by vendors' marketing messages but it's a fact.
- The so-called standards you've probably heard about — AICC, IMS, IEEE, LRN and SCORM — are not in competition with each other. One will not emerge as the winning standard; they are largely complementary.
- SCORM isn't a standard. It's a reference model for a suite of standards developed by other bodies.
- E-learning standards will not determine the quality or effectiveness of e-learning products; how vendors and developers implement standards will.

The current confusion surrounding e-learning standards is not a permanent feature of the technology or the market; it's a phase we're going through. The reason the confusion won't last is a simple phenomenon: As soon as they're published and implemented, standards become invisible. Our personal and working lives are filled with standards we never think about. Web developers never discuss HTTP or SMTP and POP; they just use them. We never think about PAL, NTSC or SECAM television; we just watch it. We don't contemplate the standards that define USB, serial and parallel port communication; we just attach devices. How much thought do you give to AAA batteries, size 9 shoes, and the books that specify CD-ROM, CD-A and DVD? Once a full set of e-learning standards is published and products that conform to them appear in the market, the current confusion about and fascination with standards will evaporate.

Why they matter

If you're new to the notion of e-learning standards, here is why they matter. During self-paced e-learning, there is an dialogue between:

- Content loaded in the learner's Web browser (client side), and
- the Learning Management System resident on a remote sever (server side).

This dialogue generates the learner's learning record and so allows managers to track progress at an individual and enterprise level. It can also affect what content is presented to the learner and in what order. Unless the content and the LMS are using the same language, the same syntax and the same vocabulary, they won't be able to communicate. Or, like a tourist with a smattering of a foreign language, they might "get by" but fail to exploit all features and functions built into the content and LMS.

Standards also give assurances to buyers about interoperability — the ability of a system or a product to work with other systems or products without special effort on the part of the customer. All content that conforms to an e-learning standard will run equally well on all LMSs that conform to the same standard.

The standards lifecycle

All standards have a development lifecycle comprised of a series of highly iterative and time consuming processes. Figure 15.1 illustrates the lifecycle for e-learning standards. It begins with a perceived need and some R&D concepts. By exposing these notions to interested consortia, draft specifications can be developed. When there is consensus about the specifications, they're exposed to labs and test beds to see whether the theory works in practice. Draft specifications should also be exposed to the market to see whether they make sense commercially. Once there's evidence that the agreed specification works, the test results — in the form of a reference model — are sent to a standards body for third-party validation, then accreditation. Once a standard has been accredited, a global standards body, like ISO, can promote it to an approved international standard — a process that can itself take a number of years.

An approved standard is sometimes called a de jure standard, that is, a standard according to law. There is another way for a standard to come into common usage — by becoming a de facto standard, that is, a standard in fact even if not by right. If an LMS or content vendor independently developed a set of proprietary e-learning standards then so dominated the e-learning

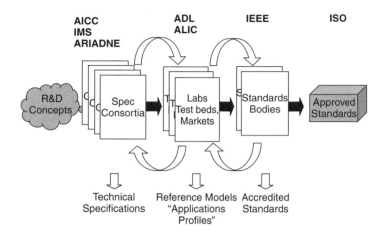

Figure 15.1 — E-learning standards lifecycle[3]
Reproduced by permission of Philip Dodds — ADL

market that their proprietary standards — developed without consultation, third-party validation, or formal approval — reached a critical mass, they would have become de facto standards.

There are many examples of important and useful de facto standards in computing: Microsoft Internet Explorer and Netscape Navigator Web browsers, the Hayes command set for modems, and Adobe's PostScript page description language for laser printers. It's possible that e-learning might embrace a de facto standard though to date no vendor has demonstrated enough muscle in the market. A de facto standard will only emerge if one vendor makes such a breakthrough in technology that all the standards work done earlier becomes obsolete. It's unlikely. All important vendors — commercially and in terms of expertise — are committed to the current standards process.

Because no e-learning specifications have so far been approved, vendors who claim that their LMS or content conforms to a standard are glossing over reality. It's more likely their product complies with some aspects of draft specifications and enhances them with proprietary features. Working out where compliance with draft specifications ends and proprietary features begin is tricky. Some proprietary features anticipate future standards but if vendors guess wrong, their proprietary features will end up as non-standard features.

Realistically, e-learning standards, like any others, will take some time to be agreed and approved. So, what approach should you take in the interim? Start by developing an understanding of the benefits e-learning standards deliver.

The benefits

The benefits that e-learning standards are being developed to deliver are sometimes described as the "-abilities":[4]

- *Interoperability*—the ability to:
  - use all features and functions of content that conforms to a standard on any Learning Management System that conforms to the same standard;
  - have content authored by different vendors and publishers—using different authoring tools—running on the same Learning Management System and exploiting all the content's features and functions;
  - share data between enterprise systems without intervention, for example, enabling data generated by an LMS to be imported by an HR or financial system—and vice versa.
- *Reusability*—the ability to author, store and manage learning content as small compatible learning objects that can be used in combination over and over as elements of different courses.
- *Manageability*—the ability to track a learner's use of and interaction with content, and to store the resulting data in an LMS or LCMS as a learning record accessible by both the learner and management.
- *Accessibility*—the ability of:
  - the LMS or LCMS to access courses, and to access and sequence learning objects through the use of metadata and packaging standards;
  - many learners to access learning content stored remotely.
- *Durability*—the ability of content to support successive releases of LMS, LCMS and database applications without recoding or redesign.
- *Affordability*—the ability to leverage standardized technologies to increase development productivity and learning effectiveness while reducing costs.

Together, these abilities will:

- allow you to protect and leverage your investment in content development;
- prevent you from being locked into proprietary technology;
- give you control over the learning value chain in your enterprise.

A pragmatic approach

If you're a learning manager or project manager, you don't have to become a standards expert. You need to know only enough to make informed decisions that won't lock you out of the specific benefits standards can deliver to your e-learning implementation. That means you should know the areas current draft standards cover:

- content metadata
- content packaging
- content sequencing
- question and test interoperability
- learner profiles
- run-time environment

Content Metadata: Metadata is data about data. When you look at a Windows folder you see metadata about each file in the folder: its name, size, type and when it was last modified. To take advantage of the power of learning objects, you need to know more about files than Windows tells you. This is how the group working on Learning Objects Metadata describe, at a high level, the additional information: "Relevant attributes of Learning Objects to be described include type of object, author, owner, terms of distribution, and format. Where applicable, Learning Object Metadata may also include pedagogical attributes such as teaching or interaction style, grade level, mastery level, and prerequisites."[5]

Content Packaging: Learning objects have no value to the learner until they are assembled into a usable form. Content packaging is about creating a uniform method for organizing learning objects into courses and collections of courses that are themselves interoperable and portable. As well as the physical files, a content package always contains a file that describes (1) the contents of the package, (2) the order in which the learning objects should be assembled, and (3) their physical location.

Content Sequencing: Content sequencing is a standard for defining the order in which learning objects are encountered by the learner. In summer 2002, a draft specification emerged for sequencing linear and simple branching content, for example, using different content sequences based on the outcome of a pre-course evaluation. Only hard-wired sequences — those defined in advance by course designers — are supported by the specification; sequencing based on forms of artificial intelligence isn't.

Question and Test Interoperability (QTI): The aim is to provide a standard format to support interoperability of questions and tests between different computer systems. QTI doesn't define how an assessment works, how questions are presented to learners, or how results are analysed. It confines itself to defining the format in which question and test data are held. QTI should make it easy for instructional designers and developers to create large question banks and for a market in tests and questions to develop.

Learner Profiles: The aim is to provide a standardized way to package information about learners. The draft specification sets out 11 broad headings under which information can be stored. The structure can be extended to include other headings like financial information. Most of the 11 headings are optional and interoperability is not part of the specification. With information about the learner organized in a standard structure, the learning experience can be customized according to each learner's profile taking location, language, age and personal preferences into account.

Run-time Environment: The aim is to create standards that ensure every conformant LMS can launch all conformant content regardless of its author. The standards will prescribe how the LMS initiates and closes its dialogue (data exchange) with the content — and collects and stores data during the session.

Who's who in standards

E-learning standards are being developed around the world by a number of bodies each with their own areas of interest but who increasingly work in collaboration.

AICC <http://www.aicc.org>

AICC was formed in 1998. The name stands for the Aviation Industry CBT Committee. The aviation industry has always been a big investor in training. It was among the first sectors to recognize that as training becomes more reliant on technology, incompatible standards can undermine investment in training; conversely, global standards can leverage investment. Because AICC was one of the first bodies to publish specifications for tracking and interoperability, their work was seized upon by businesses outside the aviation industry. For years, AICC specifications were a de facto e-learning standard.

Vendors will tell you their products are "AICC compliant". That only means they have implemented some of the nine AICC guidelines. Since different vendors can implement different guidelines, AICC compliance does not ensure interoperability. You can have problems running AICC compliant generic content from different publishers on the same LMS. Fewer vendors will tell you that their products are "AICC certified". That means an AICC-authorized independent test lab has evaluated the products and certified that they meet the specification. AICC works closely with other standards bodies and makes important contributions to the standardization of content structure and the run-time environment, that is, launching content and tracking learner activity.

IMS Global Learning Consortium <http://www.imsproject.org>

IMS stands for Instructional Management System. The project began in 1997 within EDUCAUSE, a US non-profit group dedicated to advancing higher education through IT. Subsequently, IMS became an independent membership- and subscriber-funded consortium with members from education, commerce and government organizations. IMS has two key goals:

- "defining the technical specifications for interoperability of applications and services in distributed learning
- supporting the incorporation of the IMS specifications into products and services worldwide. IMS endeavours to promote the widespread adoption of specifications that will allow distributed learning environments and content from multiple authors to work together."[6]

IMS has been a pioneer in e-learning standards and an important player in the standards process. It makes contributions in the areas of metadata and content packaging.

IEEE *<http://ltsc.ieee.org>*

When most people hear Institute of Electrical and Electronics Engineers, Inc, they think about standards for consumer electronics, but IEEE is also a leading authority in technical areas including computer engineering, biomedical technology, telecommunications and aerospace. It is involved in e-learning standards through its Learning Technology Standards Committee (LTSC) whose mandate is to develop accredited technical standards, recommended practices and guides for learning technology. Within LTSC, 20 working groups are creating separate though related e-learning standards. In the standards lifecycle, IEEE is the body with a recognized charter to create standards. It provides independent evaluation of draft specifications developed by bodies like AICC and IMS with the ultimate aim of certifying a specification, then publishing it as a new standard.

ADL *<http://www.adlnet.org>*

In 1997, the Advanced Distributed Learning initiative was launched by the US Department of Defense, the White House Office of Science and Technology and the Department of Labor. No one spends more on training than the US Government. What it wanted to see, especially for the US military, was an acceleration in the adoption of advanced distributed learning technologies — for predictable reasons:

- leveraging technology to deliver more learning faster and for less cost;
- leveraging standardization to enable interoperability;
- leveraging learning objects to enable searchable, reusable content.

Rather than duplicate work being done elsewhere, ADL's strategy has been to provide a focus for other standards bodies by harmonizing their efforts in a reference model called SCORM — Small Content Object Reference Model. Until ADL took the lead, little effort had been made to connect different standards. ADL provides both a forum and technology test bed for the integration of specifications. ADL likes to think of SCORM as a kind of bookshelf which treats each separate draft specification as a separate book. Figure 15.2 shows how different standards groups have contributed to the reference model.

By 2002, there were three books: "Book 1 (The SCORM Overview) contains an overview of the ADL initiative, the rationale for the SCORM and a summary of the technical specifications and guidelines contained in the remaining sections. Book 2 (The SCORM Content Aggregation Model) contains guidance for identifying and aggregating resources into structured learning content ... Book 3 (The SCORM Run-Time Environment) includes guidance for launching, communicating with and tracking content in a Web-based environment."[8]

It's important to understand that SCORM was written for vendors and toolmakers, not content designers and developers. Late in 2002, ADL published a draft version of *SCORM Best Practices Guide for Content Developers*.

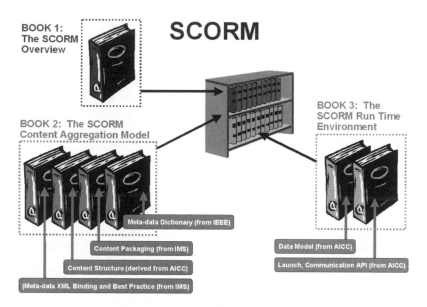

Figure 15.2 — The SCORM Bookcase[7]
Reproduced by permission of Philip Dodds — ADL

ARIADNE <http://www.ariadne-eu.org>

ARIADNE stands for the Alliance of Remote Instructional Authoring and Distribution Networks for Europe. Founded in 1997, the not-for-profit association was one of the pioneers in developing specifications for e-learning metadata and reusability. Here's how it describes its goals: "The project focuses on the development of tools and methodologies for producing, managing and reusing computer-based pedagogical elements and telematics supported training curricula. Validation of the project's concepts is currently taking place in various academic and corporate sites across Europe."[9] Along with IMS, ARIADNE contributed to the IEEE Learning Technology Standards Committee's Learning Object Metadata draft specification.

PROMETEUS <http://www.prometeus.org>

According to its Web site, "PROMETEUS is a European Partnership for a Common Approach to the Production of e-learning Technologies and Content".[10] The name stands for PROmoting Multimedia access to Education and Training in the EUropean Society. Membership is open to education authorities and institutions, businesses, training organizations, software and hardware vendors, infrastructure providers, publishers, content owners and standardization bodies. PROMETEUS describes the main goals of its members as:

- "... improving the effectiveness of the co-operation between education and training authorities and establishments, users of learning technologies, service and content providers and producers within the European Community including the Commission of the European Communities . . .

- . . . fostering the development of common European and international standards for digital multimedia learning content and services
- . . . giving a global dimension to their co-operation, and to having open and effective dialogues on issues relating to learning technologies policy with policy makers in other regions of the world, while upholding Europe's cultural interests and specificities."[11]

DCMI <http://dublincore.org>

The Dublin Core Meta-data Initiative was established in 1995 — not in Ireland but in Dublin, Ohio. The organization is ". . . dedicated to promoting the widespread adoption of interoperable metadata standards and developing specialized meta-data vocabularies for describing resources that enable more intelligent information discovery systems".[12] In other words, DCMI wants to use metadata to make things easier to find on the Internet. The organization does not focus on e-learning and sees its diverse activities as one of its strengths in developing a foundation for cross-disciplinary metadata vocabularies. However, through a memorandum of understanding with the IEEE Learning Objects Metadata working group signed at the end of 2000, a platform exists for DCMI to participate in the development of e-learning standards.

LRN <http://www.microsoft.com/elearn/support.asp>

LRN — an acronym for Learning Resource iNterchange — is neither a standards body nor a standard but it comes up often in discussions about e-learning standards. LRN is a commercial implementation by Microsoft of some e-learning specifications. Specifically, LRN supports the IMS Content Packaging 1.1 and Metadata 1.2 specifications; it also supports the SCORM 1.2 reference model.

References

1   Gates B et al (1995) *The Road Ahead* New York, Viking Penguin p 479.
2   Hodgins HW (2000) *The Confusion Around Learning Object Metadata Standards Begins to Lift* [Internet] Available from <http://www.learnativity.com/standards.html> Accessed 18 Sep 2001.
3   Dodds PVW (2002) *Demystifying SCORM* ADL Advanced Distributed Learning [Presentation] [Internet] Available from <http://www.rhassociates.com/webSlides/Demystifying SCORM.htm> Accessed 11 Jun 2002.
4   Parmentier M (1999) *ADL Technical Work Group Update for August 10–11, 1999* ADL Advanced Distributed Learning [Presentation] [Internet] Available from <http://www.adlnet.org/ADLDOCS/Presentation/ADL_Tut_99.ppt> Accessed 13 Jun 2002.
5   *Scope & Purpose* (2001) IEEE P1484.12 Learning Object Metadata Working Group [Internet] Available from <http://ltsc.ieee.org/wg12/s_p.html> Accessed 14 Jun 2002.

6   *About IMS* (2002) IMS Global Learning Consortium Inc [Internet] Available from <http://www.imsproject.org/aboutims.html> Accessed 14 Jun 2002.

7   Dodds PVW (2002) *Demystifying SCORM* ADL Advanced Distributed Learning [Presentation] [Internet] Available from <http://www.rhassociates.com/webSlides/DemystifyingSCORM.htm> Accessed 11 Jun 2002.

8   *SCORM Bookshelf Graphic* (2002) ADL [Internet] Available from <http://www.adlnet.org/adldocs/Document/SCORMBookshelfGraphic.pdf> Accessed 12 Jun 2002.

9   ARIADNE Project Public Information Site <http://ariadne.unil.ch/main.content.html> Accessed 15 Jun 2002.

10 PROMETEUS (2001) PROMETEUS home page <http://www.prometeus.org/1indexA.html> Accessed 14 Jun 2002.

11 *The Memorandum of Understanding* (1998) PROMETEUS [Internet] Available from <http://www.prometeus.org/index.cfm?PID = 282&DocID = 6&action1 = display&action2=long> Accessed 15 Jun 2002.

12 *An Overview of the Dublin Core Metadata Initiative* (2000) Dublin Core Metadata Initiative [Internet] Available from <http://dublincore.org/about/overview/> Accessed 15 Jun 2002.

16 Instructional design: must try harder

... we do not yet have a good understanding of learner–computer interactions and the communication dynamics between learner and computer ... the instructional strategies we adopt must be suitable for the technology, rather than the technology being used to imitate traditional instructional techniques. Roderick Sims[1]

What you need to know

There's little consensus about what constitutes sound instructional design (ISD) for e-learning. Traditionalists believe the old principles are universal and apply equally well to what happens on the Web as they do to what happens in the classroom. Usurpers can't understand how models developed for face-to-face learning can apply to technology-based learning, that is, self-paced courses, learning objects and simulations. Even if the usurpers are right — and I happen to believe they are — both camps have failed to produce the goods; at best, the quality of e-learning content has proved variable. At another level, there is tension not between theories of instructional design but between instructional design and business realities. Courses need to be delivered on time and on budget; many enterprises and content publishers respond by adopting a cookie cutter approach to content development.

An article written in 1996 by David Merrill, ISD guru and Utah State University professor of instructional technology was an early indicator that ISD was going wrong. In *Reclaiming Instructional Design*, Merrill described what he saw as an erosion of standards: "Too much of the structure of educational technology is built upon the sand of relativism, rather than the rock of science. When winds of new paradigms blow and the sands of old paradigms shift; then the structure of educational technology slides toward the sea of pseudo-science and mythology. We stand firm against the shifting sands of new paradigms and "realities". We have drawn a line in the sand. We boldly reclaim the technology of instructional design that is built upon the rock of instructional science."[2]

In April 2000, the debate reached a broader audience through a *Training Magazine* cover story entitled *The Attack on ISD* in which six experts launched an attack on traditional ISD models. "ISD takes too long, it costs too much," argued Fred Nickols, executive director for the Educational Testing Service (ETS) in New Jersey, "And by the time you're through, the opportunity you were trying to exploit through training has passed you by."[3] Donald Tosti, managing partner of Vanguard Consulting in California and an officer of the International Society for Performance Improvement (ISPI), observed that ISD had the effect of shutting down critical faculties: "Blind observance of ISD is a characteristic of designers who lose sight of the real problem and focus on coming up with the perfect instructional program instead of the right business result."[4] A presentation by two university professors who taught ISD rocked John Murphy, president of Executive Edge, a consulting firm in Connecticut: "There was no consideration of beginning with some business purpose in mind, some kind of impact or result that would occur because you delivered a training course. There was no mention of any expectations that some customer might have. They just drew a line around an area that they called ISD. Inside the line everything was about rules of classroom effectiveness, and four kinds of people with four different learning styles … ",[5] etc.

In September 2001, *Online Learning Magazine* fuelled the debate with an articled entitled "Out with the old — Is it time to rethink instructional design?" It quoted Rod Sims, professor of instructional technology at Deakin University in Melbourne, Australia: "Is technology simply a means to replicate face-to-face human interaction or is this a new medium for communication which requires alternative methods of design? Traditional instructional design doesn't help us ask the right questions."[6]

Things would never be the same for traditional ISD. But what is this process — or science as Merrill would have it — that unleashes such strong feelings? Merrill himself has described ISD this way: "Our quest should be to learn how to organize instructional materials and practices in a way that makes learning maximally efficient, effective and appealing."[7] In her book *Web-Based Training*, Margaret Driscoll gives a different emphasis: "Instructional systems design (ISD) is a process for developing instruction … The ISD approach acknowledges a relationship among *learners, instructors,* and *materials*."[8] Robert A.Resier, author and professor of Instructional Systems at Florida State University, offers this full-blooded definition: "The field of instructional design and technology encompasses the analysis of learning and performance problems, and the design, development, implementation, evaluation and management of instructional and noninstructional processes and resources intended to improve learning and performance in a variety of settings, particularly educational institutions and the workplace."[9]

Well-trodden ISD paths

I'm going to suggest a reason why instructional design isn't performing the way it should, at least, for self-paced e-learning courses. But before I can do that, we need to look at some of the ways ISD is being implemented.

Addie

ADDIE presents the most familiar face of instructional design. The acronym stands for five stages in a systematic approach to content development:

- Analysis
- Design
- Development
- Implementation
- Evaluation

ADDIE resembles most project management methodologies for software implementation. As a result, it feels like more of a framework for instructional design than instructional design itself. As a framework, ADDIE will deliver a level of quality commensurate with input, however, like many ISD models it fails to give clear guidance about what makes good learning content. You can follow ADDIE to the letter and still deliver mediocre content.

Bloom's taxonomy

In 1956 Dr Benjamin Bloom headed a group of educational psychologists at the University of Chicago. Bloom's group identified three overlapping domains: the cognitive, psychomotor and affective. E-learning ISD tends to focus on Bloom's cognitive domain since that's where most content operates. Bloom developed a taxonomy for classifying cognitive learning objectives in terms of intellectual abilities and skills. Figure 16.1 illustrates the six levels of classification in *Bloom's Taxonomy*; the lists of typical learning actions are not exhaustive.

Bloom's classification is also a hierarchy of complexity moving from Knowledge — the least complex — up to Evaluation. Some people group Analysis, Synthesis and Evaluation under the heading "critical thinking". Many instructional designers embrace the taxonomy because it helps them to choose the most appropriate (1) method of presentation, (2) style of assessment, and (3) delivery channel. For example, Margaret Driscoll observes that Bloom's first three levels relate to *structured information* with clear right and wrong answers; the second three, to *ill-structured complex information* requiring sets of learning strategies and tools to master.

In his Four-Component Instructional Design model, Jeroen van Merriënboer, who is head of research at the Open University of the Netherlands' Educational Technology Expertise Centre, makes a similar distinction when he refers to recurrent and non-current skills. Recurrent skills are algorithmic — applied the same way regardless of context. Non-recurrent skills are heuristic — significantly adapted according to the context in which they are used. Discriminating between structured/recurrent and ill-structured/non-recurrent can help a designer make better instructional choices about how skills are taught. As useful as Bloom's Taxonomy is as an analytic tool, it provides little guidance about how to develop high quality learning content.

SIX LEVELS OF CLASSIFICATION

	Knowledge	Comprehension	Application	Analysis	Synthesis	Evaluation
	list	summarize	apply	analyse	combine	assess
	define	describe	demonstrate	separate	integrate	decide
	tell	interpret	calculate	order	modify	rank
	describe	contrast	complete	explain	rearrange	grade
	identify	predict	illustrate	connect	substitute	test
	show	associate	show	classify	plan	measure
	label	distinguish	solve	arrange	create	recommend
	collect	estimate	examine	divide	design	convince
	examine	differentiate	modify	compare	invent	select
	tabulate	discuss	relate	select	compose	judge
	quote	extend	change	explain	formulate	explain
	name		classify	infer	prepare	discriminate
	who		experiment		generalize	support
	when		discover		rewrite	conclude
	where					compare
						summarize

(left margin, vertical:) TYPICAL LEARNING ACTION

LESS ←————————— COMPLEXITY ————————→ MORE

Figure 16.1 — Bloom's taxonomy[10]

Gagné's events of instruction

The late Dr Robert Gagné was a leader in the fields of educational psychology and instructional design. More than an academic, Gagné spent many years addressing the learning and performance needs of the US Air Force. There are many parallels in the work of Gagné and Bloom. In *The Conditions of Learning* first published in 1956, Gagné identified five domains of learning and a hierarchy of complexity for intellectual skills. Figure 16.2 compares Gagné's and Bloom's classifications.

Gagné's work is a touchstone for e-learning instructional designers who have adopted his "events of instruction", a nine-step process which creates the conditions necessary to learn:

#	STEP	INFORMATION PROCESSING
1	gaining attention	reception
2	informing learners of the objective	expectancy
3	stimulating recall of prior learning	retrieval
4	presenting the stimulus	selective perception
5	providing learning guidance	semantic encoding
6	eliciting performance	responding
7	providing feedback	reinforcement
8	assessing performance	retrieval
9	enhancing retention and transfer	generalization

LEARNING DOMAINS		COGNITIVE CLASSIFICATIONS		
Bloom	Gagné	Bloom	Gagné	
cognitive	verbal information	knowledge	stimulus recognition	LESS
	intellectual skills	comprehension	response generation	
psychomotor	cognitive strategies	application	procedure following	
	motor skills		use of terminology	COMPLEXITY
affective	attitudes	analysis	discriminations	
			concept formation	
		synthesis	rule application	
		evaluation	problem solving	MORE

Figure 16.2 — Bloom and Gagné compared

Dick and Carey

Two of the best known names in instructional design are Walter Dick and Lou Carey. In *The Systematic Design of Instruction*, Dick and Carey proposed their own instructional sequence:[11]

#	STEP
1	pre-instructional activities
	• motivation
	• objectives
	• entry behaviours
2	information presentation
	• instructional sequence
	• size of instructional unit
	• information
	• examples
3	learner participation
	• practice
	• feedback
4	testing
	• pre-test

#	STEP
5	• embedded tests • post-test follow-through • remediation • enrichment

It's easy to see the appeal of Gagné's nine-step process and Dick and Carey's sequence of instructional strategies: they provide clear guidelines for sequencing e-learning content in the cognitive domain. The mediocrity of so much e-learning content raises questions about how well instructional designers have implemented these models — have they followed them blindly assuming learning would occur automatically or applied them creatively and rigorously? I believe that increasingly e-learning will be asked to address learning in what Bloom calls the affective domain and Gagné calls the domain of attitude. Do these linear sequences apply when the focus is on affecting behaviours and attitudes, when content addresses awareness, interest, attention, concern, responsibility, the ability to listen and respond in interactions with others? Or will instructional designers need to find new dynamic models?

The ARCS model

Whether we like it or not, learners bring all the baggage of their lives to the learning process as Daniel Goleman reminds us in his influential book *Emotional Intelligence*: "The extent to which emotional upsets can interfere with mental life is no news to teachers. Students who are anxious, angry, or depressed don't learn; people who are caught in these states do not take in information efficiently or deal with it well."[12] In other words, the best instructional design in the world makes no impact on an anxious or demotivated learner. That's critical for e-learning, which is self-directed and self-paced. Employees need to be motivated to learn but, so far, motivation is something we haven't seen instructional design address.

John Keller, who teaches Instructional Systems at Florida State University, understands that motivation is the key determinant of how much effort a learner will make; this is the central teaching of the expectancy value theory. To make a worthwhile learning effort, the learner must:

- Value the task — which is why learner-centred learning needs to be relevant and solution-centred.
- Believe they can succeed at the task — which is why the learner's expectations need to be taken account of.

When true, these two conditions generate motivation. In the early 1980s, Keller published the ARCS Model of Motivational Design. It is a simple and powerful ISD model based on four sets of strategies which are outlined in Figure 16.3.

	Category	Strategies[13]	Sub-category[14]
A	Attention	Strategies for arousing and sustaining curiosity and interest	Capture Interest (Perceptual Arousal): What can I do to capture their interest? Stimulate Inquiry (Inquiry Arousal): How can I stimulate an attitude of inquiry? Maintain Attention (Variability): How can I use a variety of tactics to maintain their attention?
R	Relevance	Strategies that link to the learner's needs, interests and motives	Relate to Goals (Goal Orientation): How can I best meet my learner's needs? Do I know their needs? Match Interests (Motive Matching): How and when can I provide my learners with appropriate choices, responsibilities and influences? Tie to Experiences (Familiarity): How can I tie the instruction to the learners' experiences?
C	Confidence	Strategies that help the learner develop a positive expectation for successful achievement	Success Expectations (Learning Requirements): How can I assist in building a positive expectation for success? Success Opportunities (Learning Activities): How will the learning experience support or enhance the learner's beliefs in their competence? Personal Responsibility (Success Attributions): How will the learners clearly know their success is based upon their efforts and abilities?
S	Satisfaction	Strategies that provide extrinsic and intrinsic reinforcement for effort	Intrinsic Satisfaction (Self-Reinforcement): How can I provide meaningful opportunities for learners to use their newly acquired knowledge/skill? Rewarding Outcomes (Extrinsic Rewards): What will provide reinforcement to the learners' successes? Fair Treatment (Equity): How can I assist the learner in anchoring a positive feeling about their accomplishments?

Figure 16.3 — Part One of the ARCS Model

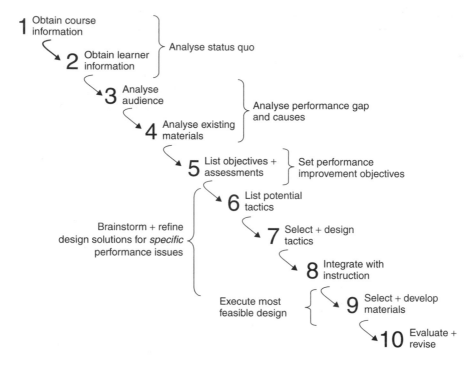

Figure 16.4 — Part Two of the ARCS Model[15]

Because ARCS is focused on motivation, it appears to align closely with the adaptive domain. The four categories and their sub-categories operate at a macro level and can be applied in conjunction with other ISD models. They are, however, only the first part of Keller's ARCS model; the second part is a 10-step process for the design of a motivational system (see Figure 16.4).

ISD and learning objects — Cisco's approach

Learning objects pose their own challenges for instructional design. The challenges arise from two characteristics of the learning object: reusability and interoperability. Together they deliver many benefits to the enterprise. However, from the instructional designer's point of view, they also take something away: context. The instructional designer of a learning object doesn't know what the learner has just experienced or will experience next. A learning object is like a railway car with no fixed place in a train, it might be the third car on one journey and the penultimate car on the next; the train might have 100 cars one day and 20 the next.

Under these conditions what is the best strategy and the best model for ISD? Can the assumption of a pre-determined sequence of learning events that many ISD models make — Gagné, Dick and Carey — be sustained with learning objects?

Should these designs be repeated over and over at different levels like a fractal? If we build each learning object to conform to the same ISD model can we assume that a course assembled from these objects will conform to the same model? In other words, does ISD work from the bottom up as well as from the top down?

In 1998 Cisco Systems realized its existing curriculum of 5-day instructor led training was monolithic and difficult to (1) update and (2) convert to e-learning. What Cisco needed was a methodology to author "database-driven objects that can be reused, searched, and modified independent of their delivery media".[16] What it came up with was the Reusable Learning Object strategy.

An appreciation of Cisco's approach to ISD and learning objects requires an understanding of the way Cisco works with learning objects. Cisco adopted a two-tier approach:

- RLO: Reusable Learning Object
- RIO: Reusable Information Object

Here is how Cisco's Internet Learning Solutions Group (ILSG) defines them: "An RLO is based on a single objective, derived from a specific job task. Each RIO is built upon an objective that supports the RLO objective ... To aid in content standardization, ILSG has chosen to further classify each RIO as a concept, fact, procedure, process, or principle. Each of these RIO types has a recommended template that authors can follow to build the RIO."[17] Here are examples of RIO classes:

Concept	What is a Router ... Dog ... Chair?
Fact	Toshiba Tecra 550CDT
Procedure	Check Email using PPP ...
Principle	When to use Layer 3 Switching
Process	How traffic flows on network[18]

The RLO-RIO nomenclature is for developers; Cisco learners know an RLO as a Lesson and an RIO as a Section. The relationship between an RLO and an RIO creates a starting point for a hierarchy of content. Figure 16.5 illustrates an example of such a hierarchy.

Cisco defines both the RLO and RIO in detail. The structure of the RLO looks like this:

- Assessment
  - Can be taken before *or* after RLO
  - Minimum of two questions per RIO
- Overview
- Introduction
  - Importance
  - Objectives

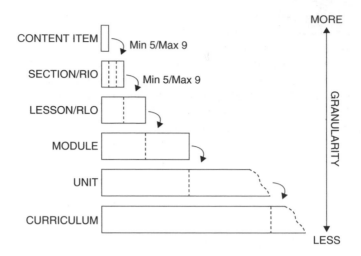

Figure 16.5—Content hierarchy based on RLO-RIO

- Prerequisites
- Scenario (optional)
- Outline

- RIOs (between five and nine)

  - Content items
  - Practice items
  - Assessment items (grouped together in RLO assessment)

- Summary

  - Review
  - Next steps (optional)
  - Additional resources (optional) (see Figure 16.6).

These are some of the metadata Cisco attaches to each RLO:

- RLO title and RLO-level objective
- Job function and job task
- Author name and owner name
- Creation date, publish date and expiration date
- Prerequisites

Earlier we looked at classifying activities in the cognitive domain. Cisco uses a combination of the classifications made by Bloom and Merrill—see Figure 16.7. From Cisco's perspective, these classifications are important because they help the RIO designer focus on the right style of activity for Practice and Assessment

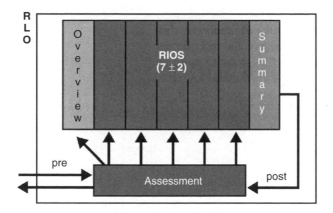

Figure 16.6— Cisco's RLO[19]

COGNITIVE CLASSIFICATIONS		
Merrill	Bloom	
remember	knowledge	LESS
use	comprehension	
	application	COMPLEXITY
	analysis	
	synthesis	
	evaluation	MORE

Figure 16.7— Cisco's approach to cognitive classification

items — and it is these two activities that, in Cisco's view, transform an RIO from information into knowledge. Remember, knowledge is actionable information.

Cognitive classification forms part of RLO metadata. Because Bloom provides six classifications to Merrill's two, Cisco designers use Bloom as a sub-set of Merrill. For example, if an author decides that an RLO comes under the Merrill classification of Use, they record that as part of the metadata then refine it with one of the five Bloom classifications Cisco associate with Use.

So far, we've seen that Cisco define five classes of RIO and that each class contains three sets of items: (1) Content, (2) Practice and (3) Assessment. Cisco

CONCEPT	FACT	PROCEDURE	PROCESS	PRINCIPLE
• Content Items	• Content Items	• Content Items	• Content Items	• Content Items
- Introduction	- Introduction	- Introduction	- Introduction	- Introduction
- Facts/o	- Facts	- Facts/o	- Facts/o	- Facts/o
- Definition	- Instructor Notes/o	- Procedure Table/e	- Staged Table/e	-Principle
- Example		- Decision Table/e	- Block Diagrams/e	Statement/o
- Non-Example/o		- Combined Table/e	- Cycle Charts/e	- Guidelines
- Analogy/o		- Demonstration/o	- Instructor Notes/o	- Example
- Instructor Notes/o		- Instructor Notes/o		- Non-Example/o
				- Analogy/o
				- Instructor Notes/o
•Practice Items	• Practice Items	• Practice Items	•Practice Items	• Practice Items
•Assessment Items	• Assessment Items	• Assessment Items	•Assessment Items	• Assessment Items

/o = optional   /e = either

Figure 16.8 — Cisco's RLO content specification

take that a stage further by defining the Content items associated with each class (see Figure 16.8).

Cisco guidelines prescribe a high level sequence for an RLO while allowing the author some freedom in the sequencing of RIOs within an RLO. There are a number of sequencing principles in ISD theory:

- known to unknown
- simple to complex
- in order of performance
- in solution order
- according to taxonomy

Some of these are reflected in Cisco's guidelines for the sequencing of RIOs:

- A Concept RIO comes before a major topic.
- Fact RIOs should be sequenced to reflect the logical flow of facts. Ideally, Fact RIOs should be anchored to a Concept, Procedure, Process or Principle RIO.
- A Procedure RIO usually comes after Concept or Process RIO.
- A Process RIO can come anywhere in a RLO sequence unless it is presented in the context of a Procedure; in that case, the Process RIO precedes the Procedure RIO.
- A Principle RIO usually follows a Concept or Process RIO.

Each RIO and RLO need to be media independent. That means each one can be rendered using any of Cisco's learning delivery channels, for example, the classroom, e-learning and print. Not every activity, interaction and media object can be rendered in every learning channel. There's no drag and drop in a print-based assessment; there's no direct observation assessment in self-paced e-learning; and no video or animation in an instructor-led class. In some cases, rendering differences are technical: a photograph needs to be rendered at a low resolution for Web delivery but high resolution for print delivery. Where differences are functional, the RIO designer provides equivalencies, for example, the instruction "drag and drop" in a Web based assessment becomes "place a check in the right box" in the print equivalent.

Cisco have developed a detailed and coherent set of standards, guidelines and templates that take account of both instructional design and learning objects requirements. Working in this disciplined environment isn't second nature even to experienced instructional designers. Recognizing the challenges, Cisco provides training for every designer who authors its RIOs and RLOs. Cisco have had more experience dealing with the instructional design challenges posed by learning objects than almost anyone else but that doesn't mean they have resolved all issues. David Wiley has written extensively about instructional design, and developed an instructional design model for learning objects. He contends that specifying the Assessment as part of the RIO structure — even though the learners accesses Assessment items at the RLO level — is a shortcoming of Cisco's approach: " ... assessment pieces must test an individual concept, fact, etc. In order to test an integrated, real world performance it would be necessary to hang an assessment off the Summary. However, this is not possible according to the strategy outlined in the white paper."[20]

I can understand both sides. Wiley wants assessments to check whether learners have integrated freestanding elements of knowledge into a useful whole that can be applied to a real-world task. Cisco believe — I'm surmising their position — that to be truly reusable an RIO needs to be freestanding and self-contained; that means Content, Practice *and* Assessment Items need to be integral parts. Wiley's concerns could probably be addressed without compromising the RIO by *adding* a second tier Assessment to the RLO Overview and Summary. This kind of detail apart, I believe Cisco's work has set the benchmark in the area. At the same time, I believe it represents the first step on a long journey during which there will be scope for revolutionary change in how instructional design is applied to learning objects.

An ISD architecture

Confusingly, "instructional design" is used to mean different things at different times in the ISD process. At a macro level, it describes an overarching system for developing and implementing performance-based instruction; at a micro level, it

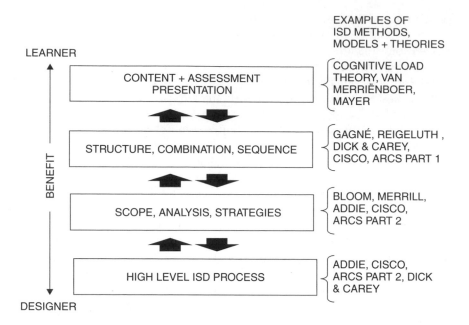

Figure 16.9 — Example of an ISD architecture

describes specific activities within the system. To make sense of all the levels at which ISD operates and of ISD itself, it might be helpful to think in terms of an ISD architecture. Figure 16.9 illustrates what it might look like.

Some content developers already work with what is in effect an ISD architecture, that is, they draw on the work of Bloom, Gagné, Merrill, Keller, van Merriënboer and others to support aspects of their instructional design. I believe organizing these strands into a formal architecture will help developers see any gaps in their approaches.

I said that I would suggest why instructional design isn't performing as well as it could and to that end I'm going to make a generalization. The two areas where ISD in the context of enterprise e-learning shows most room for improvement are:

- The need for a specific methodology to address *business* requirements — the raison d'être of e-learning.
- ISD theories and models about the *multimedia presentation* of content and assessments to learners are not being applied.

Interestingly, the two points sit at opposite ends of the ISD process: the business imperative and the engagement of learners. I'm going to address the presentation of content.

I have worked with sponsors, subject matter experts, instructional designers and Web developers at what I'll call the "presentation layer" of e-learning — where analysis, scoping and strategizing culminate in a presentation to the learner. Conversations about the presentation layer turn out to be very subjective. Instead of interest in how the learner engages with content, there are personal evaluations of colour palettes, fonts, screen layout, illustration styles, etc. Of course screen design matters—but only when it serves instructional design. For some reason, we have developed the habit of jumping straight from structure, combination and sequence to screen design. I don't think it serves the learner. What's important at the presentation layer is the embedding of knowledge and skills.

To help focus on what's important, I suggest that instructional designers and developers should become more fluent with Cognitive Load Theory (CLT). I'm sure this is already best practice in some development environments. What is surprising is that it has not reached tipping point since research findings in CLT directly address the needs and concerns of instructional designers and developers.

Jeroen van Merriënboer, an authority on CLT, puts the case like this: "Modern instructional theories tend to focus on real-life tasks as the driving force for learning ... The general assumption is that realistic or authentic learning tasks help learners to integrate the knowledge, skills and attitudes necessary for effective task performance; give them the opportunity to learn to coordinate constituent skills that make up complex task performance, and eventually enable them to transfer what is learned to their daily life or work settings ... A severe risk of all of these approaches is that learners have difficulties learning from the tasks because they are overwhelmed by the task complexity ... cognitive load theory offers useful guidelines for decreasing intrinsic and extraneous cognitive load, so that sufficient processing capacity is left for genuine learning."[21]

CLT sees learning as an information processing system; it is concerned with the transfer of knowledge from our conscious short-term working memory to our long-term memory. The limitations of our working memory—in both capacity and duration—can hamper learning. There is a third mode of memory, sensory, through which we perceive incoming messages. Together, the three modes define our human cognitive architecture (see Figure 16.10).

If working memory is the limiting factor, instructional designers need to ensure that learning content is designed to optimize what's available, as Dr Graham Cooper of Southern Cross University's School of Multimedia and Information Technology explains: "Working memory is intimately related to where and how we direct our attention to "think about something", or to process information. The biggest limitation of working memory is its capacity to deal with no more than about seven elements of information simultaneously ... Working memory capacity may be expanded slightly by mixing the senses used to present information. That is, it is easier to attend to a body of information when some of the information is presented visually and the remainder of the information is presented auditorily than it is when all of the information is presented through a single sense (either all visually or all auditorily). If the capacity of working

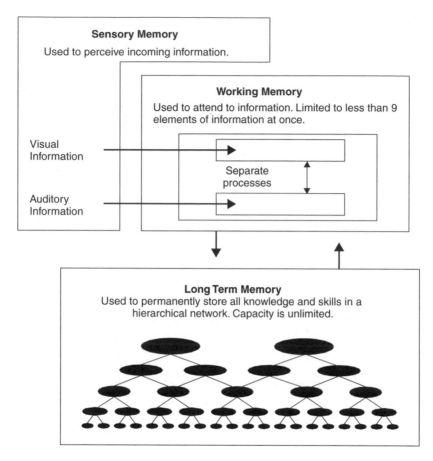

Figure 16.10 — Human cognitive architecture[22]
Reproduced by permission of Graham Cooper

memory is exceeded while processing a body of information then some, if not all, of that information will be lost."[23]

When we are learning, mental activity is imposed on our working memory. *Cognitive load* is the name for the total amount of the activity; it has two aspects: intrinsic and extraneous. Here are Cooper's explanations of each: "Intrinsic cognitive load is due solely to the intrinsic nature (difficulty) of some to-be-learned content. Intrinsic cognitive load cannot be modified by instructional design ... Extraneous cognitive load is due to the instructional materials used to present information to students ... By changing the instructional materials presented to students, the level of extraneous cognitive load may be modified. This may facilitate learning."[24] Cooper probably understates the case; there is a growing body of research supporting the view that the application of CLT improves the effectiveness of e-learning. Figure 16.11 shows how.

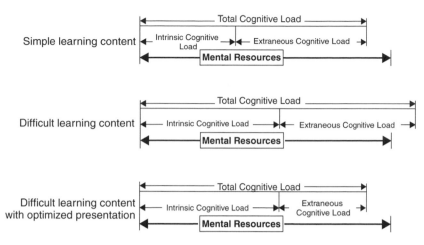

Figure 16.11— Minimizing extraneous cognitive load[25]
Reproduced by permission of Graham Cooper

The working memory has separate processors for visual and auditory information; despite the separation, humans are capable of integrating information from different senses—verbal and non-verbal, for example—into a single mental model and, so, a single meaning. This ability to make sense of mixed modality messages provides smart instructional designer with opportunities to present the total cognitive load of complex learning within the learner's mental resources. Dr Richard E. Mayer of the University of California at Santa Barbara's Department of Psychology has conducted substantial research into CLT and written extensively about multimedia and cognitive load. He understands the opportunities but warns that they don't come about by accident: " ... the instructional designer is faced with the need to choose between several combinations of modes and modalities to promote meaningful learning ... Should the explanation be given auditorily in the form of speech, visually in the form of text, or both? Would entertaining adjuncts in the form of words, environmental sounds, or music help students' learning? Should the visual and auditory materials be presented simultaneously or sequentially? ... Multimedia explanations allow students to work easily with verbal and non-verbal representations of complex systems ... presenting a verbal explanation of how a system works with an animation does not insure that students will understand the explanation unless research-based principles are applied to the design."[26]

So where does that leave the all too common practice of having a voice-over read all the text displayed on the screen? Instead of lightening the extraneous cognitive load, it induces redundant processing. Here's how Mayers describes it: "In this situation—which we call redundant presentation—the words are presented both as narration and simultaneously as on-screen text. However, the learner must devote cognitive capacity to processing the on-screen text and reconciling it with the narration — thus, priming incidental processing that reduces the capacity to engage in essential processing. In contrast, when the multimedia presentation consists of narrated animation — which we call non-redundant presentation — the learner is not primed to engage in incidental processing."[27] In self-paced e-learning, the spoken word should complement and support what's on the screen not duplicate it.

I believe CLT is a natural fit with the presentation of e-learning content and that it will resonate with smart SMEs, instructional designers and Web developers. CLT can, so the research appears to tell us, improve the effectiveness of e-learning. I'd like to see it applied as a matter of course at the top level of the architecture of instructional design.

References

1   Sims RCH (1997) *Interactive Learning as an "Emerging" Technology: A Reassessment of Interactive and Instructional Design Strategies* Australian Journal of Educational Technology Vol 13 No 1 pp 68–84 [Internet] Available from <http://www.ascilite.org.au/ajet/ajet13/sims.html> Accessed 18 Jun 2002.

2   Merrill MD Drake L Lacy MJ Pratt J and Utah State University ID2 Research Group (1996) *Reclaiming Instructional Design* Educational Technology 1996 Vol 36 No 5 pp 5–7 [Internet] Available from <http://www.coe.usu.edu/it/id2/reclaim.html> Accessed 17 Sep 2001.

3   Gordon J and Zemke R (2000) *The Attack on ISD - Charge 1: It's Slow and Clumsy* Training Magazine April 2000 Vol 37 No 4 p 42 [Internet] Available from <http://www.trainingsupersite.com/publications/archive/training/2000/004/004cvCharge1.htm> Accessed 18 Jun 2002.

4   Gordon J and Zemke R (2000) *The Attack on ISD - Charge 2: There's No "There" There* Training Magazine April 2000 Vol 37 No 4 p 42 [Internet] Available from <http:// www.trainingsupersite.com/publications/archive/training/2000/004/004cv Charge2.htm> Accessed 18 Jun 2002.

5   Gordon J and Zemke R (2000) *The Attack on ISD - Charge 3: Used as Directed, It Produces Bad Solutions* Training Magazine April 2000 Vol 37 No 4 p 42 [Internet] Available from <http://www.trainingsupersite.com/publications/archive/training/2000/004/004 cvCharge3.htm> Accessed 18 Jun 2002.

6   Shank P (2001) *Out with the Old - Is It Time to Rethink Instructional Design?* Online-Learning Magazine September 2001 [Internet] Available from <http://www.onlinelearningmag.com/new/sept01/humble.htm> Accessed 3 Dec 2001.

7   Zemke R (1998) *Wake Up! (And Reclaim Instructional Design)* Training Magazine June 1998 Vol 35 No 6 p 36.

8   Driscoll M (1998) *Web-Based Training* San Francisco, Jossey-Bass/Pfeiffer p 23.

9   Reiser RA (2001) *A History of Instructional Design and Technology: Part II: A History of Instructional Design* Educational Technology Research and Development (ETR&D) 2001 Vol 49 No 2 p 57 [Internet] Available from <http://www.aect.org/pdf/etr&d/4902/4902-04.pdf> Accessed 19 Jun 2002.

10 Bloom BS (Ed.) (1956) *Taxonomy of Educational Objectives, the Classification of Educational Goals, Handbook 1, Cognitive Domain* New York, David McKay Company Inc.

11   Dick W and Carey L (1990) *The Systematic Design of Instruction* 3rd Edition Glenview, Scott Foresman and Company In Jolliffe A Ritter J and Stevens D (2001) *The Online Learning Handbook* London, Kogan Page p 179.

12   Goleman D (1995) *Emotional Intelligence* New York, Bantam Books In Picard R Kort B and Reilly R (2001) *Exploring the Role of Emotion in Propelling the SMET Learning Process* Media Laboratory MIT [Internet] Available from <www.media.mit.edu/affect/AC_research/lc/nsf1.pdf> Accessed 20 Jun 2002.

13   Keller JM (1983) *Motivational Design of Instruction* In CM Reigeluth Ed *Instructional Theories and Models: An Overview of Their Current Status* New York, Lawrence Erlbaum Associates.

14   Keller JM (2000) *How to Integrate Learner Motivation Planning into Lesson Planning: The ARCS Model Approach* [White paper] [Internet] Available from <http://www.netg.com/research/whitepapers/kellerwp.asp> Accessed 20 Jun 2000.

15   Keller JM (2000) *How to Integrate Learner Motivation Planning into Lesson Planning: The ARCS Model Approach* [White paper] [Internet] Available from <http://www.netg.com/research/whitepapers/kellerwp.asp> Accessed 20 Jun 2000.

16   Barritt C (2001) *Reusable Learning Object Strategy Version 4.0* Cisco Systems Inc [White paper] [Internet] Available from <www.cisco.com/warp/public/10/wwtraining/elearning/implement/rlo_strategy.pdf> Accessed 22 Jun 2002.

17   Barritt C (2001) *Reusable Learning Object Strategy Version 4.0* Cisco Systems Inc [White paper] [Internet] Available from <www.cisco.com/warp/public/10/wwtraining/elearning/implement/rlo_strategy.pdf> Accessed 22 Jun 2002.

18   Barritt C and Maddocks P (2001) *The Reality of Implementing Learning Objects: Inside the Internet Learning Solutions Group* Cisco Systems Inc [Presentation] OnLine Learning Los Angeles 1 October 2001.

19   Barritt C (2001) *Reusable Learning Object Strategy Version 4.0* Cisco Systems Inc [White paper] [Internet] Available from <www.cisco.com/warp/public/10/wwtraining/elearning/implement/rlo_strategy.pdf> Accessed 22 Jun 2002.

20   Wiley DA (2001) *About the RLO strategy white paper* [Internet] Available from <http://wiley.ed.usu.edu/docs/cisco_rlo.html> Accessed 24 Jun 2002.

21   van Merriënboer JJG Kirschner PA and Kester L (2002) *Taking the Load off a Learner's Mind: Instructional Design for Complex Learning* Open University of the Netherlands [White paper] [Internet] Available from <http://www.ou.nl/info-alg-english-r_d/otec-research/publications/wetpub/papermerrienbocrcp.pdf> Accessed 25 Jun 2002.

22   Cooper G (1998) *Research into Cognitive Load Theory and Instructional Design at UNSW* University of New South Wales, Australia [Internet] Available from <http://www.arts.unsw.edu.au/education/clt_net_aug_97.html> Accessed 18 Jun 2002.

23   Cooper G (1998) *Research into Cognitive Load Theory and Instructional Design at UNSW* University of New South Wales, Australia [Internet] Available from <http://www.arts.unsw.edu.au/education/clt_net_aug_97.html> Accessed 18 Jun 2002.

24   Cooper G (1998) *Research into Cognitive Load Theory and Instructional Design at UNSW* University of New South Wales, Australia [Internet] Available from <http://www.arts.unsw.edu.au/education/clt_net_aug_97.html> Accessed 18 Jun 2002.

25   Cooper G (1998) *Research into Cognitive Load Theory and Instructional Design at UNSW* University of New South Wales, Australia [Internet] Available from <http://www.arts.unsw.edu.au/education/clt_net_aug_97.html> Accessed 18 Jun 2002.

26   Mayer RE and Moreno R (2000) *A Learner-Centered Approach to Multimedia Explanations: Deriving Instructional Design Principles from Cognitive Theory* Interactive

Multimedia Electronic Journal of Computer-Enhanced Learning Vol 2 No 2 October 2000 [Internet] Available from <http://imej.wfu.edu/articles/2000/2/05/index.asp> Accessed 24 Jun 2002.

27   Mayer RE and Moreno R (2002) *Nine Ways to Reduce Cognitive Load in Multime-dia Learning* [Internet] Available from <http://www.ou.nl/info-alg-english-r_d/otec-research/publications/wetpub/PaperMayerEP.pdf> Accessed 25 Jun 2002.

The content development process: managing e-learning's payload

17

All too often, discussions about web-based learning tend to fall back on a simplistic faith in the power of technology. Of course interactivity is a powerful draw for teachers and students alike. But dazzling technology has no meaning unless it supports content that meets the needs of learners. Report of the Web-based Education Commission to the US President and Congress[1]

... dull content—no matter how it is delivered—is not an effective way to teach people. Fortune Magazine[2]

What you need to know

When we talk about e-learning content we really mean two different things: form and content. Form can mean different things. A virtual class and a self-paced course are forms; at a deeper level, form means text or animation. Content is what the subject matter expert brings to the development process. Sometimes content is raw; it might be about a brand new technology or business process. Sometimes it arrives processed—as a book, a white paper, the transcript of a speech, a PowerPoint, even as a course in another form. The separation of form and content can be traced back to ancient Greece; Aristotle analysed the public speeches of his contemporaries by *logos*, logical content, and *lexis*, style and delivery. The Romans made the same distinction with *res* and *verba*. We have more delivery channels than the ancients but the challenge remains the same: to find the right content, then the form that expresses it best. That's what the content development process is about. This chapter focuses on developing content for self-paced courses.

Content development and the business

The best form can never compensate for poor content. As the show business adage puts it: "If it ain't on the page, it ain't on the stage." Content development begins with the business—specifically, with a performance gap that is preventing the business from achieving consistent peak performance. The objective of the content development team is simple: to close the gap. To do that, you need first to understand it and that means working with the best subject matter experts.

By definition, SMEs are scarce commodities: managers covet them; customers demand them. Unless the business understands that its contribution to content development is more than funding, the process will fail. Managers have to make SMEs available. They will only do that if they're convinced of the value of e-learning to the business and have confidence in the content development team (see Figure 17.1).

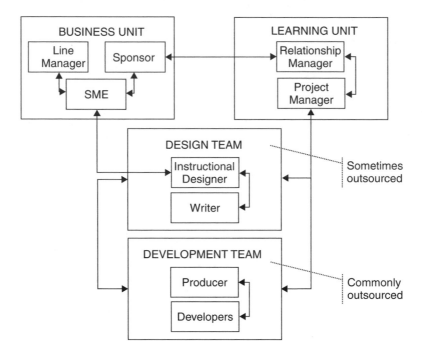

Figure 17.1 — Content development relationships

Equally, we should recognize that SMEs need to be incentivized to make a contribution. Some enterprises have been smart enough to include knowledge sharing as part of regular staff assessments. Some even set targets, for example, 20% of an SME's time on a project must be dedicated to knowledge sharing — and one of the most effective ways of sharing knowledge is to embed it in an e-learning course. Making knowledge sharing part of employee assessment means there are real rewards for supporting content development — financial and in terms of career advancement. Most SMEs are proud of the knowledge and skills they've acquired, so giving public recognition of their contributions can be another incentive for getting involved. It costs nothing to credit the SME — along with the sponsor and the development team — in each course.

Learning objects

A colleague was venting his scepticism about learning objects. "I can't imagine a situation where I would want to use them. If I had to develop a course about, I don't know—baking a pie—what use would learning objects be?" In fact, a course about pie baking provides a very good high level argument in favour of learning objects. Start by analysing the task. There are three steps: (1) prepare the crust, (2) prepare the filling, (3) bake the pie. Essentially, steps (1) and (3) are the same for every pie; the step that changes is (2). Let's say there's a known performance gap in the process of baking an apple pie. You develop each of the three steps as a learning object and store them in an object repository. Later it turns out there's also a performance gap in the process of baking cherry and rhubarb pies. Instead of having to develop two new courses, you develop two new learning objects—preparing a cherry filling and a rhubarb filling. Combine the two new learning objects with the existing learning objects for steps (1) and (3), and you have two new courses quickly and inexpensively. More accurately, you don't have three courses but five learning objects and three packaging instructions that assemble the objects according to the instructional designer's intentions.

Definitions

Technically, you can describe a learning object as a digital, tagable, shareable, reusable, modular, interoperable element of learning content. A more content oriented definition might be: the smallest discrete reusable collection of content capable of presenting and supporting a single learning concept. Since learning concepts are not of a fixed complexity, it follows that learning objects are not of a fixed size—though they should be of a fixed structure and granularity, that is, they should all be on the same level in a hierarchy of content. A simple content hierarchy is illustrated in Figure 17.2.

Warren Longmire, co-author of *Managing Web-Based Training*, supplements these definitions with a cogent description of the ideal attributes of reusable learning object content:

- "modular, free-standing, and transportable among applications and environments
- nonsequential
- able to satisfy a single learning objective
- accessible to broad audiences (such that it can be adapted to audiences beyond the original target audience)
- coherent and unitary within a predetermined schema so that a limited number of metatags can capture the main idea or essence of the content
- not embedded within formatting so that it can be repurposed within a different visual schema without losing the essential value or meaning of the text, data, or images."[3]

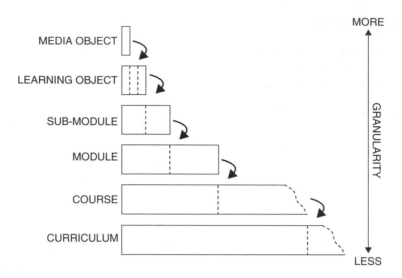

MEDIA OBJECT

LEARNING OBJECT

SUB-MODULE

MODULE

COURSE

CURRICULUM

GRANULARITY

LESS

Figure 17.2 — Simple content hierarchy

Of metaphors and similes

Wayne Hodgins, e-learning visionary and Director of Worldwide Learning Strategies at Autodesk Inc, cites Lego™ as his inspiration for learning objects: "Whether you're assembling a bridge or a house or a spaceship, you use the same Lego™ pieces. Similarly, personalized learning can use — and reuse — the same content or information "objects." Using these as the basic building blocks, the just-right assembly of personalized learning content can be easily created to form a "learning object."[4] It was a smart "sound bite" but Hodgins — who is chairman of the IEEE Learning Technology Standards Committee's Learning Object Metadata Working Group — knows better than anyone that learning objects operate at a higher level of complexity than Lego™.

Unfortunately, many people took Hodgins's simile at face value. If you listen indiscriminately to what's being said in the market, you can end up with the impression that learning objects *are* Lego™ blocks. To redress the balance, David Wiley, editor of *The Instructional Use of Learning Objects*, proposed a more complex simile — the atom — on the basis that:

- "Not every atom is combinable with every other atom.
- Atoms can only be assembled in certain structures prescribed by their own internal structure.
- Some training is required in order to assemble atoms."[5]

I'd like to suggest the train as a middle way of thinking about learning objects. Different cars are designed to carry different loads — passengers, solid freight, liquid freight; some freight is volatile, some stable, some requiring refrigeration, some needing to be kept bone dry. In the same way, learning objects are designed to carry different types of content—concepts, principles and processes, for example. Despite differences in the payload, each car must be able to connect with any other car to form a robust whole—and to run on the same gauge tracks as every other car. Whatever its content, a learning object needs to connect with any other learning object to form a seamless learning sequence—and to run on a standardized technology infrastructure. Like train cars, learning objects can be disassembled and reassembled to form new seamless wholes.

David Wiley has another objection to the Lego™ simile: "The task of creating a useful learning object system is also hindered by the idea that learning objects need to be combinable in any manner one chooses ... Software vendors and standards bodies describe their learning object related work as being "instructional theory neutral." Were this the case all would be well in learning object land. Problematically, a more accurate description of their products is "instructional theory agnostic," or in other words, "we don't know if you're employing an instructional theory or not, and we don't care' ... it is very likely that the combination of learning objects in the absence of any instructional theory will result in larger structures that fail to be instructionally useful."[6]

While I'm in favour of instructionally useful structures, I think the standards bodies and vendors are right. Technology standards should be value-agnostic; adding value is the province of the standards implementer. The International Paper Sizes Standard (ISO 216) defines a sheet of A4 as 210 mm × 297 mm. The standard cares that a sheet of A4 unfolded fits neatly into a C4 envelope; folded once, into a C5 envelope; folded twice, into a C6 envelope. Rightly, it doesn't care whether you use the sheet to make a paper aeroplane or pen a love letter.

There are a number of indicators that learning objects are the future direction of e-learning content:

- The development in 1999—and subsequent implementation—of a reusable learning objects strategy by leading Internet company Cisco Systems.
- The emphasis that e-learning standards development groups like IMS and SCORM are placing on interoperability, metadata, reusability and sequencing—all of which underpin learning objects.
- The emergence of the Learning Content Management System (LCMS) which supports the development and publishing of learning objects.

You need to decide whether your approach to content development will be (1) object oriented, or (2) course oriented. The argument in favour of object-oriented development is this: you can develop learning objects without making a full commitment to reusability, metadata and "on the fly" course assembly. On the other hand, if you adopt a course-oriented approach and later want to switch to learning objects, you'll have to rebuild all existing content. While a learning objects strategy can be implemented in phases, some upfront decisions about enabling technology need to be taken. Strictly speaking you can develop learning objects without an LCMS or CMS, however, it makes sense to implement one of the two, especially if your development plans are ambitious.

Reusability is an important benefit of an object-oriented approach; it saves time and costs. However, without metadata tagging, reuse is slow and expensive because searching for the right object to reuse is a manual activity. In practice, a repository of objects will soon grow to a size that makes manual searches impractical. On the other hand, tagging itself is time-consuming and expensive. For metadata to deliver a benefit, the tagging and searching process which supports reuse needs to be less expensive than the process of building content from scratch each time.

To help address the question of whether or not to adopt an object approach to content Robby Robson, President and CEO of Eduworks Corporation and chairman of the IEEE Learning Technology Standards Committee, provides a useful summary of learning objects' pros and cons in Figure 17.3.

Learning objects and the standards that enable them are not for everyone. Here are some circumstances where they won't deliver benefits:

- All the content you develop has a very short shelf life, so reusability isn't a consideration.
- You have no requirement for (1) an LMS or LCMS, or (2) tracking learner activity.
- Your business requirements can be met by e-learning based on simple static content with navigation restricted to hyperlinks.
- You have no requirement for using learners' interactions with content to determine sequencing, in other words, adaptive content driven by pre-assessments or competency testing.
- You intend only to license third-party content from a single publisher who will also host it.

Rapid development

Rapid development is an approach that can lead to better software products being developed faster by:

- Getting the requirements right first time.
- Early prototyping followed by iterative user tests and reviews.
- Reusing software components.
- Deferring design improvements to the next product version.
- Close teamwork.

In e-learning, rapid development is usually based on (1) template driven development, and (2) self-publishing. Templates ensure standardization across the development process. In principle, nothing should be done for the first

	Pros	Cons
Production Costs	By properly breaking content into learning objects, different parts can be maintained and updated separately. If a suitable learning object can be found, a new one does not need to be created. These are cost savers.	Changing to a learning object approach from a 'self-contained system' approach involves retooling and retraining costs.
Flexibility	As more and more standards-based learning objects become available, increased choice will translate into more flexibility for designers.	Using standards-based learning objects restricts the scope of learner information that is accessible by content if total interoperability is maintained. (Individual systems can use more than the standard learner information, but only at the cost of interoperability with other systems. Over time, more learner information will become standard.)
Pedagogy	Learning objects fit nicely into many ISD theories. Instructional templates can be created with slots for specific types of learning objects. Learning objects may encourage designers to operate in more disciplined ways with a positive effect.	Restrictions on learner information available could restrict pedagogical approaches. Approaches using lengthy discursive material may not benefit from the use of learning objects.
End User Cost	The learning object approach prevents consumers from being locked in to specific systems. As standards take hold, the market for content will take on more of the properties of a typical consumer market with lower costs and increased choice.	The cost of converting existing content to a learning object approach may be significant.
Industry Support	All leading system vendors and content producers are supporting SCORM and other standards that are based on or that complement a learning object approach.	Realistically, it is 12 to 18 months between the time the vendor community adopts an approach and the time products that implement the approach are available.

Figure 17.3—Learning objects—pros and cons[7]
Reproduced by permission of Eduworks Corporation

time. There should be a methodology and a template for every sub-process. Presentation styles and, to an extent, instructional design can be embedded in templates. Templates streamline the process of developing an early prototype. (Speed to market is a key benefit of e-learning.) Developing a prototype early allows a course to be published in phases. Release 1.0 gets time-critical learning to the people who need it as soon as possible. Enhancements in features, functions and content are made to subsequent releases published at short intervals.

Rapid development through self-publishing usually means cutting out the instructional design process and having subject matter experts author courses. There are risks. SMEs are brilliant at what they do; that doesn't mean they know anything about writing and presentation for distributed learning. You can end up with great thinking poorly expressed — a striking imbalance between Aristotle's *logos* and *lexis*. Does cutting out instructional designers and writers accelerate development by removing work from the process or does it simply move work somewhere else? And what about opportunity costs? Every hour an SME is authoring a course, he's not doing his day job — how much is that costing the enterprise? Finally, most SMEs will have no skills in authoring multimedia content. Either all self-published courses end up being text based, or SMEs need to work directly with Web developers. That can't be an effective use of experts' time.

We have to find new processes and technologies for creating effective e-learning content faster. Standardizing an instructional design architecture and presentation style goes a long way to accelerating development. Adopting and adhering to a development lifecycle is also crucial. My personal experience suggests that dramatic savings in time can be made through a fresh approach to the review process. Rapid development needs reviews that focus on essentials, comment objectively and positively, and are delivered on time. Apart from short, simple courses, I have less confidence in self-publishing as a lever for rapid development than standardization and streamlined processes.

Development costs

Development costs are largely labour and project management costs. Generally, they are assessed using one of these metrics:

- cost per learning hour
- cost per screen/page

Learning hours can only be estimated; different learners move at different speeds. The number of screens in a course can be calculated more accurately by analysing the Detailed Design. Use the metric that gives you the most accurate costings.

Complexity impacts on cost. Some developers find it helpful to rate a Detailed Design as simple, average or complex and to apply an appropriate scale of costs.

In summer 2002, the eLearning Guild conducted a Development Time Ratio survey. Respondents were asked about the *average* number of hours they took to develop a one-hour self-paced course. The results are given in Figure 17.4.

Course complexity	Development hours
Simple	117
Average	191
Complex	276

Figure 17.4 — Development time ratio[8]

Within an enterprise, the spectrum of development cost is surprisingly broad. At one end, there's a single SME based in a low-overhead branch office developing a Web-enabled PowerPoint presentation; at the other, a large development team based in a high-overhead city developing a media rich, highly interactive 40-hour course. Somewhere in the middle, a learning department employee is using an authoring system and templates to build a straightforward functional course. It's likely that the SME will spend less than 25 hours developing an hour's worth of learning; the person in the learning department might spend 80 to 100 hours. It wouldn't be unusual for the high end team to spend between 200 and 600 person hours developing content to support one hour of learning. The cost of the PowerPoint equals the SME's loaded salary plus opportunity costs. The effort of the high end team will cost hundreds of thousands of pounds or dollars.

Because development costs are labour costs, some people look to markets where labour costs are low. Asia is an obvious candidate and there are development companies in India which have experience creating e-learning content for clients based in Europe and the USA. To a degree, savings made from Asian labour costs will be offset by additional costs incurred in project management, communications, travel, time difference and — not to be ignored — cultural differences. I know people who have had very successful and cost-effective development projects based in India and others who regretted placing the work there. If your design process isn't working the way it should or is behind schedule, having a development team based on another continent will only add to your problems. Another low cost region where a skilled and experienced e-learning development community has emerged is the Canadian province of New Brunswick. Developers there work regularly for Fortune 500 companies. The exchange rate with the Canadian dollar will benefit any project based in the USA or Europe; more than that, the province has noticeably lower overheads and labour costs than most of Canada so development enjoys the benefit of the so-called "Atlantic dollar". When I made cost comparisons between development based in London and New Brunswick, London costs turned out to be approximately three times higher.

No matter where your development is based and no matter what tier of expertise you bring to bear on it, there are variables which will impact on cost:

- Quality baseline — the aesthetic standards you apply to screen design, graphics, animations, audio and video.
- Media richness — the amount of multimedia content you develop.
- Interaction richness — the quantity and quality of interactions learners have with content.
- Templates versus craft — if what's on the screen is determined strictly by templates, development will be less expensive than if developers have scope to elaborate.
- Stability of content — if a course is being developed in parallel with the development of source content (say, a new process or go to market solution), count on a lot of changes during development.
- Complexity of content — as a rule of thumb, the higher up Bloom's hierarchy of complexity, the more expensive content is to develop.
- Value to the business — sponsors will invest more in content that is critical to business success or when they have a problem that nothing else has been able to fix.
- Shelf-life — usually the cost of content development is in direct proportion to shelf-life, short shelf-life equals low cost.

Banana skins

The path to content development is littered with banana skins. There's no way to make them go away but if you know what they are and where they are, you can mitigate them.

Turnaround time for reviews

When business units have aggressive deadlines for the delivery of e-learning content, they often propose extremely short turnaround times for scheduled reviews of content, for example: "If we have the document by close of business Friday, you'll have our comments back first thing Monday morning." If you believe that the material can't be adequately reviewed in 2 days, say so up front, politely but firmly. When feedback turns up 4 or 5 days late, it's the development team who will be asked to make up for lost time. Add up all the slippage from missed review dates and you can easily lose a month out of your development schedule. Aim to define reasonable review periods in the SLA between business units and the learning department. Liase with the sponsor and your SME's line manager to ensure that time scheduled for reviews has been cleared. At the same time, the project manager should keep the SME informed of any changes to the delivery dates of content for review. Springing last minute scheduling changes on an SME whose time is over demanded will not endear them to your project.

Battle of the experts

Getting experts to agree can be a challenge. Even though two or three might broadly share a point of view, each will see things slightly differently. Those slight differences can be your undoing. It's not uncommon for there to be more than one SME involved in a content development project. Even when there is only one nominated SME, I've noticed that SMEs will share design documents with colleagues and take their feedback on board. Sometimes there is a hierarchy of experts; the real expert is too busy to review all the content so deputizes junior experts for day-to-day reviews. In both these situations, you can find yourself caught up in a battle of the experts where feedback from different sources conflicts or, worse, where one expert warns you that another expert is wrong.

Often it's impossible to bring everyone together even virtually to resolve the contradictions. You can end up not knowing what has been signed off and what hasn't. To protect yourself, you need to ensure that your SLA stipulates a single source of feedback. SMEs can argue all they want—but among themselves; you need to hear a single voice. Bring large amounts of diplomacy to bear, but insist that only feedback from the nominated source counts. If you can, agree a conflict breaking process in advance, perhaps by appointing an arbiter to rule on conflicting views—the sponsor, for example. Even the threat of arbitration can sometimes resolve conflict.

Unrealistic schedules and budgets

There is an expectation on the part of sponsors that e-learning will move at what we used to call e-speed. E-learning certainly delivers content faster than other channels but many sponsors are unaware of the complexities and time parameters of the development process. As a result, they will propose unrealistic schedules. If you are certain that applying all your energies, skills, experience, resources and determination will not ensure the delivery date is met, you need to make that point before committing yourself. I am not suggesting a complacent approach to scheduling but there really is only so much development that can take place in a given period of time. Increasing the size of the development team looks like a good idea but as IBM mega-project manager Frederick Brooks pointed out more than 25 years ago: "Since software construction is inherently a systems effort—an exercise in complex interrelationships—communication effort is great, and it quickly dominates the decrease in individual task time brought out by partitioning. Adding more men then lengthens, not shortens, the schedule."[9] Brook's observation is commonly rendered as: because one woman can produce one baby in 9 months doesn't mean that nine women can produce one baby in 1 month.

Unrealistic budgets should be resisted, too. Of course, sponsors are entitled to the best value for money they can negotiate but beyond a certain point, negotiation deteriorates into self-delusion. Unrealistic schedules and budgets are a lose–lose situation. Now matter how hard you try, you will fail to meet your sponsor's expectations. No matter how hard your sponsor drives the negotiation with you, he will end up paying the real cost of development in terms of time and money. Some learning departments think they can outsource the problem but all they're doing is moving it temporarily. It won't be long before third-party vendors will come back looking for more time and money. Present your case for a realistic schedule and budget with facts, diplomacy, patience and conviction.

Scope creep

Scope creep isn't confined to content development projects but it can be just as damaging there as elsewhere. Your first level of protection is the development of a set of interrelated and highly specific key documents: the Preliminary Design sets the scope for the Detailed Design; the Detailed Design sets the scope for software development; the budget and schedule set the financial and time parameters for the realization of the Preliminary and Detailed Designs. The second level of protection is the implementation of a change control process. Any change requested by the sponsor or SME *after* sign-off that will impact on the schedule and/or budget needs to be evaluated and documented. The change should not be implemented until the sponsor signs off the domino effect on delivery and budget. The evaluation should include risks to the overall project resulting from an extension of scope; there is a tipping point with scope creep after which its impact becomes exponential.

On some projects, I've seen change control become a disproportionately large management overhead; all I can say is, it is better than blindly making every change that's requested and arguing about the cumulative impact when the project is already running late and over budget. Of course, if a sponsor is prepared to pay for changes to the scope and to extend the delivery date, there's no reason not to implement them.

Reviews, feedback, bug reports

A number of people will review content for different reasons and at different points in the process, for example, sponsor and SME reviews, unit testing, integration testing, proofreading. Managing the output of these reviews can be challenging especially with a large course. Try to develop a standard form for everyone — possibly in Excel or Access; that way you can collate reviews under software control. Five or six people might comment on a single sub-module; you want to be able to give the developers a single document that lists all the required fixes — and you don't want to rely on cut and paste to create it. If you've implemented a CMS to support content development, you can also use it to support workflow. If the CMS has a Web interface, reviewers anywhere in the world can input comments and associate them with any component of content. Later developers can call up both the file and the comments together.

Evaluating a Detailed Design and multimedia work in progress can wrongfoot SMEs who don't work with these components on a regular basis. Putting aside some time to brief an SME—or any reviewer—about the content they need to review is a good investment of everyone's time. Explain the format of the Detailed Design and any technical phrases or abbreviations used. When introducing multimedia content for review, make sure everyone understands what phase of development it's in. What looks like shoddy work to the inexperienced eye is often just preliminary work.

There really should not be many bugs in e-learning content—especially if development is template driven. When bugs do turn up, they tend to be easy to put right. The Achilles heel of content development is the development team's interpretation of the Detailed Design. In my experience, about 80% of issues logged by reviewers have to do with interpretive issues. Does the animation reflect the process accurately? Does the diagram convey the concept accurately? Is the simulation true to life? Storyboards and prototyping can help but they just move interpretive issues to an earlier stage of the process which while making them less costly to fix doesn't make them go away.

There are ways to mitigate interpretive issues. Make sure the initial briefings by SMEs are not rushed and that there is a process in place for going back to clarify matters arising. Ask for assurances that documents which form part of the briefing are themselves accurate and up to date. Ask outright if there is anything the sponsor and SME do not want to see in the course. It helps, too, if Web developers are experienced with business content; it will help them understand the principles, processes, etc., that they are illustrating. Create an environment where asking a question is a positive action and not an admission of ignorance; too often developers suffer in silence when asking a single question would resolve their concerns about interpretation.

Something to watch out for is scope creep masquerading as feedback. When SMEs see for themselves software's potential to convey their subject, they can be tempted to exploit that potential further by developing a more involved presentation—that's scope creep. The SME isn't deliberately moving the goal posts; they just want the best presentation possible. If that means going beyond what was agreed in the Detailed Design, it's time to invoke the change control process.

Delivery

Delivering content for review—whether from a third-party development team to the learning department or from the learning department to the sponsor—is a rolling process that can turn out to be fraught with complication. Preferably, third-party developers should FTP (File Transfer Protocol) software units and courses to the learning department; in practice, enterprise firewalls don't always support FTP. E-mailing content looks a good second-best option but again limitations on the size of e-mail attachments coming into the enterprise can undermine it. I've seen content hand delivered on CD-ROMs when enterprise network policies make other options unworkable. Of course, even hand delivery becomes an issue when developers are hundreds or thousands of miles away. Given enough time and cooperation, all these issues can be overcome but if you're just starting out, they can catch you unprepared.

Similarly, providing the sponsor and SME with access to content for review can prove problematic. If possible, content should be hosted on a review server accessible on the enterprise extranet. Making the review server accessible from the enterprise intranet is easy but there are situations where busy SMEs can't access the intranet. Maybe they're working on a client site, or are themselves external suppliers with no access rights. None of these issues is insurmountable but they need to be planned for in advance.

Copyright and royalties

There's an assumption that content from libraries is inherently inexpensive. It never was the case and with the global market in IP more developed and controlled than it ever was, costs of photographs, moving pictures and music from library sources are increasing. The same is true of text based content from third-party data vendors. This doesn't mean you shouldn't use library material; it does mean you should budget for it on a realistic basis.

What you need to do

Buy or build

There are many thousands of hours of generic e-learning content available from publishers at costs significantly lower than those associated with developing custom content. You won't close all your performance gaps with "off-the-shelf" content but if some are in areas common to most enterprises or most enterprises in your sector, generic content can be worth evaluating. The bulk of generic e-learning content covers IT areas, from beginners' courses in Microsoft Office to advanced courses in network administration and programming. There is also an increasing number of courses covering non-IT areas like quality standards, customer service, finance, human resources and leadership.

Off-the-shelf content is attractive because it eliminates development lag, risk and cost — but that doesn't mean there are no trade-offs. Here are some of the points you need to consider when analysing buy versus build:

Learning Curve: Each publisher has their own user interface. If you expect staff to work with custom content as well as with content from one or more publishers, you are asking them to learn a number of e-learning interfaces. Each publisher also takes a different approach to instructional design; that impacts on the way content is presented and learning assessed. These differences can impact on learning speed and effectiveness.

Configuration: Most publishers support a degree of configuration to the presentation layer. You might be able to change colours and fonts, or insert your company logo. Configuration beyond defined parameters can be very expensive or not possible. Make sure you understand the scope of configuration that is supported.

Common Catalogue: It's best practice to provide learners with a single content catalogue. They should not have to navigate to different locations in search of the learning they need. If you are mixing custom content with content from different publishers, do not underestimate the challenge of providing a single catalogue. If you intend to use more generic content than custom, it makes sense for a publisher to provide and host the catalogue. Make sure the publishers have a detailed understanding of your catalogue requirements and a strategy and process for meeting them before committing yourself.

Localization: While the underlying principles taught in off-the shelf content might reflect those in your enterprise, it's unlikely the nomenclature for roles, processes and equipment will be the same. Some enterprises consider these differences impediments to effective learning. Most publishers provide a localization service but the associated costs can negate a proportion of the cost benefit of off-the-shelf content. If your enterprise has a policy of presenting learning in the local language, find out which languages publishers support for which courses. If you need courses translated, obtain detailed quotations in advance. Discuss the possibility of partnering on translation costs; if the courses are popular internationally, the publisher might be prepared to share translation costs.

Specifications and Standards: Whether your custom courses will be hosted on the publisher's servers or their courses on your server, you need to be sure the content is interoperable — that custom and off-the-shelf content will interact with the Learning Management System in the same way without changes having to be made. If you intend to run two brands of generic content on the same LMS seek the same assurances. Interoperability is not an issue that can be resolved by claiming compliance with e-learning specifications and standards or through discussion. Only rigorous tests will tell you what you need to know. Don't commit yourself until you are satisfied that (1) the content is interoperable, or (2) you understand the scope and cost of work required to make it interoperable.

Learning Objects: Many publishers claim their content supports learning objects; the trouble is "learning objects" means different things to different people. A discussion about learning objects is really a discussion about specifications and standards. Find out what draft standards publishers use to implement learning objects and exactly what aspects of those standards they implement. Test your custom learning objects on the publisher's servers or their learning objects on your server.

Managing development

Self-paced e-learning content development is complex and slippery because it is made up of a number of interrelated though quite different processes. To manage it you need:

- An overarching process to hold all the sub-processes and associated skills together in an effective sequence — Figure 4.7 on p. 90 illustrates a high level content development lifecycle.
- Key documents that ensure the whole team — almost invariably a virtual team — is working to the same goal.
- An approach to quality that is embedded in the super process.

There are usually four groups involved in self-paced e-learning content development (see Figure 17.1 on p. 274 to see how they are related):

- A business unit — it has a performance gap.
- The learning department — it's been asked to close the gap.
- The design team — it analyses the performance gap, then applies instructional design and writing skills to develop a solution.
- The development team — it builds the solution in software.

Traditionally, the learning department has been an internal resource — although some enterprises have started to think about outsourcing most of its work. The learning department frequently outsources design and development activity. That does not change the roles, responsibilities or processes but reinforces the need for an overarching process and key documents to keep efforts aligned.

The pivotal figure in content development is the project manager in the learning department; she is responsible for delivering content on time and on budget. The project manager reports to the relationship manager in the same department who owns the relationship with the sponsor in the business unit. Where development is outsourced, the project manager owns the commercial relationship with the third-party developer. She will have overall responsibility for the vendor selection process which includes the development of a Request for Quotation (RFQ), a project briefing document and, where appropriate, a confidentiality agreement. When a vendor has been selected, the project manager owns the contract and project work plan that consists of a schedule, project milestones and budget. Where development is outsourced regularly, there will usually be a preferred supplier list which simplifies the selection process and leverages long-term relationships.

If there is a large design team, it will be managed by a senior designer; in practice, it's common for the design team to consist of one designer and perhaps a writer or researcher. In large learning departments, there might be a head of design to set standards and oversee the output of all design teams. The design team reports to the project manager for scheduling and delivery, and to the business unit's SME for getting the content right.

Generally, an external development team is led by a producer who owns the business relationship with the production manager in the learning department. Under the producer, there is a project manager responsible for the development team delivering on time and on budget. At its centre, the development team consists of a number of Web developers with specialist skills in HTML, Java, 2D graphics, 3D graphics, Flash animations, audio, video, etc.

The development lifecycle

The development lifecycle provides the overarching process for content development. It begins when the business case for learning has been approved and ends with the delivery of a self-paced course. Figure 17.5 illustrates a typical course development lifecycle. While the diagram suggests a linear process, in practice development is almost always based on parallel processing. For example, as soon as a meaningful section of the Detailed Design is signed off, it goes into development. At any given time in the lifecycle, content will be in design, in development and in review. Almost every sub-process is a rolling process. The Preliminary Design is an important exception. Since it sets so many critical parameters, no development should take place until the whole document has been signed off internally and by the sponsor.

Key documents

The key documents that support content development perform critical functions:

- By recording the business unit's performance requirements, the instructional design strategies, and the software development requirements, key documents enable validation of the content development process formatively and summatively.
- Because they are portable and updateable, key documents enable the whole development team—usually geographically dispersed—to stay aligned with evolutions in both the vision and detailed requirements.
- Because they can be stored and searched, key documents support knowledge sharing within the e-learning development community.

Though the nomenclature varies, there are usually five key documents associated with each self-paced course:

- Business Case
- Preliminary Design

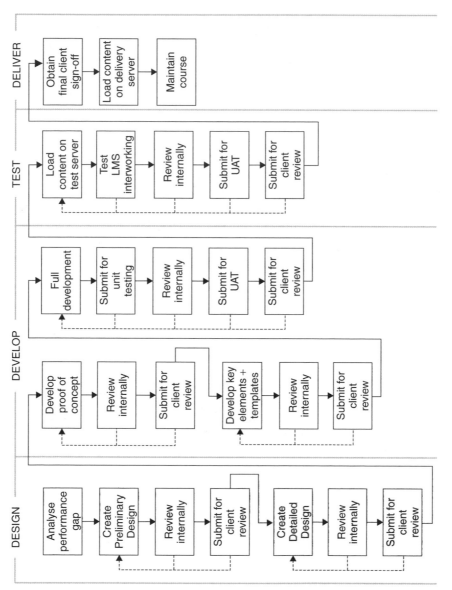

Figure 17.5 — Typical course development lifecycle

- Detailed Design
- Schedule
- Budget

Most enterprises will have their own tools and templates for schedules and budgets so I won't go into those.

Business Case

The Business Case is developed jointly by the business unit and the learning department as a pre-condition of development. From the sponsor's point of view, it ensures that:

- Learning is an appropriate method of closing the performance gap — as opposed to re-tooling or improving performance incentives.
- Development costs are broadly known upfront.
- ROI is attractive, and where required sits within centrally established guidelines.

From the learning department's point of view, the Business Case ensures that learning is aligned with the business and that projects are not started before funding has been secured.

A typical Business Case will include the following:

- a committed sponsor
- the stakeholders
- nominated subject matter experts
- the result of a performance gap analysis including:
  - the case for closing the performance gap by answering the question: are we improving something when we should be throwing it out?
  - the case for choosing learning to close the performance gap — as opposed to environmental or incentive-based remedies
  - the case for choosing e-learning to close the performance gap — as opposed to face-to-face classes or other delivery channels
- estimated content development and maintenance costs
- estimated development schedule including milestones
- an ROI case
- behavioural objectives — to set the target which Level 3 evaluation will later test, for example: "Within four months 85% of learners will have used the new process for creating a project plan."
- key project roles and responsibilities
- key project risks and mitigations
- where appropriate, localization requirements

- where appropriate, the rationale for buying an off-the-shelf course versus building a custom course
- where appropriate, a discussion of the commercial value of the course if licensed externally

Whoever funds development signs off the Business Case. In most cases, it will be the business unit.

Preliminary Design

Once the business case has been signed off, a Preliminary Design is prepared by the design team working closely with the relationship manager, business sponsor and SMEs. Performance objectives and scope of content are critical elements of the Preliminary Design. David Merrill makes a strong case for scope: "Determining the necessary and appropriate knowledge components for a given instructional goal is critical. *Determining what to teach is the most important activity of the instructional design process.* Learning cannot occur if the necessary knowledge components are missing. Learning will not be effective or efficient if the knowledge components are incomplete or inappropriate."[10] The performance gap analysis in the Business Case will point to what needs to be learned. Working with SMEs and perhaps the sponsor, instructional designers fine tune the knowledge components. The audience for the Preliminary Design includes:

- the sponsor
- the design team
- the development team

The document should be signed off by the sponsor and the SME. A typical Preliminary Design will include the following:

- a definition of the learner base:
  - size
  - business unit(s)
  - geographical location(s)
  - role(s)
  - group—for example, at the Dow Chemical Company staff fall into four groups: Global Leadership, FSFL (Functional Specialist, Functional Leader), Administration, Technicians and Technologists
  - where appropriate, competency rating
  - pre-knowledge of course content—acquired by interviewing managers and sample learners
  - age, education or other relevant characteristics

- the performance objectives, including:
  - key learning points in order of priority
  - success factor—what the learner needs to be able to do after taking the course
- especially where the course teaches a process, high-level answers to these questions:
  - *what* are we trying to do?
  - *why* are we doing it?
  - *how* do we want to do it, that is, the performance target?
- the instructional design strategies applied at each level of the course—see Figure 16.9 on p. 266 for a sample ISD architecture
- what accreditation, if any, the course leads to and the basis on which it is awarded, for example,
  - number of hours of study
  - coverage of content
  - post-assessment grade
- where appropriate, the relationship of the course to the framework of competencies in the enterprise
- nominated subject matter experts, either internal or external
- content references, for example:
  - existing learning objects
  - existing courses—whatever the delivery channel
  - videos
  - books
  - periodicals
  - CD-ROMs
  - research work
  - white papers
  - public or subscription Web sites
- creative treatment:
  - the style and personality of the course
  - special design ideas or functionality
- estimation of scale, that is, the number of
  - media objects
  - learning objects
  - modules
  - sub-modules

- assessments and questions
- study time by course, module and sub-module

- course structure and scope including names and descriptions of each learning object, module and sub-module
- tools available for download within the course, for example, templates, forms and spreadsheets — and whether they exist or need to be developed
- case studies

  - are they appropriate?
  - do they exist?
  - if none exist, are there likely candidates?

- media selection

  - any there existing media objects that could be included or adapted?
  - recommendations about which media type should be used to communicate or demonstrate each subject, for example:
    - text
    - photographs
    - graphics — with pop-up text? with voice-over?
    - animation — with voice-over?
    - schematics or flow-charts — animated?
    - video — demonstrations, interviews
    - simulations

- delivery — when the course is needed
- localization — are local versions required? how many?
- course maintenance — assumptions about shelf life and update cycle
- proof of concept — software that demonstrates the look and feel of the course, or special features and functions.

Detailed Design

Developed by the design team, the Detailed Design specifies every element of the course. It is the software developers' "script". If prototype features and functions, or a proof of concept were not included in the Preliminary Design, they can be included in support of the Detailed Design. A typical Detailed Design will include the following:

- schematic of course structure — from course home page down to sub-modules
- specification of features and functions
- storyboards of key screens and interactions
- graphic design brief including:

  - look and feel — unless prescribed by standard templates
  - list of all graphic elements

- detailed specification of each sub-module — or whatever the lowest level of granularity is, including:
  - all displayed words — proofread
  - full audio, video and animation scripts — if necessary, as separate documents
  - all assessments including:
    - descriptions of learner options and interactions
    - right answers
    - feedback for both right and wrong answers
    - strategy for building assessments from pools of questions
    - scoring strategies and passing requirements
    - adaptive content strategies for pre-assessment, if applicable — some people call this "testing out"
- description of course home page elements
- Level 1 evaluation form — which should be standardized
- supplements to generic online help files if non-standard features and functions are implemented
- to support the course catalogue:
  - keywords for course learning objects, modules and sub-modules
  - if learning objects are implemented, standard metadata tagging
  - course description for course catalogue
- where appropriate, a glossary
- where required by enterprise policy, list of links to public Web sites so permissions can be sought
- detailed production schedule developed in conjunction with project manager and software development team
- analysis of programming and production issues developed in conjunction with project manager and software development team.

Quality

Testing content just before it goes out the door might uncover all its shortcomings but it does so too late in the process to be of value. Monitoring and maintaining quality needs to be a continuous process throughout the development lifecycle. The key documents provide reference points for validation and verification — sometimes called V&V.

- *Validation* answers the questions:
  - Are we developing the right content?
  - Does the content meet the learner's requirements described in the key documents?

- *Verification* answers the questions:
    - Are we developing the content right?
    - Does each sub-process meet the specifications described in the key document developed in the *previous* sub-process?

The approach which ensures verification and validation is usually described in a V-model — see Figure 17.6. The model illustrates the relationship between validators — the key documents, processes and deliverables. One document comes from outside the development process: e-learning standards and LMS requirements.

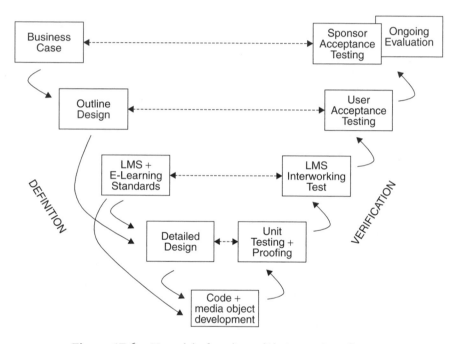

Figure 17.6 — V-model of quality validation and verification

Content wrapper

Before e-learning standards emerge, one way to ensure interoperability is to build content that is standards agnostic, then to design and build a piece of middleware that some people call a "content wrapper". The wrapper is positioned between e-learning content and the LMS. Crudely put, it speaks the language of both the content and the LMS, and acts as an interpreter for the dialogue that takes place between them (see Figure 17.7). Because your content contains no code that is LMS or e-learning standard specific, you can make it interoperate with any LMS — whatever standard it supports — by modifying the wrapper.

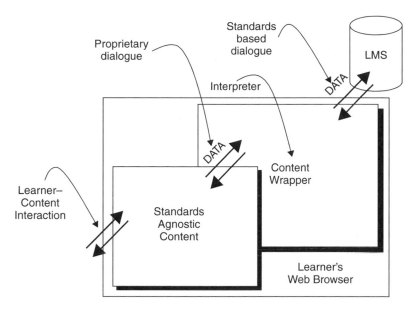

Figure 17.7—Content wrapper

The wrapper sits in an invisible frame that is part of the content frameset loaded in the learner's browser; its presence and functions are transparent to the learner. Since the wrapper is invisible, it does not constrain screen design. When the learner's interactions with content generate data—the time at which a module was started or finished, or the answer to an assessment question—the data is held in the wrapper until the learning session ends. Then using a data structure the LMS understands, the wrapper uploads the data to the server. Designing and building a wrapper is a project in its own right, but it is much less difficult, expensive and time-consuming than rebuilding all your content if you decide to conform to a different standard or change LMSs.

The content wrapper has already proved itself to be a powerful tool but I believe a more creative use of content wrappers will emerge. The first full set of published e-learning standards will be conservative and limited in scope. It's axiomatic—creating commonality means catering to the lowest common denominator. With standards published, competition between content developers will move into the arena of standards implementation. The question will be, who can wring the most value, the most learner interest, the most engaging learning interaction from plain vanilla standards? Content wrappers will prove an important weapon in the competition because they will allow content with greater complexity than the new standards support to behave—from the LMS's point of view—like standards conformant content. The market will pay attention to developers who can create wrappers that turn data outputs from their non-standard content into standards based outputs.

Authoring tools

A surprisingly wide range of tools is used to author content—from Word and PowerPoint though to Flash and Dreamweaver. Making recommendations about specific authoring tools is outside the scope of this chapter but there are some guidelines that can help you answer the question: which authoring tool should I use? A good way to start is by answering these questions:

- Who will be using the tools?
- What kind of content will they be building?

Who

Content authors fall into two camps: professional and non-professional developers. Professional developers have invested time to acquire the skills necessary to leverage high-end Web authoring tools with steep learning curves. Non-professionals might be subject matter experts or learning department staff who expect tools to have shallow learning curves and to allow them to create content quickly and easily. Tools for non-professionals tend to be "authoring systems" that take care of the housekeeping of content development and provide a limited set of pre-defined options; tools for professionals provide a comprehensive set of powerful and flexible features and functions with which to build content. Most authoring systems will cramp the style and limit the effectiveness of a professional developer; tools for professionals will bewilder and limit the productivity of the non-professional. Since it is common for content to be developed by professionals and non-professionals within one organization, you might need two sets of tools.

A suite of Web development tools used by a professional e-learning content developer might look like this:

- Macromedia eLearning Suite:
  - Dreamweaver
  - CourseBuilder
  - Authorware
  - Flash
- Adobe Photoshop
- Adobe Illustrator
- Adobe Premiere
- Adobe AfterEffects
- Adobe Acrobat
- Discreet 3ds Max
- Sonic Foundry Sound Forge
- Microsoft Visual Studio .NET

- Microsoft Visual J# .NET
- WinZip
- McAfee VirusScan
- Microsoft Word
- Microsoft Notepad

Dedicated e-learning authoring systems include Macromedia Authorware, Click2learn Toolbook and X.HLP Designer. Some authoring tools and suites are integrated with LMSs and LCMSs, for example, Knowledge Mechanics KM Studio, Saba Publisher and WBT Systems TopClass Publisher.

What

Authoring tools and systems are designed to meet specific needs. Before you evaluate tools, you should have a highly developed vision of the kind of content you expect to develop. Here are some categories and types of content:

- static content
- dynamic content
- content developed and published with or without the support of a CMS or LCMS
- learning objects
- structured courses
- assessments
- simulations
- animations
- graphics
- video
- audio

No one authoring tool can do everything though authoring systems can be fairly comprehensive. Licences for authoring systems are not cheap so you need to keep an eye on the costs of tooling up. Here are some other considerations for authoring systems:

- Is there a large user community you can turn to for peer-to-peer support?
- How many question types does it support? Some support only the basics: multiple-choice, true–false, ranking, fill in the blank, odd one out.
- Does the content require a "player", that is, a proprietary Web browser — or a large browser plug-in that learners need to download? Content should be native to Internet Explorer or Netscape and not require plug-ins.
- Does it support tagging, that is, storing metadata with content files?
- How easy is it to create simulations of software applications?
- Are any templates provided with the application?

What you should avoid is getting locked into content based on proprietary standards. Standard Web development tools generally produce open content. On the other hand, if you're thinking about purchasing an authoring system, press the vendors for information about whether the output is open or proprietary. If it's proprietary, remember you'll be locked into using that authoring system to maintain the content for as long as it is in use. The same is true if you use content authoring modules built into an LMS or LCMS. You could end up locked into delivering proprietary content through that LMS or LCMS; the only escape would be to rebuild the content using open standards.

References

1   *The Power of the Internet for Learning: Moving from Promise to Practice* (2000) The Web-based Education Commission to the President and the Congress of the United States [Internet] Available from <http://interact.hpcnet.org/webcommission/index.htm> Accessed 20 Sep 2001.

2   *Online Learning: E-Learning Strategies for Executive Education and Corporate Training* (2000) [Section] Fortune Magazine [Internet] Available from <http://www.docent.com/misc/wp_strategies.pdf> Accessed 4 Apr 2002.

3   Longmire W (2000) *A Primer on Learning Objects* ASTD Learning Circuits [Internet] Available from <http://www.learningcircuits.org/mar2000/primer.html> Accessed 23 Nov 2001.

4   Hodgins HW (2000)*Into the Future—A Vision Paper* [Report] Commission on Technology & Adult Learning [Internet] Available from <http://www.learnativity.com/into_the_future2000.html> Accessed 21 Sep 2001 p 27.

5   Wiley DA (2001) *Connecting Learning Objects to Instructional Design Theory: A Definition, a Metaphor, and a Taxonomy* In Wiley DA (Ed.) *The Instructional Use of Learning Objects* Bloomington, Association for Educational Communications and Technology [Internet] Available from <http://reusability.org/read/chapters/wiley.doc> Accessed 17 Jun 2002.

6   Wiley DA (2001) *Connecting Learning Objects to Instructional Design Theory: A Definition, a Metaphor, and a Taxonomy* In Wiley DA (Ed.) *The Instructional Use of Learning Objects* Bloomington, Association for Educational Communications and Technology [Internet] Available from <http://reusability.org/read/chapters/wiley.doc> Accessed 17 Jun 2002.

7   Robson R (2001) *Pros and Cons of Learning Objects* Eduworks Corporation [Internet] Available from <http://www.eduworks.com/LOTT/tutorial/prosandcons.html> Accessed 12 Jun 2002.

8   *The e-Learning Development Time Ratio Survey* (2002) The eLearning Guild [Internet] Available from <http://www.elearningguild.com/pdf/1/time%20to%20develop%20-Survey.pdf> Accessed 9 Jul 2002.

9   Brooks FP (1995) *The Mythical Man-Month: Essays on Software Engineering, Anniversary Edition* Reading MASS, Addison Wesley p 19.

10 Merrill D (1998) *Knowledge Objects* CBT Solutions March–April 1998 Vol 1 No 11 [Internet] Available from <http://www.id2.usu.edu/Papers/KnowledgeObjects.pdf> Accessed 18 Jun 2002.

Part V
Case Studies

PWC Consulting case study: integrating learning and knowledge

18

"The Learning and Knowledge Group is the manufacturing arm of PwC Consulting." Amy Wright, global leader of the Group, knows her claim is ironic — and accurate. "We have only one product. People. We supply people to the business. The smarter those people are, the better they deliver solutions to our customers and sell our services." For a business consultancy operating in the connected economy, Wright's focus on people is on the money. When what you're selling is thinking that's ahead of the curve, the way to differentiate your offering in a competitive market is through the quality of the people who do the thinking. The smarter the people, the better the thinking, the greater the differentiation.

Historically, the way PwC Consulting has worked smart is by developing and applying best practices with the goal of delivering projects quickly, consistently and effectively. This raises the question: how do you arrive at a best practice? There's more than one path:

- On the basis that they must be doing something right, you can study the practices of the most successful businesses in the world.
- On the assumption that they know the answer, you can ask your clients exactly what it is they need.
- Or you can examine your most successful and innovative projects and extrapolate best practices from the processes the teams applied. In other words, you can harvest the tacit knowledge learned by consultants in the field and embed it in shareable practices and tools.

PwC Consulting augments its best practices with a highly developed point of view that encompasses industry-specific insights usually arrived at through dialogue with industry leaders.

In the of autumn of 2000, Wright was appointed Global Leader of Learning and Professional Development (L&PD), in effect, the consultancy's training department where historically the focus had been on classroom learning. She set in motion a programme of realignment and reorganization. In the course of the programme, it became clear to Wright that the needs of the business and its consultants would be best served by integrating:

- Learning — including e-learning.
- Knowledge Management.
- Methods — what the consultancy calls its best practice group.

In the autumn of 2001, an integration initiative was given the green light by senior management. What follows is an examination of Wright's integration initiative which pulls together many of the themes and principles that underpin this book. The business and recent history of PwC Consulting set the context for the initiative and it's important to understand them — especially since they reveal a business in a constant state of transition over a number of years. I'm not suggesting the consultancy is somehow at fault for causing or allowing constant change. My point is the very opposite — all business is now in permanent flux. Transition isn't an event or a project, it's a lifestyle. Learning and e-learning must be designed, first, to flourish in that environment and, secondly, to help senior management respond effectively to change. The notion that implementing e-learning means figuring out what to do, setting it in motion, then walking away is deeply flawed. E-learning needs to remain in lockstep with changing business conditions and requirements.

Business background

PwC Consulting is the management consulting and technology services business of Big Five accounting firm PricewaterhouseCoopers but — for reasons beyond the control of the firm's auditing and consulting practices — that's going to change. PricewaterhouseCoopers itself was formed by the merger of Price Waterhouse LLP and Coopers & Lybrand in July 1998. As it turned out, the integration of the firms' distinct cultures proved challenging. Two years later the process was scarcely complete when the US Securities and Exchange Commission (SEC) gave the accounting profession a wake up call. In June 2000 it approved a major new rule proposal that will (1) force accounting firms to restructure radically, and (2) significantly change the independence requirements for accounting firms that audit SEC registrants. The SEC described the rule proposal as the most significant concerning auditor independence since the federal securities laws were enacted in the 1930s. From the perspective of accounting firms, the biggest impact was to limit dramatically their ability to provide services other than audit and tax services to SEC audit clients. All of a sudden, PricewaterhouseCoopers needed to get out of the consulting business.

Coincidentally, earlier that year PwC had instructed investment banker Morgan Stanley to restructure its business with a view to separating Managing Consulting Services (MCS), as the consultancy business was called at the time, from the auditing business and floating it through an initial public offering. The scenario makes sense when you recall that this was the height of the dot-com boom and investors wanted a piece of new economy businesses low in traditional assets but high in intellectual ones. A business consultancy was the natural fit.

In September 2000 the drive towards an IPO digressed when Hewlett-Packard Co. emerged with an offer to buy MCS—according to reports for a figure somewhere between $14 and $18 billion (USD). On paper, the deal worked. HP's consulting business was growing so fast, its recruitment efforts couldn't keep pace. In 1999, consulting revenue accounted for $1.5 billion of HP's $7.2 billion services revenue. At a stroke, the acquisition would grow HP's service division staff by almost 700%, an increase some analysts believed could translate into a 2000% increase in the computer manufacturer's consulting revenues. In the same stroke, PwC would comply with SEC independence requirements.

The market saw things differently. HP's share price dropped 6% on the day of the announcement—and in a weak market fell another 17% up to the beginning of November when HP pulled the plug on the deal. Still facing SEC's new requirements, PwC had no choice but to revert to its interrupted restructuring—this time in the context of a dot-com burn out.

Less than a year later, the same consulting practice, now renamed PwC Consulting, was buffeted again—along with the whole global business community—by the events of 11 September 2001. The buffeting was exacerbated throughout the autumn by Arthur Andersen & Company's self-destructive role in the Enron debacle. Accounting practices came under unprecedented scrutiny. PwC's drive towards independence accelerated. In January 2002, PwC formally announced a plan to separate PwC Consulting through an IPO. In March, PwC Consulting announced that it had begun the process of changing its name and brand identity. Against this swirling backdrop, the case study that follows was played out.

About PwC Consulting

PwC Consulting provides business consultancy to enterprises in the areas of strategic change management, process improvement and technology solutions. At the time of writing, its annual turnover for the fiscal year 2002 is estimated to be around $4.9 billion net (USD). The consultancy has about 30 000 consultants and 1200 partners based in 52 countries across six continents. Fourteen hours of flying time separate the two PwC consultants based furthest from each other. The consultancy has this global dimension because its multinational clients demand it. The business is organized into four theatres:

- Americas
- Europe-Middle East-Africa
- Asia-Pacific
- South and Central America

Within the four theatres, there are four industry-centric practice areas—the business units—each operating in the same seven service areas (see Figure 18.1).

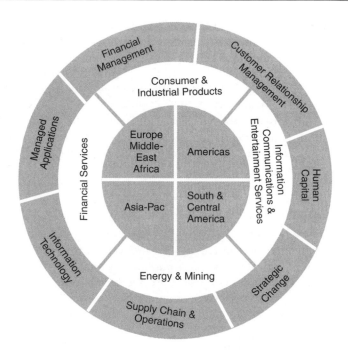

Figure 18.1 — PwC Consulting structure

Over the past 15 years, the consultancy's business has grown by 25%. Each year approximately 20% of staff leave the firm to be replaced by thousands of new joiners. Of those, many will be experienced consultants who will be ready to perform after spending just 10 to 15 days learning PwC Consulting's methods and practices. The other entrants are university graduates with no consulting experience. Their time to perform is 50 days. As a result, each year PwC Consulting invests in about 250 000 days of new joiner learning — with no balancing income.

The consultancy's most important business metric is utilization of staff — a measure of how much of a consultant's time is billed. Consultants not engaged in billable work represent a substantial overhead: 1% of utilization is worth $48 million. Even a small increase in utilization, for example, reducing graduates' time to perform from 50 days to 40, would deliver big benefits — in this example, saving the cost of 50 000 learning days each year and, more importantly, saving 50 000 days' worth of opportunity costs. Each year PwC Consulting invests about $200 million in learning. Recently, 76% of that spend has been on instructor-led learning and 24% on e-learning.

No one's home

In the context of a global business consultancy, location is a barrier to delivering learning and knowledge. When a consultant is recruited to a large project team, typically they won't set foot in a PwC premise for the next 3 months; in fact, if the project is large enough, a consultant will work exclusively at the client's site for 6 months, a year, sometimes longer. It's not unknown for consultants to move directly from one large project to the next. That means (1) consultants have little face-to-face exposure to centralized services, and (2) learning and knowledge must be delivered to consultants where they need it, that is, where they work — most often, at client sites. From the consultancy's perspective, there's a third impact: the nomadic style of working typical of a modern consultancy practice means there are few if any de-briefing opportunities. The lessons a consultant learns in the course of a project are unlikely to be captured, assessed or shared.

All of us are smarter than some of us

"How do I know," a client challenged David Dockray, managing partner for the EMEA theatre, "that I'm getting the full value of PwC Consulting's global knowledge and not just what the 20 consultants working in my office know?" The question stopped Dockray in his tracks. If in practice my client is only leveraging the knowledge of the 20 consultants he's paying for, Dockray mulled, how can I look him in the eye and tell him that engaging PwC Consulting with its global network of knowledge and skills will give his business a competitive edge? What the question had made instantly clear to Dockray was the need for a better, faster, cheaper, more consistent way of sharing knowledge and best practices — not just across projects, but countries and theatres too. The challenge, as Dockray saw it, was to engage more than 30 000 minds in every project, not just the 20 or 30 minds on the project team — and more than that, to leverage the personal knowledge networks of every consultant on the payroll. That could happen only through a process of learning and knowledge sharing that was integrated, coherent and global.

The global dimension was critical. What American consultants learn from a successful SAP implementation in a US pharmaceutical business can be applied the next day, for example, by Asia-Pac consultants on behalf of a pharmaceutical client in Japan. Because the hypothetical Japanese client benefits from everything learned in the USA, his business can achieve a significant time advantage over its competitors in the home market. It doesn't stop there. "Learnings" from both the US and Japanese projects can be leveraged in a third project, say, in Australia — and so on. With this model, consultants find themselves engaged in the kind of Learnativity spiral we looked at in Chapter 4 — see p. 84.

Integration

The integration project team gave the global board of PwC Consulting a list of eclectic suggestions for the name of the new integrated group. The board chose *Learning and Knowledge* (L&K). The integration initiative was scheduled to take one year. There was no dedicated project team though there was a programme manager in each theatre. Otherwise, everyone involved in the project also continued to execute their usual responsibilities.

Before the integration, learning had been the responsibility of the global People and Knowledge group. Knowledge Management had been a completely separate activity also under P&K but operationally responsible to business units at country level. Methods, the best practices development group, was housed within the Services Development Group. It provided products and services to support PwC consultants in winning work and delivering successful projects (see Figure 18.2).

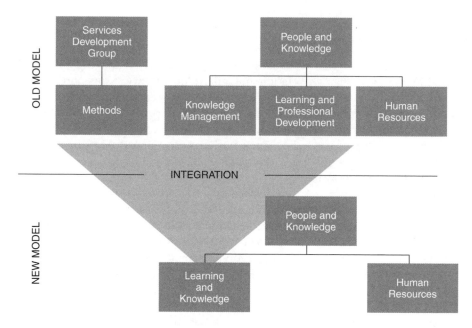

Figure 18.2 — Integration model

The drivers

The key driver for the initiative was the integration of learning, Knowledge Management, methods and activities in order to globalize and upgrade knowledge harvesting, sharing and distribution. Other drivers for integration included:

- Increasing awareness within the consultancy of the learning and knowledge resources available.
- Increasing the ease with which consultants can access the learning and knowledge resources available.
- Dismantling learning and knowledge silo activity.

- Increasing learning and knowledge efficiencies in response to a softening market.
- Leveraging technology more effectively to share knowledge and build skills.

An independent survey had shown that there was duplicated effort in the activities of LPD and Knowledge Management. While cost savings were not a driver for the integration initiative, they occurred naturally as a result of centralization of activity at theatre level. The integrated global L&K group had a staff of about 600.

In the past Knowledge Management had been driven by country and practice area. For example, there would have been a Knowledge Management database in Germany dedicated to Customer Relationship Management (CRM). All German consultants working in CRM would enter their "learnings" there. It was where they made all their knowledge searches, too. The result was a blinkered view of CRM that missed out on the tacit knowledge available in the databases of other practices and countries. Through centralization, Knowledge Management databases started to harvest and deliver at theatre and global levels.

The value proposition

The value proposition of the new integrated group was:

> To increase the value created for our clients by improving the performance of our practitioners who sell and deliver services.

At the heart of the value proposition lies a proactive approach that positions Learning and Knowledge alongside the consultancy's business units both operationally and in the board room. Wright sits on the Global and Theatre boards. She holds the pragmatic view that the head of Knowledge and Learning — or whatever that role is called in other enterprises — does not need to come from a training background. Wright believes it can be easier to gain the attention and respect of senior management if the leader comes from a business background instead. Wright was herself recruited from a client-facing role in e-business. She brought a business focus and client-centric attitude to her new responsibilities — points that were not lost on the management team and business unit leaders she works alongside. Wright is adamant that L&K should not be a support service waiting on the sidelines of business until a learning or performance gap appears, then springing into action to close it. Instead, L&K's role is to work with business units to help them achieve their goals.

L&K's value proposition is supported by six core services that the integrated group has promised to deliver to the business:

Build competencies: Develop the knowledge, skills, abilities and behaviours required for client success. Build and provide a personal curriculum. Build an environment that promotes learning as a continuous activity.

Help projects deliver effectively: Aid project teams throughout the project lifecycle — by delivering learning face-to-face and remotely, in real-time and through self-service. Develop and enhance methods and tools to help projects work smarter, faster and more competitively. Provide an integrated help desk.

Harvest and share account and project learnings: Target priority learnings. Harvest from all phases of the client service process — as rapidly as possible. Repackage learnings and best practices to provide "the best of the best". Provide research to project teams in ways most practical to practitioners.

Harvest and share business and client learnings: Build industry intelligence — point of views, trends, issues, markets, customers. Build client intelligence — products and services, people and culture, organization, processes and technology. Build performance intelligence — process, technology and organizational benchmarks.

Facilitate communities: Identify and support communities that don't formally exist in our organization structure. Make the community aware of all that is available. Facilitate the sharing of information within the community. Focus sharing on strategic priorities. Make it attractive to join and contribute to the community.

Analyse investment results: Understand the business environment we support. Understand the current/historical use of our products and services and the resulting impact. Assist our stakeholders in planning and using a new blend of our products and services. Measure the impact and report back. In practice, this service should result in consistently high investments in learning where business growth and potential lie.

To ensure these core services are on a business footing, they are embedded in a Service Level Agreement between L&K and the business units. The SLA defines exactly what business units can expect from L&K in terms of service, and sets out the associated costs. The SLA is important because it encourages business units to stop thinking about Learning and Knowledge as a group that delivers a series of one-off courses paid for on a course by course basis, and to start thinking about it as a trusted advisor who promises to keep consultants at peak performance levels — using whatever means that requires — under an annually funded service agreement.

That said, the SLA isn't a one-way street. It places obligations on the business units, too, largely in the area of resourcing. Under the agreement, business units have a responsibility to:

- Provide subject matter experts who:
  - support the development of learning content
  - present learning content in Web-based interactive collaborations
  - moderate online discussion forums
  - assess best practices before they are lodged in knowledge databases.

- Develop sound business cases for learning initiatives.
- Develop sound business cases for SMARTS accounts — more about SMARTS below.

Within the US integration team, David Stirling had special responsibility for change management. He understood that the easy part of integration was re-drawing the organizational chart; the hard part was changing people's behaviours. "The biggest challenge for L&K people," Stirling observed, "is to forget the old model, to stop thinking about themselves as purveyors of training services, and to start thinking about themselves as part of the firm's business team."

It's easier said than done. Learning and Knowledge is not a client-facing group. Members of the group can feel isolated from the everyday business of winning new work and successfully delivering projects. To help their own people engage with the new model, the integration team developed eight practical business objectives — each reflecting the belief: "We are positioned to make a significant impact on costs, revenues, and sales." Each business objective is linked to one of L&K's six core services (see pp. 309–310).

1. Reach 90% of PwC Consulting practitioners and partners with targeted training.
2. Contribute to winning 10 PwC Consulting engagements.
3. Recover $7 million of fixed operational costs from the Global Training Centre and Learning and Professional Development Centre facilities budget.
4. Increase the usefulness of Network of Electronic Interfaces (NoEIs) in the SAP, FMS and Pharmaceutical practices by 25% (Note: L&K measure usefulness through satisfaction survey results. A NoEI is a front end for knowledge databases — see p. 317.)
5. Increase the number of blended learning events by 50% over FY01.
6. Increase the number of "connected minds" in the PM and SAP communities.
7. Harvest project learnings from the strategic accounts in the SAP, FMS and Pharmaceutical practices. (Targeted number: 6 SAP, 5 FMS and 7 Pharmaceutical strategic accounts.)
8. Deliver targeted learning, knowledge and method solutions through SMARTS to 20 strategic accounts.

SMARTS

SMARTS is an acronym for Strategic and Managed Accounts: Resources, Tools and Services. The SMARTS programme is the embodiment of two of the core services the Learning and Knowledge group is committed to delivering to the business:

- Manage investments.
- Help projects deliver effectively.

SMARTS consists of the real-time delivery of customized learning to project teams working for PwC Consulting's high-value strategic accounts. Here's how it works: strategic projects are identified as candidates for becoming a SMARTS account. In the US theatre, the current target is 20 active SMARTS accounts. Because the programme is resource-intensive, there are practical limits to how many concurrent accounts can be supported. It hasn't happened yet but in time it's likely that a queue of prospective strategic accounts will form behind the active accounts. Once a account has been identified and agreed with the account partner, a SMARTS account manager from L&K is assigned to the project team. The SMARTS account manager commits 8 to 10 hours a week to the account. When you remember that accounts are ongoing over several years, the commitment is significant.

The SMARTS account manager works in partnership with the account lead and project partners. At the outset, they meet in order to:

- Discuss the account and project objectives.
- Review the members of the team and the experience they bring to the account and project.
- Establish known and anticipated skills and knowledge gaps.
- Discuss how these gaps can best be filled.
- Nominate the most likely "learnings" from the project which will need to be harvested and later shared.

Based on the output of the initial meeting, the SMARTS account manager draws up a Needs Analysis Report that specifies what L&K will both deliver to the project and harvest from it. The SMARTS account manager joins the account team, participating in regular meetings and providing ongoing support from L&K. Within this relationship, L&K often works with bid teams providing research, methods and sales support to improve sales to these accounts.

Because we don't know what we don't know, there is a danger in over-specifying what learning should be harvested. Innovative solutions can emerge out of any project and learning plans need to be flexible enough to accommodate the unexpected — both in what is harvested and delivered.

There are no dedicated SMARTS delivery teams; learning is delivered from centralized L&K resources. SMARTS focuses on blended learning using a mixture of e-learning, Web-based collaborative learning and, where necessary, instructor-led learning. Many of the online collaborative sessions are recorded so consultants can access them asynchronously. The SMARTS team identifies appropriate self-paced e-learning content; to facilitate the use of and access to e-learning, it develops custom "learning paths" for project team members.

To minimize time away from projects, SMARTS provides learning in small bites. If the SMARTS account manager and project partner decide that instructor-led learning needs to take place on the client site, L&K will provide the instructor and content — usually organized in 2- to 3-hour sessions that give consultants the flexibility to complete project tasks and acquire new learnings. On-site delivery means the opportunity costs traditionally associated with face-to-face learning are driven out while face-to-face benefits are driven in.

Funding

A Learning and Knowledge budget is agreed annually at global board level. From the global budget, each business unit is allocated a number of learner days with a cost attached to each day. The allowance is always just a little less than a business unit might hope for—simply to position learning as a scarce resource that should not be squandered. Each business unit leader divides its allocation of learning across its seven service areas. In the course of a year those allocations can be moved between service areas but not increased.

Whatever the delivery channel—classroom, online collaboration or e-learning—content is always developed centrally and funded out of a central learning budget. Development is not charged to business units. Where content has been developed then delivered exclusively to one business unit, delivery costs are charged to the unit.

At business unit level, the focus is on client-centric delivery—that means all learners in a class are engaged on the same account. Even though it foregoes cross-fertilization of ideas between accounts, this hothousing of account teams has been shown to produce the best solutions to client issues.

Where delivery is global—for example, new joiners learning or a course on project management applicable across the practice—delivery as well as content development costs come out of the central learning budget. With content delivered globally, there's no account segregation. Learners in one classroom or in one Web collaboration can come from a number of accounts, giving opportunities for knowledge sharing across accounts and theatres.

Centrally-financed content delivered globally tends to fall under the headings of technology, teamwork and knowledge sharing. Content delivered at theatre level tends to take the form of:

- The SMARTS programme.
- Instructor-led learning delivered in a PwC premise or hired facility, for example, an hotel.
- Instructor-led learning delivered in a central learning facility like PwC Consulting's learning centre in Tampa.
- Collaborative learning which always means Web-based sessions using CentraOne.

Where a theatre or country has localization requirements, for example, the need to translate a course developed in English into a local language, the localization is paid for by the country.

So, the funding of learning can be summarized like this::

- Content development: funded centrally.
- Content delivery: funded centrally for global learning needs.
- Content delivery: funded locally — that is, at theatre, country, or business unit level — when it meets local learning needs.

SMARTS is funded differently. Every business unit receives an annual allocation of funds to cover activity under the SMARTS programme. The allocation is scaled to fund two SMARTS-supported projects. That number isn't carved in stone and could be adjusted as the programme develops. If the cost of learning requirements for SMARTS accounts in a business unit exceed the annual allocation, the business unit must fund the difference. Annual allocations have been carefully calculated, so topping up the SMARTS budget should be required only in cases where a project team is over-delivering to the client or asking for learning which is beyond what the project needs. So far that hasn't happened.

Evaluation

There are two conditions that must be met before learning and knowledge receive the attention they deserve in an enterprise: (1) a learning and knowledge representative sits on the board, and (2) there is a demonstrable return on investment. With the first condition already met, the Learning and Knowledge group pay close attention to ROI.

L&K calls evaluation *Performance Metrics*. The driving metric is *time to utilization* which defines the time gap between the learning event and the application of what was learned. The outer edge of acceptability is 6 months. Where time to utilization is overly long, there are two likely explanations:

- The learning was not effective — in other words, there is a quality issue.
- The learning was not relevant or solution-centred which can be a quality issue but is just as likely to be a management issue.

It's a management issue if learners are allowed or directed to take the wrong courses, that is, courses not aligned with the learner's immediate business needs. L&K conducted a time to utilization survey and discovered that only 25% of learning had been utilized within 6 months. That meant $150 million a year was being invested in just-in-case learning when what the fast-paced consultancy business really needed was just-in-time learning. L&K next surveyed learners to find out if there was a quality issue with the learning that was being delivered. Learners told L&K quality was not an issue.

So the wrong learners taking the right courses was the reason time to utilization was not what it should have been. When that phenomenon was examined more closely, it turned out that business units were not as engaged in monitoring and guiding who was taking what courses as they could have been. Ideally, each consultant's annual appraisal will include the discussion and agreement of a personal learning path for the following 6 months; in a project driven environment, it can be hard to see learning needs beyond that point. Managers had found it challenging to make time to discuss, design and monitor individual learning paths.

L&K decided the best way to make business units pay more attention to how they were using learning was to remind them of its financial value. Business unit leaders were told to share their annual learning budget across their seven services as numbers of learning days, for example, 600 instructor-led days to Financial Management services and 450 to Supply Chain and Operations services. The allocation of days then cascades down to the level of line managers who own operational responsibility for learning spend. Now, when a consultant asks his manager to go on a 5-day course, everyone from the learner right up to the business unit leader understands that those days are coming out of a limited resource. There is no attempt to discourage learning but there is a requirement to demonstrate that requested learning is aligned to real business needs. What L&K have done is to create a check on relevancy at both the supply and demand ends of the learning chain:

Supply: Business units need to submit a business case to L&K for the development and delivery of learning.

Demand: Learners need to submit a business case to their line managers to participate in learning.

As a result, the *time to utilization* metric changed dramatically in just one year—from 25% of learning utilized within 6 months to 60%. That change represented a saving of millions of learning dollars. It's tempting to draw the conclusion that regardless of the language used, these savings resulted from a curtailment of learning. What invalidates the conclusion is the fact that the controls and time to utilization metric apply only to high value classroom learning and collaborative learning on the intranet, not to self-directed, self-paced e-learning. There's more about this distinction in Hierarchy of Needs on p. 318.

The time to utilization metric is tracked by a sequence of surveys across a sample of learners. The first survey is conducted 6 weeks after the learning event. It's followed by one survey each month until the learner declares they've applied what they've learned. You'll remember from Chapter 3—ROI, Metrics and Evaluation—that this approach is classic Kirkpatrick Level 3 which evaluates learners' behaviours: can the learners go out and do it? Has their behaviour changed as a result of learning?

Knowledge Management

L&K doesn't talk about Knowledge Management—it talks about *learning and knowledge*. Learning knowledge, skills and practices from a shared knowledge base is not viewed as separate or different from learning from a self-paced e-learning course, a moderated Web collaboration or a classroom course. L&K accept that different skills are needed to design, develop and deliver learning events — whether synchronous or asynchronous — than those required to facilitate the exchange of knowledge, but that's only a difference in *how*; the more important *why* is common to all these learning activities: to deliver smarter consultants to PwC Consulting's clients.

To understand how their consultants really leveraged knowledge sharing, L&K asked them. A survey revealed that the most effective learning was facilitated by an informal buddy network. If consultants needed to learn something, they picked up the phone and called someone they trusted. The survey results reflected a known practice that Ikujiro Nonaka and Hirotaka Takeuchi describe in *The Knowledge-Creating Company*: "In reality, informal groups evolve among individuals seeking to solve a particular problem or pursuing other commonly held objectives. Membership in these groups is decided by individuals' abilities to trade practically valuable information. Orr (1990) argues that members exchange ideas and share narrative or "war stories," thereby building a shared understanding out of conflicting and confusing information."[1]

For PwC consultants, having a personal relationship with the source of information turned out to be as important as the information itself. "Why should trust be of particular value in the knowledge driven economy?" asks Charles Leadbeater in *Living on Thin Air*. "Trust has become so valuable because we need it more and yet it has become more elusive: demand has gone up while traditional sources of supply have contracted. Trust has become more important because it fosters the co-operation and risk-sharing that promote innovation and flexible response to change in a global economy."[2]

Often the trusted buddy was engaged on a different project. That happens because there are a number of unique roles in each project. There is, for example, only one programme manager. If the programme manager needs to consult a buddy who is a peer, that person is going to be engaged on another project where she is the only programme manager. That means there is a dispersed community of programme managers who have a potential for trust in each other but who have no process to help them make the connections that can develop into relationships and, in turn, the sharing of what they know and learn. Programme managers are just one example of potential communities that for one reason or another do not occur naturally. Recognizing the importance of what the survey had revealed, L&K responded by including Facilitate Communities as one of its six core services.

The facilitation happens in two ways:

- First, by maintaining face-to-face learning — classroom and Web based — despite the high costs associated with it. Continuing with our example, when a group of programme managers working on different accounts in different theatres are brought together for a global course on project management, cross-fertilization of ideas occurs naturally. So does the creation of personal networks that will lead to an ongoing exchange of ideas and methods.

- Secondly, by establishing a dedicated intranet site where communities, like programme managers, can post questions and share knowledge. These intranet sites are owned and actively maintained by L&K, updating them with regular postings of news and information of interest to each community.

Consultants who use the sites are a needs-driven community. That's important — adults learn most effectively when what they are learning is relevant, applicable to their daily work and problem-centred. Participation in these intranet communities is voluntary and there is no obligation on participants to contribute. Like forums on public Web sites, the community is made up of a relatively small group of vocal contributors and a larger group of "lurkers" — people who learn by observation but make few contributions. L&K does not become involved with the content on these sites, for example, editing user contributions. That is the work of subject matter experts. Within each community there is a group of volunteers who moderate the exchanges and manage and control the quality of information posted there.

Tacit knowledge, what an enterprise's employees have learned *first hand* about their work, is the most valuable knowledge an enterprise possesses. Writing in 1998, the Institute for the Future was unequivocal in its valuation of tacit knowledge: "In times of great transition and turn-over, like the past decade of downsizing and reengineering, tacit knowledge goes out the door with the workers. In the new knowledge economy, however, it's precisely this tacit knowledge that will give companies their competitive advantage. Companies must find formal ways to nurture this knowledge and pass it around, or they won't make it into the next century."[3] The trouble is, precisely because it is first-hand knowledge, increasingly, no manager and no central body in an enterprise is in a position to make qualitative judgements about tacit knowledge. Today, peers are best placed to make judgements about what constitutes best practice — which is why PwC's online communities are self-moderating.

PwC Consulting maintains eight global knowledge databases organized around core topics like Business Practices and Marketing. To give the stored data greater focus, it can be viewed through industry- or service-specific filters called Network of Excellence Interfaces or NoEIs. Since the content underpinning NoEIs consists of postings and documents from consultants in the field, there is a danger the databases will become uneven collections of random thinking instead of a structured entry point to the best ideas in the consultancy.

When a consultant does a search on an issue they're dealing with, what they don't need is 800 hits on entries of variable quality. One hit will do the job — as long as it's the right hit. Quality control measures need to be in place to keep the databases centres of excellence. iAnalytics is one of the solution areas within PwC Consulting. The leaders of iAnalytics recognized the need for quality control in their own NoEI and set up a group tasked with ensuring that only best of breed ideas were published there. But what makes an idea best of breed? As we've seen, there is no single arbiter to consult; instead, useful judgements are the outcome of rigorous debate by informed peers.

It's no secret that achieving consensus among a group of experts is characterized by volubility and garrulousness. In other words, experts like to argue among themselves. Within the iAnalytics community, the upside to this noisy debate was the creation of an ad hoc virtual forum — whose members are working subject matter experts — for the exchange and testing of best practices. When something is published in the iAnalytics NoEI, consultants can be confident that it reflects the best thinking in the consultancy. With that high quality resource in place, no iAnalytics project team needs to reinvent the wheel — and every team is able to build on best practice.

Hierarchy of needs

A large part of the attraction of working for a global business consultancy like PwC Consulting is the quality of learning available. Everyone arrives with high expectations. All learning, however, is not of equal value to the business. We've seen how L&K took steps to ensure their learning aligned with their business needs. But when you look at learning from a consultant's point of view, it's about more than being prepared to perform at peak level throughout projects. Learning is also (1) the key to a successful career path, and (2) a way of acquiring interesting knowledge and skills for which a consultant has no immediate application. The Learning and Knowledge group could see that a hierarchy of learning needs existed within the consultancy (see Figure 18.3).

The highest need is for project-driven learning and knowledge. Without successful, profitable projects the business will fail and any other learning needs become immaterial. However, if *all* learning has a project focus, consultants will feel their longer-term career-driven learning needs aren't being looked after. A consultant might want to improve her interviewing and team leadership skills even though she is years away from leading a major project team. So ranked below project learning is the consultant's need for learning that can enable career advancement. And below career-focused learning is the need for the learner simply to pursue what interests them about the business they're in — whether that's an entry level course about Java or an advanced course about e-procurement.

Instructor-led training is the most expensive to develop and deliver; self-paced e-learning, the least expensive. Other delivery channels sit within those cost parameters. PwC Consulting scales its investment in learning in proportion to the hierarchy of learning needs. Project-driven learning is supported by four learning channels:

- The high-investment SMARTS programme.
- Expensive instructor-led learning.

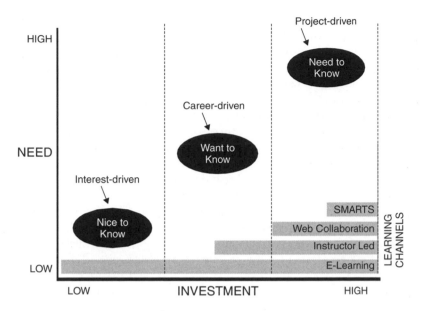

Figure 18.3—Hierarchy of learning needs and investment

- Web-based moderated collaboration using CentraOne, in effect, online instructor-led learning.
- Self-paced e-learning courses—relatively inexpensive to buy or custom develop and deliver.

Career-driven learning is supported by e-learning and some instructor-led learning. It forms part of a consultant's personal learning path and is discussed in the course of their annual review. While project-driven learning is typically planned only 6 months in advance, career-driven learning can be planned a year in advance, even longer. Interest-driven learning is supported by e-learning and consultants are encouraged to take as many of the 4000 self-paced courses available to them as they have the interest and time to pursue. Nothing is done to restrict interest-driven learning to areas in which the learner is currently or likely to be engaged—nor to evaluate either its effectiveness or whether it generates a return on investment. By contrast, high-investment, project-driven, client-centric learning and knowledge is painstakingly evaluated.

Blended learning

Blended learning, the use of a mix of delivery channels available in an enterprise's learning value chain, figures in PwC Consulting's learning model. It's one thing to talk about mixing channels to meet a learning need but I always wonder about what drives the proportions of the blend. Is it considerations of cost, instructional design, expediency? Here's how it works in PwC Consulting.

In order to access their annual learning budgets, business units need to present a business case to the Learning and Knowledge group for each learning initiative they have in mind. The business case includes a cost analysis of what the business unit views as the most appropriate learning delivery channels — how much of the money applied for will be spent on instructor-led learning, how much on Web-based collaboration, and how much on e-learning. Learning and Knowledge has a vision of the relative amounts that should go into the consultancy's overall blend; this information is made available to business units in the form of guidelines. L&K has no expectation that every learning initiative will fit neatly into the target blend; what's important is meeting the overall target.

There are two related drivers for channel selection. The first is *time to market*; the second, *shelf-life*. L&K favours two channels for learning that needs to be delivered fast in order to be relevant. One is Web-based collaboration where subject matter experts make live interactive presentations of urgently needed learning. The other is e-learning content authored by subject matter experts themselves using L&K's custom-built rapid development tool. Learning Object Creator, as it is known, requires a level of skill not much more advanced than that required to build a PowerPoint presentation — a skill which is ubiquitous in the consultancy. In contrast, L&K would discourage a business unit from investing in a large self-paced e-learning course to deliver time-critical learning. It isn't only a cost consideration; the real overhead is the time taken to develop large high quality self-paced courses. The corollary is also true. Learning content with a long shelf-life — for example, content on a one-year or 18-month review cycle — is a good candidate for a self-paced e-learning with all the development overhead that carries. Of course, the point of a blended solution is that different aspects of learning content can be delivered though different channels. If some of the content is very stable, it can be committed to a self-paced course or mini-course. The volatile content, on the other hand, would be best handled through moderated online collaborations and self-paced content developed using the Learning Object Creator. Content that falls between the two might be delivered though the classroom.

Postscript

It's a cliché of the information economy that the only constant is change — and like many clichés, this one is true. In the summer of 2002 in the wake of spectacular accounting irregularities at Enron, WorldCom and Xerox, PwC Consulting accelerated its plans to separate from PricewaterhouseCoopers. At the beginning of May, PwC filed a registration statement with the US Securities and Exchange Commission for an initial public offering scheduled for early August. At the beginning of June, PwC Consulting raised eyebrows with the announcement that the new public company would trade under the name "Monday". Another striking change of direction occurred at the end of July, when computer giant IBM announced it would acquire PwC Consulting and integrate it with the Business Innovation Services unit of IBM Global Services. On 2 October 2002, IBM bullishly announced that the expeditious acquisition was complete. PwC Consulting had become IBM Business Consulting Services.

Both IBM and PwC Consulting have considerable experience with internal and client-facing e-learning. It will be fascinating to watch how that experience is integrated and leveraged, and how the world's largest business and technology consultancy engages the minds and knowledge networks of its global team of consultants.

References

1   Nonaka I and Takeuchi H (1995) *The Knowledge-Creating Company* New York, Oxford University Press p 90.

2   Leadbeater C (2000) *Living on Thin Air— The New Economy* 2nd edition London, Penguin Group p 152.

3   *From Information To Knowledge: Harnessing The Talent Of The 21st-Century Workforce* (1998) Institute for the Future [Internet] Available from: <http://www.iftf.org/html/iftflibrary/humanresources.html>. Accessed: 20 Mar 2002.

19 BP case study: embedding an e-learning capability

Just as we are committed to developing and extending our portfolio of business activities, so we are committed to developing and enhancing the capability of those individuals through programmes of education and training, enabling them to fulfil their personal potential to the maximum. They represent our human capital.
Lord Browne, BP Group Chief Executive[1]

No company can ... extract the deep value from within its human and hard assets—without developing and sharing its knowledge, experience, ingenuity, values and strategic purpose across the company. In other words, no organization can harness its own complexity without developing the capacity to learn from itself.
John Leggate, BP CIO and Group VP, Digital Business[2]

"If we get it right," opined David Appleton, BP's Manager of Digital Learning, "we'll put ourselves out of a job within two years." To understand why one of the people responsible for e-learning in the world's second largest and most profitable oil company believes that implosion equals success, you need to know something about the corporate culture of BP.

Business background

In the late 1980s in an attempt to transform the business from a regional multilayered monolithic operation to an adaptive and flexible enterprise capable of responding to new challenges, BP restructured itself from 11 business units into three business streams (BPX, BP Oil and BP Chemicals) in three regions (Europe, America and the Far East). Even so, head office in London still boasted 86 committees and each year each of the group's six managing directors attended more than 100 committee or board meetings. It was common for financial proposals to require 15 signatures before they could be presented to management. More change was required.

BP entered the 1990s with a new chairman and CEO, both determined to make the business more agile. One of the first acts of Robert Horton, the new chairman, was to launch Project 1990—designed to reduce the cost of complexity throughout the BP Group, to define a suitable Group Head Office, and to reposition the corporation in terms of approach, style and business base for the next decade. The same month he became chairman Horton was quoted by *The Financial Times*: "Corporations which achieve the greatest success will be those which are prepared, and able, to respond rapidly, flexibly and imaginatively... What I'm trying to do is to simplify, refocus, make it clear that we don't need any longer to have hierarchies."[3]

At the time, the head of the BPX (exploration and production) business stream was John Browne, now Lord Browne and the current Group Chief Executive. Under Project 1990 Browne initiated a major division reorganization with the aim of meeting the new challenges of oil exploration by releasing the creativity of his people. Browne's agenda was to:

- eliminate layers of redundant management and associated support services
- focus on business units
- shift responsibility from the chain of command to line managers

Browne set out to realize those aims by operating within six broad culture guidelines:

- people
- openness
- teamwork
- simplicity
- trust
- empowerment

The effect was to move BPX from "command and control" management to facilitated management — known within BP today as "leading from the wings" — with decision-making responsibility and authority pushed down to the front lines. Seven layers of management were replaced by four. Browne facilitated change through evaluation workshops where employees identified ways to eliminate bureaucracy, simplify operations and improve performance. Of the three business streams executing Project 1990 it was BPX that demonstrated the most visible results despite the fact that, like the rest of BP, it was grappling with a recession and weak oil prices.

In 1991, Browne adopted another strategy for BPX which was to become a characteristic of the new BP — outsourcing. Significant aspects of IT operations, systems development, systems maintenance and telecommunications were outsourced to a handful of key providers. Under the agreements, the providers were expected to collaborate so closely among themselves that what was delivered to BPX was not standalone services but a single seamless service.

Both the changes set in motion by Horton and the BPX culture of the early 1990s have exerted a significant influence on BP Group culture ever since. In 1994, John Browne became CEO of BP. Today, after 10 years of evolution, BP is a decentralized and lean global business that operates in a highly entrepreneurial environment. Here's how Browne described the new BP: "We have built a very flat team-based organization that is designed to motivate and help people to learn, We've divided the company into lots of business units, and there is nothing between them and the nine-member executive group to whom they report."[4] In 2002, 110 of these empowered business units were operating within four business streams:

- Exploration and Production
- Gas, Power, Renewables and Alternatives
- Refining and Marketing
- Chemicals

At the axis of these business units sits the Global Business Centre which sets context and direction—and defines the boundaries within which the business units operate. Each business unit has a "performance contract" with the Global Business Centre which forms the basis of quarterly performance reviews. Though independent, business units understand it is in their interests to learn from each other; in the absence of a chain of command, a strong culture of networking and knowledge sharing has developed—increasingly facilitated by technology.

In January 1999, John Leggate took over as CIO of the newly merged BP-Amoco and brought with him his passion for organizational learning. As a key part of the process of learning from the outside, Digital Business in BP occasionally holds Colloquia where internal and external experts present case studies and new ideas—and lead discussions about how BP might learn from them. After a watershed Colloquium in 2000, BP faced up to the challenges of digital business with a framework designed fully to align activity with BP Group strategy. Key elements of the framework included:

- Simplicity and Decluttering: The Common Operating Environment (COE)
- Integration and Transparency: The BP Intranet
- Leveraging the Business Units: Sharing and Collaborating
- Living on the Web

The Common Operating Environment

As a result of mergers and acquisitions, BP's infrastructure was a patchwork of networks, standards and applications. Instead of facilitating the easy exchange of data and knowledge, the infrastructure inhibited it. An enterprise-wide commitment to a Common Operating Environment (1) simplified the process of data and knowledge exchange on a global basis, (2) simplified support by reducing the range of hardware and software in use, and (3) increased reliability through the simplified infrastructure that resulted.

Recently, the further acquisition of Arco and Castrol introduced a diversity of desktop environments across the Group. In line with the COE all desktops were upgraded to a common standard—providing all employees with the same user interface to access information resources.

The BP intranet

A robust global intranet was seen as a necessary tool for a business based on the free flow of information, the sharing of learned lessons, and optimizing resource allocation. The intranet would have to conform to and support the COE, be flexible and reasonably future-proof, and conform to Internet standards in order to optimize connectivity — making BP easier to work with for customers, partners and suppliers.

Knowledge sharing and collaborating on the digital network

"Most activities or tasks are not one-time events. Whether it's drilling a well or conducting a transaction at a service station, we do the same things repeatedly," Lord Browne has observed. "Our philosophy in BP is fairly simple: Every time we do something again, we should do it better than the last time."[5] For that to happen, knowledge has to move quickly and efficiently from one business unit to another; that can happen only when people are open to knowledge sharing and work comfortably in virtual teams across continents and time zones.

Virtual Teamwork takes advantage of the COE and the BP intranet to deliver:

- More effective sharing among business units.
- High productivity networks.
- Formation of teams with remote team members.
- Transfer of data and information with understanding.
- Codifying and storage of learning through video and multimedia methods.

In the context of this chapter what is interesting about these three aspects of BP's Digital framework is how they set the stage for the introduction of e-learning.

E-learning: Early drivers

BP sees itself as a knowledge business. It has 110 000 employees working in over 100 countries. Of those, 70 000 have dedicated desktop or laptop computers. Employees without their own systems have access to shared systems. In fact, most BP employees are guaranteed intranet access so they can take advantage of *myHR*, BP's comprehensive online tool for the delivery of HR services. These high level facts alone establish BP as a natural candidate for an e-learning implementation. Like many organizations, the seeds of e-learning within BP had less to do with enterprise level strategy and more to do with tactical learning needs. In 2000, BP had two critical learning initiatives: (1) the global implementation of a standardized desktop, and (2) a push to increase Web skills and e-literacy with collaboration applications like Microsoft NetMeeting and Outlook in order to leverage Virtual Teamworking. A remark by the CEO in an interview in the *Guardian* created a sense of urgency around these projects: "What you can say about the new economy is that it changes the way we work. Email has long been mission critical, but six months from now you will have to be web-literate to even survive within BP."[6] The two learning threads were brought together in an E-Business project funded by Digital Business.

Digital Business is the enterprise-wide group with responsibility for all digital systems, processes, the e-agenda and business process transformation. Through outsourcing, it provides and supports centralized infrastructure services across the group and specific application services to all business units. The outcome of the E-Business project team's efforts was *WebLearn*, an intranet portal for all e-learning about Digital Business across the group (see Figure 19.1). In 2000, it was only a concept; in 2001, *WebLearn* offered 200 courses in five languages and had about 15 000 registered learners who between them took about 25 000 self-paced courses. Because the skills gap was with standard business applications, learning content was licensed from generic content publishers. With the portal in place and the E-Business project team winding down, the success of *WebLearn* — driven by a strong marketing campaign, both face-to-face and through digital delivery — made people consider the potential of e-learning to deliver more than basic digital skills. The need to embed an e-learning capability in all business units was recognized and from the ashes of the project rose Digital Learning sponsored and funded by Digital Business.

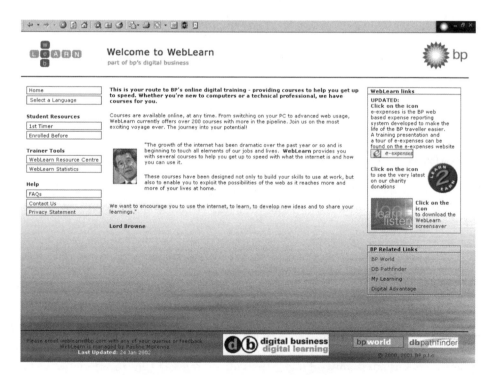

Figure 19.1 — BP's *WebLearn* home page

It's worth reflecting on the previous sentence. The perceived need was not for an e-learning group or centralized e-learning capability. In a global organization as large as BP, a centralized e-learning resource would not have been a cost-effective method of reaching the significant learner population—nor would it have been aligned with the autonomy of business units. The correct solution for BP was to embed an e-learning capability within business units.

The used of the word "embed" is not arbitrary; within BP, it has a specific meaning. The Learning Stages is a well known four-part model: (1) unconscious incompetence: I don't know what I need to learn; (2) conscious incompetence: Now I know what I need to learn; (3) conscious competence: I have learned what to do; (4) unconscious competence: I do it automatically.[7] In BP, to embed a capability means unconscious competence: "At this stage the business team takes the lead and links what they are doing to their routine business processes. Meanwhile the experts take the role of advisors, and introduce new tools where appropriate."[8] Digital Learning was funded centrally as a service to business units but that didn't mean Digital Learning was going to develop and distribute e-learning for the business; it meant Digital Learning existed to help business units learn how to develop and distribute e-learning for themselves. That Digital Learning is funded by Digital Business is interesting, too. In most enterprises, e-learning is owned by the learning group or HR. In BP, Digital Business took the initiative with e-learning because the initial driver had been closing a digital skills gap.

Its subsequent funding of Digital Learning was an entrepreneurial action, providing seed money, if you like, for an initiative it believed the whole group would benefit from. It would be easy to assume that Digital Business is so rich the investment in e-learning wouldn't be felt. It would also be wrong. With a heavily outsourced organization and a high proportion of Digital Business spend appearing in the budgets of business units, central funding is a notable exception. When Digital Business picked up the $1.7 million tab for one year of Digital Learning operations, it represented a significant spend item.

BP's learning structure

In BP there is a group level Learning and Development Committee (L&D) whose membership is drawn from the Executive Committees of the business streams. L&D, like all BP enterprise management committees, sets policies, standards and targets—and creates processes to ensure that people achieve or adhere to them. Below L&D is the operational group: BP Global Learning and Development Network. The network is made up of Content Owners Learning and Development Professionals, Infrastructure Owners and Others. Infrastructure Owners are Digital Business who own the technical infrastructure and Group HR who own the learning infrastructure. Content Owners are, mainly, Digital Business for technical skills and Group Technology for petrotechnical skills, plus Finance, HSE and Group HR who are responsible for leadership and soft skills learning. There is a Learning and Organizational Development Group whose focus is departmental leadership training and specialist training. The Learning and Development Network also liases with Knowledge Management and Communications.

Current drivers for e-learning

The key driver for e-learning across BP is cost savings through effectiveness and efficiency. To shed some light on that driver, it's helpful to recall the definitions of Knowledge Management guru Karl-Erik Sveiby: "Efficiency is calculated solely on input variables; effectiveness is calculated with both input and output variables. Efficiency measures show how well an organization is using its capacity...Effectiveness measures how well an organization is satisfying the need of those it serves."[9] BP understands that e-learning is not the solution to all learning needs but where content and e-learning are a good fit, e-learning can deliver at least the equivalent of face-to-face learning for much less cost and with greater flexibility.

A second driver for e-learning is its power to transform a business by changing the way its people learn. It's far too early to judge whether e-learning will have the same kind of positive impact on BP as did Knowledge Management but e-learning's potential (1) to develop its people to peak performance and readiness to compete, and (2) to increase organizational agility by sharing knowledge and skills across the group quickly and efficiently are important drivers.

The third driver is blended learning, that is, leveraging face-to-face learning for aspects of content best suited to the classroom, and leveraging e-learning for aspects best suited to a self-paced self-directed approach. Typically, BP use blended learning to bookend classroom learning with prerequisite and follow-up content delivered through e-learning. There is a recognition in BP that 20% of its learners are natural e-learners while the remaining 80% take some convincing. With a culture based on leading from the wings, it's counterproductive to insist that people use e-learning.

What's interesting in BP is that blended learning can also happen within the classroom. An instructor might spend part of a session using traditional face-to-face learning but then ask learners to work with an e-learning course. At the end of the day, the instructor will tell learners who haven't finished the self-paced course or who want to go back and review parts of it, they can carry on learning at their desktops. A moderated introduction can convert a good proportion of the reluctant e-learners in the room.

The fourth driver is educating the value chain. In an enterprise built around outsourcing, it's essential that vendors are as much members of the e-learning community as staff. For e-learning to realize its potential to transform a business, BP's customers will need to become e-learners too. In the Refining and Marketing business stream, staff of independent petrol station operators — BP's customers — have already taken the same e-learning courses as staff of BP-run petrol stations.

The fifth driver is compliance. Increasingly, BP staff are required to comply with training standards in HSE (Health Safety Environment), Security and Ethics. E-learning is a natural cost-effective channel for the delivery of much of this learning.

Digital learning: what and how

David Appleton's comment at the beginning of this chapter might be starting to make sense. His mandate was to make his department redundant by ensuring that within 2 years the business units knew enough about e-learning and felt confident enough to develop and deliver it themselves.

The dominant initiative within Digital Learning is called E-Learning Capability. In 2001, the initiative played midwife to 30 e-learning projects that together created almost $30 million in value through cost savings and increases in productivity, for example, shorter time to competence. E-Learning Capability's objectives in 2002 were to:

- Support the adoption, development and implementation of e-learning initiatives.
- Provide a centre of expertise for the exploitation and adoption of e-learning.
- Provide a network of best of breed suppliers to support the development of e-learning programmes.

To meet these objectives, E-Learning Capability developed a set of products and services.

E-Learning Toolkit: Delivered through an intranet site, the toolkit provides guidelines, tools, recommendations and consultancy to business units developing e-learning projects. (There's more about the toolkit on p. 330–332.)

E-Learning Vendor Network: Digital Learning has built a global network of vendors who understand the BP culture and are capable of developing high quality, cost-effective e-learning to meet the needs of business units. Vendors have not only been vetted, they are project-ready. Contract templates for each vendor are available to business units. A vendor database contains information about each vendor and as the number of projects a vendor works on grows, project evaluations will form part of its record.

Catalyst for E-Learning: E-Learning Capability markets the benefits of e-learning to high value areas within the group. Typically, these are functional groups with enterprise-wide responsibility—Health Safety Environment, Security, Finance and Ethics. A Vendor Expo delivered another form of marketing by introducing vendors to functional groups and business units. E-Learning Capability also delivers interactive online presentations across the intranet covering e-learning technology and processes. In its role as catalyst, Digital Learning supports e-learning projects through three tiers of service. The service tier available to a project is at the discretion of Digital Learning who make a judgement based on (1) the size of the project—the bigger the project, the greater the risks and rewards, and (2) the visibility of the project—the larger and more dispersed its learner base, the more impact a project can have in promoting the adoption of e-learning across BP. As long as Digital Learning is funded centrally, there is no charge for these services.

> *Tier 1*: This is a hands-off service which simply directs the project owners to the not insubstantial resources available on the E-Learning Toolkit intranet site.

> *Tier 2*: In addition to the resources on the intranet site, Digital Learning provides occasional consultancy in the form of *peer assists*. Peer assists are a common knowledge sharing tool within BP: "Stated simply a peer assist is a meeting or workshop where people are invited from other teams to share their experience, insights and knowledge with a team who have requested some help."[10] In an e-learning context, a peer assist might consist of reviews of key project documents and plans, or help with the selection of a content vendor or developer.

> *Tier 3*: Here a resource from the Digital Learning team is assigned to the project for its duration to provide ongoing support and consultancy.

E-Learning Delivery: Digital Learning also has a responsibility to develop a hosting and technical infrastructure for e-learning. In the past, standalone e-learning projects made their own arrangements for content hosting. If content was licensed from an e-learning publisher, typically, it would be hosted on the publisher's servers. In practice, content could be hosted anywhere. It is a characteristic of BP culture to allow a number of competing solutions to develop until a clear leader emerges; at that point, everyone is expected to adopt the solution that has shown itself to be the best. An ASP model for hosting and LMS services is emerging as the solution of choice. The LMS is owned and operated by Exult, BP's external HR vendor. New e-learning offerings will be hosted in this outsourced environment; existing content will be migrated to it. A single centralized LMS will facilitate the development of an enterprise-wide course catalogue. Regional e-learning portals will be brought under the umbrella of a single enterprise e-learning portal called *myLearning*.

The E-Learning Toolkit

To help meet its objectives, E-Learning Capability developed an intranet site designed to make its E-Learning Toolkit available to all business units and central service groups. In Internet jargon, this site is always "under construction". The core of the knowledge available there was acquired during the development of *WebLearn* but as each new e-learning project generates new learned lessons, they're added to the site. This is an example of how technology allows learning from one business unit to be shared quickly and efficiently with others (see Figure 19.2).

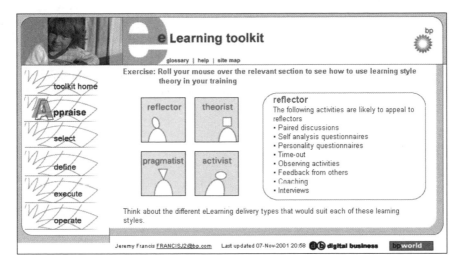

Figure 19.2 — BP's *E-Learning Toolkit* — appraise stage

The structure and navigation of the site have been designed to reflect BP's high-level project management process which most e-learning projects would be expected to follow:

- Appraise
- Select
- Define
- Execute
- Operate

At each level on the site, there is information, lessons learned and download-able tools appropriate to the project phase.

Appraise: This is a pre-project discussion phase in which a number of key questions are addressed: Is your business unit or service group ready for e-learning? Is your content a good fit with e-learning? Would a face-to-face or blended solution be more effective? Is your content aligned with your business goals? There is also support for the development of a business case for the project — and project planning tools to help with phases, timescales and checkpoints.

Select: Here there are tools and templates designed to help the project team assess, select and manage the e-learning vendors they need. The quality and technology parameters of e-learning also need to be analysed. Does the team understand what determines good e-learning? Does it understand (1) the limits of BP's e-learning infrastructure, (2) the learning standards that have been implemented, and (3) the appropriate instructional design for the project?

Define: This is the first stage after a project has been given the green light. Project planning tools are available as well as tools to help the team define project roles and responsibilities.

Execute: Here there are tips about what to avoid, case studies and implementation planning advice covering technical assurance, user acceptance testing (UAT), roll out communications and delivery.

Operate: The project team can access guidelines about monitoring and evaluating their projects.

The E-Learning Community

The Toolkit intranet site is frequented by an e-learning community which by the middle of 2002 had grown to 130 members. There's no criteria for joining — anyone with an interest in e-learning can register themselves. Bearing in mind that Digital Learning's mandate is to embed an e-learning capability across the group, it's notable that there were already more community members than business units — and according to David Appleton, 35 members had already achieved "expert" status. That's an interesting number, too, roughly equal to the number of projects that have been supported by Digital Learning. If each project delivers one e-learning expert, the goal of embedding an e-learning capability across the group is within reach.

The members of the community can communicate with each other at a peer-to-peer level using a dedicated instance of *Connect*, BP's "... searchable intranet repository, through which all staff [can] search for people with relevant knowledge and experience. Additionally, they [can] easily create a personal home page rich in content, which in turn would be accessible to anyone with network access."[11] *Connect* is often referred to as BP's Yellow Pages. Although the community intranet site is owned and operated by Digital Learning, *Connect* allows community members to share knowledge quickly and efficiently, without reference back to E-Learning Capability.

Routes to market

Each business unit has a Business Information Manager (BIM) who is more or less the equivalent of an IT director in a standalone business. Each BIM owns their business unit's relationship with Digital Business; it's through this relationship that Digital Business understands the IT needs of its customers. Since Digital Learning is a part of Digital Business, BIMs are also the primary interface between the business and e-learning. E-learning projects are initiated both through BIMs and the Global Learning and Development Network. To catch all inquiries, Digital Learning maintains an active relationship with the L&D Network.

As part of its catalytic role, Digital Learning also takes a proactive approach to its market by talking to content owners like HSE, Security and Finance. Appleton believes there's a lot of potential for e-learning in areas like Security which is an increasingly large concern for high-profile global enterprises. The challenge in these areas is changing behaviours — people know they should back up data and change passwords regularly but there's a gap between knowing and doing. It's a gap Appleton believes e-learning has the potential to close.

Digital Learning also approaches high profile projects within the group — frequently funded and controlled by a functional group — to find out whether there are learning needs associated with the project that e-learning is well positioned to meet.

Putting it into practice

Intercompany Process is Digital Learning's current benchmark case study. The genesis of the Financial Group initiative was an awareness of shortcomings in the hugely complex inter-company accounting transactions which led to a high error rate. The driver for the initiative — and the e-learning which supported it — was the potential for interest savings in capital which previously had been tied up while errors were corrected.

The e-learning content was distributed globally to 4000 learners who — because BP's accounting processes are outsourced — were largely staff of Big Five accounting firms like PricewaterhouseCoopers and Accenture. Content was hosted on BP's extranet so vendors who work outside the BP firewall could access it. PwC who have the contract for BP's European accounting provided subject matter expertise. Digital Learning's role was to provide Tier Three support — consulting the project team in the areas of hosting, tracking and localization. Content was developed and launched in English then translated into five languages.

Content development followed a rapid prototyping model. Once the prototype had been signed off, development to completion took only 6 weeks. The form of the content was self-paced learning — six modules delivering two and half hours of study plus downloadable tools.

One of the project's learning objectives was to deliver time to competency with the new programme in 3 months. In practice, time to competency was achieved in just 6 weeks — that meant savings began to appear 6 weeks earlier than expected. Because of the high value of transactions, the improvement in time to competency contributed to an impressive ROI.

The future for digital learning

At the end of year two, the Digital Learning project will wind down and the resource will cease to exist in its present form. The strong results delivered through early e-learning programmes like Intercompany Process have encouraged the group to begin developing a longer term learning vision and strategy (see Figure 19.3). There is also the potential for greater alignment — possibly even integration — of e-learning with Knowledge Management. There might also be a group requirement for ongoing e-learning consultancy especially for functional service groups.

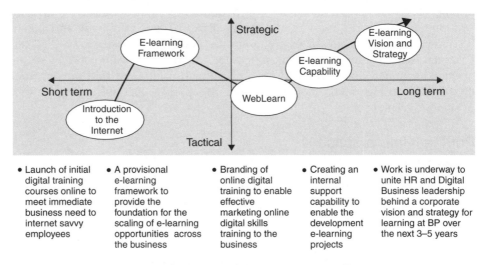

• Launch of initial digital training courses online to meet immediate business need to internet savvy employees	• A provisional e-learning framework to provide the foundation for the scaling of e-learning opportunities across the business	• Branding of online digital training to enable effective marketing online digital skills training to the business	• Creating an internal support capability to enable the development e-learning projects	• Work is underway to unite HR and Digital Business leadership behind a corporate vision and strategy for learning at BP over the next 3–5 years

Figure 19.3 — BP's E-Learning Journey[12]

For these reasons, David Appleton believes there is a need for some form of coordinating management. A new e-learning body could be financed by business units, service groups and content owners. At the time of writing, its shape is up for grabs. With BP's bias for outsourcing, one scenario calls for a very small internal group supported by a network of external vendors with e-learning expertise — the large business consultancies, for example. In the same way that business units now work with Digital Learning and a network of approved external e-learning content publishers and developers, in the future they could work with external e-learning consultants. In addition to supporting business units and functional groups, these consultancies could work with the internal e-learning group to facilitate the development of a long-term group-wide e-learning strategy led by Group HR.

The least likely scenario is that BP will decide to back-pedal on its interest and investment in e-learning — not in an organization where the Group Vice-President of Digital Business holds beliefs like these: "Learning is done largely through bringing people together, and our technology makes that learning more efficient and effective. So we have web-based learning tools, self-service courses, chat rooms where information and best practices can be exchanged; and web-casting to bring teams together or to extend the benefits of our knowledge to other stakeholders — suppliers, for example, on whom we rely heavily to understand our needs more precisely. Again, there are any number of ways in which learning and technology are coming together to grow the knowledge base that is one of our principal assets."[13]

References

1 Brown J (2001) *BP Annual Report 2001* [Internet] Available from <http://www.bp.com/downloads/downloads.asp?category=1> Accessed 1 May 2002 p 13.

2 Leggate J (2001) *Learning in the Digital Era—The Strategic Imperative* [Presentation] The Society for Organizational Learning, Atlanta [Internet] Available from <http://www.bp.com/centres/press/s_detail.asp?id=143> Accessed 1 May 2002.

3 Financial Times 20 March 1990 In Tan B (1996) *Strategic Reorganization and Deployment of Information Technology in British Petroleum* [Case Study] National University of Singapore [Internet] Available from <http://www.comp.nus.edu.sg/~cs4251/Case2.doc> Accessed 1 May 2002.

4 Prokesch SE (1997) *Unleashing the Power of Learning: An Interview with British Petroleum's John Browne* Harvard Business Review September–October 1997.

5 Prokesch SE (1997) *Unleashing the Power of Learning: An Interview with British Petroleum's John Browne* Harvard Business Review September–October 1997.

6 Murphy P and Macalister T (2000) *Sharp Pressed Man—Interview: Sir John Brown, Chief Executive, BP* Amoco The Guardian Saturday April 15 2000 [Internet] Available from <http://www.guardian.co.uk/Archive/Article/0,4273,3986525,00.html> Accessed 4 May 2002.

7 Gordon T (1977) *Teacher Effectiveness Training T.E.T. Instructor Guide Solana Beach*, Gordon Training International pp 4–14.

8 Collison S and Parcell G (2001) *Learning to Fly–Practical Lessons from One of the World's Leading Knowledge Companies* Oxford, Capstone Publishing Limited p 171.

9 Sveiby K-E (1997) *The Intangible Assets Monitor* [Internet] Available from <http://www.sveiby.com.au/IntangAss/CompanyMonitor.html> Accessed 25 Sep 2001.

10 Collison S and Parcell G (2001) *Learning to Fly–Practical Lessons from One of the World's Leading Knowledge Companies* Oxford, Capstone Publishing Limited p 58.

11 Collison S and Parcell G (2001) *Learning to Fly–Practical Lessons from One of the World's Leading Knowledge Companies* Oxford, Capstone Publishing Limited p 105.

12 *BP eLearning Credential* (2002) [Presentation] Accenture.

13 *Learning in the Digital Age: An Interview with BP's John Leggate* (2001) Pegasus Communications Inc Newsletter [Internet] Available at <http://www.pegasuscom.com/levpoints/leggate.html> Accessed 16 Dec 2001.

The Royal Bank of Scotland Group case study: delivering in an immature market

20

If you just close a bunch of branches, you save something like 20 million quid [$30 million] but if you invest correctly in a good IT platform, the savings can run to $500 million. Fred Goodwin, Group Chief Executive, The Royal Bank of Scotland Group[1]

Technology based learning is a crucial pillar to The Royal Bank of Scotland Group's strategy to improve its business through its people — by providing more efficient and effective training solutions. Brian McLaren, Head of Training and Online Learning, The Royal Bank of Scotland Group[2]

In 1998 the main plank in The Royal Bank of Scotland's distance learning platform consisted of weekly live television broadcasts delivered to its 650 branches by satellite — an approach which the training industry knew as "business television". These transmissions were supplemented by training content distributed either on VHS cassettes under the internal brand *Learning Curve* or in book format from a central resource library. Branch staff learned about rate changes, product launches and job vacancies through paper-based communications called *Focus Circulars*. The corporate intranet was limited to the bank's head office locations throughout the organization; surprisingly, branches were excluded. By 2002, the bank was delivering more than 300 hours of custom e-learning content — developed at a cost of about £2 million a year — through a dedicated training and communications network to around 2000 dedicated learning workstations in branches across the UK. The self-paced e-learning content was supported by an innovative virtual classroom application. The speed and scale of change was dramatic. Reflecting on the achievement, David Buglass, the bank's Manager of Learning Infrastructure, observed, "We have been able to deliver an e-learning infrastructure and substantial amounts of content in what we saw, especially in the early days, as an immature market."

Seen from a distance, most e-learning implementations tend to look similar. Critical differences only become apparent on close examination. The Royal Bank of Scotland is an exception. It has gone about every aspect of e-learning implementation in a very individualistic way that has moved the bank to the forefront of e-learning in the UK — and the bank's e-learning initiative shows no sign of coasting.

Business background

Outside the UK, The Royal Bank of Scotland Group is hardly a household name — perhaps it should be. In 2002, ranked by market capitalization the Group was the second largest bank in the UK and Europe, and the fifth largest in the world — ahead of Deutsche Bank, J.P. Morgan Chase, Barclays and UBS. Again ranked by market capitalization, the Group was larger than US corporate giants Ford Motor Company, Boeing, Du Pont, 3M and McDonalds. The bank has grown dramatically through a series of acquisitions, the most significant in March 2000 when it beat off arch rival Bank of Scotland to complete a hostile takeover of what was then Britain's largest bank — National Westminster — at a cost of £21 billion. Group Chief Executive Fred Goodwin later commented, "It was a significant achievement ... NatWest was double our size, the financing structure was unique. And it was the biggest ever hostile financial services transaction of its type."[3] The impact on the Group was seismic. The following year operating profit increased by 32%. Over the years 2000 and 2001, Group operating profit increased by 73%. By April 2002 the Group employed around 106 000 staff worldwide and had generated an annual income of about $60 billion.

The Group is organized into five client-facing businesses or operating Divisions:

- Retail Banking
- Wealth Management
- Retail Direct
- CBFM (Corporate Banking and Financial Markets)
- Manufacturing

In addition to its Divisions, the Group has three companies whose brands enjoy a high profile in their markets:

- Direct Line Group
- Ulster Bank Group
- Citizens Financial Group Inc (US)

What the bank calls the Centre is made up of five group and corporate functions which provide services to the operating divisions:

- Legal and Regulatory Affairs, Group Secretary
- Strategy
- Finance, Risk and Internal Audit
- Communications
- Human Resources

Approximately 30% of staff work in Retail Banking and 20% in Manufacturing.

Learning background

Before 1998, learning in the bank's branches was driven by instructor-led training supported by weekly live television broadcasts, training programmes on VHS and paper-based bulletins. While the approach worked, it was recognized to be disjointed. A second, more worrying training characteristic was increasingly apparent: the quality and quantity of training across the branches was not consistent. Where branch managers appreciated the value of training, staff were well served; where managers lacked commitment, staff were poorly served.

In the spring of 1998, the Director of Corporate Affairs initiated a review of communications between head office and branches. The resulting report called for the implementation of a dedicated communications infrastructure linking all branches with head office using ISDN lines and incorporating the existing satellite television network. Each branch would be equipped with one or more dedicated multimedia workstations — called Training and Communication PCs or TCPCs — connected to what was in effect a group-wide intranet.

At the same time, the Human Resources group was pointing to the absence of a training infrastructure as a barrier to the implementation of a Web-based self-service style of learning it believed essential for the delivery of consistent training messages to support the Group's future growth and development. The intersection of infrastructure requirements was serendipitous. The HR group heard about the Corporate Affairs group's plans for a new network and recognized that it could also be used for the delivery of e-learning. HR developed a business case for a shared network and successfully presented it to Corporate Affairs. The two groups then worked together to present a joint business case to the board for an investment in a dedicated Training and Communications Network (TCN) to serve the Retail Banking Division.

The business case

Consistent training messages delivered through self-paced e-learning and an interactive virtual classroom were at the heart of the HR group's business case; improved and standardized communication, at the heart of Corporate Affairs. The two strategies were aligned with each other and with the bank's business requirements. The bank's new emphasis on a retail business model and growth through acquisition demanded a higher order of communications and focused, consistent learning across the group. Attracting the best people was also essential to ensure the bank's success, however, exit interviews revealed that lack of training was one of the top two reasons why staff were leaving.

Cost saving was another driver. The business case offered more learning for less money. The HR team compared the cost of delivering e-learning with costs associated with traditional training, that is, the cost of running training workshops, the opportunity cost of attending workshops away from the branch, travel and accommodation and subsistence. The total cost of implementation and roll out of the new TCN was budgeted at £5 million. ROI was calculated using the formula:

$$\frac{\text{number of staff} \times \text{travel} \times \text{accommodation} \times \text{expenses}}{\text{total cost of roll out (infrastructure and content)}}$$

It produced a 7:1 return on investment, or seven times more learning for the same money — that meant £15 million worth of learning delivered at a cost of £2 million. Additional benefits cited by the business plan included:

- Reduced learning time.
- Increase in learning on offer.
- Reduced staff turnover and recruitment costs.
- Clear and accountable learning deliverables.

The bank's board signed off the joint business plan.

A custom LMS

A rigorous evaluation of the LMS market in 1998 led the implementation team to conclude that no product had the combination of maturity and functionality the bank needed. Rather than compromise, the team decided to design and build a custom LMS based around its specific requirements including:

- Learning Record:
  - Support a personal record of learning activity including:
    - Self-paced e-learning courses
    - Workshop learning (instructor led)
    - Learning Resources Direct
- Self-Paced E-learning:
  - Launch a course
  - Track start and completion date in personal record
  - Track the learner's progress at page level in personal record
  - Support an assessment engine
  - Manage bookmarks
  - Track assessment outputs in personal record
- Workshop Learning:
  - Present a catalogue of workshops customized according to the learner's role
  - Support online self-registration
  - Display dates and places available
  - Confirm workshop registration by e-mail
  - Track workshop starts and completions in personal record

- Learning Resources Direct:
  - Support the central library of books and CD-ROMs
  - Support online keyword search
  - Support online booking requests
  - Track borrowings in personal record

Because of the immaturity of e-learning standards at the time, the LMS was not designed to be standards conformant but was standards aware. All bank e-learning content is custom content, so standards and interoperability have not been the burning issues they are in other enterprise implementations. The LMS was integrated with PeopleSoft using a nightly batch process to update staff lists.

By 2002, it had become clear to the bank that the LMS market had matured since the initial product evaluation. The bank began a rigorous gap analysis to assess whether third-party LMSs could meet all current and future requirements.

Virtual Classroom

The bank developed its own innovative, integrated Virtual Classroom solution that used (1) the TCN's ISDN lines to deliver the user interface and data, and (2) the bank's "business television" satellite network to deliver live video (see Figure 20.1). At first, the integration proved more challenging than expected — a risk associated with any custom development — but in the end, Virtual Classroom successfully delivered:

- Broadcast-quality one-way video — emanating from the bank's purpose-built television studio in Edinburgh.
- Video and two-way audio at the desktop.
- A PC-based interface.

Virtual Classroom proved a powerful communications and learning tool. Change management programmes helped branch employees transition smoothly and effectively from face-to-face learning to e-learning. The application is owned by the bank's Group Communications area and supported by Group Technology with assistance from the developers, Arel Communications.

Implementation

From day one, implementation was a collaborative effort. A virtual team of about 40 with members from both inside and outside the bank was assembled for a Project Definition Workshop. By the end of the meeting, key players had a clear understanding of their own roles and responsibilities and those of other team members with whom they would have to work closely and swiftly. Here's how high-level responsibilities were assigned:

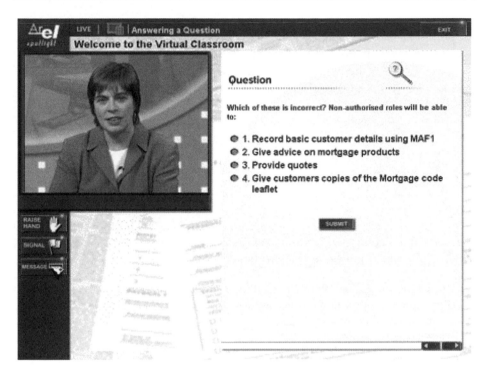

Figure 20.1 — Royal Bank of Scotland's Virtual Classroom

HR Development (HRD)	Project management of both internal and external resources for the development of self-paced content
Retail Network Support	Course content subject matter experts
Corporate Affairs	Developers of video sequences included in self-paced courses and Virtual Classroom sessions
HR Information	• content publishers • project managers for the LMS design
HR Systems Development	• technology consultants to internal and external resources • LMS developers

With (1) a new infrastructure, (2) a custom LMS, (3) the Virtual Classroom custom application, and (4) 100 hours of content being developed in parallel, communications and clarity of roles and responsibilities were essential. A detailed project plan set out milestones and dependencies, and underpinned the harmonious interworking of the virtual team. The HR Development project manager had the responsibility of publishing a weekly team report listing tasks completed during the current week and tasks scheduled for the next. Attendance at weekly project meetings was mandatory. E-mail, phone calls and videoconferences kept members informed and their efforts synchronized.

In October 1998 the bank's board signed off the Training and Communications business case; in October 1999 the new infrastructure, LMS, Virtual Classroom and content went live with a learner base of 20 000 located in 650 bank branches and sites.

Content

The first tranche of learning content was aimed at two client-facing roles within the bank: Customer Advisers and Customer Service Officers. The bank invested £475 000 in developing content for the former and £900 000 for the latter. Content focused on the competencies and skills associated with each role. Courses drew on the bank's learning value chain to deliver:

- E-learning modules with interactive activities, assessments and multimedia — audio and video audio accessed from local CD-ROMs to optimize performance (see Figure 20.2).
- Face-to-face workshops.
- Work observations.
- Learning events from external providers.

Access to e-learning is primarily through the enterprise intranet, called Insite, and the TCPC workstations installed in branches because so far that's where the majority of learners have been. However, Insite supports dial up access so self-paced e-learning is available anywhere a learner has intranet access — providing the learner has a copy of the multimedia CD-ROM that supports the course they want to take. Offsite access has not been a driver for e-learning in the Retail Banking Division but will become increasingly important as e-learning spreads through other operations and businesses in the group.

The bank does not have a central e-learning content development budget; operating Divisions and Group functions pay for the development of the learning they need. During implementation, content development was sponsored by the Retail Banking operating Division and development teams were led by an HR Development project consultant. Subject matter experts were provided by Retail Network Support. Instructional design and content development were the responsibility of external vendors. Development budgets were negotiated with vendors by the team's project consultant.

By 2002, the amount of e-learning content provided by the bank had increased to 300 hours, around 250 dedicated to the Retail Division and the rest spread between Corporate Banking and Financial Markets, and Manufacturing. The initial emphasis was on delivering e-learning content to client-facing staff; there are now plans to widen the curriculum to include process and product learning.

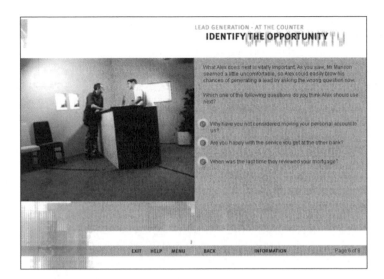

Figure 20.2—Royal Bank of Scotland self-paced content

In 2003, the bank plans to double its annual investment in content development. In preparation for the increased workload, the bank spent one year rigorously evaluating external development vendors before appointing six of the candidates to its preferred supplier panel. The appointments are for 2 years and the bank is looking not just for content development but for strategic partnerships as Brian McLaren, Head of Training and Online Learning, explained: "The introduction of a preferred panel of suppliers gives us the back up which we require to support e-learning activity across a much-enlarged Group … It also provides the suppliers the unique opportunity to live within our culture and help shape our e-learning thinking as we progress forward with our growth plans."[4]

The LMS has not been used to launch and deliver generic e-learning content; though the bank does license some content from NetG, it is delivered on CD-ROM. The bank has been considering the use of generic e-learning content to meet requirements for basic business skills.

National Westminster acquisition

Acquiring a bank twice its size posed many challenges for The Royal Bank of Scotland. For e-learning, the priority was the harmonization and integration of both banks' employees. The bank's learning initiative was quickly rolled out across National Westminster Bank. The number of TCPC multimedia workstations on the TCN increased from 650 to around 2000. One thousand new satellite installations were required to support Virtual Classroom.

The bank's custom LMS proved its scalability by absorbing 30 000 new learners in 1600 NatWest branches with no degradation in performance. After the acquisition, the LMS was upgraded to (1) make it more robust, and (2) support learning objects. At the same time, all e-learning content was rebuilt using an object-oriented approach. Working in partnership with its external content developers, the bank developed a custom standard for learning objects that took account of draft e-learning standards emerging at the time. The move to learning objects was driven not by technology but by a business requirement. Forbes Magazine sets the scene: "When RBS makes an acquisition, it refrains from slapping its logo on everything in sight. In almost all cases, the original brand's identity is maintained. The NatWest name has remained on branches years after the merger."[5]

What the Group needed was the ability to develop brand-free learning content that could be used in any of its UK-based banks: The Royal Bank of Scotland, National Westminster Bank and Ulster Bank. Later, when a learner calls up content, local branding would be inserted in real time. Learning objects made this automated customization possible. The bank is also considering leveraging its substantial investment in learning content by forming a publishing partnership with its preferred supplier panel in order to license non-proprietary content to the Financial Services market. A brand-free, object-oriented approach to content development facilitates generic publishing and enables licensees to customize the presentation of content.

The acquisition of NatWest also had an impact on ROI. Over 5 years, tangible benefits worth £22.5 million will be realized across the Group.

Relationship with the business

To be successful, learning must have a close relationship with the business. In The Royal Bank of Scotland the pivotal role in that relationship is the HR Business Partner who acts as a conduit between Group HR and (1) the operating Divisions, and (2) Group functions. HR Business Partners offer a full HR consultancy. The role includes educating the business about the benefits of e-learning and how to recognize when a learning need might be best met by self-paced or virtual class e-learning. Internal marketing, however, has proved one of the least successful aspects of the bank's learning initiative. "What we've accomplished in e-learning is probably better known outside the bank than it is by the operating Divisions," admits David Buglass, "but we're working on turning that round."

Working with their HR Business Partners, Operating Divisions own the responsibility for identifying gaps in skills and competencies, however, once a development project is signed off it is always managed by HR Organization-Development who provide the sponsor with a virtual content development team made up of:

- a Business Training Consultant
- a Project Consultant (project manager)
- a subject matter expert

- an external developer from their panel of six preferred vendors
- an internal systems developer

Evaluation

The bank has yet to implement a formal learning evaluation process but a Performance Measurement team is focusing on the development of processes to (1) measure the real cost of learning and (2) calculate ROI based on personal and sales performance. The aim is to link investments in specific learning projects with product sales. Meanwhile, other indicators point to the impact the e-learning initiative has had. Exit interviews have begun to show that training ranks as only the seventh most important reason for leaving the bank; before the implementation of e-learning it was one of the top two reasons.

Each year the Group conducts a employee opinion survey of all staff; it's the most visible and important element of an ongoing process of employee communication and consultation. In 2001, 75% of employees responded either on paper or online. The figure was up 8% on the previous year and the highest response rate ever; in fact, it was significantly higher than the average for large corporate organizations. Senior management acknowledge that e-learning deserves some of the credit for the increasingly positive survey results.

Future developments

In 2002 The Royal Bank of Scotland launched a number of initiatives designed to determine the future shape of e-learning in the Group. By the end of the year, the bank will have a vision for future developments that builds on its innovative approach and early successes. Pieces of the vision are already forming.

No formal Knowledge Management processes or resources have been implemented anywhere within the bank. KM is now being evaluated with a view to future implementation. The Group has almost 250 external vendors supporting its learning value chain. To ensure the Group optimizes its learning spend and receives the best possible service levels from its suppliers, a project has been implemented with a mandate to rationalize the supply of learning products and services, and to create standard procurement processes.

Recognizing the increasingly diverse nature of businesses and roles within the Group, the bank's vision for e-learning is moving towards multi-channel delivery of learning content. Choice is the driver. The Group expects its employees to be proactive in shaping and maintaining their own development. Providing a broad range of delivery channels is one way the bank will facilitate self-service learning. Staff will be able to access content through the channel that best matches their role and work pattern. Dedicated learning workstations, laptops, handheld devices, WAP-enabled devices, downloadable briefings from SMEs in the form of MP3 files — anything that effectively delivers engaging learning messages to learners is under consideration. Traditional delivery channels will continue to form part of the mix. Learning Resources Direct, the bank's central reference library of books and CD-ROMs, will be upgraded to create an environment inspired by the richness and interconnectedness of Amazon.com.

The key business driver for The Royal Bank of Scotland is continued growth through acquisition. More than anything else, all future developments must help the bank—and its learning—to be acquisition-ready. At short notice, Group HR needs to be able to roll out its learning network across any newly acquired business and realize one of e-learning's key promises: to streamline post-acquisition harmonization—of product lines, staff skills and competencies, operational processes, systems and applications and corporate culture. Learning needs to be a partner in the acquisition process. In The Royal Bank of Scotland, that's what it's gearing up to be.

References

1   Christy JH (2002) *The A List— Pro-Choice— Banking* Forbes.com 15 April 2002 [Internet] Available from <http://www.forbes.com/global/2002/0415/043.html> Accessed 20 May 2002.
2   *AdVal Group preferred training supplier to The Royal Bank of Scotland* (2000) [Press release] [Internet] Available from <http://www.adval.co.uk/press/03nov2000.htm> Accessed 20 May 2002.
3   Robinson K (2001) *Right, said Fred, Both of Us Together* The Banker Issue 901 April 2001 [Internet] Available from <http://www.thebanker.com/art2apr01.htm> Accessed 20 May 2002.
4   *Royal Bank of Scotland Group appoints AdVal Group plc as a Preferred Supplier for e-Learning and other Services* (2002) Adval Group plc [Press release] [Internet] Available from <http://www.adval.co.uk/press/10May2002.htm> Accessed 20 May 2002.
5   Christy JH (2002) *The A List— Pro-Choice— Banking* Forbes.com 15 April 2002 [Internet] Available from <http://www.forbes.com/global/2002/0415/043.html> Accessed 20 May 2002.

21

The Dow Chemical Company case study: high commitment, high ROI, high volume

... we'll begin implementing our comprehensive People Strategy, ensuring we continue to develop the very source of the competitiveness that makes us strong today, and the innovation that will build our future—our people. Michael D Parker, President and CEO, The Dow Chemical Company[1]

To ensure that all people have common basic skills and adequate training to be able to perform their designated tasks, each Dow business identifies the training programs necessary to perform the work tasks, reviews training effectiveness and maintains training records of the learning acquired. Training courses that teach basic quality skills, concepts and terms are available for Dow people in all functions. The Dow Quality Management System Manual[2]

One of the criticisms of e-learning you'll hear again and again is how few self-paced courses are ever completed. There's an interesting debate to be had about whether the criticism is valid but it's one they won't be having at Dow. "It's not unusual for us to see 7000 course completions in a week," observed Sonya Davis, one of the Global Project Leaders in Dow's HRD Strategic Center. In 2001 learners at Dow clocked up around 630 000 hours of e-learning. What is it about the way Dow goes about e-learning that has generated take-up on this scale?

Business background

Dow describes itself as "a leading science and technology company that provides innovative chemical, plastic and agricultural products and services to many essential consumer markets."[3] In August 1999, Dow announced it would merge with the Union Carbide Company; 18 months the merger was realized to create the world's second largest chemical company. Headquartered in the American state of Michigan, Dow had annual sales of $28 billion in 2001 and served customers in more than 170 countries. Until 1995, the business had been organized vertically around locations not processes. The predictable result was a lack of standardization, redundancy of effort and an absence of knowledge sharing. The business was reorganized to reflect a global vision and operation. Now Dow operates about 20 businesses organized in six process-focused Segments:

- Performance Plastics
- Performance Chemicals

- Agricultural Products
- Plastics
- Chemicals
- Hydrocarbons and Energy

Central functions like Environmental, Health and Safety, Human Resources and Public Affairs have a global responsibility for serving the business units.

In 2002 the company had about 43 000 employees and 10 000 full-time contractors organized into 10 geographic regions. The bulk of employees are based in North America — around 25 000. Europe accounts for some 12 000, Latin America 3000, and Asia Pacific 2500. Staff are organized into four groups:

- Global Leadership
- FSFL (Functional Specialist, Functional Leader)
- Administration
- Technicians and Technologists

Anyone who is part of a cross-discipline team is required to speak English; in practice, that means technicians and technologists are not. In all, there are about 12 languages spoken across Dow's global operation.

In 2002 the company had about 40 000 workstations worldwide, all with a common desktop called Dow Workstation providing access to the same information systems and sources. Every day these workstations process about 160 000 external e-mail messages — 90 000 inbound, 70 000 outbound. There are 450 sites on Dow's intranet; the company added three times as many new sites in 2001 as it had in 2000.

Historically, Dow's success has been built not just on innovation but on the management and leverage of the company's substantial intellectual property. Theo Walthie, Business Group President, described the breadth of the company's knowledge base: "... Dow has an information pool that is 22 terabytes deep. If you have no idea how big that is, just imagine a football field covered with sheets of regular office paper, filled with information. Now stack more sheets on top until each stack is six and a half feet high. That's when people say we are "in over our heads"! But, even then, you only have one terabyte of information. Dow alone had 17 of these football fields — and that was before we acquired Union Carbide!"[4] On the same occasion, Walthie listed five fundamental drivers of change and competitive advantage for the petrochemical industry at the start of a new century:

- Sustainable Development
- Climate Change
- Chemicals Policy
- the dynamics of Hydrocarbons and Energy
- the continuous evolution of Technology

Learning background

Much of the learning that happens within Dow is focused on environment, health and safety. Employees need to comply with strict training requirements — and not just once but continuously. All production staff, for example, have to re-take a course on the use of fire extinguishers every year. The annual cost of delivering an enterprise-wide programme of compliance training in the classroom was significant:

- over $3 million in delivery costs
- over $5 million in class materials, and
- over $20 million in salary costs

The reorganization of Dow which began in 1995 had a big impact on Human Resources; for the first time, it had global responsibilities. PeopleSoft Human Resources Management System was installed in 1996 and the following year, HR launched *People Success Finder*. This online system provided employees with easy access to global career information, training resources and job opportunities. It pointed to a solution for a new global requirement: the need to deliver consistent training messages about health and safety, soft skills, products, and legal and policy regulations to a global business with staff in more than 30 countries. In 1998 Dow created an enterprise-wide e-learning initiative with equal support from Human Resources, who led the project, Environmental, Health and Safety, and the manufacturing segments. *learn@dow.now*, Dow's brand name for e-learning, went live in January 1999 as part of the already successful *People Success Finder* system. Implementation followed a big bang approach with a fully-functional system available to all learners from day one. Courses, however, were phased in as they became available.

Learning Management System

Dow's requirements for an LMS included:

- Flexibility
- Fast implementation
- Easy course creation and language translation
- Open and scalable architecture
- Ability to deliver courses globally across changing regulations, local requirements, and in multiple languages
- Ability to deliver online assessments and a complete learning audit trail for regulatory compliance and certification

Thirty products were evaluated. In the end, Dow chose an LCMS not an LMS: WBT's TopClass 4. (See p. 178 for the difference between LMS and LCMS systems.) It's SCORM compliant and supports an object-oriented approach to learning content. Dow used its in-house IT resources to implement TopClass. A strategic decision was taken to store tracking data for each learner with their personnel record, so the LCMS was integrated with PeopleSoft. Classroom training is also tracked with data entered in PeopleSoft manually. The learning record maintained by TopClass is used to confirm regulatory compliance though Dow does not use the LCMS or PeopleSoft to track the expiry of compliance certificates. That responsibility lies with a plant's Learning Coordinator who works with employees to keep all their required certifications current.

Maintenance and day-to-day operation of the LCMS is the responsibility of the HRD Resource Center. While TopClass has released two further versions since the LCMS was first implemented, so far Dow has not upgraded its system. Potential benefits don't seem to justify costs in project management and IT resources. It's hard to argue with Dow's "if it ain't broke, don't fix it" approach. No one else is driving TopClass harder or achieving greater learning success and cost savings.

With the benefit of hindsight, there's a feeling that the voice of the learner was not given a platform during implementation; the result is a learning system that's a little too administration-centric when it should be learner-centric. On the plus side, Dow has made an investment in usability by partnering with WBT to translate TopClass into seven languages. Dow always delivered e-learning courses in a number of languages, now the environment in which learners access courses is localized too.

ROI and evaluation

Dow made headlines with its e-learning ROI. *learn@dow.now* cost $1.3 million to set up and $600 000 in annual licensing and operational costs. In its first year of operation, the investment generated hard returns of $34 million out of a total spend of $100 million. In year two, hard returns had grown to $45 million. At Dow hard returns refer to money that was being spent but no longer is, for example, venue hire, salaries, materials; soft savings reflect notional savings like opportunity costs. Neither opportunity costs nor travel costs were included in calculating annual savings achieved through e-learning. However, calculations took account of learning equivalencies — e-learning takes 40% to 60% less time than its classroom equivalent to achieve the same learning.

When presenting a business case for *learn@dow.now*, the implementation team had to follow the capital approval methodology set out by corporate finance including a 3-year investment plan. David Kepler, Dow's CIO, applied a value strategy to the project: "We started with the business result that we wanted to achieve and then built the system necessary to achieve those results, so we did it in the most affordable way."[5] The original estimate for cost saving was $5 million a year. It was enough to get sign off but significantly underestimated the effectiveness of a global e-learning implementation. Cost per learner per course had been running at $95; with the implementation of *learn@dow.now* it dropped to $11. In fact, the e-learning initiative is generating the highest ROI value stream of any IT project ever implemented at Dow—and only one other site on the corporate intranet gets more hits.

No evaluation programme has been developed for *learn@dow.now*; the same evaluation methodology applied to classroom learning is applied to e-learning. In practice, that means Level 1 and some Level 3 evaluation. Level 1 asks every learner if they enjoyed the learning experience and whether they believe they will apply what they've learned. Level 3 consists of a 360° evaluation of a sample of learners to understand whether behaviours have changed as a result of learning.

Content

When *learn@dow.now* was launched, 15 courses were available. By the end of year one the number had increased to 98. In 2000, the course catalogue swelled to 426 self-paced courses; the following year, to more than 500. By the end of 2002, learners will be able to choose from more than 600 courses. When you consider that 80% of content is custom developed, the course catalogue represents a substantial investment in cost, time and resources. Of course, Dow has the satisfaction of knowing its courses are used. Course completions in year one numbered 24 492; in year two, around 150 000; in year three, around 315 000. *CIO Magazine* was so impressed by the scale of e-learning in Dow, it presented *learn@dow.now* with its Enterprise Value Award which acknowledges the power of an IT initiative to transform enterprises, industries and society as a whole. One of the magazine's judges observed: "What won them the award was the scale of the system. The sheer number of classes that they've offered and the number of people that have been trained are remarkable."[6]

Most instructional design and content development is outsourced to five developers who enjoy preferred vendor status. Content development can be project managed by a Project Leader from the HRD Strategic Center, or a business unit or group function Project Leader. Some content is developed internally using TopClass Publisher, Macromedia Dreamweaver and Microsoft FrontPage; some of the external developers also use TopClass Publisher. Because all content is developed using an object-oriented approach, Dow has built up a library of reusable learning objects.

Generally, content is developed in US English and later translated into seven languages: Dutch, French, German, Italian, Portuguese, Spanish and UK English. Some courses are also available in Chinese, Indonesian, Japanese and Thai. At Dow, localization doesn't mean just translation. Care is taken to localize the names of job roles, processes and equipment. To a degree, e-learning is disadvantaged by the requirement for localized content. Some business units and group functions find the cost and time scales onerous, especially when the learner base is small, and look to other learning channels for a solution.

Off-the-shelf content is used for business and soft skills learning. Preference is given to publishers whose content is localized. NetG and Intellinex are among the publishers who supply content to *learn@dow.now*.

How learning is managed

There is no dedicated e-learning group in Dow. Project Leaders in the HRD Strategic Center have responsibility for specific e-learning projects but manage other projects too. Around 20 HR Business Partners provide the link between HR and the business. Business Partners provide an overall HR consultancy to business units; as part of that work, they are proactive in promoting the benefits of e-learning to business leaders and directors. Larger business units and group functions have their own learning leaders, some with a dedicated staff of five or six.

Business units have the option of working independently or with HR to meet the learning needs of their people. They can commission custom e-learning content, buy synchronous learning services, and license generic e-learning courses — even contract with publishers to host the content. Inevitably, this leads to some redundancy of effort and spend across the enterprise. There is a Learning Leadership Network whose aim is to share knowledge, coordinate effort and provide direction but not all business units and group functions participate. The situation is not typical of Dow's operations which are standardized and focused through strategies emanating from the centre.

When a business unit chooses to work with HR, the process follows these lines. A business unit becomes aware of an apparent learning gap in its operations. Through its HR Business Partner, the business unit engages a team from the HRD Strategic Center (1) to carry out a learning gap analysis, and (2) based on the nature of the content, to recommend one or more learning channels best suited to closing the gap. It's recognized that some learning content — leadership skills and safe driving are examples — benefits from a face-to-face learning experience. Even when the bulk of a course is delivered by instructors, it can be bookended with online resources — pre- and post-assessments, prerequisite and follow-up content — in order to minimize time spent in the classroom. When e-learning is a key part of the solution, an HRD Strategic Center Project Leader forms a virtual development team made up of a business unit sponsor, subject matter experts from the business unit, and one of the five preferred external content developers. While project management and consultancy are provided by group HR, other development costs are met by the business unit.

So far Dow has not focused on educating its suppliers and customers. Suppliers who work on site and have a Dow Workstation have access to *learn@dow.now*; many take advantage of the resource. Dow has recently introduced an extranet for clients called *My Account@Dow*. The extranet means that Dow has a platform for delivering e-learning to customers but for the time being that's just an aspiration.

Learning respect and responsibility

Dow is unequivocal about respect for people: "We believe in the inherent worth of people and will honor our relationships with those who let us be part of this world: employees, customers, shareholders and society."[7] In 2000, William Stavropoulos, who was CEO at the time and is now chairman, decided that all Dow staff should take a comprehensive course in respect and responsibility as soon as possible.

When the content was assembled, the course turned out to last 6 hours. It didn't take long to work out that it would take a full year to deliver the course in classrooms and at a cost of $20 billion. Neither the time frame nor cost were viable. To get past the time–cost barrier, content was developed as a self-paced e-learning course and successfully delivered through *learn@dow.now* to 40 000 employees in just 5 months and at a total development and delivery cost of $450 000. The Respect and Responsibility course generated more than 11 000 hours of e-learning per month. Employees of the newly acquired Union Carbide Company also took the course which has become mandatory for all new joiners and employees of acquired businesses.

Future directions

There's every indication that the volume of self-paced e-learning at Dow will continue to grow. Dow is looking to the e-learning market for best practices and optimal platforms for managing and delivering content on new larger scales. At the same time, Dow is looking to add synchronous learning to its Web-based delivery channels. In 2002, two virtual classroom applications were trialled, both on a standalone basis with no attempt to integrate them with the LCMS.

Of course, a much bigger enterprise-wide challenge lies in store — integrating e-learning channels with Dow's well established Knowledge Management system. Whatever direction e-learning at Dow moves in, care needs to be taken to ensure that the qualities of learner-centred learning that have delivered such high ROI and high take-up are not lost: relevancy, authenticity, solution-centering, self-direction and -pacing, and localization.

References

1   *2001 Annual Report* (2002) The Dow Chemical Company [Report] [Internet] Available from <http://www.dow.com/financial/2001ann/161-00562.pdf> Accessed 28 May 2002 p 5.

2 *The Dow Quality Management System Manual–Condensed Edition* (2000) The Dow Chemical Company [Internet] Available from <http://www.dow.com/about/aboutdow/qualinit/index.htm> Accessed 28 May 2002.

3 *Fast Facts about Dow* (2002) The Dow Chemical Company [Internet] Available from <http://www.dow.com/dow_news/press/pre_fast.html> Accessed 28 May 2002.

4 Walthie T (2002) *Fundamental Drivers of Change and Competitive Advantage* [Presentation] CMAI World Petrochemical Conference 21 February 2002 [Internet] Available from <http://www.dow.com/dow_news/speeches/20020320_walthie.htm> Accessed 28 May 2002.

5 Overby S (2002) *The World's Biggest Classroom CIO Magazine* 1 February 2002 [Internet] Available from <http://www.cio.com/archive/020102/dow_content.html> Accessed 17 Mar 2002.

6 Overby S (2002) *The World's Biggest Classroom CIO Magazine* 1 February 2002 [Internet] Available from <http://www.cio.com/archive/020102/dow_content.html> Accessed 17 Mar 2002.

7 *2001 Annual Report* (2002) The Dow Chemical Company [Report] [Internet] Available from <http://www.dow.com/financial/2001ann/161-00562.pdf> Accessed 28 May 2002 p 22.

Part VI
Future Directions

22 Future directions: where e-learning is headed

I think e-learning has just moved from something that was an experiment — a very healthy experiment three or four years ago — to main line. I think we're at the very early stages of really understanding the power it has. It's no longer a question of whether it will be effective or how much it can increase productivity; it's just a question of degree. John Chambers, CEO, Cisco Systems[1]

As its enabling technologies mature, the Internet will fade from view. But the impact of the Net on individuals as consumers, employees, and citizens will continue to expand as the power of information becomes ubiquitous. David M. Cooperstein, Forrester[2]

What you need to know

Standardization

In the short to medium term, standardization is the most important direction e-learning will move in. Standards will enable all the components of e-learning to work together seamlessly right out of the box; they will enable e-learning systems to interoperate with other systems in the enterprise. By enabling e-learning systems in *different* organizations to interoperate, standards will deliver high value content economically and allow the enterprise to educate its value chain of employees, suppliers and customers. E-learning vendors understand the importance and urgency of standards; the market cannot mature without them. All the important e-learning vendors actively support the standards initiatives that are in place. Implementing and delivering e-learning needs to become as straightforward and commonplace as implementing and delivering e-mail. And it will.

Consolidation

Along with standardization, there will be consolidation in the e-learning market. Consolidation will remove some of the confusion that dogs e-learning. Too many vendors have similar offerings. It's normal for enterprises to issue RFPs to as many as 20 or 30 LMS vendors. When the proposals arrive, it takes a substantial effort to clarify the differences between vendors' products. In an effort to differentiate their offerings, LMS vendors add more modules with more functions and features—which only makes selection more difficult. A fragmented e-learning market also makes enterprises uncomfortable. When making a significant investment in improving the performance of its global workforce, an enterprise wants the reassurance of knowing they've made the investment in a company with the same scale of capitalization and management skills as itself.

There has been some consolidation already—LMS vendors have acquired LCMS vendors, for example—but it needs to happen on a much bigger scale. Enterprise ERP and HRIS vendors need to move into e-learning not with the tentative steps they've taken so far, but with a commitment to market dominance. The summer of 2002 saw indications that the commitment was emerging. In April, PeopleSoft announced it was adding an LMS module to its offering. At the end of July, PeopleSoft acquired Teamscape Corporation, a small LMS vendor, and announced it would release "a fully integrated enterprise learning management solution" before the end of the year. When you recall that integrating a third-party LMS with enterprise HR and financial systems has been a major component of e-learning implementation, this was important news to enterprises running PeopleSoft. In May, SAP and Siemens announced they would jointly develop and market a comprehensive software solution designed for corporate universities and human resource development and training institutions; no date was given for the release of the product. An agreement in July between IBM Learning Services and the Thomson Corporation pointed to an end-to-end technology-content partnership. IBM has a strong range of e-learning systems and has deployed e-learning internally with great success; Thomson styles itself as the world's largest provider of corporate and professional learning solutions. Together IBM and Thomson will boast the world's largest e-learning sales force and support team. While the presence of enterprise vendors removes some of the confusion in the e-learning market, there will still be a place for some smaller vendors—to serve small to medium-sized enterprises and to provide competition for larger vendors through nimbleness, innovation and service.

When the technology sector of e-learning settles, the focus will shift to the content sector. Consolidation has begun there too. In June 2002, SmartForce, a generic content publisher and, with an annual income of around $200 million, the largest e-learning vendor, announced it would merge with SkillSoft, another large generic content provider. The deal was completed in early September. The new company, which trades under the name SkillSoft, has a combined catalogue of more than 3000 courses and a global client base of about 2800. E-learning analysts gave the merger the thumbs up. With SmartForce's emphasis on IT content and SkillSoft's on soft skills, the two companies had never been real competitors. Their approach to content, however, is quite different and their challenge is to develop a fully integrated catalogue that reflects the new entity.

The one area where there is less need for consolidation is custom content development. There are and will continue to be larger and smaller content developers; that should suit everyone. The large generic publishers will out-source some of their development to these smaller businesses as will those LMS vendors that provide custom content as part of their offering. Enterprises will continue to contract custom content developers directly, matching vendors' skills and resources with specific content requirements. The challenge for content developers is to work their way onto approved supplier lists.

Simulation

Harvey Smith, lead designer of the award-winning computer game "Deus Ex", has a vision of where simulations are headed: "The games of the future will rely heavily on much more complex, high fidelity world representations that will allow for more emergent behavior and unforeseen player interactions. Taken together, these next-generation design paradigms are not simply improvements over older models, but represent a fundamentally different approach to simulating real-world physics, handling artificial intelligence and interface usability."[3]

Some people believe that high fidelity simulations will emerge as e-learning's "killer app" with the power to build must-have demand. Elliott Masie, head of The Masie Center e-learning think tank, is one of them: "Simulation is the ultimate goal of e-Learning: to create an environment where learners can practice, fail, succeed and learn in a rich and realistic setting."[4] So is Clark Aldrich, ex-Gartner e-learning analyst turned simulation developer: "I would consider simulations to be the front-runner for creating broad, sharable, e-learning experiences. Until that happens, e-learning will remain a niche industry. But once that happens, e-learning will change the world."[5]

The US Army thinks simulation works. It spent over $7 million and three years developing a video game called "America's Army" which has been described as "The Sims" with barracks, M-16s and military prison. The game was launched on 4 July 2002 and within 36 hours several hundred thousand copies had been downloaded from 110 servers. The aim of the game is to teach potential recruits what it really means to be a soldier from training camp through to field missions (see Figure 22.1).

The flight simulator sets the standard for simulations. It's realistic, real time, and allows the user an infinite number of interactions. In the enterprise environment, simulations hold out the promise of the ultimate business modelling: learners live out a strategy before putting it into action. Hi-fi simulations are all about immersive, experiential learning. Feedback doesn't come in the form of a text message but through behaviours in the simulated world: a scowl on one of the character's faces or a crucial deal that fails to go through. Lessons learned through realistic feedback tend to be remembered. It's normal for pilots in fight simulators to experience increased heart rate and cold sweat when instructors deliberately

Figure 22.1 — "America's Army" simulation
Source: America's Army

put them into emergency situations. Managers could do the same thing with crisis business scenarios: "Okay, how would you get out of this?" The Shell Oil Company famously uses planning scenarios not to predict the future but to help the company understand the forces shaping the global energy market. Imagine the impact if the scenarios could be played out in hi-fi simulations instead of with documents, spreadsheets and databases (see Figure 22.2). Imagine the potential for hi-fi, real-time simulations in medical schools.

So far, simulations have been luxury items for organizations with deep pockets and there is no reason to expect that rapid, inexpensive development will become a reality any day soon. However, enterprises might be driven to use simulations despite the costs. Many university graduates joining enterprises today arrive with years of e-learning experience behind them. Their expectations of enterprise e-learning are high. What is going to happen when the young people who are growing up in the rich realistic worlds of computer games like "Majestic", "Age of Empires", "Baldur's Gate", "The Sims", "Roller Coaster Tycoon" and "Deux Ex" cross the corporate threshold? Will they be engaged by text and graphic expositions, and multiple choice assessments? Not a chance. Not all learning needs to take place inside simulated realities but expect simulations to figure increasingly in the future of e-learning.

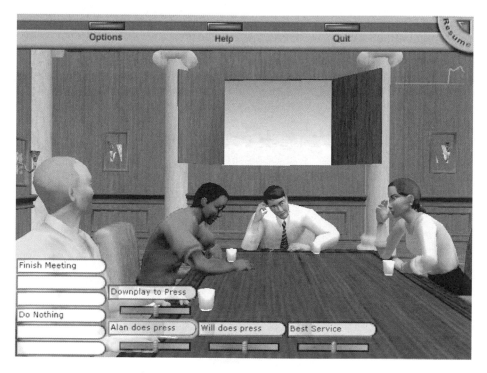

Figure 22.2 — "Virtual Leader" simulation
Reproduced by permission of SimuLearn Inc

Mobilization

Ultimately, just-in-time learning means mobile learning or, as it's called, m-learning. Learners shouldn't be dependent on a physical network connection to learn any more than they should depend on one to make a telephone call. M-learning at its simplest means enabling learners to download self-paced e-learning courses to their laptops so they can study offline. But taken further, m-learning changes the nature of e-learning. Instruction delivered on PDAs for service personnel working on customers' sites blurs the line between working and learning. When a customer buys a system, instead of giving them a print-based manual, give them a PDA with the manual pre-loaded and instructions on how to update it from the Internet. Give new joiners a PDA and every day beam "Today's Lesson" into it without a physical connection. As WAP-enabled devices have faster connections and bigger displays with better resolution, "what you need to know when you need to know it" takes on a new reality. Use handheld devices to distribute personalized guidance from coaches and mentors. No single learning channel is right for all styles of content but wireless devices have an important role to play in bringing learning to the learner.

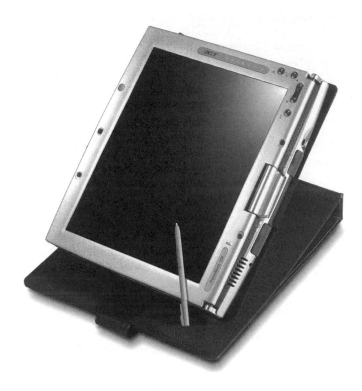

Figure 22.3—The Tablet PC
Source: Acer

If you asked me whether a single wireless device has the power to change the nature of the e-learning experience, I'd say, Yes, the Tablet PC—a cross between a laptop and a PDA (see Figure 22.3). It's too early to tell whether the Microsoft-backed concept will find a market but the latest incarnation of the Tablet PC is receiving good reviews in the press and has attracted the right kinds of partners including Acer, Adobe, Autodesk, Corel, HP, Fujitsu Siemens, NEC, SAP and Toshiba. The Tablet PC's tactile quality, both in the way it can be held like a writing pad—it weighs around three pounds—and its pen-and-ink handwriting-recognition engine, gets the learner closer to content and opens up the possibility of new kinds of interactions. The high resolution display can be used in both portrait and landscape formats to suit different kinds of content. The Tablet PC also promises speech recognition that will allow the system to be used as a dictating machine that turns speech into text. I know that new technology arrives with a lot of caveats and progresses through a series of stumbles. I also know that e-learning should be needs- and not technology-driven. But the Tablet PC looks like delivering the kind of m-learning environment I'd like to be developing content for.

Permeation

This is a vision of e-learning in the enterprise in which the learning value chain simultaneously delivers many different forms of learning at many different levels of granularity. The cumulative effect is a workplace permeated by learning. In this scenario, e-learning is so closely aligned with the enterprise's strategic vision and so relevant to each employee's tasks that it becomes indistinguishable from work. E-learning technologies make learning an integral part of every business process. Doing requires learning and learning requires doing; they are different facets of the same activity. For some people in some enterprises, this is almost a reality. The challenge is to make it universal.

Permeation should be a long-term objective of every learning organization although it can't be defined by specific volumes of content or numbers of learning channels. Permeation starts to happen at the tipping point where the number of learning opportunities in an enterprise equals the tasks at hand. I know it's achievable, even inevitable — I just need a little more time to work out the metrics.

References

1   Galagan PA (2002) *Delta Force* T+D Magazine July 2002 [Internet] Available from <http://newsroom.cisco.com/dlls/delta_force_t_d_magazine.pdf> Accessed 26 Jul 2002.

2   Cooperstein DM (2001) *The Ubiquitous Internet* Forrester TechStrategy February 2001 [Abstract] [Internet] Available from <http://www.forrester.com/ER/Research/Report/Summary/0,1338,11702,FF.html> Accessed 3 Aug 2002.

3   Smith H (2001) *The Future of Game Design: Moving Beyond Deus Ex and Other Dated Paradigms* [Presentation] Multimedia International Market, Montreal October 2001 [Internet] Available from <http://www.igda.org/Endeavors/Articles/hsmith_printable.htm> Accessed 16 Nov 2001.

4   Franklin P (2001) *The Wonderful World of Simulations* ISPI The Networker Newsletter Vol 17 No 1 [Internet] Available from <http://www.svispi.org/networker/2001/0101a1.htm> Accessed 4 Aug 2002.

5   Aldrich C (2002) *A Field Guide to Simulations* [White Paper].

Appendix 1: E-learning newsletters

Newsletters and mailing lists are free and easy ways to stay in touch with the latest thinking and news about e-learning.

Big Dog's Human Resource Development Page
Very good reference site and newsletter from Donald Clark
<http://www.nwlink.com/~donclark/hrd.html>

Dispatch
E-learning research, news and notes from Brandon-Hall
<http://www.brandonhall.com>

E-Clips from The eLearning Guild
Clips of what's new and interesting, and a guide to the weekly *eLearning Developers' Journal*
<http://www.elearningguild.com>

E-Learning Guru
Newsletter — and Web site — featuring trends, case studies and interviews from Kevin Kruse
<http://www.e-learningguru.com/>

E-learning NewsLine
Weekly news, trends and insights from *E-Learning Magazine*
<http://www.elearningmag.com>

e-News™
Bi-weekly news and research from The Corporate University Xchange
<http://www.corpu.com>

eCLIPSE
Monthly newsletter about e-learning people, systems and environments from the excellent E-Learning Centre
<http://www.e-learningcentre.co.uk/eclipse/default.htm/>

ElearningPost
Daily news and links about corporate learning, community building, instructional design and knowledge management from an excellent Web site
<http://www.elearningpost.com>

Fastrak
Mailing list for new tips and tools for trainers and communicators
<http://www.fastrak-consulting.co.uk/tactix/fastline.htm>

IT Training Magazine
IT skills issues and developments
<http://www.train-net.co.uk/home/index.cfm>

Knowledge Notes
A free, weekly newsletter published by ThinkEquity Partners, a research-centred boutique investment bank
Subscribe by e mailing: Knowledgenotes@thinkequity.com

Learning Circuits Express
A free information service from Learning Circuits, ASTD's online magazine about e-learning
<http://www.astd.org/virtual_community/td_magazine/elist.html>

Line Zine Newsletter
Monthly supplement about the best thinking on learning, performance, knowledge and human capital in the new economy from a high-quality Web site
<http://www.linezine.com>

News, Resources and Trends
A focus on new dimensions in education technology for faculty and administrators from Syllabus Press
<http://subscribe.101com.com/syllabus/>

Online Learning E-News
Information and ideas from VNU Business Media
<http://www.vnulearning.com/freeenews.htm>

Online Learning E-Reviews
News and dialogue about e-learning products from VNU Business Media
<http://www.vnulearning.com/freeenews.htm>

Play for Performance
Seriously fun activities for trainers, facilitators, performance consultants and
managers from Sivasailam (Thiagi) Thiagarajan
<http://www.thiagi.com/pfp-register.html>

T + D Extra
A free information service from T + D Magazine published by ASTD
<http://www.astd.org/virtual_community/td_magazine/elist.html>

TechKnowledge® E-Learning Tips Newsletter
Tips, strategies and ideas from the speakers and participants in the ASTD
TechKnowledge® Conference & Exposition
<http://www1.astd.org/tk03/emailnewsletter_signup.aspx>

TechKnowLogia
The International Journal of Technologies for the Advancement of Knowledge
and Learning — heavyweight but very good
<www.TechKnowLogia.org>

TechLearn Trends
Training, e-Learning and Collaboration Updates from Elliott Masie
<http://www.masie.com>

The Education Economy
News about corporate, post-secondary and pre-K-12 learning markets from
Eduventures.com
<https://www.eduventures.com/signUp/tier0SignupPage1.cfm>

Training Directors' Forum E-Net
Discussion-driven newsletter for training managers from VNU Business Media
<http://www.vnulearning.com/freeenews.htm>

VUG
Monthly newsletter covering the Internet University movement from the Virtual
University Gazette
<http://www.geteducated.com/vugaz.htm>

Work-Learning Research E-newsletter
Will Thalheimer's practical research-based information on learning and
performance
<http://www.work-learning.com/subscribe_to_newsletter.htm>

Appendix 2: Online resources

Here are some of the e-learning resources you can find in the biggest library in the world.

ALN
The Web of Asynchronous Learning Networks
<http://www.aln.org>

Advanced Distributed Learning Network (ADLNet)
The home of the SCORM reference model
<http://www.adlnet.org>

ADVISOR® E-Learning Articles
<http://www.advisor.com/Articles.nsf/vTechLookup!OpenView&RestrictToCategory=e-Learning>

Association for Educational Communications and Technology
Don't miss the quarterly publication (members only)
<http://www.aect.org>

ASTD
American Society of Training and Development
<http://www.astd.org>

AT&T Learning Network
<http://www.att.com/learningnetwork/>

BAOL
The British Association for Open Learning
<http://www.baol.co.uk>

Bibliography of Educational Technology
Excellent resource with links to Amazon.com — maintained by Dr Badrul Khan,
associate professor and Director of Educational Technology Leadership Cohort
program at The George Washington University
<http://bookstoread.com/e/et/de.htm>

Brandon-Hall E-Learning Consultancy
<http://www.brandon-hall.com>

Bryan Chapman's E-learning Stock Tracker
<http://www.brandon-hall.com/public/ticker/>

Cambridge Research — E-Learning Project
E-learning research project at Cambridge University
<http://www.jims.cam.ac.uk/research/subject_groups/elearning.html>

CETIS
The Centre for Educational Technology Interoperability Standards
<http://www.cetis.ac.uk>

Chief Learning Officer
Regularly includes good e-learning articles
<http://www.clomedia.com/default.asp>

Distance Learning Course Finder
The world's largest online directory of e-learning courses from 130 countries
<http://www.dlcoursefinder.com/US/>

Distance Learning Notes
E-learning reference site
<http://distancelearn.about.com>

Distance Learning on the Net
Glenn Hoyle's e-learning links
<http://www.hoyle.com/distance.htm>

E-learning: The Magazine of Distributed Learning
<http://www.elearningmag.com>

e-Learning Centre
Excellent UK-based reference site
<http://www.e-learningcentre.co.uk/eclipse/default.htm/>

E-Learning Research Center
CIO Magazine's guide to e-learning
<http://www.cio.com/research/elearning/>

E-Learning Start4All
Comprehensive e-learning links page
<http://e-learning.start4all.com>

e-LearningGuru.com
Kevin Kruse's collection of e-learning resources
<http://www.e-learningguru.com>

E-LearningHub.com
<http://www.e-learninghub.com>

eArmyu.com
US Army e-learning programme
<http://www.earmyu.com>

EducateU.com
E-learning courses from Dell Computers
<http://www.learndell.com>

EducationGuardian: E-learning
Guardian newspaper's e-learning coverage
<http://education.guardian.co.uk/elearning/>

EIfEL European Institute for E-Learning
<http://www.eife-l.org/En/>

eLearn Magazine
<http://www.elearnmag.org>

eLearning Forum
Silicon Valley-based e-learning community
<http://www.elearningforum.com>

ETV
The European Training Village
<http://www.trainingvillage.gr>

European eLearning Directory
Guide to European e-learning vendors
<http://www.elearning-directory.com>

GAZEL Global Arizona E-Learning
Globalized E-Learning Association
<http://www.gazel.org>

GEM
The Gateway to Educational Materials
<http://www.geminfo.org>

IEEE Learning Technology Standards Committee
<http://ltsc.ieee.org>

IMS Global Learning Consortium
<http://www.imsproject.org>

Instruction and Assessment on the World Wide Web
Thelma Loom's excellent survey of LMSs, LCMSs and other e-learning elements
<http://www.student.seas.gwu.edu/~tlooms/assess.html>

Internet Time Group
Jay Cross's e-learning reference site
<http://www.internettime.com>

Learnativity
Wayne Hodgins's and Marcia Conners's excellent reference site
<http://www.learnativity.com>

Learning Ericsson.net
Free access to Ericsson's e-learning about telecommunications
<http://learning.ericsson.net/eeonline/index.shtml>

Learning On Screen
The Society for Screen-Based Learning
<http://www.learningonscreen.co.uk>

LearningBites
Interesting commentaries on e-learning
<http://www.learningbites.net>

Lguide Generic Content Reviews
<http://reviews.lguide.com>

MIT OpenCourseWare
Project to develop free online access to nearly all of MIT's courseware
<http://ocwmit.edu>

MSN eLearning Center
<http://encarta.msn.com/elearning/dcfault.asp>

National Center for Education Statistics
Part of the US Department of Education
<http://nces.ed.gov>

NB TeleEducation
Distance education resources from the Government of New Brunswick
<http://teleeducation.nb.ca>

NB Training
Government of New Brunswick site listing content developers in the province
<http://www.nbtraining.com>

Office of Training Technology
The US Navy's reference site for e-learning
<http://www.ott.navy.mil>

Online Learning News Blog
<http://people.uis.edu/rschr1/onlinelearning/blogger.html>

Online Learning White Papers
Reference site from VNU Business Media
<http://www.lakewoodconferences.com/whitepapers.htm>

SUfI — Scottish University for Industry
Scotland's public e-learning for individuals and businesses
<http://www.scottishufi.co.uk>

Technology-based Training Supersite
 <http://www.tbtsupersite.com>

The "No Significant Difference Phenomenon"
Thomas Russell's collection of studies about technology based learning
<http://teleeducation.nb.ca/nosignificantdifference/>

The European Commission: eLearning
<http://europa.eu.int/comm/education/elearning/>

The Institute of IT Training
UK-based professional body for IT training professionals
<http://www.iitt.org.uk>

The Instructional Use of Learning Objects
The online version of David Wiley's book about learning objects
<http://reusability.org/read/>

The Learning Lab
Describes itself as "a centre of excellence for learning technologies"
<http://www.learninglab.org.uk>

The Masie Center
<http://www.masie.com>

The Node Learning Technologies Network
Canadian reference site with emphasis on e-learning in universities
<http://www.node.on.ca>

Trainingmag.com
Incorporating *OnlineLearning Magazine*
<http://www.onlinelearningmag.com>

Training Media Review
Objective reviews of training content and technologies
<http://www.tmreview.com>

TrainingZONE — E-learning
E-learning reference site and forum
<http://www.trainingzone.co.uk/zones/elearningzone/>

Ufi: University for Industry
UK government's e-learning for individuals and businesses
<http://www.ufi.com>

University of Wisconsin — Milwaukee: Center for International Education
Learning Objects Reference Site
<http://www.uwm.edu/Dept/CIE/AOP/learningobjects.html>

USDLA: US Distance Learning Association
Don't miss the excellent monthly journal; there is a journal archive on the site
<http://www.usdla.org>

VNU Business Media
<http://www.vnulearning.com>

WBTIC Web-Based Training Information Center
<http://www.wbtic.com>

World Wide Learn
Global e-learning portal
<http://www.worldwidelearn.com>

Appendix 3: Glossary

A

Adaptive Learning

Self-paced e-learning courses that adapt to the learner's pre-knowledge of the content or specific learning needs based on a course pre-assessment or a competency assessment.

ADDIE

A high level instructional design model based on the steps: Analysis, Design, Development, Implementation and Evaluation.

ADL (Advanced Distributed Learning)

A US Department of Defense initiative to accelerate the development and adoption of integrated e-learning standards.

AICC

An acronym for the Aviation Industry Computer-Based Training Committee, an international association that has developed draft e-learning standards for the aviation industry. For a time, AICC's draft standards were the only ones available.

Andragogy

Andragogy is to adults what pedagogy is to children. It describes the theory of how adults learn.

Animation

Animation uses a sequence of slightly different static images to trick the human eye into believing it is seeing motion. In e-learning, animation can be applied to explain complex ideas and processes.

API (Application Program Interface)

APIs allow one computer program to make requests of a second computer program or operating system. A common use of APIs to customize an off-the-shelf application like a Learning Management System.

Application

Application is another name for a computer program. Learning Management Systems and authoring tools like Dreamweaver are e-learning applications.

ARCS

ARCS is a high- and medium-level instructional design theory that emphasizes learner motivation. The name is an acronym for Attention, Relevance, Confidence and Satisfaction.

ASP (Active Server Pages)

ASP is a programming environment specific to servers running Microsoft operating systems which allows developers to author dynamic content on the Internet. Typically, an ASP script pulls content from a database then displays it in an HTML framework.

ASP (Application Service Provider)

An Application Service Provider is a business that makes Web-based applications running on its own servers available to other individuals and enterprises. Some Learning Management Systems are available through an ASP model.

Assessment

Generally, an assessment is a way of finding out whether learning has taken place or measuring how much learning has taken place. Other assessments measure a learner's pre-knowledge of the content.

Asynchronous

This term is applied to a process which is not completed in real time. E-mail is asynchronous; a telephone conversation isn't. In an e-learning context, self-paced courses are asynchronous learning; there is a time lag between the authoring process and the learning.

Authoring

Authoring describes a structured approach to the development of course content. Some people use it to describe only the work Web developers do; others, to include the development of course designs.

Authoring Tool

An authoring tool is a software application used by Web developers to produce course content in software.

Authoring System

An authoring system is a suite of integrated proprietary authoring tools, sometimes designed for non-expert users. They tend to offer greater ease of use but with less flexibility than open tools.

B

Bandwidth

Bandwidth describes a communications channel's capacity for carrying information. In an e-learning context, bandwidth often refers to the capacity of an enterprise's infrastructure to carry e-learning content to learners.

Bespoke Learning Content

Bespoke content is a British expression that describes content developed to close a specific performance gap in a specific enterprise. Americans call this *custom content*.

Blended Learning

Blended learning describes the practice of delivering learning through a combination of channels, usually face-to-face classroom learning alongside e-learning.

Bookmarking

In e-learning, bookmarking refers to a Learning Management System's ability to remember where a learner left off in a course and to jump back to that position at the start of the next learning session.

Browser

See Web Browser.

C

Catalogue

In an e-learning context, a catalogue is a listing of all courses available from a Learning Management System.

CBT (Computer Based Training)

Computer-based training is an umbrella term for the process of using computers to manage and deliver learning content. It tends to mean different things to different people and has an old-fashioned connotation.

Chat

Chat is synchronous online communication using a system called Internet Relay Chat (IRC). People refer to "chat rooms" where users can meet and engage in multiple simultaneous conversations. Chat technology does not have a place in e-learning. Instant Messaging technology is a better way of implementing real-time peer-to-peer communication.

Chunking

Chunking is an ugly way of describing the process of breaking down content and delivering it in small, easily assimilable units.

Classroom Based Training

This expression describes training that takes place in a physical classroom led by an instructor. It's also called *instructor-led training* and *face-to-face learning*.

CMI (Computer Managed Instruction)

An early name for what today we call a Learning Management System or Learning Content Management System.

CMS (Content Management System)

A CMS is a software that wraps a layer of intelligence around a database in order to streamline the workflow associated with developing and publishing Web content. It can be integrated with a Learning Management System.

Curriculum

A curriculum is a predefined set of courses, learning objects and learning events designed to meet a known business requirement in an enterprise, for example, making new joiners performance ready. Learners can have personal curricula which take account of their long-term career path as well as short-term requirements.

Custom Learning Content

See Bespoke Learning Content.

D

Delivery Channel

In e-learning, a delivery channel is a method of delivering learning, for example, classroom-based learning, asynchronous self-paced e-learning, synchronous virtual classrooms and peer-to-peer collaboration.

Design

Design is used to describe a number of activities that have little in common — from course design to screen design. In e-learning, it is generally used to describe instructional design.

Developer

A developer is more accurately described as a Web developer, someone with the skills to turn a course design into Web-based software. The term is sometimes used to describe an instructional designer, graphic designer, writer, etc.

Distance Learning

Distance learning describes synchronous online learning that takes place without the instructor being physically present.

Distributed Learning

Distributed learning defines asynchronous online learning that takes place anywhere and any time it is needed.

E

EPSS (Electronic Performance Support System)

EPSS describes learning and support that is integrated with the application it supports. The Windows paperclip is a common but crude example. EPSS is the ultimate form of just-in-time learning.

Evaluation

Evaluation describes a systematic process for ascertaining whether learning has been successful from performance, investment and business perspectives.

Extranet

An extranet is a private network based on Internet protocols that is accessible only to individuals and organizations who have appropriate logon rights. Extranets allow enterprises to deliver e-learning to suppliers, partners and customers outside the corporate firewall.

F

FAQ (Frequently Asked Questions)

Web speak for a document that answers users' frequently asked questions. In an e-learning content, FAQs are useful tools for supporting e-learning systems and courses.

Firewall

A firewall describes a method of allowing a private network's users — for example, users of an enterprise intranet — to access the public Internet while restricting users on the public Internet from accessing the private network.

Frameset

A frameset is a collection of Web pages displayed simultaneously in a Web browser. The way the pages are presented is determined by information held in the *controlling frame* which is not displayed.

FTP (File Transfer Protocol)

FTP is an Internet protocol that supports the transfer of files between local and remote computers. It is commonly used to upload content to and download content from Internet servers.

G

Generic Learning Content

Generic content is developed and published by third parties who anticipate the learning needs of a broad range of enterprises. A typical generic course might help a learner to improve their PowerPoint skills. Generic content is also called *off-the-shelf content*.

Granularity

In the context of e-learning, granularity is a way of describing the relative size of units of learning. The greater the granularity, the smaller the learning units or objects.

H

Hard Skills

Hard skills have well defined processes, actions and outcomes. In e-learning, hard skills are often synonymous with IT skills.

Hosting

(1) Hosting describes the activity of an Internet Service Provider in providing the technology platform for an enterprise's Web-based learning system. (2) Hosting describes the process of running an application or content from an Internet server. The server is said to be hosting the application or content.

HRD (Human Resource Development)

(1) HRD describes the investment by an enterprise in its staff through organized learning experiences—like e-learning—in order to improve employee performance. (2) HRD describes the whole training and development field and profession.

Human Capital

Human capital describes the value of all the knowledge, attitudes, skills and competencies held by an enterprise's employees. Human capital is owned not by the enterprise but by the individuals who possess it.

HTML (HyperText Markup Language)

HTML is the standard programming language used to build Web pages. Web browsers display a Web page by interpreting the instructions embedded in HTML code.

I

IEEE (The Institute of Electrical and Electronics Engineers)

IEEE is an international standards body. Its Learning Technology Standards Committee works to develop technical standards for e-learning.

ILT (Instructor-Led Training)

See Classroom Based Training.

IMS (Instructional Management System)

The IMS Global Learning Consortium is a coalition of academic, commercial and government organizations working to develop a set of open standards for e-learning.

Infrastructure

Infrastructure describes the physical hardware in an enterprise that provides connections between computers and between users. It can include telephone lines, Internet connections, satellite links, routers, aggregators and repeaters.

Instant Messaging

Instant Messaging (IM) describes synchronous peer-to-peer largely text-based communication using Internet technologies. Some IM applications support file transfers, shared whiteboards, and voice and video communications.

Instructional Design (ISD)

Instructional design describes a systematic process for designing learning content.

Instructional Designer

An instructional designer selects and applies a learning methodology to create a design for learning content. Many instructional designers also write the text in a course.

Interactivity

Interactivity describes the engagement of a learner in learning content through interactions with the content.

Internet

The Internet is a global network of networks. Parts of the Internet can be accessed freely by any users; other parts have restricted access. No one owns the Internet; it is a public, cooperative, self-sustaining facility.

Internet Explorer (IE)

Internet Explorer is Microsoft's Web browser, the most popular in the world by an increasingly large margin.

Interoperability

Interoperability describes the ability of a system to work in conjunction with other systems readily and effectively. In the context of e-learning Interoperability describes the ability of learning content to run on different Learning Management Systems without modification.

Intranet

An intranet is a network based on Internet technologies and standards and owned by an organization. It is usually connected to the public Internet. Most e-learning is delivered through intranets.

IP (Internet Protocol)

IP is an international standard for addressing and sending data across the Internet.

ISO (International Organization for Standardization)

The ISO is an international federation of national standards bodies. The aim of the various e-learning standards bodies is to achieve ISO recognition for the standards they are developing.

IT (Information Technology)

IT is an umbrella expression that describes both computers and their capability to process information.

J

Java

Java is a object-oriented programming language developed by Sun Microsystems and intended to be completely interoperable. Applications authored in Java can run on a standalone basis or be launched from within an HTML document.

Java Applet

A small Java program that runs on the Internet or an intranet and is launched through a Web browser.

JavaScript

While JavaScript is a scripting language it has nothing to do with Sun's Java. JavaScript is simpler. It enables a Web browser to interact with the user, for example, to change the colour of text when the cursor moves over it.

Just-in-case Learning

This is a tongue-in-cheek description of learning curricula based on information rather than needs. Just-in-case learning is a bad investment; there's no guarantee it will ever be used.

Just-in-time Learning

Just-in-time learning describes the ability of a learner to access just what they need to know when and where they need to know it. It is the holy grail of e-learning.

Just-too-late Learning

This is a tongue-in-cheek description of what happens far too often: great learning content is delivered just after it was needed.

Knowledge Management (KM)

Knowledge Management describes a systematic process for capturing tacit knowledge within an enterprise and making it accessible to anyone who needs it.

L

LCMS (Learning Content Management System)

An LCMS is an application that combines some of the learning management functions of a Learning Management System with the content management functions of a Content Management System.

Learner

A learner is the end user of e-learning.

Learning Object

A learning object is a self-contained reusable unit of e-learning content. An enterprise can derive value from learning objects when they are organized by a metadata classification system and stored in a CMS or LCMS.

Learning Objective

A learning objective is a clear specification of a measurable behavioural outcome of learning. It is also used during the evaluation of learning effectiveness.

Link

A link describes a URL that is embedded in a Web page. The presentation style of the link should inform the user that it is a connection to additional information or a way of navigating through content.

LMS (Learning Management System)

A Learning Management System is an application that automates many of the processes associated with e-learning. Typical functions include learner registration, progress tracking and storage of assessment results. An LMS hosts and maintains the course catalogue, custom learning content and generic learning content.

Localization

Localization describes a process in which content is adapted for delivery to different countries or regions. More than translation, localization takes account of local culture, tradition and practices.

M

M-learning

M-learning is short for mobile learning. In Europe, m-learning usually refers to the delivery of learning content to handheld wireless devices. In the USA, it can sometimes mean disconnected learning—learning on a laptop even when no connection to the Internet is available.

Mentoring

Mentoring describes a learning process in which less experienced employees are matched with more experienced employees. Mentoring can be formal or informal, face-to-face or virtual.

Metadata

Metadata is data about data. In an e-learning context, it is usually used to describe tags embedded in learning objects so they can be searched for and retrieved intelligently.

Multimedia

Multimedia describes content which is not text, for example, video, audio, animation, photographs and graphics.

N

Navigation

Navigation describes the process of moving through content on the Web. You can navigate within a page or between pages. Navigation is usually effected by clicking on links. User-friendly, self-explanatory navigation is a hallmark of good e-learning content.

Netscape Navigator

This is the name of Netscape's Web browser. By the middle of 2002, less than 5% of Web users were browsing with Navigator.

O

Off-the-shelf (OTS) Learning Content

See Generic Learning Content.

Offline

Offline describes working with a computer that does not have an active connection to a network.

Online

Online describes working with a computer that has an active connection to a network.

Online Learning

Online learning is another way of saying *e-learning*.

Outsourcing

Outsourcing describes the transfer or delegation of the operation and day-to-day management of a business process to an external service provider. In an e-learning context, outsourcing usually refers to using an Application Service Provider for LMS services and/or to host content.

P

Performance Gap

Performance gap describes the difference between required and actual performance.

Personalization

In an e-learning context, personalization is about tailoring the learning experience and content to the needs and profiles of individual learners.

Plug-in

Plug-in describes software that extends the functionality of a Web browser. Plug-ins are sometimes required to display proprietary e-learning content or multimedia content not native to Windows, e.g. QuickTime and Real Audio or Video.

Protocol

Protocol describes a set of rules — sometimes standards — that govern how data is exchanged between computers and applications. E-learning standards define protocols for the exchange of data between the learner's Web browser and the Learning Management System.

R

Repurpose

Repurpose describes the process of adapting existing learning content so it can be delivered through a different channel than originally intended. An instructor-led course could be repurposed for self-paced e-learning.

RFP (Request for Proposal)

An RFP is a document distributed to vendors by an enterprise inviting them to bid for defined products and services.

RIO (Reusable Information Object)

A RIO (say *ree-oh*) describes a collection of content, practice and assessment items that meet a single learning objective. A number of RIOs are combined to form a Reusable Learning Object. This approach was defined by Cisco Systems.

RLO (Reusable Learning Object)

(1) *See* Learning Object. (2) In Cisco's e-learning scheme, an RLO is a collection of RIOs supported by an overview, a summary and assessments.

ROI (Return on Investment)

Return on investment is usually expressed as a ratio or percentage of benefit to investment. In e-learning, there's an initial ROI calculation for implementation then a series of ROI calculations for each course developed.

S

SCORM (Sharable Content Object Reference Model)

Developed by the US Department of Defense's Advance Distributed Learning (ADL) initiative, SCORM describes a model for e-learning standards that produces small, reusable, interoperable learning objects.

Self-paced Learning

Self-paced learning describes learning that is initiated and scheduled by the learner and taken at a pace that reflects their (1) capacity to learn and (2) prior knowledge of the content. Asynchronous self-paced learning courses are the backbone of e-learning.

Sequencing

Sequencing describes the process of arranging learning content into the optimal order for effective learning.

Simulation

Simulation describes an approach to learning which engages the learner in a realistic highly interactive representation of a device, process or situation on the basis that the best way to learn is to do.

Skill Gap

Skill gap describes the difference between required and actual skill levels.

Skill Gap Analysis

A skill gap analysis studies the difference between required and actual skill levels to identify the nature of and reason for the gap. The outcome of the analysis is usually a recommendation for a programme of learning to close the gap.

Subject Matter Expert (SME)

In an e-learning context, the Subject Matter Expert, usually appointed by the course sponsor, brings their expert knowledge to bear on the design and development of learning content.

Soft Skills

Soft skills are not based on well defined processes, actions and outcomes. Examples include communication and presentation, leadership and management, and team building. Another name for soft skills is *business skills*.

Streaming Media

Streaming media technology is a response to limited and variable bandwidth. Playback of audio, video and animation files begins as soon as a minimum amount of data has been downloaded. Subsequently, playback and download happen simultaneously.

Synchronous Learning

Synchronous learning describes a real-time or "live" online learning event in which all participants—typically, an instructor and a number of learners—are all logged on to the system at the same time.

T

TCP/IP (Transmission Control Protocol/Internet Protocol)

The basic communication protocol of the Internet. All communication between computers on the Internet uses TCP/IP.

U

URL (Uniform Resource Locator)

A URL is the standard form of address for a page located on the Web, an intranet, or an extranet. Here's an example: http://www.adlnet.org

Usability

In the context of e-learning, usability is a measure of how easy it is for a learner to use the interface to navigate, access content and achieve their goals.

User Interface

User interface describes all the hardware and software with which a user interacts with a computer. In e-learning, the hardware configuration is usually a given, so the only aspect of the user interface designers and developers can influence is what the learner sees on the screen.

V

Virtual Classroom

Virtual classroom describes an e-learning application that allows an instructor to present content to and interact with a number of learners who are all logged into the application at the same time.

VoIP (Voice over IP)

VoIP uses Internet technology to allow people with Internet access to talk to each other — without telephone systems.

W

WAP (Wireless Application Protocol)

WAP is a set of communication protocols that standardize how wireless devices — cellular phones and PDAs, for example — can access the Internet. WAP provides a platform on which to build m-learning.

WBT

WBT is an acronym for Web Based Training. WBT is seldom used any more; people use *e-learning* instead.

Web Browser

A Web browser is an application that allows users to navigate the World Wide Web and to view Web pages containing a mix of text, graphic, audio, video and animation. All e-learning courses are viewed in a Web browser.

World Wide Web (WWW)

The World Wide Web is one aspect of the Internet. Using a Web browser, users can navigate from one World Wide Web site to another, from one page to another. The World Wide Web popularized the Internet because it supports an attractive mix of text, graphics, audio and video.

Wrapper

Wrapper describes software that sits between learning content and the Learning Management System. Acting as an interpreter, a wrapper allows data generated by content to be understood by the LMS and vice versa.

Index